Employment, Technology and Economic Needs

Employment, Technology and Economic Needs

Theory, Evidence, and Public Policy

Edited by

Jonathan Michie

Professor of Management, Birkbeck College,
University of London

and

Angelo Reati

Commission of the European Community, Brussels, Belgium

Edward Elgar

Cheltenham, UK • Northampton, MA, USA

Published by
Edward Elgar Publishing Limited
8 Lansdown Place
Cheltenham
Glos GL50 2HU
UK

Edward Elgar Publishing, Inc.
6 Market Street
Northampton
Massachusetts 01060
USA

A catalogue record for this book
is available from the British Library

Library of Congress Cataloguing in Publication Data
Employment, technology, and economic needs : theory, evidence, and
    public policy / edited by Jonathan Michie, Angelo Reati.
    "In association with the European Association of Evolutionary
Political Economy."
    Includes bibliographical references and indexes.
    1. Full employment policies—European Union countries—Congresses.
2. Unemployment—European Union countries—Congresses. 3. Labor
supply—Effect of automation on—European Union countries—
Congresses. 4. Labor supply—Effect of technological innovations
on--European Union countries—Congresses. 5. Labor supply—European
Union countries—Regional disparities—Congresses. 6. Hours of
labor—European Union countries—Congresses. I. Michie, Jonathan.
II. Reati, Angelo. III. European Association of Evolutionary
Political Economy.
HD5764.A6E494 1998
331. 1'094—dc21   97–52043
                                                            CIP

ISBN 1 85898 680 X

Printed and bound in Great Britain by Bookcraft (Bath) Limited.

Contents

Figures

Tables

Contributors

Eileen Appelbaum, Economic Policy Institute, Washington, DC, USA

Susan Baines, Department of Social Policy, University of Newcastle upon Tyne, Newcastle upon Tyne NE1 7RU, UK

Eugenio Benedetti, University of Padova, 'M. Fanno' Department of Economics, Via del Santo 33, I-35123 Padova, Italy

Fred Block, University of California at Davis, USA

Antonio G. Calafati, University of Ancona, Department of Economics, Via Pizzecolli, 68-60121 Ancona, Italy

Charles M.A. Clark, Department of Economics, St John's University, Jamaica, New York 11439, USA

Sara Davies, Department of City and Regional Planning, University of Wales College of Cardiff, PO Box 906, Cardiff CF1 3YN, UK

Charles Edquist, Department of Technology and Social Change, Linköping University, Linköping, Sweden

Leif Hommen, Department of Technology and Social Change, Linköping University, Linköping, Sweden

Ray Hudson, Department of Geography, University of Durham, Durham DH1 3LE, UK

Catherine Kavanagh, Department of Economics, University College Cork, Cork, Republic of Ireland

Michael Kitson, St Catharine's College, Cambridge, UK

Jeff Manza, Department of Sociology, Pennsylvania State University, USA

Maureen McKelvey, Department of Technology and Social Change, Linköping University, Linköping, Sweden

Jonathan Michie , Birkbeck College, University of London, UK

Kevin Morgan, Department of City and Regional Planning, University of Wales College of Cardiff, PO Box 906, Cardiff CF1 3YN, UK

Christos Pitelis, Judge Institute of Management Studies, Cambridge, UK

Marco Rangone, University of Padova, 'M. Fanno' Department of Economics, Via del Santo 33, I-35123 Padova, Italy

Angelo Reati, Commission of the European Communities, Brussels, Belgium

Ronald Schettkat, University of Utrecht, Department of Social Economics, The Netherlands

Werner Sengenberger, Employment and Training Department, ILO, Geneva, Switzerland

Marc R. Tool, Professor Emeritus of Economics, 5708 McAdoo Avenue, Sacramento, CA 95819-2516, USA

Andrew Tylecote, Department of Economics, University of Sheffield, 9 Mappin Street, Sheffield S1 4DT, UK

Jane Wheelock, Department of Social Policy, University of Newcastle upon Tyne, Newcastle upon Tyne NE1 7RU, UK

Preface and acknowledgements

This book emerged from the annual conference of the European Association of Evolutionary Political Economy (EAEPE) held in November 1996 at the University of Antwerp-RUCA on the theme of 'Work, unemployment and need: theory, evidence, policies'. Our thanks therefore go to the 1996 EAEPE Conference Organizer, Julien van den Broeck, and other EAEPE officers: Robert Delorme, John Groenewegen, Geoffrey Hodgson and Andrew Tylecote. We are also grateful to all the authors for having responded so fully and quickly to editorial suggestions in revising their papers. Our editing of the chapters benefited from the discussions at the conference and we are therefore grateful to all the participants, and in particular for comments from Alain Lipietz, David Musson, Patricia Northover and Grahame Thompson. Francine O'Sullivan, Dymphna Evans and their colleagues at Edward Elgar did an excellent job as usual in turning the manuscript around quickly.

Jonathan Michie would also like to thank Robyn May, for help with preparing the manuscript and, for having put up with weekend editing, Carolyn, eight-year-old Alex and two-year-old Duncan.

JONATHAN MICHIE
ANGELO REATI

Introduction: Towards an alternative theory and policy on employment

Jonathan Michie and Angelo Reati

One can give to the poor only if one does not take from the rich.
(The Pareto criterion)

CLASSICAL POLITICAL ECONOMY AND NEOCLASSICAL ECONOMICS

The shared concern of the chapters in this book – which are revised versions of a selection of papers from the 1996 conference of the European Association of Evolutionary Political Economy – is to go beyond the neoclassical theory of employment and present sounder policy guidelines to solve the unemployment problem.

After twenty years or so of neoclassical-inspired economic policy in European countries, the scourge of unemployment remains. In official statistics unemployment has fallen but, unfortunately, this is not because of any fundamental changes in reality but rather the result of several artefacts. At the same time, poverty, social exclusion and inequality have grown considerably. Neoclassical economists object that we still have unemployment because the policies they advocate have not been implemented with sufficient strength. This argument is a *non sequitur*: it could be fully disproved only if the state were to play no role at all in regulating the economy – something which is inconceivable in a modern society.

The problem with neoclassical theory is that it provides a wrong diagnosis of the causes of the stagnation which started in the 1970s and, therefore, the remedies which follow can only worsen the problem. Neoclassical theory relies on the postulate that the capitalist system, if left as free as possible, is able to produce continuous growth and employment. Recessions can be caused only by accidents (like the oil shocks) or errors in economic policy. To correct for such errors we need competition and flexibility – particularly in the labour market – and, in general, a withdrawal of the state from the economy.

1

In fact, far from being an accident, such cyclical fluctuations are part of the normal functioning of capitalism. If we want to understand the evolution of actual economies – and to propose policies – it is not enough to investigate only the tendencies which determine the long-term dynamics of capitalism. We must also consider the phases of growth and stagnation, as well as the role played by institutions. On this point non-mainstream political economy has provided two fundamental contributions. First, the long-wave theory, whose origins date back to 1913 (van Gelderen) and 1925 (Kondratieff), on which see Freeman (1996), van Duijn (1983) and Mandel (1995). And secondly, the theory of 'regulation' developed in France in the 1970s (*l'école de la régulation*, on which see Boyer and Saillard, 1995) as well as in the USA (the Social Structure of Accumulation, on which see Bowles *et al.*, 1986, and Gordon *et al.*, 1983).

Starting from the historical observation that capitalist economies had experienced a quite regular recurrence of 25–30-year periods of sustained growth followed by periods of stagnation of similar duration, the long-wave theory suggests that one of the main causes of these long upswings has been a radical change in the technological basis of society, which produces a cumulative process of growth led by investment (Schumpeter, 1977; Kleinknecht, 1987). However, to be effective, this accumulation of capital needs to be sustained by an appropriate institutional framework. For instance, during the post-Second World War long wave, the systemic relationships which made such a regime of accumulation possible were collective wage bargaining linking wages to productivity, the formation of a 'social consumption norm', and the welfare state, as well as the institutional framework for competition and the monetary and credit relationships.

Long stagnations have set in when these technological revolutions have become exhausted; the slowdown in output creates mass unemployment, and a mismatch appears between the mode of regulation and the underlying economic cycle. Thus it is not surprising that the short-term Keynesian policies of demand management – which were suitable for regulating the economy during the long expansion – were no longer effective in the stagnation phase. Such stagnations have ended when the system succeeded in adopting a new accumulation regime, rooted in a new technological basis, and in finding an appropriate mode of regulation. In other words, it is necessary to rematch institutions with the techno-economic sphere, and this implies a long process of trial and error.

On the basis of the preceding analysis, the all-out labour market flexibility preached by the neoclassicals as *the* solution to the unemployment problem can be seen to be rather inadequate at best. However, we should distinguish between a 'positive' and a merely 'negative' kind of labour market flexibility. By 'positive' flexibility we mean the flexibility which is directly targeted at job creation, and whose effectiveness can be measured immediately with reference to its success in meeting this goal. It is, for instance, the flexibility required by the continuous shifts of the labour force from the declining to the expanding sectors in periods of structural change, or the flexibility which is needed to implement a reduction of working time as a remedy to unemployment.

Other forms of flexibility are 'negative' as their effects on employment are dubious or even positively harmful. This is particularly true of the flexibility whose essential aim is to submit workers to capital, such as making jobs more precarious, imposing part-time working, or unconstrained dismissals. Making it easy to hire and fire will only facilitate exit from and entry into the labour market, with no necessary impact on the actual level of employment.

Another example of 'negative' flexibility with dubious effects on employment are the measures which increase inequality, such as wage cuts, particularly at the bottom of the scale; for example, the OECD (1996) found no clear correlation between, on the one hand, employment and unemployment rates for the low-skilled and, on the other, the incidence of low-paid labour.

These 'negative' forms of labour market flexibility represent an important obstacle to the diffusion of the present technological revolution in computer and information technologies. For successful implementation of these technologies at the enterprise level a close involvement of the labour force is desirable, involving trust and participation. Such conditions are hampered by short-term labour contracts with no guarantee of stability. Also, in a highly flexible labour market, enterprises have less incentive to train their personnel, since part of the benefits from such investments may accrue to their competitors.

Innovation is also jeopardized by downward wage flexibility in a double sense (Kleinknecht, 1996):

1. low wage increases lead to the maintenance of obsolete equipment, since they allow old vintages of capital stock to be replaced more slowly, reducing the competitiveness of an economy; and
2. low wage levels depress effective demand and thereby discourage product innovations – the innovations which are the most promising for job creation.

In spite of a diversity in emphasis, heterodox political economy suggests several broad lines of economic policy for employment, which depart from the neoclassical recipes: [1]

- to maintain growth and keep pace with international competitiveness, public authorities should take measures to foster innovation and its diffusion. This implies support for basic science and R&D as well as specific actions to overcome obstacles to the diffusion of innovations, particularly at the organizational level of enterprises;
- to facilitate the structural change induced by the current technological revolution on computer and information technologies, the state should engage in vocational training and skill formation, and skill upgrading for the entire population;
- to create favourable economic conditions for employment, in the present circumstances governments should implement expansionary Keynesian policies, and wages should keep pace with productivity; and
- inequality should be reduced, not only for reasons of social justice but also because inequality is harmful for growth (Persson and Tabellini, 1994).

This minimum common denominator of the heterodox approach is enriched by a range of specific proposals to cope with the present employment crisis. Some of these are presented in Part IV of this book, and range from the provision of a basic income for all to the reduction of working time, to the development of the non-profit sector. Others have been presented elsewhere, such as the recent proposals for a public investment-led programme to create a million good-quality new jobs in the UK through a modest increase in taxation or borrowing (Kitson *et al.*, 1997). Let us now see how these issues are addressed in the book.

A RECONSTRUCTION

Part I analyses the political economy of the institutions governing employment. It starts with an examination by Calafati of the question of unemployment and disequilibrium, in which it is shown that institutions can create adjustments which do not necessarily require (downward) wage flexibility. The crucial question is how policy-makers perceive unemployment. If it is seen as entailing a waste of resources and a distorted distribution of the social product then this calls for action on demand management and income redistribution through the welfare state, supplemented by policies to adapt labour supply to labour demand. If, on the contrary, the distribution of the social product is not deemed to be unsustainable, then market transactions may be left unregulated, with persistent unemployment.

The role of economic policy is analysed in Chapter 2 by Michie and Pitelis, who argue that while much macroeconomic theory and policy analysis assumes – explicitly or (more often) implicitly – perfect competition, when it comes to industrial and regulatory issues the realities of imperfect competition, industrial concentration, market shares and so on have to be addressed. And more fundamentally, the 'market' is shown (even if this is not always admitted) to be not so much free as constructed, created by legislation and regulation. They therefore argue not only that economic policy needs to be pursued in a coherent fashion on both the demand and supply sides, but also that a common theoretical framework needs to be adopted, recognizing the realities of market structure and the importance of institutions.

The need for an expansion of industrial capacity is emphasized by Kitson and Michie in Chapter 3, with reference to the UK experience. Advanced economies, they argue, require a healthy manufacturing sector in order to generate sufficient exports to pay for necessary imports and because of the symbiotic relationship between the manufacturing and the service sectors. In the UK, Thatcher's excesses led to deindustrialization with the result that the relatively poor growth of manufacturing hampered the development of the overall economy. If the UK is to compete effectively in the international arena in the future, this investment shortfall in manufacturing will have to be reversed. One of the tasks of the Labour government should therefore be the creation of new institutions to foster investment in skills and technology, inter-firm co-operation, and better relations between employers and employees.

In Chapter 4, Appelbaum and Schettkat analyse the institutions for wage bargaining, with three broad models of: (a) decentralized bargaining, where wages are negotiated between individual companies and employees; (b) centralized bargaining, where national unions and employers' associations bargain over the whole economy (the 'corporatist' model); and (c) branch bargaining, setting minimum sectoral standards which may be modified at a lower level. At individual company level, unions are constrained by competition in the product market; at the central level unions are aware of the macroeconomic influences of their action, and therefore are more inclined to take into account possible adverse effects of their claims. The econometric analysis provided by the authors suggests that a developed 'corporatist' system, similar to that of Scandinavian countries, is probably the most favourable for promoting employment.

In Part II of the book, devoted to the issue of technology and innovation, Reati starts by addressing the controversial question of the medium/long-term prospects for employment in the light of the radical innovations in computer and information technology. A careful consideration of the characteristics of this technological revolution shows that, while we should expect growth in output, the most likely future trend for employment is stagnation or even decline. This is because the scene is dominated by process innovations, which have a net job-reducing effect, and there are no signs of a reversal of the situation in the next few years, with product innovations taking the lead.

This question of product innovations is deepened in the subsequent two chapters. Noting that the conditions for an upsurge of product innovations are more extensive and difficult to satisfy than those required for process innovations, Tylecote (Chapter 6) examines the specific impediments to the first type of innovations. The first comes from depressed and uncertain demand: while a process innovation may well pay even if demand is static, the rate of return expected on launching a new product is highly sensitive to demand conditions. The other main obstacle stems from the relationship with those who finance the innovation. It is not easy for lenders to judge the degree of novelty of the innovation and to determine the amount of resources to devote to it. To this is added the question of appropriability: can the firm ensure that the bulk of the returns from the innovation accrue to shareholders, or does the innovation tend to involve large spillovers to other stakeholders?

In their review of existing theory and empirical research on the employment effect of innovations, Edquist *et al.* (Chapter 7) go beyond the usual distinction between product and process innovations by introducing the notion of organizational process innovations and by considering also the different impact of these innovations in manufacturing and services. Empirical research has shown that, in general, process innovations have a net job-reducing effect, while for product innovations the opposite holds. Thus, technological trajectories which are either labour-saving or employment-generating can arise according to the balance between the two kinds of innovations. This, in turn, depends on the characteristics of industrial and service sectors. For instance, in manufacturing, product innovations usually originate from R&D-intensive sectors, and a similar outcome is found in services.

The two case studies presented by Davies and Morgan (Chapter 8) – of Wales in the UK and of the Ruhr area in Germany – show that regional unemployment cannot be eliminated by regional innovation strategies alone, but that such policies may be necessary preconditions for breaking the cycle of structural decline, joblessness and poverty. New institutions can foster innovation and long-term competitiveness by generating trust and constructing collaborative networks which can safeguard existing jobs and companies.

Most of the chapters in Part III are inspired by the 'regulation school' approach, confirming its usefulness for understanding current problems and for suggesting remedies.

In Chapter 9, Benedetti and Rangone examine the transformation of the employment relation which results from the transition to post-Fordism – a regime where the stock exchange, rather than the factory, represents the symbol of the wealth of nations. The change in working activity, which loses most of its physical nature to become abstract, goes together with a deterioration of the welfare prospects for individuals and their families: workers' rights no longer possess their previous status of natural rights, and instead become ancillary to industrial restructuring. Within this framework, social acceptance of change depends on the fact that workers' expected rewards from the future situation outweigh the benefits of maintaining the present situation. Such an outcome requires a new regulatory setting and, since macroeconomic constraints make the opportunity to compensate possible losses rather occasional, social conflict cannot be excluded. Noting that measures to combat unemployment which rely upon the market mechanism are unlikely to work, the authors conclude that the new system of regulation should promote non-market solutions to the welfare aspects of structural unemployment.

One of the neoclassical recipes for the unemployment issue is to develop a 'risk society' by inducing households to create their own jobs through small business activities. In Chapter 10, Wheelock and Baines present the results of a case study of 104 micro-enterprises in the business services sector in two UK urban areas (Newcastle upon Tyne and Milton Keynes), to show how such a way of responding to insecurity arising from the threat of unemployment is played out in the daily lives of families. It appears that, while micro-businesses can help to maintain social relations by reinstating aspects of old ways of working (the greater dependence on family), this is not without social costs. The main one is 'self-exploitation' in the form of extremely long and often inconvenient hours of work, which brings pressures on personal relations and risks of family breakdown.

In Chapter 11, Hudson maintains that the unemployment problem should be treated within the context of a new sustainable regime of accumulation centred on environmental protection. In this mode of regulation, the distribution of social output should shift from inherited wealth and position in the wage labour market to a distribution which relates more closely to the socially useful work that people carry out. An essential means for achieving this objective is a fiscal system based on eco-taxation, with the revenues raised forming the basis for a citizen's income and public expenditure.

This idea of a basic income for all also emerges from Clark and Kavanagh's discussion of alternative explanations of Irish unemployment

(Chapter 12). In the developed world, they argue, the problem of scarcity has been fundamentally solved, and it does not make sense to pursue growth at all costs to absorb unemployment. The solution lies in distribution rather than in production, with increasing participation of people through socially useful activities and not necessarily waged employment in the market sector of the economy. This brings us to the proposals of Part IV.

Tool (Chapter 13) opens the policy agenda of Part IV by explaining that employment is indeed a human right which has the same philosophical and political status as the rights defined in the UN Universal Declaration of Human Rights. Work is, in fact, an essential factor of social integration and participation, and exclusion from work implies exclusion from mainstream society. Thus, public authorities have the obligation to create job development plans to ensure that 'every adult who wants to work ... be assured of paid employment at a livable wage in the private or public sector'.

The perspective of the International Labour Organization – which, among the international institutions, is one of the more progressive and open-minded – is presented by Sengenberger who sets out a policy agenda for full employment with a five-point strategy centred on growth (Chapter 14).

Broader and more radical prospects are offered in the last two chapters. Manza and Block discuss basic income schemes (Chapter 15), while Reati argues that a true solution for the unemployment problem can be found in a generalized reduction of working time, which would assist the secular downward trend of this variable (Chapter 16).

Concerning the first point, there are two extreme positions. On the one hand, there are those who advocate an unconditional full basic income grant – given to everybody, poor or rich – in order to make work really optional (Van Parijs, 1995). Since fundamental needs are covered by basic income, each individual can freely choose whether to work for further income. On the other hand, there are those who conceive basic income schemes as a means to fight poverty. This is the attitude taken by Manza and Block, who propose such a measure through a 'negative income tax', that is, an income supplement that would guarantee all US adult citizens an annual income of $6,000 in 1990 dollars (plus a supplement for children). These benefit levels are designed to bring all households within about 90 per cent of the Federal poverty line.

On the second topic, Reati works out the conditions under which the reduction of working time could serve the purpose of eliminating unemployment. He also shows that, when capital is operated at higher levels of utilization and there is a concomitant growth of productivity, it is even possible to reach full employment without cutting wages (and without inflation).

NOTES

1. By heterodox we refer to theories inspired by the classical approach, focusing on production and not just exchange, as is the case for neoclassical economics (Pasinetti, 1986).

REFERENCES

Bowles, S., Gordon, D.M. and Weisskopf, T. (1986), 'Power and profits: the social structure of accumulation and profitability in the postwar US economy', *Review of Radical Political Economics*, **18** (1–2), 132–67.

Boyer, R. and Saillard, Y. (eds) (1995), *Théorie de la régulation. L'État des savoirs*, Paris: La Découverte.

Freeman, C. (ed.) (1996), *Long Wave Theory*, Aldershot, Hants: Edward Elgar.

Gordon, D.M, Weisskopf, T.E. and Bowles, S. (1983), 'Long swings and the non-reproductive cycle', *American Economic Review*, **73** (2), 152–7.

Kitson, M., Michie, J. and Sutherland, H. (1997), 'The fiscal and distributional implications of job generation', *Cambridge Journal of Economics*, **21** (1), 103–20.

Kleinknecht, A. (1987), *Innovations Patterns in Crisis and Prosperity: Schumpeter's Long Cycle Reconsidered*, London: Macmillan.

Kleinknecht, A. (1996), *Is Labour Market Flexibility Harmful to Innovation? Notes from a Recent Debate in The Netherlands*, Discussion Paper TI 96-37/6, Rotterdam and Amsterdam: Tinbergen Institute.

Mandel, E. (1995), *Long Waves of Capitalist Development: A Marxist Interpretation*, 2nd edn, London: Verso.

OECD (1996), *Employment Outlook*, Paris: OECD.

Pasinetti, L.L. (1986), 'Theory of value: a source of alternative paradigms in economic analysis', in M. Baranzini and R. Scazzieri (eds), *Foundations of Economics: Structures of Enquiry and Economic Theory*, Oxford: Basil Blackwell, 409–31.

Persson, T. and Tabellini, G. (1994), 'Is inequality harmful for growth?', *American Economic Review*, **84**, 600–21.

Schumpeter, J.A. (1977), *Il processo capitalistico: cicli economici*, Turin: Boringhieri (translation of the abridged version of *Business Cycles*, first published in 1939).

Van Duijn, J.J. (1983), *The Long Wave in Economic Life*, London: Allen & Unwin.

Van Parijs, P. (1995), *Real Freedom for All: What, if Anything, Can Justify Capitalism?*, Oxford: Oxford University Press.

PART I

The Political Economy of Employment
and Unemployment

1. Labour supply and unemployment

Antonio G. Calafati*

INTRODUCTION

If the economic system is considered a 'self-regulating system', the appearance of unemployment should influence labour supply and labour demand so as to reduce the magnitude of unemployment. A self-regulating system is a system endowed with adjustment mechanisms which make disequilibria *transient*.

Two quite different classes of adjustment mechanisms have been considered in economics. The first class refers to adjustment processes based on price–quantity interrelations. The second class refers to adjustment processes based on parametric (institutional) modifications. The first class of adjustment mechanisms – price–quantity fluctuations in response to exogenous shocks, or disequilibrium states – has played a central role in the interpretation of unemployment. Indeed, the 'dis-connection' of this mechanism in the labour market has often been proposed as the cause of persistent unemployment. In contrast, institutional adjustment (or evolution), notwithstanding the importance that it has gained in different scientific paradigms in the last decades, has not been extensively used to interpret and explain unemployment. However, by affirming that in contemporary societies the adjustment mechanism which relies on the flexibility of wages is 'disconnected', the relevance of institutional evolution for the interpretation and explanation of unemployment becomes hard to question.[1]

In this chapter I shall address the issue of the relationship between institutional evolution and unemployment in modern market economies. In order to deal with the issue of institutional evolution – and institutional

* I am indebted to Ulrich Witt for his suggestions and encouragement while writing this chapter. I am also grateful to Paolo Ramazzotti, Marco Rangone and Stefano Staffolani for their comments on earlier drafts. Finally, I wish to thank Angelo Reati to whom I owe many helpful remarks, from which the chapter has greatly benefited. I am also indebted to St Antony's College (Oxford) and the Institut für Arbeitmarkets-und Berufsforschung (Nürnberg) where I conducted part of the research for this chapter. Financial support from MURST and CNR is gratefully acknowledged.

adjustment – it is necessary to consider carefully the dichotomy between formal and informal institutions, which raises the fundamental question of the meaning of 'self-regulation' for an artificial system. Modern economies are 'artificial systems', to the extent that some of their parts – for instance, formal norms constraining private contracting – are introduced through public decisions. In modern societies, then, the role of collective decisions in the sphere of institutional evolution is of central importance.

In a society endowed with a collective-decision mechanism a state of disequilibrium is relevant not only because it is perceived by individuals: policy-makers too perceive and react to disequilibrium states. If social interaction does not induce an institutional evolution which makes disequilibrium transient the economy may still attain a position of equilibrium if policy-makers react to disequilibrium by determining the 'right' kind of institutional modification. Such a system may be still regarded as a self-regulating system to the extent that the policy-maker is considered a part of the system and the 'calibration' of the system he or she performs is effective.[2]

By introducing the regulation of the system performed by collective decisions a second fundamental issue emerges: which are the disequilibria to which the policy-maker reacts? With regard to the issue of unemployment this is an important and pertinent question. In fact, the interpretation of unemployment as a disequilibrium state is not straightforward in the context of policy-making. Unemployment may be interpreted as a waste of resources. Unemployment may also be considered inefficient for the distortion in the distribution of the social product that it entails. Moreover, unemployment is, in most frameworks, an event which is interrelated to other events (for example, inflation).

The second issue I shall address in this chapter is the relationship between unemployment and the welfare effects of unemployment. I shall argue that the reaction of policy-makers to the 'unfairness' of the distribution of the social product brought about by unemployment is of crucial importance in explaining the kind of institutional evolution 'induced' by unemployment. I shall also argue that there are peculiarities of individual societies which 'filter' the effects of unemployment on the distribution of the social product. Because of specific institutional features, societies differ greatly in the effects that the same amount of unemployment has on the intertemporal distribution of the social product. Therefore, the institutional evolution which is relevant for an interpretation of the phenomenon of unemployment encompasses also the formal and informal institutions that govern distribution.

After developing an institutionalist metatheory of labour supply in the next three sections I shall then turn to explicate the relationships between the notions of 'unemployment' and 'disequilibrium'. In the final two sections I shall address the issue of the mechanisms which regulate labour supply and the welfare effects of unemployment.

INDIVIDUAL UTILIZATION OF TIME AND LABOUR SUPPLY

The utilization of time is the basis of the metatheory[3] of labour supply which I shall present in the following pages. I shall use three categories to describe the utilization of time by an unspecified individual agent: paid work (A); housework (H); consumption (L).[4] The usual distinction in behavioural sciences between the *actual* utilization of time and the *desired* utilization of time is introduced for any individual in the population who can control the function of allocating his or her time. This distinction is made necessary by the existence of constraints, stemming from social interaction, which limit the set of structures of time utilization that an individual can actually achieve.

By definition, in the following framework individual labour supply is given by A, where $\hat{A}$ and $\bar{A}$ are respectively *potential* and *actual* individual labour supply, and $D \equiv (\hat{A} - \bar{A}) \geq 0$ is a measure of the individual disequilibrium in this sphere.[5]

A basic question is the interpretation and evaluation of the individual and aggregate effects of a state of disequilibrium as defined above. To explicate this question it seems useful to turn to the analysis of the internal interrelations of the components which make up the structure of time utilization.

The cornerstone of the structure of time utilization is to be seen in the 'consumption process'. Individual welfare can be interpreted as a network of 'individual final states' – that is, 'goods' – *in which the individual wishes to be for a certain length of time* (the length of time being technically determined by the nature of the goods). Hence, following the fund-flow approach, the consumption process can be interpreted as a production process:[6] the consumption process may be interpreted as a subcategory of the more general production process. The consumption process is the final stage of the whole production process (when it is fully vertically integrated).

What distinguishes this stage of the production process is that it cannot be further disintegrated by substituting one's time with the time of other agents in the production (consumption) function. An agent may decide to drive to the theatre or to take a taxi. But that agent, and nobody else, has to sit down and follow the performance. There is a 'consumption process' when an interaction between an individual agent (body–mind) and physical elements takes place such that the time of the individual cannot be replaced by any other factor of production.

To perform the consumption process an individual needs a set of elements that can be grouped into three categories: (a) the flow elements (commodities and services) produced through housework; (b) the flow elements obtained through exchange from the market; (c) the fund elements.

Both the commodity content (capital intensity) and the time content (time intensity) associated with the consumption process put a constraint on the magnitude that the other elements of the structure of time utilization can assume – and vice versa. Given relative prices,[7] any increase in individual labour supply logically implies a change in the consumption pattern: *it must lead to choosing a network of final goods (final states) which is less time-intensive or to substituting self-produced commodities with commodities bought in the market.*

There are practical limits to the commodity content of the consumption patterns of human beings. However, the range of the commodity content of the consumption process is very wide – and it is culturally determined. Of course, for the individual, there is an economic limit. But this limit does not prevent the individual from setting the amount of paid work offered at a level *which would allow him or her to attain a 'very high' commodity content.*

I shall now introduce the hypothesis that individuals (being rational) tend to use all their time – that is, idleness is a forced or pathological state. Therefore, individuals choose a consumption structure that leads to a utilization of all their time. But the actual structure of time utilization of an individual at time t is the result of a specific 'adaptation process' that involves his or her whole structure of time utilization and consequently its consumption (Figure 1.1).

Given relative prices, the adaptation process towards the actual pattern of consumption is constrained by the fund elements to which the individ-

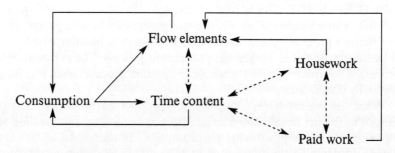

Figure 1.1 The interdependency between consumption and the utilization of time

ual has access, and by the fact that no goods can be generated – final states attained – without a certain amount of flow elements (which in modern societies cannot be totally self-produced).

An individual rationed in the labour market can react by moving to a pattern of consumption with a higher time content, and by increasing the self-production of the flow elements he or she uses in the consumption process. On the other hand, by reducing the time content of the consumption process an individual will be in a position to increase his or her labour supply.[8]

The adaptation process described above normally implies a learning process and sometimes it can even imply a change in the desired pattern of consumption.[9] The malleability of consumption is a factor of fundamental importance in this process of adaptation – and it is a consequence of the lexicographic ordering of goods that individuals follow.

Each individual evaluates the outcome of the adaptation process, and makes plans on how to change his or her consumption pattern. But this outcome can also be evaluated on the basis of the criteria of social justice collectively chosen. Hence, a very important issue in advanced societies, in which this process plays a crucial role, is to judge from a normative point of view the equilibrium position attained.[10]

NON-MARKET TRANSACTIONS AND INDIVIDUAL UTILIZATION OF TIME

The individual structure of time utilization is also rooted in the network of non-market transactions in which the individual is embedded. Individual agents are normally 'parts' of a social network with which a 'set of non-market transactions' is associated. In order to simplify the analysis I shall briefly consider only two classes of non-market transactions, namely those related to the family and to the state.

If the whole transaction network of an individual agent is taken into account, it can be easily inferred that market exchanges of work-time do not play the key role that is often implied. The assumption that the exchange of one's work-time is the generalized way of obtaining the commodities required to implement the self-production process and the consumption process should be relaxed. It is more a consequence of the incompleteness of the categorical system most economists use to describe the economic process than a useful heuristic hypothesis. In fact, non-market transactions allow part of the population to command the needed amount of commodities, totally or partially, without having to perform paid work. It follows that the redistributive patterns prevailing within the social networks in which the individual operates – the family and the state – must play a role in individual decisions concerning the structure of time utilization. Therefore, the redistributive function of the family and of the state has to be taken as the starting point of an analysis of labour supply.

A family is a network of emotional relationships, typically of a non-economic nature, with which a network of economic relationships is associated: (a) non-market transactions of property rights; and (b) team production and joint ownership of funds. The family operates also on the basis of a set of informal norms which governs the allocation of the time of the family members – and which regulates access to the funds owned collectively by the family.

There is a basic interdependency in the structure of time utilization by the family members.[11] Accordingly, for a given family the aggregate labour supply cannot be explained as the sum of independent individual choices. The total labour supply emerges from the equilibrium position of the family unit. The search for this equilibrium is constrained by the set of norms that governs the redistributive function that it performs, by the set of capital stock (and hence technology) on which individual and collective self-production processes are based and, finally, on prices.

The set of norms that governs the redistributive function changes over time, being an aspect of cultural evolution: a family can obviously move from one pattern of behaviour to another. It is also different in different societies. (The technology of self-production differs too as a consequence of accumulation of fund elements and technical progress.) Consequently, *the structure of time utilization of the family evolves over time as an effect of changes occurring in this set of norms* – and not only because of changes in individual values and motivation.

The family may decide to reduce the amount of paid work performed because some of its members wish to move to patterns of consumption with a higher time intensity and a lower commodity content. Or it may reduce the amount of self-production because some of its members wish to move to patterns of consumption that require more expensive inputs and hence decide to increase the total paid work offered in order to reach the needed (higher) income. The effect on total labour supply of the two changes is rather different.

As well as the family, the state too performs a redistributive function by supplying collective services, by allowing access to artificial and natural funds, and by redistributing resources. The range and depth of this function differs fundamentally from one country to another and has changed radically during the last four decades in many countries. The set of norms that shapes the redistributive function of the state by modifying the set of 'exchange entitlements' an individual can acquire, affects the utilization of time by individuals and, consequently, the total labour supply.[12]

Under the constraints and opportunities associated with the redistributive functions of the social networks to which a person belongs, the individual structure of time utilization of the family members converges towards a specific pattern through the kind of adaptation process described in the previous paragraph. The difference is given by the fact that the norms governing the division of labour and redistribution within the social network play a key role in this adaptation process.

CULTURAL CHANGES AND LABOUR SUPPLY

On the basis of the analysis carried out in the previous pages, one can affirm that the *individual labour supply* depends on the desired pattern of consumption, that is, on the desired structure of time utilization. To move from individual to total labour supply the *diffusion* among the population of specific patterns of time utilization and patterns of consumption have to be considered. Therefore, to understand the evolution of labour supply over time it is necessary to analyse the diffusion of specific patterns of time utilization within the population.

Any population can be described at time t in terms of the diffusion of a certain set of structures of time utilization.[13] The evolution of the overall utilization of time by the population – and hence of aggregate labour supply – is then to be understood in terms of the modification of the relative diffusion of the set of ideal-typical structures of time utilization.

As I stressed above, a given utilization of time is best interpreted as a behavioural pattern, that is a system of actions to be performed. The symbolic representation of an action or system of actions may be called a norm (or an institution).[14] By definition, a norm may be interpreted as an abstract pattern of behaviour (or action) to which an individual may decide to conform or not. The interest in conceptualizing the behaviour of individuals using the notion of the norm stems from the fact that it makes it possible to describe the population in terms of its normative orientation, that is in terms of the number of individuals following specific systems of norms.[15] The dynamics of labour supply can then be interpreted in terms of the propagation of norms.[16]

The speed of the propagation process of the set of relevant norms is very important in order to understand the trend in labour supply and unemployment in advanced countries. It is to be compared with the speed with which the number of jobs potentially available grows over time. The issue of the pace of the propagation process is related to the approach to be followed to study the propagation process itself. The standard approach of contemporary evolutionists is to represent the propagation process by modelling some kind of 'symmetrical interchanges of behaviour' taking place in 'absolute time'. It is questionable whether the resulting differential equation is a description or an explanation of the process. However, the institutionalist tradition offers a different methodological perspective to analyse the propagation process.

What is needed for a long-term analysis of the labour market is an explanation of the dynamics of labour supply. In fact, what is required in order to understand, and not only describe, the trend of labour supply is an interface which would allow economists to use as inputs for their analyses 'stylized descriptions' of the institutional and cultural changes that have taken place in a society over a certain period of time (and of which the trend in the labour supply is a consequence[17]). If the economic system is conceptualized as an 'open system', the evolution of institutions and values can be connected – on the basis of a linear or cumulative circular causal relationship – with the outcomes of economic interactions.[18] A systemic approach seems to be very useful to supplement the standard analysis of institutional evolution.

I shall now consider three stylized patterns of the structure of time utilization, just as an example. Their relative diffusion among the population seems to be relevant to the explanation of the evolution of the labour supply in industrial societies over the last four decades. They can be called respectively: (a) the 'acquisitive orientation'; (b) the 'parity orientation'; and (c) the 'work orientation'.

In the case of the acquisitive orientation, there is a tendency to increase the amount of the total paid work offered by the family in order to have a pattern of consumption with the highest possible 'commodity content'. Therefore, a family with an acquisitive orientation reduces the time intensity of consumption, decreases the amount of housework *and increases labour supply* – regardless of the level of welfare already attained. By postponing consumption the family can further increase current labour supply.

The 'parity orientation' within the family has marked the last four decades to the same extent as the acquisitive orientation. This expression refers to the constant reduction of housework and time content of the consumption process of women: a reduction necessary to accommodate an increase in the amount of paid work they perform outside the family.[19] This evolution in the values and attitudes of women leads to a great difference in their activity rate, and hence in the labour supply.[20] A world of increasing participation rates by women was not the world envisaged by social sciences and social thought until the 1940s.

The 'work orientation' is playing an increasing role and it is an evolution that will probably affect the labour market very markedly in the next decades too. With the term 'work orientation' I refer to the desire to exchange one's time on the market for reasons other than the quantity of exchange entitlements one wishes to obtain. There are two aspects to take into consideration. First, disutility of work does not apply in modern society to all agents and to all jobs. This phenomenon might have two causes: (a) the reduction of working time; (b) the improvement of working conditions. In a growing number of cases *working is a good*, that is a 'final state' in which one wishes to be. Working may be a good for different reasons. It may depend on the relationship between the personality and features of the social network to which the individual belongs. The relationship between aspiration, education and performing paid work also plays a role. In many instances, working means implementing a coherently pursued life plan. Moreover, working can be *the prevailing mode of integration in the social network.*[21]

The three ideal-types just considered have to be seen as some possible elements of a set of ideal-typical structures of time utilization that could be used to describe the population at a specific moment of time in relation to the objective of studying labour supply. Changes in the relative diffusion of the patterns of time utilization chosen to describe the population may be called 'cultural evolution'.[22] As shown in Figure 1.2, the trend in the labour supply may be said to be caused by cultural evolution in the sense that it depends on the relative diffusion of a specific set of structures of time utilization. In turn these structures are norms (of behaviour) and studying the propagation process can be interpreted as studying the changing normative orientation of the population.

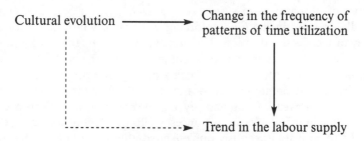

Figure 1.2 The dynamics of labour supply

UNEMPLOYMENT AND THE EVOLUTION OF THE ECONOMIC SYSTEM

Leaving aside short-term fluctuations in the level of economic activity, labour demand can be seen as rooted in the amount and type of artificial funds accumulated in the economy, in which technical progress is incorporated. The constellation of factors which governs the accumulation of funds and technical progress belongs to a sphere of social interaction which seems different from the sphere which is relevant, according to my statements above, to the interpretation of labour supply.

Unemployment in advanced industrial societies with no wage flexibility may then be interpreted as a *discrepancy* (or inconsistency) between the *desired* commodity content of the consumption plans of the population and the level of *accumulated* artificial funds and organizational knowledge in the economy.

Therefore, unemployment is a state of the world that might well be observed. The elemental and traditional questions here are: Are there feedback loops linking unemployment to the supply and demand of labour? What is the nature of these feedback loops? Reliable and effective *negative retroaction chains*, on the side of both labour supply and labour demand, would make the system a self-regulating system.

Before turning to answer these questions it is appropriate to call attention to the differences between the 'virtual retroaction' implicit in the operation of the price mechanism and the 'real retroaction' on which institutional evolution is based.

First, it must be taken into account that the existence of institutional adjustment mechanisms for a given economy in a certain period does not imply that states of disequilibrium are not observable. A 'correct' institutional evolution is an evolution that makes a state of disequilibrium transitory or temporary: it has the effect of reducing the magnitude of disequilibrium. A 'wrong' institutional evolution stabilizes or even enlarges the magnitude of disequilibrium. Institutional evolution is, first, a matter of propagation of systems of norms among the population and, secondly, of introducing (and enforcing) exogenously introduced norms by way of a collective decision. The propagation process follows a pattern that is specific to each norm and determined against the background of a set of *de facto* conditions. Even if such a propagation process goes in the right direction, it cannot by any means be assumed that it will end within a short time or even instantaneously. On the contrary, it might prove to be very slow in many relevant instances. Collective actions too cannot be assumed to be instantaneously implemented after observing the disequilibrium state. Moreover, the same process of individual orientation to the new norms needs time. In an economy that relies on institutional evolution to cope with states of disequilibrium it is quite normal to observe, for given periods of time, states of disequilibrium.

Secondly, by definition, any adjustment mechanism 'perceives' the state of the system as a 'disequilibrium state' only when the difference between the actual and the desired magnitude of the pertinent variable reaches a given threshold. Before institutional evolution is set in motion, the degree of disequilibrium must be 'significant'. Therefore, for example, only when the level of unemployment reaches a given 'threshold value' does it start to affect institutions.

The notion of 'threshold' is a key concept to understand how feedback loops operate. However, the determination of the magnitude of the threshold is a complex question. In the case of totally artificial systems the threshold of the control mechanism of the systems is determined by design. In the case of natural systems, for instance ecosystems, it may not be so easy to discover. In the case of individual human beings and societies, too, the thresholds in the retroaction processes which characterize these systems are difficult to detect and determine. For instance, for how long must an individual look for a job before deciding to give up the search? And how high must unemployment be before policy-makers decide to react in one way or another? As far as human beings and social systems are concerned there may even be a change in the magnitude of this threshold over time. This aspect is quite important when we consider the action of calibration of the economic system performed by the policy-maker. The threshold may be raised or lowered through a collective decision.

In an economic system that evolves over time, labour supply may progressively become higher than labour demand. When this *difference* is perceived by the adjustment mechanisms – assuming that there are effective adjustment mechanisms – it begins to decrease. To the extent that the retroaction is brought about by a collective decision, the moment in which the adjustment process begins depends on the value of the threshold, which is determined by a collective decision too (see Figure 1.3).

It is necessary to stress that a self-regulating economic system *may experience persistent unemployment*. Only in a world where self-regulation is ensured by 'virtual negative retroaction' are disequilibria not observable.[23] By contrast, in a world where 'real retroaction' operates, persistent unemployment is an observable phenomenon which has a magnitude associated with three 'parameters': first, it depends on the length of time it takes unemployment to reach the threshold value, secondly, it depends on the value of the threshold, thirdly, it depends on the length of time of the adjustment process.

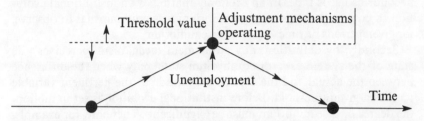

Figure 1.3 Threshold value, pace of adjustment and persistent unemployment

But before turning to the question of the existence of a feedback loop between unemployment and labour supply it is necessary to interpret the concept of unemployment against the background of the adjustment process discussed above.

Unemployment is measured by statistical offices. But the operationally defined notions of unemployment, to which such great importance is given in the policy debate, has constantly been a source of misunderstanding. When unemployment is measured on the basis of the standard practices it is in fact agents' plans that are referred to, and it is not possible to say whether these plans are equilibrium plans or not; that is, it is not possible to affirm to what extent they incorporate the constraints stemming from social interactions. Indeed, a problem of interpretation arises when the behavioural dimension of labour supply is retained *and* the adjustment mechanisms are not operating in virtual time. As a matter of fact, in a Walrasian framework the term 'unemployment' – a state of 'disequilibrium' – describes a virtual state of the labour market while the adjustment process *is taking place*. Since the adjustment process takes place in 'virtual time', the term 'unemployment' (and 'disequilibrium') by definition has no empirical content. According to the standard paradigm disequilibrium states are not observable. Hence, statistical offices cannot measure unemployment: they can only measure 'voluntary unemployment' – which by definition is not a disequilibrium state.

If adjustment processes are considered to take place in 'real time' – as in Figure 1.3 – the adjustment process has a time length and unemployment has an empirical dimension. Statistical offices are really measuring unemployment. However, a fundamental question arises: What are they actually measuring when they measure unemployment?

From the previous analysis a straightforward interpretation of unemployment follows: individuals have preferences as to their structures of consumption that cannot be turned into reality. When statistical offices measure unemployment, then, they are measuring the number of individuals for which the actual consumption structure (utilization of time) is different from their desired consumption structure. They are measuring the number of individuals who are not implementing their consumption plans. But social scientists have to find out which kind of equilibrium – or degree of order – stems from the attempts of individual agents to accomplish their plans: individual plans in themselves do not convey any information on the degree of disequilibrium. In fact, the operationally defined notion of unemployment cannot be taken as a measure of disequilibrium without many caveats. The difference between the actual consumption process of individuals and a standard consumption process – introduced as a normative judgement – ought to be taken as a measure of disequilibrium. In the Classical and Keynesian tradition unemployment causes by definition unsustainable patterns of consumption, and then disequilibrium states. But the effects of persistent unemployment on the consumption patterns of the population can be turned into an empirical question – especially when an affluent market society is under consideration (and one with a developed 'welfare state').[24]

UNEMPLOYMENT, PERMANENT UNEMPLOYMENT AND RELATIVE POVERTY

Once 'real time' is introduced, independently from the type of the feedback loops governing the supply and demand of labour, the relationship between the concepts of 'unemployment' and 'disequilibrium' becomes more complex. Even though there is a negative feedback effect at work, the fact that the adjustment process requires time has profound implications.

There is no *a priori* justification for assuming that while the adjustment process is taking place – assuming that it is taking place, for the sake of the argument – all the unemployed at time t will be also unemployed at time $t + k$. Instead, in principle it may happen that all the unemployed at time t are employed at time $t + k$.

In other words, when 'real time' is introduced the notion of unemployment has to be supplemented with that of 'permanent (or long-term) unemployment'. By shifting from virtual to real time, the interpretation of a state of disequilibrium in the labour market is not straightforward. Indeed, what matters is not simply 'being unemployed' at time t, but rather the length of time during which an individual has been unemployed at time t.

For this simple but none the less crucial reason the magnitude of 'unemployment' does not convey any significant information to policy-makers as to the effects of unemployment on the welfare of the population. But in order to know the structure that links aggregate unemployment to the welfare of the individuals making up the population it has always been necessary to interpret unemployment.

Since equilibrium in the labour market has two dimensions – one referring to optimal (or full) utilization of resources and the other referring to a 'fair' distribution of social product – it may be appropriate to speak of 'equilibrium' even in a situation of unemployment: it depends on how the ensuing distribution of the social product is evaluated.

The distribution of the social product, given the wage structure, depends, first, on the distribution of total work-time (labour demand) required by the market sector among the population; secondly, it depends on the existing pattern of redistribution. Even without taking into account the features of the redistribution taking place through non-market transactions it is clear that the standard notion of unemployment does not convey any significant information about the distribution over time of total work-time and, *a fortiori*, about the distribution of the social product.

Unemployment is not at all incompatible with equilibrium once equilibrium is interpreted as intertemporal equilibrium in the distribution of the total paid work required for the whole economic process. In principle, the possibility cannot be ruled out that the labour market – understood as the negotiation process of paid work – has the capacity to redistribute intertemporally among individuals the amount of paid work actually demanded over a given period.

The distinction between unemployment and long-term unemployment introduces a second level at which negative retroaction could be found.[25] The system might be endowed not only with a mechanism to reach aggregate equilibrium in the labour market, but also with a mechanism ensuring a 'fair' intertemporal allocation of available jobs among potential workers: a mechanism that brings about a turnover among the people employed.[26] If such a mechanism were at work, the labour market would retain the feature of assuring a 'fair' redistribution of the total paid work among the active population.

A society in which there is permanent unemployment may still be considered to be in equilibrium to the extent that a fair distribution of the social product is attained.[27] In any market society the distribution of the social product relies to a great extent on non-market transactions. Although the relevance of non-market transactions seems to be obvious,[28] economists have not always been ready to acknowledge it. To simulate the effects of a 'perfect' labour market, a society should be endowed with mechanisms which ensure that the ongoing economic process takes place under the following condition regardless of the actual state of the labour market:[29] all individuals should have a consumption structure such that their level of welfare is above the poverty line.

Since not all the population is employed, this condition may be ensured only if there is the necessary amount of redistribution of resources. This crucial redistributive function is in most countries characteristically performed by the norms which govern the personal interaction *within the family*. If the distributive role of the family is considered, the ongoing process should take place under the following condition: the family should have an amount of resources sufficient to put all members of the family above the poverty line – once the redistributive function has been performed. A society in which unemployment is equal to zero is, in terms of fairness of distribution of the social product, 'equivalent' with a state in which the number of poor is equal to zero. The redistributive function of the family is in most advanced countries supplemented by that of the state ('welfare state'). In fact, it can be affirmed that the redistribution of the social product has constantly been at the centre of the policy agenda since the Second World War.

As shown in Figure 1.4, it is necessary to address the 'transformation' in the notion of disequilibrium brought about by the separation of the issue of full (or optimal) allocation of human resources from the issue of the fair distribution of the social product. As I shall stress in the following section, each level is embedded in a specific set of norms, therefore economic systems – and the evolutionary pattern of every economic system – are distinguished from each other in terms of how they perform at each of the three levels.

The relationship between unemployment and relative poverty (let us assume relative poverty as a measure of the distortion in the distribution of social product) differs greatly from one social system to another. Two social systems with the same level of unemployment may have rather different levels of 'permanent unemployment', and the same level of permanent unemployment may produce different levels of relative poverty. From this perspective, a policy-maker interested in the welfare implications of unemployment should measure these welfare implications directly and not infer them from unemployment.

In order to understand the effects on the distribution of the social product of a state of disequilibrium in the labour market, the notion of a 'filter' may prove useful. In this context a 'filter' may be defined as a set of institutional features which reduce or amplify the signals coming from a different subsystem of the social system. Societies with the same level of permanent unemployment, for instance, may differ strongly with regard

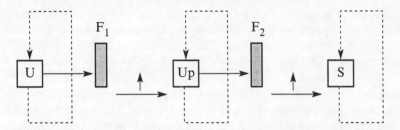

Figure 1.4 Systems of norms which regulate the effects of unemployment

to the 'unfairness' of the distribution of social products because of the norms governing welfare redistribution within the family, or because of the redistribution performed by the state: the extension and effectiveness of the welfare state is not equal in all industrial economies.

The 'filters' that transform a given level of unemployment into a different amount of permanent unemployment and a given level of permanent unemployment into a certain amount of relative poverty are made up of systems of norms which are partially artificial.

THE REGULATION OF LABOUR SUPPLY

The main conclusion reached so far is that the interrelation between labour supply and unemployment is not the only sphere in which to address the issue of disequilibrium and in which to look for mechanisms of self-regulation. However, by no means does this imply that the link between unemployment and labour supply is unimportant in understanding the dynamics of economic systems. Over the last two decades regulating (or constraining) labour supply has not been at the centre of policy-making. However, the regulation of labour supply was and might again be in the future of central importance.

Although economists are familiar with at least two kinds of 'spontaneous institutional evolution' which tend to reduce labour supply when unemployment is greater than zero, the link between unemployment and labour supply *has an essentially artificial nature*: labour supply reacts to unemployment as a consequence of 'actions of calibration' decided by collective agents.

One well-known mechanism which self-regulates unemployment is based on the circular causation between unemployment and population growth. The endogeneity of population has been one of the most discussed hypotheses from the time of Adam Smith until the beginning of the twentieth century. One of the most dismal aspects of Classical political economy was in fact its attempt to look at population as an endogenous variable. However, by the time of Wicksell it was well established that population growth had to be regarded within economics as an exogenous variable.[30] When looking at population growth from a modern perspective, the hypothesis of a link between unemployment and population has to be relaxed.[31]

A second 'spontaneous' circular causation is that implied in the behaviour of a 'discouraged worker', a phenomenon which has attracted some attention.[32] It is an interesting example of institutional evolution based on adaptive preference. Suppose that a relevant number of individuals follows the following rule in changing their desired structure of time utilization: the amount of paid work they offer at time $t + 1$ is equal to zero if they were unemployed at time t. Individuals no longer wish to exchange their time if they do not get jobs within a certain interval of time (a month, a year). In a society in which individuals follow this rule, unemployment is a self-destructive phenomenon. (It may be interesting to observe, however, that one of the reasons why this kind of adjustment does not take place for every individual may be the 'dissatisfaction' with the welfare content of the consumption pattern towards which the individual would converge if unemployed.)

In spite of their attractiveness, these two mechanisms have not played a significant role over the last four decades. On the contrary, collective action has deeply influenced the evolution of labour supply operating in two quite different spheres of social interactions. First, collective actions have constrained the relationship between population and paid work offered in terms of hours per year. Secondly, collective actions have greatly influenced the level of population regulated by immigration (and emigration).

Indeed, there are three collective norms whose modification has played a fundamental role in constraining the supply of labour: (a) the age of retirement; (b) the minimum working age; (c) the length of the working day. Labour supply – which can now be measured in units of time offered in the market, and not in terms of the number of individuals who offer part of their work-time in the market – is constrained by these norms.

Undoubtedly, the normative value of these parameters has undergone a significant change in this century, but their values have not changed so much in the last two decades. Whatever the interpretation of these norms,[33] it is none the less apparent that the trend followed by such parameters has been pointing in the direction of reducing labour supply, that is the amount of work-time offered in the market by the population. (In Europe, at least, the evolution of the labour force determined by changes in participation rates has been overwhelming since the 1960s: the increase in participation rates has reversed and not simply counterbalanced the effects of the trends of the above-mentioned norms.)

Governments have also influenced population levels by regulating immigration (and, whenever possible, emigration). Although the subject has been widely studied, economists tend to underrate the role played by (net) immigration in equilibrating (and disequilibrating) the labour market. In most European countries immigration accounted for the necessary increase in the labour supply during the 1950s and 1960s. What is interesting is the peculiar dynamics of net immigration, due to its substantial and non-economically determined asymmetry. Democratic societies cannot afford to take into consideration 'induced' emigration as a way of reducing labour supply. Even in the mild form of economic incentives to emigrate, public policies aimed at fostering emigration appear to be unacceptable. Many countries have even attempted to stimulate the emigration of foreigners in various ways. These policies, which for moral and political reasons were not pursued convincingly, did not prove successful and were abandoned.[34]

Regardless of the important question of asymmetry just stressed, control of immigration ought to be regarded as the most important policy

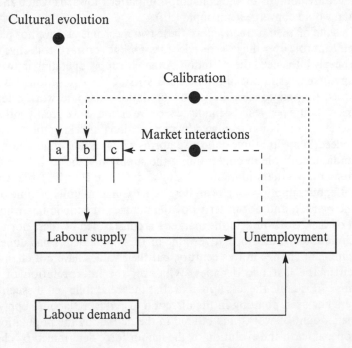

Figure 1.5 Levels of interactions between unemployment and labour supply

measure devised and implemented in the postwar period to reduce the state of disequilibrium in the labour market in industrial societies.

The level of labour supply observed at time t is the outcome of a process of cultural evolution and collective regulation. On the basis of the analysis carried out in the previous paragraphs there are three classes of norms (institutions) within the set of exogenous and endogenous norms governing labour supply (see Figure 1.5).

Class 'a' is made up of norms which are determined by cultural evolution – and are not influenced by the state of the labour market.[35] Women's attitudes to the amount of paid work they desire to perform is a notable example of the role played by cultural evolution in the labour market over recent decades in many industrial societies. This evolution has followed a pattern which is unrelated to the state of the labour market.

Class 'b' contains parameters whose trend is influenced by the state of the labour market through collective decision. The length of working time and the minimum working age, for example, are exogenous norms whose magnitude can be calibrated by policy-makers.

And finally there is the class 'c' which contains norms whose relative diffusion changes spontaneously as a reaction to the appearance of unemployment in the economic system. A change of preferences such as occurs in the case of the discouraged worker is an example of this class of norms.

UNEMPLOYMENT AND THE POLICY-MAKING PROCESS

I have sketched above a framework to address the issues of calibration and 'natural' negative retroaction in the sphere of labour supply. Calibration brought about by collective decisions more than the operation of 'natural' feedback loops emerged as the more effective level of regulation. It is now important to stress and make clear that calibration and the operation of natural counteractive feedback loops do not exhaust the issue of self-regulation.

Calibration operates as in Figure 1.6. The decision-maker observes the impact of the change in the institutional setting and introduces a new change if the *actual* impact is different from the *desired* impact.

Calibration (that is, setting the magnitude of exogenous variables at the desired level) is not the only way to modify the system which is relevant in the context of self-regulation. A second way is to build adjustment mechanisms into the system; that is, to insert *artificial* counteracting feedback loops or to eliminate the obstacles to the working of existing *natural* counteracting feedback chains. Instead of regulating the system from outside, the decision-maker endows the system with a control device.[36] A notable

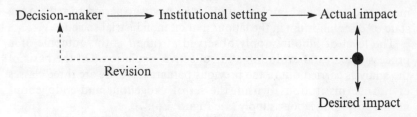

Figure 1.6 Calibration in the sphere of institutional evolution

and pertinent example is the counteracting feedback loop created by introducing unemployment benefits (see Figure 1.7).

The introduction of unemployment benefits closes the loop, creating
an artificial adjustment mechanism. To build the mechanism into the
system is a collective decision, but once inserted, the mechanism operates
automatically on the basis of individual rational behaviour.

There is a further level of collective intervention which must be considered with reference to institutional evolution. An economic system may
be modified by reducing the interdependencies within the system. The
decision-maker, by introducing or eliminating certain norms, may 'cut'
unwanted linear causal relationships or disconnect undesired cumulative
interdependencies. The introduction of a national health service, for
instance, makes the amount of health service an individual can consume
independent of his or her income and, hence, of the position he or she
has in the labour market. By removing the causal relationship between
unemployment and the reduction of the consumption of health services,
the welfare effects of unemployment are greatly reduced.

An important example of unwanted reinforcing feedback loops is
given by the effect on skills and motivation to learn of remaining unemployed. Training for the unemployed and similar policies aim to interrupt
the operation of this positive feedback loop.[37]

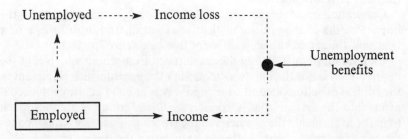

Figure 1.7 Unemployment benefits as a built-in counteracting feedback loop

The kinds of intervention I have now discussed are pertinent for each of the spheres indicated in Figure 1.4: unemployment, long-term unemployment and relative poverty are determined by their specific sets of linear and circular causal relationships. The two sets of institutions making up the 'filters' are also subject to the same kinds of intervention.

Once the systemic dimension of unemployment is stressed, the role played by the policy-making process in the regulation of the economic system makes the issue of interpreting unemployment quite complex. From a systemic perspective there are no reasons why policy-makers ought to evaluate unemployment in isolation. Rather, they should evaluate simultaneously a constellation of features of the economic process, associated with unemployment, which are in principle interdependent (see Figure 1.8). Having often relied on a strictly 'closed system', the hard fact that policy-makers evaluate an interdependent system and not only the labour market has been underrated. But it is a question that cannot be avoided. Moreover, since by definition this evaluation process has a political dimension, history plays an important part.

There is a second issue to consider. The structure that links the set of features (or state of the system) shown, as an example, in Figure 1.8, is made up of linear and circular causal relationships. As implied by the previous analysis, this structure is to be regarded neither as fixed nor as natural. The structure of the system is artificial to the extent that, as previously stressed, there are artificial institutions. Then, a constructivist approach to unemployment is unavoidable: not simply the scale of the economic process but also the structure of the system can be changed.

For some decades after the Keynesian revolution and the Neoclassical synthesis, the complexity of the issue of self-regulation with regards to unemployment was often neglected. The Keynesian approach to unem-

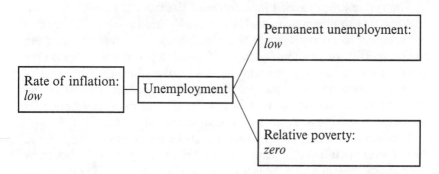

Figure 1.8 Unemployment and its constellation of hypothetical effects

ployment – similar to the approach stemming from the Neoclassical synthesis[38] – has for many years underrated the relationship between unemployment and other states of the system. In a complex and evolving economic system to interpret unemployment as a 'disequilibrium state' is no longer obvious (whereas it is obvious if one moves from the Walrasian or Keynesian paradigm). It depends on the theoretical perspective from which policy-makers observe the state of the economic system and on the set of values from which they evaluate the state of the system.

An economic process which is associated with high unemployment but with low permanent unemployment and low inflation may be regarded by a policy-maker as desirable. Therefore, instead of reacting to unemployment, the decision-maker may react to long-term unemployment and decide to reduce, for instance, unemployment benefits and to implement training measures for the unemployed. Moreover, it may be interested in the degree of relative poverty and react to this feature of the economic process.

For some decades there was a prevalence of policies of demand regulation and expansion of the welfare state. In terms of Figure 1.4 it is clear that these two policies, implemented to combat unemployment, belong to a much larger set of possible policies. In fact, it seems hard to deny that during the past decade in many countries there has been a shift in the attention of policy-makers towards a different subset of policies. A large number of institutional modifications are being implemented which aim at changing the relation between unemployment and long-term unemployment, and particularly at having an economic process which produces a lower level of long-term unemployment starting from the same level of unemployment. To create an economic system able to generate very low permanent unemployment – whatever the level of unemployment is – seems to be the new policy paradigm.

The systemic approach I have followed has made it possible to show that reacting to unemployment is not the only strategy of policy-makers with respect to unemployment. They may look at unemployment from the perspective of the consequences of unemployment and focus on the unfair distribution of the social product rather than on the waste of resources (reduction of social production). Policy-makers may assign no importance to 'unemployment as a waste of resources' and care only about the distortion in the distribution of the social product.[39]

Furthermore, the system of values that the policy-maker maps on to the structure that links the features of the economic process is chosen by the political system and is subject to change over time.

CONCLUSION

In this chapter I have addressed the issue of self-regulation in relation to the phenomenon of unemployment, for an economy with fixed wages. I have argued that an economy where wages are fixed is by no means to be regarded as an economy where there are no adjustment mechanisms. In fact, in a market economy institutional evolution can be seen, at least in part, as influenced by counteractive feedback loops. In principle it can be assumed that some of these loops ('natural loops') are established in the economic system as a consequence of the patterns of private interactions taking place among individuals. However, other loops are created by collective decisions. In an economic system which is largely artificial – in the sense that individual behaviour is embedded in a web of formal norms – rational policy-makers react to disequilibrium states in two ways. First, they calibrate the system changing the institutional setting. Secondly, they insert artificial negative feedback loops, that is they change the *structure* of the system.

After developing a metatheory of labour supply I addressed the issue of the relationship between labour supply and unemployment. I came to the conclusion that in an economic system characterized by ongoing institutional evolution labour supply does not react spontaneously to the appearance of unemployment in a significant measure. Nevertheless, labour supply is embedded not only in a web of informal norms but also in a web of formal norms. Therefore, there are different norms that could be changed by the collective decision-maker in order to adjust labour supply so as to reduce unemployment. There is much scope for calibration in this sphere.

I have also questioned the often implicit hypothesis that unemployment is by definition a disequilibrium state. In fact, unemployment can be seen in terms of a waste of resources and in terms of a distorted distribution of the social product. I have argued that the relationship between unemployment and the distributive effects of unemployment is very complex, with a variety of institutional features of social systems playing an important role. If unemployment is not causing an unsustainable distribution of social product, it could not be regarded by policy-makers as a disequilibrium state. Unemployment may not induce a calibration in labour supply, for instance, because policy-makers do not perceive it as a disequilibrium.

However, the institutional evolution of the economic system might be influenced by a 'distortion' in the distribution of the social product. But these 'distortions' or 'disequilibrium' might not influence the institutions governing the level of unemployment, but rather the institutions regulating the effects of unemployment on the distribution of the social product.

I have argued that these effects can be analysed within two spheres. First, there is the relationship between unemployment and long-term unemployment. Secondly, there is the sphere of redistribution of the social product where the family and the state play a crucial role.

I have not analysed the adjustment mechanisms which may be found in these two spheres. I have, however, suggested that by considering these two spheres the issue of self-regulation in relation to unemployment becomes much more complex than it is normally considered to be. First, there are two sets of norms, that I have named 'filters', partly natural and partly artificial, that transform a given level of unemployment into a certain level of relative poverty. Being made up also of collective norms such filters may be objects of calibration. Secondly, both long-term unemployment and relative poverty might be influenced by negative and positive feedback loops. Again, negative feedback loops may be natural or artificial.

Finally, I have stressed that to conceptualize a given state of the world as a 'disequilibrium state' is a normative judgement. Moreover, in an economic system, the states of the subsystems are interrelated. A constellation of interdependent states associated with unemployment – and not only unemployment – is normally evaluated by the policy-maker. Unemployment may persist because the policy-maker does not react by calibrating the system in a way that would reduce unemployment but would also worsen the state of other subsystems.

The current impasse on the issue of unemployment is caused by the transition which policy-making is experiencing. Aggregate demand management and collective redistribution (welfare state) were the two levels at which unemployment and the welfare effects of unemployment were tackled for some decades after the Second World War. In recent times unemployment has come to be seen as related to the states of other subsystems – inflation or features of labour negotiations, for instance – while the private transaction process (market and non-market transactions) has come to be regarded as more efficient than collective transactions to achieve the desired degree of redistribution. Having a normative dimension, these shifts are hard to question. However, it may be worthwhile stressing that they certainly imply a radical transformation of modern societies, and the transition towards this new structure is a complex question.

NOTES

1. An effective analysis of the reasons why in modern societies the labour market does not clear through wage flexibility is presented in Solow (1990). By generalizing the 'wage efficiency theory' and the 'insider–outsider theory' Solow puts forward an explanation of the fact that wages are not flexible, based on the rationality of a specific set of norms

governing the behaviour of individuals in the labour market. However, Solow neglects a question of fundamental importance. A system in which markets clear through price changes is a system with an extraordinarily high degree of 'resilience': shocks of any magnitude are absorbed by the system, which is able to attain a new equilibrium position. To the extent that equilibrium is what matters and the system has a high degree of resilience we do not need to care about the magnitude and nature of shocks. But if the mechanisms which make the system 'resilient' are disconnected the (disequilibrium) state of the system at time t may be understood only in terms of the nature and magnitude of shocks occurring at time $t - k$. To understand the nature, frequency, relevance and magnitude of these shocks becomes the only way to construct an explanation of the state of the economic system. Moreover it may be said to be exactly the scope of the 'theory of institutional evolution'. Solow can bypass this question simply because, although he gives a role to norms in his framework, he does not consider the evolution of the normative orientation of the population over time. But how believable is it to consider as given all the social norms which seem to be relevant to understand the state of the labour market in the last four decades? When the state of a system over a long period is considered to assume a given normative orientation it seems to be inappropriate.

2. A modification of an artificial part of the system may be called a 'calibration of the system' (on the concept of calibration see Bateson, 1979, ch. VII). If it is assumed that there is a calibration of the economic system such that the system will reach an equilibrium position, unemployment (or any other state of disequilibrium) may be interpreted as a consequence of the inability or unwillingness of policy-makers to calibrate the system.

3. A metatheory is a web of causal relationships which is 'open', that is it allows the occurrence of the event to be explained, and also a limited set of other events (compare Right, 1971). By adding a state of the world present at time $t - 1$ (or an event occurring at time $t - 1$) only the event to be explained can be caused by the modified causal relational structure. In so doing the metatheory is then turned into a theory. This way of constructing an explanation is typical of much institutionalist thinking. For an analysis of Hirschman's methodology from this perspective, see Calafati (1996).

4. Compare Juster and Stafford (1991).

5. I am not taking into consideration the case in which individuals are forced to work *more* than they wish.

6. Throughout this chapter I shall interpret the production process following Georgescu-Roegen's fund-flow model (Georgescu-Roegen, 1971).

7. Assuming no wealth, transfers or access to credit.

8. An individual can increase labour supply also by postponing consumption.

9. The adaptation process is generated by the 'mechanisms of integration': see Parsons and Shils (1959, pp. 133–42).

10. The set of exchange entitlements of an individual is not to be linked only to his or her actual structure of time utilization, and more specifically to A, but also to the relative market value of A. In modern societies at least the labour market is 'segmented'. Individual agents can move towards a 'higher' segment of the labour market – and hence towards a higher wage for unit of time.

11. For an institutionalist approach to the study of the family, see the important studies presented in Anderson *et al.* (1994).

12. On the notion of 'exchange entitlements' see Sen (1981, ch. 1, Appendix A).

13. The elements of this set will have an ideal-typical character, and their construction is the first step to be taken in order to accomplish a research strategy grounded on the methodology of 'population thinking'. Although it is not often stressed, 'population thinking' in social sciences requires a greater attention to be given to the categorial framework which will be used in the explanation process. For a restatement of the importance of the shaping of concepts and categories in social science, and therefore of description, see Runciman (1983).

14. See Dopfer (1991, 1994). In the text 'institutions' and 'norms' are synonymous (some authors consider an institution a behaviour grounded in a norm: compare Crawford and Ostrom, 1995). However, I believe that the notion of 'norm' – for instance as

presented in Right (1963) – should be taken as the basis of the analysis. It has a more precise semantic meaning than the term institution. Moreover, and more importantly, the notion of 'norm' lies in the overlapping area of different social sciences, playing a crucial role in any interdisciplinary research programme. With the expression 'institutional evolution' I refer to a change in the normative orientation of the population. A change in the normative orientation – which can be driven by different kinds of reasons (compare Dopfer, 1994) – manifests itself in the form of a higher number of people following a given norm (or system of norms). Institutional evolution does not require normative innovation, that is the emergence of a new norm: it can be only a matter of diffusion of norms already existing and followed. Institutional evolution, however, requires in some cases institutional innovation too: it is the case of collective norms. With collective norms it is a case of diffusion (number of people who decide to abide by the norm) and of normative innovation. Institutional innovation, then, is rooted in changes taking place in the individual systems of action and in the collective system of action.

15. One can then follow different approaches: either to rely on the research strategy implied in the notion of 'embedded behaviour' – compare Granovetter (1985) and Wrong (1961) – or to assume a cost–benefit perspective (as in the new institutional economics and also in some strands of evolutionary thinking in economics). The two approaches are not mutually exclusive. An interesting approach to this fundamental question has been developed in Dopfer (1994).

16. If, as in many studies of the propagation process, a symmetric exchange of behaviour over time is assumed, the propagation process may be described analytically as in Witt (1989).

17. Compare Kapp (1961, 1976a).

18. On the 'open system character' of the economic system, compare Kapp (1976b). A general treatment of the notion of an 'open system' is to be found in Bertalanfy (1969). The interpretation of the economic system as an 'open system' is the hallmark of much interdisciplinary research done in economics during the last four decades by such authors, among others, as Georgescu-Roegen, Myrdal, Hirsch, and Hirschman.

19. The important aspect to observe is that there are significant differences between the European countries as to the actual diffusion of this norm of behaviour. Clearly in most countries there is still scope for a further diffusion of the cluster of norms that lies behind this evolution.

20. As to the reduction in the time content of the consumption process of women, for instance, Veblen's description of the leisured class can be compared with the attitude towards work in many contemporary societies: see Veblen (1989).

21. Certainly an education that aims specifically at acquiring the skill to be used in the workplace will greatly increase the number of people in society who see working activity as a way of fulfilling their life plans and not only as a means of access to a certain amount of exchange entitlements.

22. To consider the linkages between cultural evolution and the evolution of the economic system is the vantage point of the institutionalist paradigm. Ayres's (1944) work is a notable and early example of the utilization of this approach, which has been developed, among others, by G. Myrdal, K.W. Kapp, F. Hirsch and A.O. Hirschman.

23. 'Persistent unemployment has been a persistent problem for economic theory' (Solow, 1990, p. 28). In fact, in the neoclassical paradigm a self-regulating system cannot be in a state of disequilibrium.

24. A country in which this issue has been widely investigated from an empirical perspective is certainly Germany: see, for instance, Strittmatter (1992) and Hess *et al.* (1991).

25. On the notion of 'permanent' or 'long-term' unemployment see, for instance, Benoît-Guilbot and Gallie (1994).

26. The often implicit importance given to this aspect is reflected in the explicit importance of the rate of jobs created and destroyed. The hypothesis that unemployment is transitional is more likely to be correct in a world where people keep changing jobs because workplaces are continuously 'destroyed' and 'generated'.

27. In order to highlight the welfare implications of labour market disequilibrium the category of 'person's resources' as developed in Sen (1992) may supplement the 'entitlement approach' (Sen, 1981).

28. The role of non-market transactions in market economies was stressed by Polanyi (1944) in his classical work. It has assumed a central importance in contemporary discussions on the notion of inequality (see Sen, 1992).

29. It seems justifiable to assume that in an industrial (affluent) society a distribution of the social product *does* exist according to which all members of the population are above the poverty level (however defined). This may not be true in a 'backward' country.

30. This change of perspective has important consequences, which have been often underrated, for instance, by growth theory. In the second half of this century there has been a 'population cycle' in most advanced countries. Population changes have been a continuous source of significant shocks to which the economy has had to adjust. Standard growth theory rules out these sources of shocks assuming a constant rate of population growth (and an unchanging age structure within the population).

31. Although not often stressed in public discussion of unemployment, different governments expect to solve the current problem of unemployment through demographic change, and hence they are prepared to live for at least two decades with unemployment. Some governments may be even looking with fear at the coming shortage of potential labour supply. This position seems to be held by the Deutsches Institut für Wirtschaft (1990), which sees present unemployment as temporary (in the meaning in which this word was used in classical political economy).

32. The empirical relevance of the phenomenon of the discouraged worker is well known, but there is no general agreement on its interpretation. The 'discouraged worker' may be still considered an 'unemployed individual'. In most countries total unemployment is measured with and without discouraged workers. It is not a technical issue. It is a matter of interpreting the exchange of one's own work-time as a 'right' or not.

33. Introducing collective norms forces us to introduce the notion of the normative orientation of the population: see Witt (1986); Vanberg (1986). In this case the problem seems to be the authority of the collective agent to interfere with the spontaneous process of norm propagation. This is a difficult issue. If a population with a strong normative orientation is considered, one can study the evolution of the parameters governing labour supply as the consequence of collective decisions. Otherwise these parameters can be considered as natural norms, that is norms emerging from private interactions. The collective decisions concerning them can then be considered as a ratification of the diffusion of such norms among the population.

34. See Werner and König (1984); Hönekopp (1987).

35. Certainly not in the time span which is relevant for the policy-making process.

36. If an artificial control device does not operate as expected it can be revised or calibrated. In fact, one can also speak of calibration with reference to a modification of a control mechanism (an interacting set of parts) and not only as a modification of a part of the system.

37. The effect of an undesired reinforcing feedback can also be counterbalanced by building into the economic system counteractive feedback loops operating on the same elements of the system.

38. Compare Solow (1990, ch. 3).

39. For a forceful criticism of this position, see Lunghini (1995).

REFERENCES

Anderson, M., Bechhofer, F. and Gershuny, J. (eds) (1994), *The Social and Political Economy of the Household*, Oxford: Oxford University Press.

Ayres, C.E. (1944), *The Theory of Economic Progress*, Chapel Hill, NC: University of North Carolina Press.

Bateson, G. (1979), *Mind and Nature: A Necessary Unity*, London: Wildwood House.

Benoît-Guilbot, O. and Gallie, D. (eds) (1994), *Long-term Unemployment*, London: Frances Pinter.

Bertalanfy, L. von (1969), *General System Theory*, New York: Braziller.

Calafati, A.G. (1996), 'Albert O. Hirschman and the complexity of economic systems', Annual Scientific Meeting of Società Italiana degli Economisti, ms.

Crawford, S.E. and Ostrom E. (1995), 'A grammar of institutions', *American Political Science Review*, **89** (3): 582–600.

Deutsches Institut für Wirtschaftsforschung (1990), 'Angebot an Arbeitskräften in Deutschland auf längere Sicht', *Wochenbericht*, **49**: 679–90.

Dopfer, K. (1991), 'Towards a theory of economic institutions: synergy and path dependency', *Journal of Economic Issues*, **2**: 535–50.

Dopfer, K. (1994), 'How economic institutions emerge: institutional entrepreneurs and behavioral seeds', in Shionoya, Y. and Perlman, M. (eds), *Innovation, Technology, Industries, and Institutions: Studies in Schumpeterian Perspective*, Ann Arbor, Mich.: University of Michigan.

Georgescu-Roegen, N. (1971), *The Entropy Law and the Economic Process*, Cambridge, Mass.: Harvard University Press.

Granovetter, M. (1985), 'Economic action and social structure: the problem of embeddedness', *American Journal of Sociology*, **91** (3): 481–510.

Hess, D., Hartstein, W. and Smid, M. (1991), 'Auswirkungen von Arbeitslosigkeit aus die Familie', *Mitteilungen aus der Arbeitmarkt- und Berufsforschung (IAB)*, no. 1: 178–92.

Hönekopp, E. (ed.) (1987), *Aspekte der Ausländerbeschaftigung in der Bundesrepublik Deutschland*, Nürnberg: IAB.

Juster, F.T. and Stafford, F.P. (1991), 'The allocation of time: empirical findings, behavioral models, and problems of measurement', *Journal of Economic Literature*, **29**: 471–522.

Kapp, K.W. (1961), *Toward a Science of Man in Society: A Positive Approach to the Integration of Social Knowledge*, The Hague: Martinus Nijhoff.

Kapp, K.W. (1976a), 'The nature and significance of institutional economics', *Kyklos*, **29** (2): 209–32.

Kapp, K.W. (1976b), 'The open system character of the economy and its implications', in Dopfer, K. (ed.), *Economics in the Future: Toward a New Paradigm*, London: Macmillan.

Lunghini, G. (1995), *L'età dello spreco. Disoccupazione e bisogni sociali*, Turin: Bollati Boringhieri.

Parsons, T. and Shils, E.A (eds) (1959), *Toward a General Theory of Action*, Cambridge, Mass.: Harvard University Press.

Polanyi, K. (1944), *The Great Transformation*, New York: Rinehart & Winston.

Right, G.H. von (1971), *Explanation and Understanding*, Ithaca, N.Y.: Cornell University Press.

Right, G.H. von (1963), *Norm and Action: A Logical Enquiry*, London: Routledge & Kegan Paul.

Runciman, W. (1983), *Treatise on Social Science*, Cambridge: Cambridge University Press.

Sen, A. (1981), *Poverty and Famines. An Essay on Entitlements and Deprivation*, Oxford: Clarendon Press.

Sen, A. (1992), *Inequality Reconsidered*, Oxford: Clarendon Press.

Solow, R.M. (1990), *The Labour Market as a Social Institution*, Oxford: Basil Blackwell.

Strittmatter, F.J. (1992), *Langzeitarbeitslosigkeit im Wohlfahrtsstaat*, Nürnberg: IAB.

Vanberg, V. (1986), 'Rules and choice in economics and sociology', *Jahrbuch für Neue Politische Ökonomie*, 7: 146–67.

Vanberg, V. (1986), 'Spontaneous market order and social rules: a critical examination of F.A. Hayek's theory of cultural evolution', *Economics and Philosophy*, 1: 75–100.

Veblen, T. (1989), *The Theory of the Leisure Class. An Economic Study of Institutions*, New York: Macmillan.

Werner, H. and König, I. (1984), *Ausländbeschäftigung und Ausländerpolitik in einegen westeuropäischen Industriestaaten*, Nürnnberg: IAB.

Witt, U. (1986), 'Evolution and stability of cooperation without enforceable contracts', *Kyklos*, **38**: 245–66.

Witt, U. (1987), *Individualistische Grundlagen der Evolutorischen Ökonomik*, Tübingen: J.C.B. Mohr (Paul Siebeck).

Witt, U. (1989), 'The evolution of economic institutions as a propagation process', *Public Choice*, **62**: 155–72.

Wrong, D. (1961), 'The oversocialized conception of man in modern sociology', *American Sociological Review*, **26** (2).

2. Demand- and supply-side approaches to economic policy

Jonathan Michie and Christos Pitelis*

INTRODUCTION

Conventionally, demand-side (macro) and supply-side (competition and industrial) policies are examined separately, usually by specialists in different areas of economics. The methodological assumption is to regard the other side (demand or supply, respectively) as given.

This situation is not satisfactory. Demand- and supply-side policies should not be seen as just non-mutually exclusive; rather they should reinforce each other. Moreover, from the theoretical point of view it is important that both types of policies should be based on a common conceptual framework. Traditionally, this has not been the case. Notably, while industrial policies in the West have been based on the assumption of imperfect competition, macro-international trade policies were assuming perfectly competitive markets. On the other hand, the new international trade theories and Michael Porter's approach to the competitiveness of nations do support the need for an integration of demand- and supply-side policies.

The aim of this chapter is to take a further step in this direction. The next section considers the current macroeconomic policy agenda, and the subsequent two sections discuss industrial policies and strategy and the demand- and supply-side dichotomy, respectively. The final section concludes.

THE CURRENT MACROECONOMIC POLICY AGENDA

Economic policy in the European Union (EU) in the late 1990s is stuck on the path laid down by the Maastricht Treaty, which was drawn up in the late 1980s' era of economic growth, falling unemployment and con-

* We are grateful for comments from participants of the 1996 EAEPE conference and in particular to Angelo Reati.

cerns about rising inflation. The idea of pursuing active macro-economic and industrial policies has given way to an adherence to monetarism, privatization and labour market deregulation. At a macroeconomic level the resulting growth in low pay, poverty and unemployment has placed an increasing burden on the public purse. And at the industrial level productive efficiency is harmed by the resulting instability in the labour market – particularly within the increasingly low-paid sectors – and the loss of incentives for producers to upgrade their productive systems. A vicious circle of low-wage, low-productivity, low-investment activity is generated, leading to loss of competitiveness and growing unemployment, with the increasing burdens on the exchequer provoking yet further moves down the recessionary spiral. Yet any suggestion of fiscal and monetary policies to combat unemployment has consistently raised the spectre of high inflation in the minds of policy-makers.

This spectre receives its support from the idea that there is a unique 'non-accelerating inflation rate of unemployment' (the NAIRU): in other words, the assertion that there is one particular level of unemployment at which inflation stabilizes. The relationship between unemployment and changes in earnings variously measured is plotted for Britain in the 1980s in Michie and Wilkinson (1992), and the results could not be more at variance with the notion of a predictable relationship between the two variables.[1] The historical evidence for any credible relationship between the level of joblessness and the rate of inflation is thus fragile at best.

This NAIRU theory is a version of Milton Friedman's 'natural rate of unemployment' developed by the economists Richard Layard and Stephen Nickell. They argue that, as unemployment falls, the 'bargaining wage' demanded by workers rises whilst the 'feasible wage' which employers can afford to pay does not rise with output. This failure to rise of the wage which employers can afford to pay as output rises is based on one or both of two seriously flawed arguments.

First, it is supposed that as firms increase their level of output, productivity fails to rise, and may fall. But the opposite is usually the case: in economic expansions output per head generally rises (it increased 20 per cent between 1984 and 1990 in the UK). This increase in productivity is explained by the fact that capital is operated at a higher level of utilization as demand increases, and firms invest in more modern and productive equipment. The more reasonable assumption that productivity and hence the 'feasible wage' increases with output destroys one of the bases for the NAIRU law. If increased capacity utilization and, over the longer term, an increased and more technologically advanced capacity allow a growth of the feasible wage, then there may be no unique 'equilibrium' point (NAIRU) with only that one level of unemployment associated with non-accelerating inflation. Thus even if the bargaining and feasible wages happened to coincide at a given level of unemployment, if unemployment falls with the feasible wage, increasing (due to increased productivity) more than the increase in the bargaining wage, then such a model would actually predict that the reduction in unemployment would result in inflation falling rather than rising.[2]

The second string to the NAIRU bow is the argument that firms have to cut prices to sell more. By enabling firms to lower prices, cuts in wages and other employment costs allow them to sell more and to increase employment. But the size of the market of a firm (and hence the employment it can offer) is determined by, amongst other things, its price *and* the price of its competitors. If the workers employed by that firm accept a lower wage so that the firm can retain its monopoly profits at a lower price, it will be able to increase its output and its market share but only at the expense of other firms and the employment they offer. But, of course, if all firms lower their wages there will be no change in relative prices and no increase in demand. In fact, if this happens, the chances are that demand will decline because a general fall in wages relative to prices will have reduced the purchasing power of wage income.

Full Employment

Throughout the 1950s and 1960s almost all countries enjoyed full employment, meaning that anyone who wanted a job was generally able to find one. There was of course always some registered unemployment as people changed jobs, but the long-term involuntary unemployment of the interwar period had gone. All this came to an end in the early 1970s. So while full employment is certainly possible, it will require a fundamental change in government policy globally. However, there are various arguments that suggest full employment may not even be a desirable objective.

First, it has been argued that unemployment may be necessary to make those in employment work harder. This ignores the rapid economic and social progress made during the 25 years 1948–73 when there was full employment and economic growth was faster than it has been since; the response to wide job opportunities was a progressive workforce upgrading. Compare that with the cost of the enforced idleness and the enormous loss of prospects for those entering the labour market since the mid-1970s. Secondly, it is sometimes objected that not everyone wants a full-time job. But the point is that people should be given that opportunity and choice, along with the possibility of part-time work. Thirdly, there are environmental constraints. This means that we should think about the type of economic growth we want, not just the amount. But there is no reason to suppose that environmentally friendly economic progress is less labour-intensive than a more environmentally unfriendly path; or that the physical environment will in any way be served by a progressive degeneration of the social environment.

There is a separate argument that full employment is no longer possible, however desirable, because new technology is allowing huge increases in productivity so that fewer workers are actually needed. This is simply wrong. There is no evidence at all of an increase in the rate of growth of labour productivity over the past two decades; on the contrary, if anything it has been slower. Moreover, even a casual glance at the world today would indicate that public and private needs place few constraints on employment whatever the improvement in technology. There may be problems with the willingness or ability of present forms of political, social and economic organization to meet even the basic requirements of the majority of the world's population but that does not disguise the want.

A Policy Agenda

The industrial world – especially Europe – is in the grip of an unemployment crisis which bears worrying similarities to the situation before the Second World War: in the 1920s the world economy was highly volatile with unprecedented stock market and currency speculation. Organized labour was on the retreat and wage cutting and labour market deregulation was the order of the day. The consequent effective demand problems were exacerbated by the collapse of commodity prices in the early 1920s which benefited industrial profits but ruined agriculture. This unstable economic base collapsed in 1929 when the world financial system was completely disrupted by the Wall Street crash and industry was undermined by the Great Depression, against which national governments proved individually and collectively powerless.

Economic orthodoxy, then as now, held trade unions, state labour market regulation and social welfare payments responsible for unemployment, and preached against state intervention to counter joblessness and for balanced budgets. When translated into policies these notions, by deepening the recession and multiplying social deprivation, had the opposite to the predicted effect and the consequent widening of the credibility gap led to weak and vacillating governments. In Britain, the Labour government split over policies which cut pay, reduced unemployment benefit levels and introduced means testing, policies which were finally implemented by the National Government led by Ramsay MacDonald. In Germany six million unemployed, widespread poverty and cuts in unemployment pay paved the way to fascism and ultimately to the Second World War.

The lessons learned from this débâcle, at the level of economic theory and public policy, laid the groundwork for the postwar prosperity. National governments committed themselves to full employment and a welfare state policy which included health, social security, education and housing. In the labour market, collective bargaining was encouraged, minimum employment rights guaranteed and industrial training was strengthened. At the international level agreements on finance and trade were concluded which were designed to encourage international commerce but which were targeted at currency speculation and the problems of chronic surplus countries. These were reinforced at the national level by controls on international capital movements.

Contingency plans were made for the stabilization of commodity prices but these made little headway after the end of the Korean War crisis when the collapse of raw material prices turned the terms of trade in the favour of industrial countries. The purpose of these policies was to create a framework of rules for encouraging creativity of free enterprise whilst prohibiting the strong predatory and exploitative tendencies in capitalism.

This national and international collectivist effort created the promise that poverty would at last be lifted. This promise was most fully realized in those countries of northern Europe which most completely adopted the co-operative state model; no more so than in Sweden where the Social Democratic Party embraced the 'wage solidarity' with 'active labour market' policies formulated by the trade unions so that labour effectively managed capitalism (on which, see Michie, 1994). At the international level the growth in the market of industrial countries helped to create new opportunities for economic development. The real failure of the postwar period was at the international level. This can be explained by the dominant economic power of the USA and that country's continued adherence to the notion that capitalism operates at its best when completely unrestricted. This philosophy came to pervade the workings of the international agencies (IMF, World Bank and GATT) and subverted their role as agents working for world economic stability.

This combination of, first, the lack of any effective stabilizing international institutions and, second, the progressive decline in the economic power of the USA played a major part in recreating the sort of international finance and trade volatility last seen in the interwar years. This undermined the ability of national governments to exercise control and destroyed the credibility of the policies which formed the basis for postwar economic prosperity. The return to the pre-Keynesian orthodoxy in macro-economic management completed the circle. Restrictive monetary policies, intensified competition for shares in markets which were growing more slowly than productive potential, and unrestricted currency speculation interacted to recreate world recession.

Unemployment today is not therefore the result of the working of mystical economic laws regulating wages. Nor is unemployment the result of there being too little work that needs to be done to employ fully all those who seek employment. Both private need and public squalor are on the increase. The physical environment needs to be improved; more work should go into education, health and public services generally; and housing and other infrastructure work would in almost all countries be welcomed. Yet there is continuous pressure for cuts in taxes, for lower wages, and for reduced social welfare contributions to be matched by cuts in government expenditure. The argument is that if the rewards to capital were increased, then enterprise would be stimulated. But after a decade or more of 'putting capital first' in most EU states, where is the evidence of the renaissance?

A massive shift of income and wealth towards the rich took place on a global scale throughout the 1980s and continued through the 1990s. Reversing this by increasing employment, cutting unearned speculative gains in the interest of benefiting creative enterprise instead, and reducing the differential between the highest and lowest paid would relieve pressure on public finances as people are raised out of state dependency and as the costs of administering the tax/benefit system fall.[3] Increased purchasing power of the developing countries globally, and of the mass of consumers in Europe, would allow demand to grow alongside supply. It is also within this context that the need for training should be seen as training for jobs which are actually being created in the real economy and which will be sustained beyond the life of the associated training programme. Just as economic development can suffer from skill shortages, so training can suffer from lack of genuine job opportunities.[4]

The lessons of history have to be relearned. Just as today's economic orthodoxy represents a retreat by political commentators and ruling elites back to repeating the free market dogmas of the 1920s, so we need to remember the lessons learned at such enormous costs from the resulting Great Depression and the rise of fascism. At the international level those lessons included the need for really effective international agreements: not to 'set free' capital but rather to stabilize trade flows and restrict speculative activities.[5]

INDUSTRIAL POLICIES AND INDUSTRIAL STRATEGY

Western theoretical perspectives on competition and industrial policies have been squarely based on the concepts of 'monopoly welfare losses' and the theory of comparative advantage. According to the former, departures from the perfect competition ideal tend to be pervasive and lead to welfare losses. Accordingly, the government should strive to rese-cure the perfectly competitive ideal through suitable competition and industrial policies. Granting this, everyone can benefit by specializing in products where they face least comparative disadvantage and trading in international markets. It is worth noting here that these two cornerstones of western policy are based on diametrically different assumptions of imperfect competition and perfect competition, respectively. Moreover (and in part relatedly), western governments were soon to 'discover' the benefits of large size, namely, the 'American Challenge' thesis. Accordingly, industrial policies allegedly drawing on the welfare losses argument were often found to support mergers and more generally the acquisition of large size, especially in the 1960s and 1970s. Large 'national champions', moreover, were often nationalized companies.

As if this inconsistency were not enough, the 1980s then witnessed the 'return to the market', deregulation and privatization, in direct response to observed 'government failures'. Interestingly, this was accompanied by a return to the 'benefits of small size' view, accompanied by policy mea-sures to support small- and medium-sized enterprises (SMEs). It is hardly surprising in this framework that western policies have been described as *ad hoc*, discontinuous, inconsistent, lacking a .coherent theoretical frame-work, and failing to amount to an industrial strategy (on which, see Pitelis, 1994).

In contrast to the west, the Far Eastern economies successfully moved from import substitution to export promotion by creating competitive advantages. The state played an important role in this process, including the use of managed competition and managed trade. The effect which such industrial, trade and macroeconomic policies – which are aimed at enhanc-ing an economy's growth rate – will have on other economies will depend on a number of factors.

Thus, consider an industrial strategy including the following elements:

1. Build the institutions and mechanisms to generate acceptance of the objective of growth given the existing distribution of income.
2. Adopt policies of selective protectionism, managed trade and con-trolled liberalization.
3. Ensure that domestic firms (including transnational corporations) are investing at home, repatriating profits, and in general abiding by the rules of the accord (in behaving nationalistically).
4. Play the competitive bidding game with foreign multinationals to attract them away from rival countries.

5. Support small and medium-sized enterprises to exploit their relative advantages and the synergies between them and large firms, and potentially provide a pool of domestic competitors against foreign multinational corporations.
6. Provide a suitable and stable macroeconomic environment by targeting real variables and providing an appropriate productive infrastructure including investment in 'human capital' (skills, education, training) and support for R&D, particularly of the type favouring targeted sectors and firms.

This might be characterized as a Machiavellian strategy since it aims explicitly to gain advantages at the expense of others. Most critics of any such policies tend to point to practical difficulties, such as the possible retaliation by other countries. However, the objectives of such a strategy can also be questioned as being too concerned with redistributing wealth towards the economy in question rather than with the issue of how to generate wealth. Instead, an industrial strategy should aim to contribute to global welfare, and to reduce global inequalities and inequities. Such an approach would move away from seeing competitiveness in a static neoclassical sense, viewing it instead in a dynamic way. Such an industrial strategy would try to encourage inter- and intra-firm competition so as to nurture conditions favourable to the creation of new ideas, techniques, products, processes and organizational and institutional forms, and would aim to enhance the information-providing attributes of economic organizations (including firms and markets).

A dynamic industrial strategy of this type should provide incentives, support mechanisms and appropriate institutions for achieving dynamic competitiveness. Conditions necessary for it are addressing 'state' capture by sectional interests (Pitelis, 1994) – in part through striving for conditions of contestability in private and political markets – and a plurality of institutional and organizational forms, including for example support for small and medium-sized enterprises. Devising feasible, consistent, sustainable strategies which nurture dynamic efficiency and enhanced welfare is a challenge still to be tackled. But one important element would be the nurturing of institutions, mechanisms and organizations which foster dynamic efficiency, productivity and growth.[6]

One reason why a focus on institutions and dynamic efficiency can lead to global welfare improvements is quite straightforward and derives directly from the notion of (and need for) productivity. The most important determinants of productivity are human skills and incentives, technology and innovativeness, and economies of scale, scope, learning and time. All these depend on the institutional setting, including the definition and enforcement of property rights, which can reduce the costs of transacting. Relatedly, these can lead to reductions in the costs of production (transformation) through the very initiation of the process of production taking place, thus leading to the economies highlighted above.

The exact measures which need to be taken to achieve global welfare improvements will vary according to the conditions prevailing in each country. It is beyond the scope of this chapter to pursue a full analysis of these issues, but some observations may be of use. First, there is a need for international co-operation to ensure that (inter)national policies are at least not inconsistent and mutually undermining. In this context, any policy which improves productivity can be useful, such as education, skills, technology and innovation, public sector efficiency improvements, and so on. However, the need to ensure competition also suggests the need to support SMEs. In order to achieve economies of transformation, often related to large size, there should be measures facilitating the 'clustering' of SMEs (on which, see Best, 1991). 'Clusters' of SMEs can also be a potent source of indigenous development for less-favoured regions, countering a dependence on transnational corporations (TNCs). Technology transfer through foreign direct investment (FDI) should be pursued in conjunction with 'clustering'.

Of course, the appropriate policy mix will vary from country to country. But the aim of sustainable growth can certainly be pursued through a plurality of institutional and organizational forms designed to achieve, first, the successful exploitation of dispersed knowledge; secondly, the benefits of competition which can derive from this (and from appropriate competition policies), thirdly, technology and skills transfer through FDI and the parallel exploitation of the benefits of clustering; and finally, the amelioration of the problem of state capture. Recent recognition by the EU – and EU member states, including the UK – of the need for and benefits of a focus on dynamic competitiveness, achieved through measures such as education and the promotion of skills, technology and innovation, and public sector efficiency improvements, as well as support for (clusters of) SMEs, are a step in the right direction, yet still fail to derive from a coherent theoretical framework able to address among other things the issues of globalization and TNCs, of distribution and of convergence. These issues are explored in more detail elsewhere (see Pitelis, 1996); here our focus is on the link between supply-side (industrial) and demand-side (macro) policies.

THE DEMAND AND SUPPLY SIDES

The Current Dichotomy

While much macro-economic theory and policy analysis assumes – explicitly or (more often) implicitly – perfect competition, when it comes to industrial and regulatory issues the realities of imperfect competition, industrial concentration, market shares and so on have to be addressed. Indeed, the licensing of new telecommunications companies in the UK by the telecommunications regulator OFTEL (Office of Telecommunications) is not presented just as a move towards a more perfectly competitive market but also as a means of influencing the behaviour of the incumbent firm, encouraging a reduction of costs towards what is happily admitted to be the natural monopolist's declining average cost curve. And that is in the industry which, of all the privatized utilities, must stand most chance of moving towards a competitive market situation. In many of the other regulated industries it is admitted that the network functions will remain natural monopolies. Certainly, the job of the regulators is to license new operators, but in most cases the end goal is not a perfectly competitive market but rather an oligopolistic one. And the purpose of having the new firms is not simply because of the role they play in creating a competitive market but also to assist the regulator in actually regulating the behaviour of the incumbent, much as yardstick competition has been used to provide additional information regarding running costs and the like. On top of this, the resulting competition itself has to be regulated in most of these industries.

These processes are analysed in detail elsewhere (Michie, 1995, 1997); the point here is that the assumption of perfectly competitive markets which underlies much macroeconomic policy has to be explicitly abandoned when it comes to analysing actual industrial and regulatory issues. Here the realities of monopolistic and oligopolistic cost structures and corporate behaviour have to be acknowledged. And more fundamentally, the 'market' is shown (even if this is not always admitted) to be not so much free as constructed, created by legislation and regulation.[7]

Deflationary Macro-policies and Industrial Capacity

Demand expectations and risk both play important roles in firms' decisions about expanding capacity. Firms need to be confident that demand will grow at such a rate as to validate any expansion of their capacity; but experience in recent years has made managers cautious about overestimating future sales, as the penalties for doing so tend to be much greater than for losing potential business by failing to expand.[8] The real problem about encouraging investment in new capacity is that of risk: not that the cost of its output is higher, as the neoclassicists continually imply when suggesting that lower wage costs are needed to make it viable – new plant is, if anything, more efficient then existing plant. The key question is how to reduce this risk and how to make firms more willing to take it. Once this is recognized as one of the central problems of economic policy today, attention will focus on the various means by which this can be effected: the government's own economic strategy, the institutional factors determining the supply of capital, interest rates, company taxation and so on.[9]

Driver (1996) demonstrates that firms have become more cautious about investing in new capacity in recent years. He analyses the answers to the Confederation of British Industry (CBI) Industrial Trends Survey questions on capacity utilization and factors limiting capital expenditure and their implications for 'capacity stance' – that is, the ratio of planned capacity to expected demand. Over the last 20 years the capacity stance has tightened, with firms implicitly accepting higher levels of restraint on output due to insufficient capacity. Using the required rate of return in relation to the cost of capital as a proxy for reluctance to take on risk, Driver shows that there is evidence of growing caution about the risks of installing additional capacity. Means must be found to tackle this.[10]

The creation of new and more advanced industrial capacity requires new investment, yet the need to drive up investment rates is often diverted in policy debates on to the question of how to increase savings; this has been a particularly dominant argument in the USA, and is damaging when it switches attention away from the need actually to create capacity. Pollin (1996) therefore refutes this argument at both the theoretical and empirical levels, showing that the supposed shortage of savings is an illusory constraint to the creation of new capacity and a return to full employment. Expanding investment and output will themselves tend to generate additional saving out of the newly created wealth.

'Clusters' and Macro-policy

Attention has recently focused on the important role of 'clusters' of SMEs in economic development (see Pyke *et al.*, 1991; Best, 1991). Management gurus such as Michael Porter (1990) have lent weight to the idea of the benefits of such 'clustering'. In partial response, clustering is fast becoming an important part of the industrial policy agenda of the EU. This is welcome for the reasons described above, despite the EU's lack of any coherent framework underlying its support for (clusters of) SMEs. However, support for (clusters of) SMEs has an extra interesting dimension since, if it is to be pursued seriously and consistently, it requires a compatible macro-policy. That supply-side policies should be at least not contradicted by macro-policies (and vice versa) should be self-evident; yet it is hardly addressed. When applied to the case of (clusters of) SMEs this points to the need for macro-policy to pay attention to the actual needs of SMEs. In contrast to TNCs, SMEs are often more locally dependent. Accordingly, they are hit more harshly by deflationary policies at the domestic level which adversely affect domestic demand conditions, and by high interest rate policies which increase the cost of capital (which is a major constraint on the expansion of SMEs). By virtue of their locational flexibility, large TNCs are less affected by the domestic policies of each particular government. It follows that theory, evidence and the EU's declared objective to support (clusters of) SMEs require a macro-policy of low inflation and interest rates, competitive exchange rates and a healthy level of effective demand. Deflationary policies risk undermining these requirements, thus introducing an inconsistency between the declared supply-side objectives and the actual demand-side policies.

CONCLUSION

The key to sustainable growth and a return to full employment is to ensure both a continuous expansion of demand and for this to be matched by increased output rather than by inflation or, in the case of individual countries, trade imbalances. *Genuine* supply-side policies – that is, policies which really will lead to an increased and more efficient supply of goods and services, rather than the deflationary and deregulatory policies which are so often mistermed 'supply-side', simply because they are being promoted in the context of a disregard for demand conditions – require an expansion of industrial capacity, and of economic capacity more generally.

The growth process involves 'hysteresis' – that is, history matters – and economies can get locked into vicious cycles of decline. Thus, for example, whatever the supposed increased static efficiencies of free market policies, if these weaken the manufacturing sector of an individual economy, such as Britain, then there is the risk of a destabilizing process that will inhibit growth. Hence the need for industrial policies.[11] Likewise, trade policies are also central to any growth strategy;[12] as are policies to control the operation of multinationals. Thus Cowling and Sugden (1996) argue that an industrial strategy should be seen in particular within the context of the increased role in the global economy – and in the economies of most individual countries – of transnational corporations. Not only has the potentially disruptive effects of transnational corporations increased the need for a conscious industrial policy to be developed by government – at local, regional, national and transnational levels – but such strategies need to be developed and implemented as part of a conscious effort to increase the extent of democratic involvement in the workings of the economy.

Trends towards increased globalization – with capital becoming ever more footloose and individual transnational corporations ever more unaccountable – risk exacerbating current inequalities, and threaten to perpetuate the present high levels of unemployment. It is in this context that the increased inequalities which have been witnessed over the past 15 years or so, globally and within individual countries, can best be tackled: not simply by redistribution alone, but by an egalitarian growth strategy which creates the conditions, including the necessary expansion in economic capacity, to overcome poverty and inequality. Creating additional industrial capacity will not be a simple task, but it is essential for achieving any substantial reduction in unemployment. In recent years theory and evidence point to the need for an industrial strategy which fosters (clusters of) SMEs – now a declared objective of the EU. That SMEs are more locationally dependent than TNCs points to the need for a macro-policy to support healthy demand-side conditions, and for an integration of supply- and demand-side policies at the domestic, European and global levels.

NOTES

1. This is consistent with Screpanti's (1996) findings on the non-uniqueness of NAIRU; Screpanti also finds that employment rather than unemployment is of more relevance for analysing the behaviour of wage increases.
2. For a discussion of the behaviour of wages and productivity over the business cycle, see Michie (1987).
3. The sums involved are calculated by Kitson *et al.* (1997a, 1997b), demonstrating that the net cost of a public sector-led expansion, even one involving an ambitious increase in public provision and hence expenditure, would be far lower than the gross cost.
4. These points are argued in detail in Michie and Wilkinson (1994, 1995).
5. For a discussion of economic and employment policy in the context of international business and foreign direct investment, including the influence of multinational enterprises, see Porter (1994) and the various authors in Michie and Grieve Smith (1995), in particular Kozul-Wright (1995); Porter challenges the idea that globalization has made geography unimportant, and Kozul-Wright, in addition to making similar points to Porter, reports a wealth of new data on multinational investment and other activities, and discusses the policy implications of these developments. For an analysis of the 'globalization' of the activities of multinational firms, see Archibugi and Michie (1997b, 1998) and Howells and Michie (1997a, 1997b); and on the implications of this for national systems of innovation, see Archibugi and Michie (1997a).

6. On which see Pitelis (1994) and Michie and Grieve Smith (1996, 1997).
7. On the processes of regulatory and contractual intervention to create – or at least proxy – markets, see Deakin and Michie (1997a, 1997b).
8. Business strategy is also being subjected to various constraints emanating from financial markets; in particular, the new-found enthusiasm for shareholder activism poses risks for economic performance when firms are pressured to deliver short-term results and dividend payments. Even the tying of management renumeration to corporate results through share options and the like can have perverse effects. All this is inhibiting the creation of new capacity and preventing the adoption of high-performance work systems (see Appelbaum and Berg, 1996).
9. These points are argued in detail by Grieve Smith (1996).
10. In the UK the operation of corporate taxation needs to be reconsidered. The elimination of free depreciation and the reduction of corporate tax rates have adversely altered the balance of risk between profiting from expansion and losing from overcapacity (see Driver, 1996).
11. The implementation of appropriate industrial policy is described by Best and Forrant (1996), where 'appropriate' is taken to mean not just an industrial policy which is grounded in a detailed knowledge of the region for which it is being developed, but also one which recognizes that the ability of industry to innovate will be constrained by the time it takes to move from concept development through to final marketing, so that reducing the length of this cycle becomes key to creating an innovative industrial sector.
12. On which, see Kitson and Michie (1995a, 1995b).

REFERENCES

Appelbaum, E. and Berg, P. (1996), 'Financial market constraints and business strategy in the US', in J. Michie and J. Grieve Smith (eds), *Creating Industrial Capacity: Towards Full Employment*, Oxford: Oxford University Press.

Archibugi, D. and Michie, J. (1997a), 'Technological globalisation or national systems of innovation?', *Futures*, **29** (2): 121–37.

Archibugi, D. and Michie, J. (eds) (1997b), *Technology, Globalisation, and Economic Performance*, Cambridge: Cambridge University Press.

Archibugi, D. and Michie, J. (eds) (1998), *Technology, Trade, and Growth*, Cambridge: Cambridge University Press.

Best, M.H. (1991), *The New Competition: Institutions of Industrial Restructuring*, Cambridge: Polity Press.

Best, M. and Forrant, R. (1996), 'Creating industrial capacity: Pentagon-led versus production-led industrial policies', in J. Michie and J. Grieve Smith (eds), *Creating Industrial Capacity: Towards Full Employment*, Oxford: Oxford University Press.

Cowling, K. and Sugden, R. (1996), 'Capacity, transnationals and industrial strategy', in J. Michie and J. Grieve Smith (eds), *Creating Industrial Capacity: Towards Full Employment*, Oxford: Oxford University Press.

Deakin, S. and Michie, J. (1997a), 'Contracts and competition: an introduction', *Cambridge Journal of Economics*, **21** (2): 121–5.

Deakin, S. and Michie, J. (1997b), 'Contracts, competition, and governance', in S. Deakin and J. Michie (eds), *Contracts, Co-operation, and Competition: Studies in Economics, Management, and Law*, Oxford: Oxford University Press.

Driver, C. (1996), 'Tightening the reins: the capacity stance of UK manufacturing firms 1976–1995', in J. Michie and J. Grieve Smith (eds), *Creating Industrial Capacity: Towards Full Employment*, Oxford: Oxford University Press.

Grieve Smith, J. (1996), 'Rebuilding industrial capacity', in J. Michie and J. Grieve Smith (eds), *Creating Industrial Capacity: Towards Full Employment*, Oxford: Oxford University Press.

Howells, J. and Michie, J. (1997a), *Technological Competitiveness in an International Arena*, Economic and Social Research Council, Centre for Business Research Working Paper WP52, Cambridge: CBR.

Howells, J. and Michie, J. (eds) (1997b), *Technology, Innovation, and Competitiveness*, Aldershot, Hants: Edward Elgar.

Kitson, M. and Michie, J. (1995a), 'Trade and growth: a historical perspective', in J. Michie and J. Grieve Smith (eds), *Managing the Global Economy*, Oxford: Oxford University Press, ch. 1.

Kitson, M. and Michie, J. (1995b), 'Conflict, cooperation and change: the political economy of trade and trade policy', *Review of International Political Economy*, **2** (4): 623–57.

Kitson, M., Michie, J. and Sutherland, H. (1997a), 'The fiscal and distributional implications of job creation', *Cambridge Journal of Economics*, **21** (1): 103–20.

Kitson, M., Michie, J. and Sutherland; H. (1997b), '"A price well worth paying"?: the benefits of a full employment strategy', in J. Michie and J. Grieve Smith (eds), *Employment and Economic Performance: Jobs, Inflation, and Growth*, Oxford, Oxford University Press.

Kozul-Wright, R. (1995), 'Transnational corporations and the nation state', in J. Michie and J. Grieve Smith (eds), *Managing the Global Economy*, Oxford: Oxford University Press, ch. 6.

Michie, J. (1987), *Wages in the Business Cycle: An Empirical and Methodological Analysis*, London: Frances Pinter.

Michie, J. (1994), 'Global shocks and social corporatism', in R. Delorme and K. Dopfer (eds), *The Political Economy of Complexity*, Aldershot, Hants: Edward Elgar.

Michie, J. (1995), 'Institutional aspects of regulating the private sector', in J. Groenewegen, C. Pitelis and S.-E. Sjostrand (eds), *On Economic Institutions: Theory and Application*, Aldershot, Hants: Edward Elgar.

Michie, J. (1997), 'Network externalities: the economics of universal access', *Utilities Policy* **6** (4): 317–24.

Michie, J. and Grieve Smith, J. (eds) (1995), *Managing the Global Economy*, Oxford: Oxford University Press.

Michie, J. and Grieve Smith, J. (eds) (1996), *Creating Industrial Capacity: Towards Full Employment*, Oxford: Oxford University Press.

Michie, J. and Grieve Smith, J. (eds) (1997), *Employment and Economic Performance: Jobs, Inflation, and Growth*, Oxford: Oxford University Press.

Michie, J. and Wilkinson, F. (1992), 'Inflation policy and the restructuring of labour markets', in J. Michie (ed.), *The Economic Legacy, 1979–1992*, London: Academic Press, ch. 9.

Michie, J. and Wilkinson, F. (1994), 'The growth of unemployment in the 1980s', in J. Michie and J. Grieve Smith (eds), *Unemployment in Europe*, London: Academic Press, ch. 1.

Michie, J. and Wilkinson, F. (1995), 'Wages, government policy and unemployment', *Review of Political Economy*, **7** (2): 133–49 (special issue on 'High Unemployment in Western Economies').

Pitelis, C.N. (1994), 'Industrial strategy: for Britain, in Europe and the world', *Journal of Economic Studies*, **21** (5): 1–92.

Pitelis, C.N. (1996), 'Policies for competitiveness: the new learning', University of Cambridge, mimeo.

Pollin, R. (1996), 'Saving and finance: real and illusory constraints on full employment policy', in J. Michie and J. Grieve Smith (eds), *Creating Industrial Capacity: Towards Full Employment*, Oxford: Oxford University Press.

Porter, M.E. (1990), *The Competitive Advantage of Nations*, New York: Free Press.

Porter, M.E. (1994), 'The role of location in competition', *Journal of Economics of Business*, **1** (1): 35–9.

Pyke, F., Berattini, G. and Sengenberger, W. (1990), *Industrial Districts and Inter-firm Cooperation in Italy*, Geneva: International Institute for Labour Studies.

Screpanti, E. (1996), 'A pure insider theory of hysteresis in employment and unemployment', *Review of Radical Political Economics*, **28** (3): 93–112.

3. Deindustrialization, unemployment and government policy: the UK experience

Michael Kitson and Jonathan Michie*

INTRODUCTION

There is a mood among many mainstream economists that, whatever Thatcher's excesses, she at least laid the conditions for what is now a reasonable economic performance for the UK with a relatively low level of unemployment; that something had to be done in 1979 to break trade union power; and that the incoming Labour administration should therefore pursue a 'steady as you go' course. We would argue that these views are variously wrong, miss the point, or at least are dangerously complacent.

First, some facts and figures. Looking at the output performance of the whole economy, despite the benefits of North Sea oil and the unsustainable Lawson boom, GDP grew at a rate of only 2.4 per cent between the peak years of 1979 and 1989. What was particularly damaging were the effects of Thatcherite economic policy on the manufacturing sector. Over the same ten years 1979–89, UK manufacturing output grew by a total of only 15 per cent – an average growth rate of barely 1 per cent a year. By 1992 output had fallen back to around 1973 levels.

But does focusing on output levels overlook a productivity miracle which could be said to have turned the situation round in the 1980s? Certainly, manufacturing productivity grew in that decade, but first, this was largely due to job cuts rather than to increased output, and these jobs were not being lost in a period of full employment when the labour would be taken up productively elsewhere. Secondly, part of the increased output per person was actually due to a one-off increase in labour inputs per person through increased production-line speeds, reduced break times and so on, not acknowledged in the official productivity calculations. Thirdly, the official productivity figures are constructed using a single

* We are grateful for comments from the participants of the 1996 EAEPE conference.

price deflator for both output and input prices; when the appropriate deflators are used, the 51 per cent increase in labour productivity recorded between 1979 and 1989 falls to 34 per cent (Stoneman and Francis, 1992). And fourthly, what productivity growth there was went disproportionately into increased profits rather than reduced output prices – which could have increased market share, with higher output and employment than was in fact experienced, along with a healthier balance of payments and lower inflation – and the increased profits went dispro-portionately into dividend payments rather than investment. So UK productivity levels still lag behind the other leading industrialized coun-tries. Productivity growth has been largely wasted: it has been used to cut employment and increase dividends rather than to develop new products and expand output.

It is true that the investment record of UK manufacturing has been relatively poor for decades; the point is that it has been even worse since 1979. It has thus continued to be a major cause of Britain's indifferent growth performance, constraining technological progress and the expan-sion of demand. The cumulative effect of this record has resulted in British workers lacking the plant and machinery used by their counter-parts in the other major industrialized countries. But does it *matter* that in the UK during the 1980s growth was so skewed towards services, par-ticularly financial services, and the construction of shopping malls for the sale of what were increasingly becoming imported manufactured goods? We would argue that yes, it does. Advanced economies require a large and competitive manufacturing sector in order to generate sufficient exports to pay for necessary imports and because of the symbiotic relationship between the manufacturing and service sectors.

This chapter therefore argues, first, that deindustrialization can be a serious problem for advanced industrial economies (and not just for the industrial sector itself); secondly, that the UK in particular is suffering from the adverse impacts of deindustrialization and that the key reason for the relatively poor performance of UK industry has been underinvest-ment in manufacturing; and thirdly, that underinvestment and deindustrialization have been allowed to persist due to the lack of any strong modernizing force within British society, the trade union move-ment having been too weak to force through any such modernization, and government policy having been at best rather ineffectual and at worst positively harmful. The reasons for this policy failure lie in Britain's eco-nomic history and in the consequently distorted nature of both the economy and society. This fundamental problem, then, of a lack of any strong modernizing force has if anything been exacerbated since 1979.

DOES MANUFACTURING MATTER?

As income rises and economies approach industrial maturity it can be expected that manufacturing employment shares fall and manufacturing (current price) output shares rise and then fall (Cosh *et al.*, 1994). It is however, important to recognize that the process of deindustrialization may not just reflect positive factors, such as rising income and industrial maturity, but may also reflect negative factors such as an uncompetitive or small manufacturing sector. In this regard, negative deindustrialization will not only be reflected in falling output and employment shares (although these shares may fall more rapidly in countries suffering negative as opposed to positive deindustrialization), but in low growth (of manufacturing and total output) and an inability to maintain external trading equilibrium. Furthermore, it may be possible for positive deindustrialization to lead to negative deindustrialization, as shifting sectoral shares may result in the domestic manufacturing sector being unable to reap the benefits of rapid productivity growth.

In neoclassical economics, divergences from 'equilibrium' can be rectified through price adjustment and/or the correction of market failures. In reality, economies do not behave like this. History is important (as recognized in recent path-dependent models) such that the quantity and quality of factors of production accumulated from the past determine what can be produced in the immediate future. This is inconsistent with conventional equilibrium theory, which asserts that an economy is constrained by exogenous variables which remain stable over time (Kaldor, 1985). Additionally, it implies that it is difficult and expensive to reverse many economic decisions. If a factory is closed or if a market is lost it is difficult to regain the *status quo ante*. Also, the impact of economic shocks may not only have a once and for all impact on long-run capacity but may lead to cumulative changes. Thus as Allyn Young stated, forces of economic change are endogenous:

> They are engendered from within the economic system. No analysis, of the forces making for economic equilibrium, forces that we might say are tangential at any moment of time, will serve to illumine this field, for movements away from equilibrium, departures from previous trends are characteristic of it. (Quoted in Kaldor, 1985, p. 64)

As the UK's House of Lords Select Committee on Science and Technology reported: 'Manufacturing industry is vital to the prosperity of the United Kingdom. ... Our manufacturing base is dangerously small; to achieve adequate growth from such a small base will be difficult' (House of Lords, 1991, p. 3). The relative decline of manufacturing in the UK has been greater than the norm for the OECD countries. In terms of percentage shares of value added, the UK manufacturing sector contributed 13.3 per cent less in 1993 than it did in 1960, compared to an average fall across the OECD of 9.3 per cent. In terms of employment shares, the manufacturing sector's contribution fell by 19.9 per cent across the same period, compared to an average fall across the OECD of 7.3 per cent.

Manufacturing output in the UK is barely higher today than it was 20 years ago. The picture is one of rising output up to 1973, followed by a sharp fall to 1975, and subsequent recovery in the second half of the 1970s (generally taken as peaking again in 1979 although the annual index averages to a lower overall figure over 1979 than for 1978). The deep recession of the early 1980s was followed by a weak recovery, leading straight into the Lawson boom, taking manufacturing output to a new peak in 1989 before falling again in the early 1990s' recession. Meanwhile productivity grew in every year apart from 1975 and 1980, even when output fell. There has been an almost continual decline in manufacturing employment from its peak level in 1966.

Compared with France, Germany, Italy, the USA and Japan, the UK is the only country of the six with a lower average level of manufacturing output over the years 1979–89 than over the years 1973–79, and was also the only country to experience a fall in output between the years 1973 and 1979. (Between 1979 and 1989 this average growth returned to a positive figure, albeit lower than in any of the other countries apart from France.[1]) A similar picture emerges for manufacturing employment, with the UK being the only one to experience a fall between 1964 and 1973; while others saw employment fall between 1979 and 1989, none did so at the rate experienced in the UK, and during 1973–79 only Germany and Japan experienced a faster rate of job losses and, as indicated above, in both cases this was due to strong productivity growth rather than simply output loss, as was the case for the UK. Looking at the three peak-to-peak periods of 1964–73, 1973–9 and 1979–89, Britain was at the bottom of the league table of the six countries in two of the periods, and second bottom in the third. This poor record on manufacturing output resulted in declining manufacturing employment.

Looking at the average annual growth of manufacturing output for the six countries between the peak years 1964 and 1989, the UK is firmly at the foot of the performance league. Taking the overall growth figure to 1992, while the level of manufacturing output was more than 30 per cent higher by the end of the 20-year period in Germany, and almost 70 per cent higher in Japan, in Britain the overall growth was barely 1 per cent; that is, the absolute level of manufacturing output in 1992 was hardly different from that achieved in 1973. Between the peak years of 1964 and

1989, the average annual growth of manufacturing output was 6.6 per cent in Japan, 3.9 per cent in the USA, 3.7 per cent in Italy, 2.9 per cent in France, 2.7 per cent in Germany, and only 1.5 per cent in the UK. Over the ten-year peak-to-peak period 1979–89, manufacturing output grew by a total of only 15 per cent, an average cumulative growth rate of barely 1 per cent a year (before dropping back in 1992 to around the same level as it had been in 1973).

The relatively poor growth of manufacturing has led to slower growth of the whole economy. During the post-Second World War period the UK growth rate has been consistently less than that achieved by the other major capitalist countries: the norm has been for it to be approximately two-thirds of that achieved by the 'world' group. Even during the 'Golden Age', from 1950–73, the UK's growth rate of 3.0 per cent looks mediocre compared with the average growth rate of 4.6 per cent achieved by the leading capitalist countries.

An assessment of the UK's relatively poor growth rate performance must be tempered by consideration of different levels of income. It may be expected that growth rates will differ because countries have different per capita income levels. Countries with relatively low income levels may have relatively higher growth rates as they have the potential to appropriate technologies and organizational techniques from the leading countries. This process, even allowing for the fact that it may be both erratic and confined to countries at broadly similar stages of industrialization, cannot explain Britain's inferior growth performance. The UK's poor growth rate has been associated not just with other industrialized countries catching up with the UK GDP level, but with those countries overtaking that level. In 1950 the UK was the second richest European economy, by 1973 it was seventh, and by 1992 it was eleventh. During the period 1950–73, the UK had the lowest growth rate of the 16 European economies. During the period 1973–92, when all growth rates slowed, its growth rate ranked joint twelfth, only two countries having an inferior growth performance.

Two important points are clear: first, the decline in manufacturing employment in the UK *cannot* be explained solely by shifts in consumption patterns, or by other sectors' requirements for labour. The loss of manufacturing jobs has been accompanied by a deteriorating performance in manufacturing trade and by a rise in unemployment. And second, manufacturing has not experienced rapidly rising output as a result of productivity growth but, on the contrary, a stagnant trend in output, with productivity growth hence translating not into output growth but instead into job losses.

CAUSES OF UK DEINDUSTRIALIZATION

The key evidence presented in support of the Thatcher shock is the improvement in productivity (see Crafts, 1996, and Eltis, 1996; and for an opposing view, Kitson and Michie, 1996). Yet, we would argue, there was no productivity miracle during the 1980s – any such picture is a mirage. During all three peak-to-peak periods since the mid-1960s the growth of the UK's manufacturing gross capital stock has been inferior to that of the other major industrial nations. This is most evident during the 1979–89 period, when, although there was a worldwide slowdown in the growth of manufacturing investment, the UK was the only country of the five not to experience any growth in the manufacturing capital stock. This has left a legacy of a relatively low level of capital in UK manufacturing. Capital per worker in the UK is significantly below that of the USA and Germany; the gap with these two countries (and France) has been widening since the mid-1960s. In addition to a lack of investment, much of that which has taken place has been cost-cutting rather than capacity-enhancing. Thus while for the vast majority of OECD countries the growth rates of both total and industrial R&D were much higher in the 1980s than in the 1970s, the most notable exception to this was the UK (see Archibugi and Michie, 1995, table 1).

The three 'positive' aspects of the UK government's record since 1979 are usually said to be: improved industrial relations; privatization and deregulation; and an improved tax system. On industrial relations, we would not regard the government since 1979 as having made a positive contribution. Strike levels in the 1980s and 1990s have been far lower than in the 1960s and 1970s internationally – not just in Britain. The main reason is of course widespread unemployment. The anti-trade union legislation in the UK has certainly made it easier to cut wages. But the problem with wage cutting is that it develops a dependency on cheap labour on the part of employers and reduces pressure for improved managerial efficiency, better training, new investment and other means of enhancing productivity. There is little limit to the reduction of unit labour costs by these means but they are actively discouraged when firms have opportunities for low wages and poor working conditions. Moreover, in a world where competitive success increasingly requires co-operation in production to make the best use of new technologies and to achieve the required product standards, employment policies which have a contempt for basic rights have the opposite effect by alienating workers.

Secondly, privatization and deregulation has led to 'cream skimming'. New entrants are not interested in investing where the incumbent is inefficient, but where there are quick profits to be had. This has had the perverse effect of a government, elected in 1979 on a pledge of reducing the degree of regulation, instead overseeing a massive increase. And the results of such regulation have included the banning of BT from offering cable TV through its network, with the result that the majority of the UK cable TV industry – a sector in which Britain held an early technological lead – is now in American hands. In a comparison of the G7 countries, recent OECD research found the UK to have the best performers in only two sectors of the economy (across manufacturing and services): namely, the nationalized postal service and railways. Whether this will survive privatization remains to be seen.

Thirdly, UK governments since 1979 have added to the regressive effects of their labour market policies on the distribution of income by their tax and social welfare policies. The elimination of higher tax brackets, the switch to indirect taxation and increases in national insurance contributions have favoured the rich. Meanwhile, the least-well-off have been hit by the elimination of the earnings-related elements from unemployment and sickness pay; by the break in the link between social welfare and earnings, and in some cases from inflation; and by the restrictions on eligibility for out-of-work benefits. Low pay and labour-force instability are major obstacles to effective training and personnel policy. Targeting training at the unemployed to get them into jobs with low-paying firms in need of undervalued labour to keep obsolete equipment in operation and outdated product lines profitable is a waste of training resources. Such firms need skills which are specific to outdated technology and are therefore effectively obsolete. For firms to benefit from having a trained and motivated workforce they need assurances that their competitor firms will also be committing equivalent resources to the training, health and safety, and other measures involved. This assurance can be achieved through a combination of government regulation setting certain standards, along with trade union organization capable of enforcing these standards and building upon them.

POLICIES TO REVERSE UK DEINDUSTRIALIZATION

If the UK is to compete effectively with the major industrialized countries the investment shortfall will have to be reversed. UK macroeconomic policy since 1979 has resulted repeatedly in an overvalued exchange rate and high interest rates. Industrial policy has been ineffectual, with little attempt to use the public sector as a modernizing force.[2]

The most obvious cases of sterling being overvalued as a result of macroeconomic policy were, first, the effects of the Thatcher government's initial monetarist policies in 1979–80 and, secondly, membership of the exchange rate mechanism (ERM). Additionally, erratic monetary policy and volatile interest rates have discouraged investment and business confidence. This was particularly apparent during the early 1980s when high interest rates created cash flow problems for many companies, leading to bankruptcies and plant closures as well as contributing to the appreciation of sterling and the squeeze on exports. The Cambridge Small Business Research Centre survey into business performance in the 1980s indicated that a third of all firms identified interest rate policy as the most important negative government policy. Overall, firms believed that government policy had hindered their performance. A high proportion of firms considered that they had received *no* help from government during the 1980s. The attack on trade union rights has been at best an irrelevance to the real failings of British industry; and encouraging a 'hire and fire' mentality will only exacerbate short-term attitudes and behaviour. The increased inequality which has been part and parcel of this agenda has also proved a costly burden on society and the economy.

The UK economy requires a new institutional framework that will provide the 'social capital' necessary for capitalism to prosper. Currently in the UK the dominant institutions, which have evolved from and are embedded in a divisive class system, have created obstacles to growth (Olson, 1982). Change is necessary, requiring not only reform of existing institutions but the creation of new institutions that will foster investment in skills and technology, inter-firm co-operation and better relations between employers and employees. The first requirements are to discard economic policies based on unrealistic theories and to accept that, in advanced industrialized economies, economic efficiency and growth will improve in a society based on fairness and equity.

NOTES

1. For a discussion of the exceptionally poor performance for France, see Halimi *et al.* (1994).
2. As Postmaster-General from October 1964 to August 1965, Tony Benn concluded the following: 'This highlights in my mind one of the great difficulties of being a socialist in the sort of society in which we live. The real drive for improvement comes from those concerned to make private profit. If, therefore, you deny these people the right of extending private enterprise into new fields, you have to have some sort of alternative. You have to have some body which wants to develop public enterprise but our present Civil Service is not interested in growth. It is geared to care and maintenance' (Benn, 1987, p. 264, diary entry for 28 May 1965).

REFERENCES

Archibugi, D. and Michie, J. (1995), 'The globalisation of technology: a new taxon-omy', *Cambridge Journal of Economics*, **19** (1): 121–40; reprinted in Archibugi and Michie (eds), *Technology, Globalisation and Economic Performance*, Cambridge: Cambridge University Press, 1997.

Benn, T. (1987), *Out of the Wilderness: Diaries 1963–67*, London: Hutchinson.

Cosh, A.D., Hughes, A. and Rowthorn, R.E. (1994), '*The Competitive Role of UK Manufacturing Industry, 1950–2003: A Case Analysis*', University of Cambridge mimeo.

Crafts, N. (1996), 'Deindustrialization and economic growth', *Economic Journal*, **106**: 172–83.

Eltis, W. (1996), 'How low profitability and weak innovativeness undermined UK industrial growth', *Economic Journal*, **106**: 184–95.

Halimi, S., Michie, J. and Milne, S. (1994), 'The Mitterrand experience', in J. Michie and J. Grieve Smith (eds), *Unemployment in Europe*, London: Academic Press, ch. 6.

House of Lords (1991), *Report from the Select Committee on Science and Technology*, London: HMSO.

Kaldor, N. (1985), *Economics Without Equilibrium*, New York: M.E. Sharpe.

Kitson, M. and Michie, J. (1996), 'Britain's industrial performance since 1960: underinvestment and relative decline', *Economic Journal*, **106**: 196–212.

Olson, M. (1982), *The Rise and Decline of Nations*, New Haven, Conn.: Yale University Press.

Small Business Research Centre (1992), *The State of British Enterprise: Growth, Innovation and Competitive Advantage in Small and Medium Sized Enterprises*, Cambridge: Small Business Research Centre, University of Cambridge.

Stoneman, P. and Francis, N. (1992), 'Double deflation and the measurement of output and productivity in UK manufacturing, 1979–1989', Warwick Business School Discussion Paper.

Young, A. (1928), 'Increasing returns and economic progress', *Economic Journal*, **38** (152): 527–42.

4. Institutions and employment performance in different growth regimes

Eileen Appelbaum and Ronald Schettkat*

INTRODUCTION

Although the OECD countries are all capitalist market economies, their institutional settings as well as their economic performance varied substantially in the 1970s and 1980s. Therefore, whether institutions matter is not controversial in economics, but rather the question is which institutional arrangements best support the performance of the economy. Many economists became interested in understanding how institutional differences influence economic performance. However, the industrialized economies varied less with respect to GDP growth than with respect to employment (see Figure 4.1). This suggests that differences in GDP growth rates are not sufficient to explain variations in labour market performance. One of the most obvious candidates for the explanation of differing economic performance in market economies is the wage-bargaining system, which differs remarkably between countries.

Wage-bargaining can take place at several levels. At one extreme, individual companies and employees may negotiate the wage (decentralized bargaining), whereas at the other extreme, national unions and employers' associations may bargain over wages for a whole country (centralized bargaining). Countries can occupy any position on this continuum. Traditionally economists favoured the decentralized model of wage-bargaining because it is best suited to achieving efficient allocation in perfectly competitive markets. But this may not be the case in an imperfect world where asymmetric information, transaction costs, uncertainty, interdependence of actions and so on exist and where employers and unions have market power. In such an imperfect world – which has gained

* Earlier versions of this chapter gained substantially from critique and comments by Wendy Carlin, Andrew Glyn, Richard Jackman, Guenther Schmid, and David Soskice. We are grateful for research assistance by Susanne Fuchs, Alice Wurche, Keinan Tang and Yan Yuan.

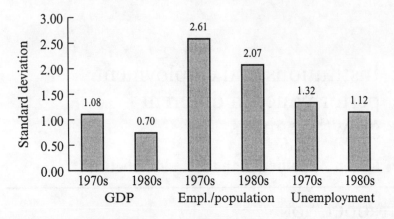

Source: Based on OECD statistics.

*Figure 4.1 Standard deviations of growth rates of GDP, employment to
        population ratios, and unemployment rates*

importance in economic theory – even centralized wage-bargaining
systems can produce a superior economic performance, as recent theoretical and empirical work suggests. Political scientists have discussed these
issues under the label 'corporatism', and more recently economists have
taken up this discussion, often under the label 'wage-bargaining and economic performance'.

The general result in this literature is that institutions have a strong
influence on labour market performance, but the specific relationship
between wage-bargaining institutions and economic performance remains
unclear. Some economists take the view that more organized wage-setting
increases the ability to compensate for external shocks, and thus reduces
the non-accelerating inflation rate of unemployment (NAIRU). This view
of a negative linear relationship between the centralization of wage-
bargaining and unemployment has been challenged in recent work, which
argues that both centralized and decentralized wage-bargaining systems
are able to produce favourable employment outcomes through wage
restraint although this is achieved in each case through completely different mechanisms. In a decentralized bargaining system wage restraint is
achieved by market pressure, whereas in the centralized system the central
wage negotiator internalizes the negative effects of overly high wage
increases and thus acts as if the market co-ordinates wage-setting.
Countries with wage-bargaining at an intermediate level, such as branch-
level negotiations, suffer from the market power of organized labour,
which does not internalize negative feedback effects. These countries,
therefore, experience a poorer employment performance.

Usually, the literature discusses the employment and unemployment impacts of the aggregate real wage and does not explicitly deal with the wage structure; nor does it discuss the employment structure of economies with respect to industries. However, the industrialized economies differ enormously concerning the industry composition of employment and wage differentials. Therefore, a second effect of wage-bargaining institutions on wages, namely on inter-industry wage dispersion, may also be important. The argument is that wage-bargaining institutions affect wage dispersion and, through this mechanism, affect employment growth in industries with below-average rates of productivity growth. In the last two decades or so, the industrial economies have exhibited a negative or at best zero correlation between productivity growth and employment growth by industry (Figure 4.2) (Appelbaum and Schettkat, 1995). This contrasts with the positive correlation which Salter (1960) and others, such as Kaldor (1987), described as characteristic of industrialized economies earlier this century, and which provided the underlying rationale for the Swedish (Rehn and Meidner) model of wage and industrial policy.[1] Under the new circumstances, aggregate employment growth depends on the expansion of employment in lower productivity growth industries (mainly consumer services).

This change in the growth regime coincided with rising unemployment; that is, with disequilibrium in the labour market. In this context, labour market institutions became increasingly important. In the earlier conditions of near-full employment, and with nominal wages and employment rising most strongly in high productivity growth industries, there was little scope for institutional differences among countries to affect outcomes. As an inverse relationship began to develop between employment growth and productivity growth, however, whether an overall increase in employment could be achieved came to depend on an expansion of industries with lower productivity growth. Institutional differences between countries then became important, as different institutional settings have been more or less successful in promoting employment growth in lower productivity growth industries, usually services.

In this chapter we discuss theories of wage-setting in industrialized economies as well as efforts to measure those institutional arrangements that affect wage-setting. We investigate the relationship between wage-setting systems and wage dispersion and employment performance. Our conclusion is that overall employment growth was weakest in the 1980s in those countries that lacked both high inter-industry wage dispersion and highly developed corporatist institutions. In addition, we argue that a broader definition of corporatism (see pp. 77–9) that includes co-ordination with government may affect employment growth in publicly provided or subsidized services.

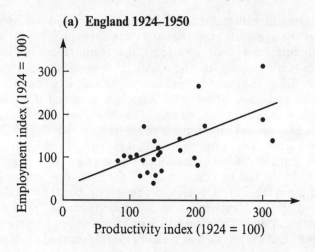

(a) England 1924–1950

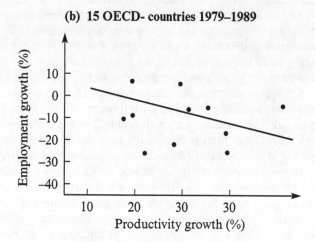

(b) 15 OECD- countries 1979–1989

Sources: (a) Slater (1960), (b) Appelbaum and Schettkat (1995).

Figure 4.2 The relationship between growth of productivity and employment in manufacturing industries

WAGE-BARGAINING SYSTEMS AND ECONOMIC PERFORMANCE: THEORY AND MEASUREMENT

Theoretical Considerations

Wage-bargaining can take place at (a) the firm (establishment) level, (b) the branch level, and (c) the national level. In a decentralized bargaining system, unions or even individual workers negotiate the wage with single employers (single-employer or decentralized bargaining). At the branch level, unions and employers' associations negotiate (multi-employer bargaining) while at the national level the peak organizations of unions and employers negotiate (centralized bargaining). In practice, bargaining can occur on more than one level (multi-level bargaining) with the national or the branch-level agreements setting (minimal) standards which may be modified at lower levels.

Increasing centralization of wage-bargaining can have two different effects: with increasing comprehensiveness, unions gain market power which may be used to push up wages and working standards; at the same time, bigger organizations encompass larger groups, that is, the negative effects of wage-bargaining become endogenous. These two effects thus work in different direction, and Mancur Olson's (1982) theory suggests that special-interest groups are most damaging when they have gained a certain amount of power but little responsibility. An encompassing organization can exist at different levels but it always requires that the membership over which the organization has effective authority be coterminous with the population that will bear any adverse consequences of action (Crouch, 1992). This has allowed economists (Calmfors and Driffill, 1988) to argue that wage-bargaining at the company level (decentralized) but also at the national level (centralized) leads to favourable macro-economic outcomes, such as low unemployment and inflation rates. Economies with an intermediate level of wage-bargaining, however, suffer from union power which does not internalize negative effects. These countries are therefore expected to produce less-favourable macro-economic outcomes.

Calmfors and Driffill (1988) argue that both extremes (countries with decentralized and with centralized bargaining systems) achieve positive employment results through wage restraint, although by different means. Company-level unions are constrained by competition in the product market[2] but they can externalize the negative effects of their actions. Company unions thus have limited power but they do not carry the burden of negative effects, that is they are in a free-rider position with respect to negative effects which do not affect their membership. A centralized union, on the other hand, can expect its policy to influence the macro-economy, that is, the negative effects of wage-setting will affect the union's members directly. If workers lose their jobs and depend on benefits, these benefits will be financed by members of the union and hence overly high wage increases will directly affect members' net wages. Similarly, if wage rises induce inflation this will directly affect the real wage of the union's members. Therefore, it is argued that centralized unions (and employers' associations) will take the macro-economic effects of their action into account because there is simply no outside world to which negative effects can be shifted. A branch-level union, in contrast, has market power but it externalizes the negative effects of its action. This relation between external effects and the centralization of wage-bargaining is illustrated by the hump-shaped curve in Figure 4.3.

So far the theoretical argument has been developed for a closed economy. The impact of increased competition should have flattened the trade-off curve between centralization of the wage-bargaining system and likely negative effects.[3] In the extreme case, when foreign products are perfect substitutes for domestic products, national institutions would become irrelevant and the upper curve in Figure 4.3 would become horizontal. In effect a national industry has no more power over price-setting than a competitive firm.

The hump-shaped relation between centralization of the bargaining system and possible negative effects is under debate for other reasons as

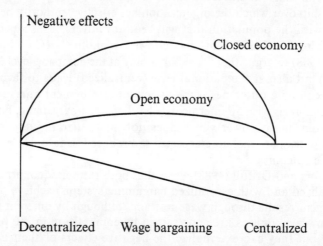

Figure 4.3 The possible relationship between negative effects and wage-bargaining systems

well. A linear negative relation is the proposed alternative. Michael Bruno and Jeffrey Sachs, Richard Layard, Stephen Nickell and Richard Jackman, as well as David Soskice all assume such a linear negative relationship. The more centralized (Soskice uses the term 'co-ordinated' and Bruno and Sachs use 'corporatist') a bargaining system is, the more it takes account of macro-economic impacts. This view is supported by the fact that the share of wage costs increases with aggregation. The share of wage costs in output is roughly 20 per cent at the firm level but at the aggregate level it is about 70 per cent (Nickell, 1988). This suggests that the impact of the negative effects of wage-setting falls monotonically with aggregation. In other words, the more encompassing the organizations are, the more they take the negative effects of their action into account. As the degree of corporatism increases the micro horizon widens to the macro horizon (linear falling curve in Figure 4.3).

Measurement

Many efforts have been made to measure the degree of co-ordination in wage-bargaining, or, more generally, the institutional factors which affect responsiveness of wage-setting to macro-economic conditions. Union density was used to explain variations in economic performance between countries (see, for example, Blanchflower and Freeman, 1992) but there are also efforts to measure 'corporatism'.[4] Whereas it is relatively straightforward to measure union density,[5] it is more difficult to measure the degree of corporatism. The problems are manifold: (a) no standard definition of corporatism exists; (b) it is often difficult to quantify institutional features; (c) combining different variables in one indicator causes problems.

Many of the researchers who have developed indices for corporatism have a deep institutional knowledge of some countries, but there remains a substantial subjective component in their classifications. In addition, the definition of corporatism used differs between studies (see Table 4.1 for a brief characterization of the indices). It is therefore not surprising that the various indicators differ substantially and that some countries are classified as highly corporatist by some authors, whereas others classify them as non-corporatist (Figure 4.4).[6]

Institutions are often regarded as very stable, and most studies on corporatism and economic performance were published in the early and mid-1980s and refer mainly to the 1970s. Since then, however, substantial changes have taken place in some countries. In Sweden, centralized bargaining disappeared in the early 1980s, in the UK the unions' influence diminished, and New Zealand switched from multi-employer to single-employer bargaining. However, there is no uniform trend to more

Table 4.1 A brief characterization of indices representing wage-bargaining systems

Comprehensiveness index based on OECD data	Coverage and bargaining level (Schettkat, 1995a)
Soskice	Covert and overt co-ordination of unions and employers' associations
Calmfors and Driffill	Centralization of unions and employers' organizations
Bruno and Sachs (Crouch)	Centralization of unions, shop-floor representation, employers' co-ordination, existence of works councils
Blyth	Level of bargaining, union and employers' co-operation
Schmitter	Organizational centralization and the number of unions
Cameron	Centralization of unions, control capacity of central organization, union membership
Tarantelli	Degree of ideological and political consensus of unions and employers, centralization of bargaining, regulation of industrial conflict
Lehmbruch	Influence of unions in the policy formulation process
Lijphardt and Crepaz	Average of several other indices
Layard, Nickell and Jackman	Unions' plus employers' co-ordination

decentralized bargaining. In some countries wage-bargaining became more centralized and many countries did not change at all (see, for details, OECD, 1994).

The theoretical debate suggests that an index which characterizes wage-bargaining needs to capture the *coverage* and the *level* at which wage-bargaining takes place. Even centralized wage-bargaining will have little effect if only a small proportion of workers is covered. Some authors use union density to capture the share of the workforce affected

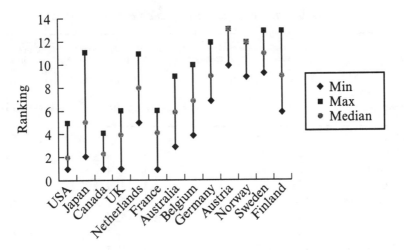

Note: Only countries available in each study are included.

Sources: Calmfors and Driffill (1988), Bruno and Sachs (1985), Blyth (1987), Cameron (1984), Tarantelli (1986), Lijphardt and Crepaz (1991), Schettkat (1995a).

Figure 4.4 Ranking of countries by different indices of 'corporatism'

by collective bargaining as an estimate of coverage. High union density leads by definition to high coverage, but as the example of France shows (see Table 4.2), high coverage can be achieved even with low union density through legal extension of collective agreements (for an overview, see Hartog and Theuwes, 1993).[7] The level at which wage-bargaining takes place is still important. If the agreements are extended to the whole economy, bargaining parties might be expected to take macro-economic effects into account. This will be the case if negotiations take place at the national level, no matter how high the union density rate. If only specific parts of the workforce are organized, collective negotiations may be biased in favour of the organized workers.

Both variables, the bargaining level and the coverage rate, have the advantage that they can be 'easily' measured, that is to say such an index does not so much rely on subjective classifications as do many other efforts to classify bargaining systems. Bargaining level and coverage are combined in the comprehensiveness index displayed in Table 4.2.[8] The advantage of this index is that it captures the components regarded as most relevant in the theoretical literature and in addition both components can be measured objectively. Most importantly, data for the 1970s and the 1980s are available for both components for most countries. This makes it possible to account for changes in the wage-bargaining systems.

Table 4.2 Bargaining indices, union density and wage differentials

	Comprehensiveness				Calmfors/ Driffill ranking[a]	Union density (% of labour force)		Earnings inequalities[b]	
	Values		Ranking[a]					D9/D1	D9/D1
	1970–80	1980–90	1970–80	1980–90	1970s	1975	1985	1980	1990
	(1)	(2)	(3)	(4)	(5)	(6)	(7)	(12)	(13)
USA	26	18	1	1	2	22.8	18.0	4.8	5.6
Japan	28	23	2	2	4	34.4	28.9	3.0	3.2
Canada	37	38	3	3	1	34.4	35.9	4.0	4.4
Switzerland	106	106	4	6	3	32.9	28.8		2.7
New Zealand	134	134	5	7	8	50.1	47.3	2.9	3.0
Portugal	140	198	6	16	n.a.	52.4	51.6	3.6	3.5
UK	140	47	7	4	5	48.3	45.5	2.8	3.3
Netherlands	152	142	8	9	10	38.4	28.7	2.5	2.6
Spain	168	136	9	8	n.a.	30.4	16.0	n.a.	n.a.
France	170	184	10	14	6	22.8	16.3	3.3	3.3
Australia	176	80	11	5	7	56.0	56.5	2.8	2.8
Belgium	180	180	12	12	9	55.3	54.3	2.4	2.3
Germany	182	180	13	13	11	36.6	37.4	2.7	2.5
Austria	196	196	14	15	15	56.1	48.6	3.5	3.5
Norway	225	225	15	17	14	52.7	55.7	2.1	2.0
Sweden	249	166	16	11	13	82.1	94.2	2.0	2.0
Finland	285	143	17	10	12	67.4	68.6	2.5	2.5
Correlations									
D9/D1(1980)	–0.71	–0.52	–0.65	–0.45	–0.61	–0.68	–0.58	1.00	
D9/D1(1990)	–0.75	–0.63	–0.72	–0.57	–0.68	–0.65	–0.55	0.98	1.00

Notes

[a] Low rankings = low degree of comprehensiveness (centralization).

[b] From OECD, *Employment Outlook 1996*; earning inequality specifics: US from *Employment Outlook 1993*, Canada 1981, New Zealand 1984, Portugal, Netherlands 1985, Belgium 1986, Germany 1984, Norway 1979, 1991.

Sources: Data on the comprehensiveness index: Schettkat (1994); union density: OCED, *Employment Outlook*.

The most dramatic change to decentralization occurred in the UK, where unions' influence and coverage declined in conjunction with a shift to single-employer bargaining during the 1980s. These changes have moved the UK to the less-centralized end of the spectrum. Australia moved from being a middle-ranking country to being a much less co-ordinated country, mainly because the level of co-ordination shifted to the company level. Substantial changes also occurred in the Nordic countries, where both Sweden and Finland gave up centralized wage-bargaining, as is clearly shown in the change in the index between the 1970s and the 1980s. Norway, on the other hand, remained an economy with centralized wage-bargaining.

BARGAINING SYSTEMS AND WAGES

Aggregate Wage Flexibility

Wage-bargaining institutions can influence employment and unemployment through two channels: (a) a co-ordinated wage policy may lead to wage restraint in the overall economy; and (b) centralization may have an impact on wage differentials and the wage structures (the ranking of industries by wages). Originally the discussion of corporatism and economic performance was not related to wage structure but rather emphasized the behaviour of the aggregate wage. Flanagan *et al.* (1983), Bruno and Sachs (1985), Calmfors and Driffill (1988) and Soskice (1990) all discuss the impact of wage-bargaining institutions on aggregate wage restraint and on inflation, employment and unemployment. The main argument is that wage restraint is best achieved in corporatist bargaining systems although there is dissent as to whether this a linear (Bruno and Sachs, 1985; Soskice, 1990; Layard *et al.*, 1991) or a non-linear relationship (Calmfors and Driffill, 1988).[9]

Bruno and Sachs, for example, focused on the ability of economies to absorb external shocks, such as the oil price increases in the early and late 1970s, and argue that corporatist countries are likely to achieve a better economic performance than non-corporatist countries because they are able to follow an accommodatory wage policy: that is, inflationary pressure is lower and thus reduces the NAIRU which allows for higher employment and lower unemployment. In addition to the degree of corporatism (as measured by the Calmfors–Driffill index) Layard *et al.* (1991) argue that the characteristics of the unemployment insurance system (replacement ratio and benefit duration) are important in explaining variations in the responsiveness of wage-setting to unemployment across countries. Using regression analysis of the responsiveness of wage-setting to unemployment, these authors find a negative linear relation to the centralization index of Calmfors and Driffill.[10]

Wage Differentials

Only a few studies of bargaining systems and economic performance take wage dispersion into account (Freeman, 1988; Rowthorn, 1992; Appelbaum and Schettkat, 1993, 1995) although 'equal pay for equal work' is part of almost any union's programme and more comprehensive unions are expected to enforce such a concept on a broader scale than are less comprehensive unions. In the literature, however, it is seen that unions can have a positive and a negative impact on wage differentials. Unions raise the wages of organized workers and thus raise the wage differential (Friedman, 1962), but they may also increase standards and thus reduce wage differentials (Blanchflower and Freeman, 1992). At the firm level, union–non-union wage differentials differ substantially from 0.22 in the USA to 0.07 in Austria (ibid.), suggesting that unions can have a different effect depending on their type of organization (company unions as in the USA, centralized unions in Austria).

In cross-country comparison,[11] wage differentials decline with increasing union density. Not only the degree of unionization but also wage-bargaining institutions are expected to have an impact on wage differentials. Sweden, for example, was a country ranking high on the comprehensiveness scale and was known for its solidaristic wage policy which was intended to reduce wage differentials between industries and skill groups (Meidner and Hedborg, 1984; Flanagan, 1987). Sweden's wage differentials are still outstandingly low, although they have increased through the 1980s. The USA, on the other hand, is the leader in wage dispersion and has the least-comprehensive wage-bargaining system. Austria has a high value on the comprehensiveness index but at the same time wage differentials there are very high (see Table 4.2). Austria, however, seems to be an outlier, because countries with a high comprehensiveness tend to have low wage differentials. One explanation for the Austria–Sweden difference that has been put forward is the different historical development of the corporatist arrangements in the two countries (Therborn, 1992). In Sweden, corporatist institutions – highlighted by the Saltjöbadan agreement (Meidner and Hedborg, 1984) – developed as a solution to industrial conflicts which were damaging economic performance. In contrast, the Austrian labour movement was more markedly based on consensus after the Second World War (Guger, 1992). In general, however, wage-bargaining systems are associated with wage differentials in a negative linear way: low-ranking countries on the comprehensiveness scale have high wage differentials and high-ranking countries have low wage differentials (see correlation coefficients in the lower panel of Table 4.2).

It may be concluded from these exercises that wage-bargaining institutions seem to be very important for inequality. Less-comprehensive bargaining systems and less-centralized bargaining systems allow more easily for earnings inequality. These results support Richard Freeman's (1996) call for a policy to strengthen institutions in order to prevent inequality from rising further in the USA. The results, however, will also please those who see institutions as rigidities which prevent economies from creating employment.

UNEMPLOYMENT AND EMPLOYMENT TRENDS

The non-linear relationship of the impact of wage-bargaining institutions on unemployment (hump-shaped) and employment (U-shaped) were discovered in the 1980s (Calmfors and Driffill, 1988; Freeman, 1988; Rowthorn, 1992). Calmfors and Driffill proposed a theoretical explanation for these non-linear relations in which extremes of the wage-bargaining institution scheme do well because they create aggregate wage restraint (see discussion above). However, Rowthorn, using the Calmfors–Driffill index, discovered that these relationships hold for the 1980s but cannot be found for the early 1970s when almost all industrialized countries experienced full employment.

In Table 4.3 we display regression analysis for unemployment rates and employment to population ratios (employment rates) on the comprehensiveness index and on the Calmfors and Driffill index. In line with Rowthorn's results (based on the Calmfors–Driffill index), we do not find empirical evidence for a non-linear relation between the wage-bargaining system (with either index) and employment to population ratios or unemployment rates for the early 1970s. If anything, there is a negative, linear relationship between the unemployment rate and the index. This changes in the 1980s, when the hump-shaped (U-shaped) relation for unemployment (employment) emerges. This is most clearly seen if changes in the rates rather than levels are used (lower panel of Table 4.3). In other words, the relationship between wage-bargaining systems and unemployment (employment) seems to have changed substantially from the early 1970s to the 1980s.[12]

Why is it, then, that the hump-shaped relation can be found in the 1980s, but that it is not apparent during the full-employment period of the early 1970s?[13] Although institutions may have changed substantially, it is unlikely that the structures in the economy created by these institutions have changed as rapidly.[14] In view of the fact that most employment growth has occurred in service industries and that some services are

Economics of employment and unemployment

Table 4.3 Regression analysis of labour market performance on wage-bargaining systems

Dependent variable	Independent variables			Summary statistics		
	Constant	CompR70-U	CD-U	R^2	F	N
Level						
Unemployment rate						
1970–3	2.89	−0.18		0.06	0.86	15
	[1.05]	[0.18]				
	3.32		−0.28	0.15	2.3	15
	[1.25]		[0.21]			
1985–9	2.02	1.00		0.41	9.11	15
	[1.58]	[0.33]				
	3.13		0.74	0.23	3.78	15
	[1.81]		[0.38]			
Employment to population ratio						
1970–3	71.31	−0.92		0.12	1.75	15
	[3.35]	[0.70]				
	69.69		−0.54	0.04	0.55	15
	[5.35]		[0.73]			
1985–9	77.65	−2.53		0.42	9.33	15
	[3.97]	[0.83]				
	74.67		−1.84	0.22	3.67	15
	[4.60]		[0.96]			
Changes						
Unemployment rate						
70/80	−0.87	1.18		0.67	26.67	15
	[1.09]	[0.23]				
	−0.19		1.02	0.5	13.11	15
	[1.34]		[0.28]			
Employment to population ratio						
70/80	6.34	−1.61		0.38	8.1	15
	[2.71]	[0.57]				
	5		1.3	0.25	4.3	15
	[3]		[0.63]			

Notes
1. CompR70-U = ranking of countries according to the comprehensiveness index of the 1970s (see Table 4.2) in U-shape form: to the highest and lowest ranking countries the lowest values were assigned. To countries in the middle the highest values were assigned.
2. CD-U = ranking of countries according to the Calmfors–Driffill index, in U-shape form.
3. Levels refers to average of the rates for the indicated period.
4. Changes are computed as follows: 70/80 = average for the period 1958–89 minus 1970–73. The linear version of the indices was never significant.
5. The real values of the comprehensiveness index (Comp) produced slightly different results, but rankings are displayed for comparison with the Calmfors–Driffill index.
6. In brackets: heteroscedastic consistent standard errors.

Table 4.4 Co-ordination and comprehensiveness

Co-ordination (Layard *et al.*)	Comprehensiveness 1970–80		
	Low	Medium	High
Low	USA Canada	UK New Zealand	
Medium	Japan Switzerland	Australia Spain Netherlands France	Belgium
High			Germany Austria Finland Sweden

Co-ordination (*Layard et al.*)	Comprehensiveness 1980–90		
	Low	*Medium*	*High*
Low	USA Canada UK New Zealand		
Medium	Japan Switzerland	Australia Spain Netherlands	France Belgium
High		Sweden	Germany Austria Finland

Notes
1. Co-ordination according to Layard *et al.* (1991, pp. 52–3, table 6) computed as employers' co-ordination (1 to 3) plus union's co-ordination (1 to 3); low = 1 and 2; medium = 3 and 4; high = 5 and 6.
2. Comprehensiveness as computed in Table 4.2; actual values for the indicated period divided by the average of 1970–80 (both periods); low < 0.8; medium = 0.8–1.2; high > 1.2.

suffering from the 'cost disease' (Baumol, 1967), some institutional settings may have made expansion easier than others. But it remains a puzzle
why the two extremes, the decentralized and the centralized bargaining
systems, achieved similar results. An explanation may be sought in differences between public and private sector growth. Employment in services
with low productivity growth rates may be traded in private markets if
wages have sufficient downward flexibility. This may overcome the negative demand effect of rising relative prices in these services. Thus, in
countries with less-centralized wage-bargaining systems, which usually
have lower wage dispersion, employment expansion may have taken place
in privately provided consumer services.[15] But economies with comprehensive bargaining systems and low wage differentials also experienced high
employment growth mainly in industries which provide services to consumers as well (Scharpf, 1990), but here employment and service provision
is publicly organized (financed or directly provided). Public provision

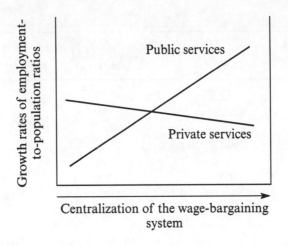

Notes
Private services: community, social, personal, recreational.
Public services: public administration, government sector according to national accounts.
CD = rankings according to Calmfors and Driffill (1988).
Regressions:
average growth rate of private services = 1.5 − 0.08 CD; R^2 = 0.37, F(1,8) = 4.8
　　　　　　　　　　　　　　　　[0.19] [0.03]
average growth rate of public services = −0.25 + 0.23 CD; R^2 = 0.48, F(1,8) = 7.6
　　　　　　　　　　　　　　　　[0.42] [0.08]
Heteroscedastic consistent standard errors in brackets.

*Figure 4.5 Behind the U-shape: stylized relations between private and public
service employment growth and the wage-bargaining system*

(demarketization: Glyn, 1992) overcomes the negative effect of rising relative prices for consumer services and thus allows for employment expansion in these industries without high wage differentials. These considerations are supported by the positive linear relationship between the indices representing wage-bargaining systems and the ratio of public employment to population, and the negative relationship to the ratio of private service employment to population, respectively (see Figure 4.5).[16]

These trends in private service employment and public employment seem to be the major differences in the stylized employment development in countries with centralized and decentralized wage-bargaining systems. High wage dispersion allowed for an increase in private service employment even in jobs which do not have high productivity growth, but this means of employment creation was not available in the countries with centralized bargaining systems. Here public employment expansion was the solution to the employment problem; that is to say, it was less the integration of different interest groups in the bargaining system itself (corporatism in the narrow sense) than the interaction with government (corporatism in the broadest sense) which underlay the favourable employment trends.

CONCLUDING SUMMARY

In this chapter we discussed the impact of wage-bargaining institutions on labour market performance as measured by the employment-to-population ratio and the unemployment rate. We found a U-shaped (hump-shaped) relation between the degree of centralization of the wage-bargaining system and the employment-to-population ratio (unemployment rate) in the 1980s but not in the early 1970s. The widely discussed non-linear relationship between centralization of the wage-bargaining system and labour market performance was mainly the result of developments which occurred during the 1970s and 1980s. Unemployment rose little – although from different levels – in economies at the decentralized end but also at the centralized end, whereas the middle experienced substantial increases in unemployment and low growth rates of employment.

Michael Bruno's and Jeffrey Sachs's argument that inflationary pressure is reduced by aggregate wage restraint and thus that the NAIRU declines with the degree of corporatism in a linear way may hold for the 1960s and early 1970s. But inflation was not a major problem in the 1980s, economic growth was much lower and unemployment was in general higher than in earlier periods. In the 1980s, wage differentiation was probably more important for employment growth in the private sector than aggregate wage restraint, which is almost automatically achieved by high unemployment. The underlying employment trends are very different in countries with decentralized bargaining and those with centralized bargaining systems, although both increased employment in services in the 1980s. It is private, market-orientated employment that expanded in countries with less-centralized bargaining systems while in countries with centralized bargaining systems it was mainly public employment which expanded and which raised tax rates. Countries with an intermediate degree of centralization in the wage-bargaining system, however, did not experience the employment growth of the extremes but tried to hold unemployment down by a reduction of labour supply (through early retirement, for example). But high transfers are costly as well, and consequently tax rates rose here also, but without the advantage of additional production, consumption and employment.

NOTES

1. The designers of the solidaristic wage policy (Gösta Rehn and Rudolf Meidner, see Meidner and Hedborg, 1984) argued the it generates a shift to more productive activities and hence a stronger rise in aggregate productivity growth compared to the market outcome. This policy works perfectly well as long as employment in high-productivity growth industries grows, which was characteristic of industrial development (Salter, 1960). By setting wage increases in every industry at a level equal to productivity growth in the median industry, space is created for relative price reductions in industries with above-average productivity growth rates, where wages rise less than productivity. This allows for market expansion and employment expansion in these industries. At the lower end, however, wages rise more than productivity and relative prices increase, which causes contraction of markets and employment in these industries. The policy runs into trouble, however, if employment in high-productivity growth industries ceases to expand. Then the positive employment impact in high-productivity growth industries does not occur and at the same time jobs in low-productivity growth industries disappear.
2. If a union and an individual employer bargain over the wage, the trade-off between wage increases and employment strongly depends on the price elasticity of demand for the firm's product. Most firms are confronted with competitors who provide products which serve as substitutes. At the extreme, in an atomistic, perfectly competitive market, firms face a completely price-elastic demand so that cost and subsequent price rises will reduce the demand for the specific firm to zero. Therefore, in perfectly competitive markets the trade-off between wage increases and employment at the firm level is quite clear and will be recognized by company unions in wage-bargaining.
3. Danthine and Hunt (1994) discuss this effect for economic integration, such as the integration of the European Union.
4. In some work corporatism refers to the wage-bargaining system only, whereas in others it is used to characterize the concerted action of organized labour, capital and government. Lehmbruch (1984) identifies three standard definitions of corporatism:

   1. the development and strengthening of centralized organizations with an exclusive right of representation;
   2. the privileged access of centralized organizations to government;

3. social partnership between labour and capital to regulate conflict between both groups and co-ordination with government.

The first definition is the one most in line with debates in economics on wage-bargaining. The third definition is the most comprehensive and includes governments, and it underlies the classification of some political scientists.

5. For measurement problems of union density, see, for example, Visser (1991).
6. Soskice (1990) criticized the Calmfors and Driffill index on the grounds that wage policy can be co-ordinated without being formally centralized and without a central union. Rowthorn (1992) also argues that co-ordination of wage-bargaining does not necessarily depend on formal structures but the unions may co-ordinate wage bargaining outside of formal structures, as is the case with covert co-ordination, for example in Germany where the metalworkers' union set the benchmark for wage increases in other industries (see Meyer, 1990; OECD, 1994).

   Soskice claims that it is wage co-ordination by employers which makes Japan a co-ordinated economy. In the Soskice index, therefore, Japan is classified as an economy with co-ordinated wage-setting although it has a formally decentralized bargaining system. Some Japanese firms are closely connected in corporate groups (*keiretsus*, Aoki, 1988), mainly in the manufacturing sector where large export-orientated firms dominate. However, the six major corporate groups (*keiretsus*) in total cover only 4.8 per cent of all employees (ibid., p. 121). According to Layard *et al.* (1991, p. 52) employers' co-ordination of wage policy in Japan is middle ranking (see also the Layard/Nickell/Jackman index in ibid., Tables 3.2 and 3.3).
7. As France in the summer of 1995 shows, even unions which organize only a fraction of the labour force may have substantial power.
8. The comprehensiveness index is obtained as the product of the coverage rate and the bargaining level (1,2,3). Countries with a high coverage and centralized bargaining show a high score, whereas those at the other extreme (that is, low coverage and decentralized bargaining) have a low score.
9. Freeman (1988) actually critizes Calmfors and Driffill because they regress unemployment and employment performance on their centralization index but the effect is transmitted via wages which are not modelled.
10. This result is confirmed by the comprehensiveness index. It raises the responsiveness of wage-setting to unemployment in its linear form but fails to do so in its U-shaped form (Schettkat, 1995b).
11. Of course, wage differentials are difficult to compare between countries because gross and net wages may differ substantially as do the services the public sector provides.
12. It is not true, however, that countries with low increases in unemployment rates achieved this through reduced labour force participation. On the contrary, labour supply and unemployment performed better in countries at the extremes of the bargaining system than in the intermediate countries.
13. The sensititivity of the aggregate wage-setting process to unemployment supports a positive linear relationship with the comprehensiveness of the wage-bargaining system (see Layard *et al.*, 1991; Schettkat, 1995b).
14. Although wage-bargaining institutions changed over time, wage differentials did not change substantially when countries moved to less-centralized bargaining. Decentralization seems to be connected to rising wage differentials, but this is a slow process and the bargaining structure of the 1970s still explains international differences in wage differentials in the 1980s quite well (Schettkat, 1995b).
15. It must be kept in mind that while international comparative analysis is able to account for institutional variety, at the same time the number of available variables is very small, which limits the possibilities for analysis.
16. The distinction between private sector service employment and public sector employment is, of course, only a rough approximation for the theoretical arguments made for the expansion of the two sectors.

REFERENCES

Aoki, M. (1988), *Information, Incentives, and Bargaining in the Japanese Economy*, Cambridge: Cambridge University Press.

Appelbaum, E. and Schettkat, R. (1993), *Employment Developments in Industrialized Economies*, Discussion Paper I–101, Wissenschaftszentrum Berlin.

Appelbaum, E. and Schettkat, R. (1995), 'Employment and productivity in industrialized countries', *International Labour Review*, **134** (4–5): 605–23.

Baumol, W. (1967), 'Macroeconomics of unbalanced growth: the anatomy of the urban crisis', *American Economic Review*, **57**: 415–26.

Blanchflower, D.G. and Freeman, R. (1992), 'Unionism in the United States and other advanced countries', *Industrial Relations*, **31** (1): 307–23.

Blyth, C.A. (1987), *Interaction between Collective Bargaining and Government Policies in Selected Member Countries*, Paris: OECD.

Bruno, M. and Sachs, J. (1985), *Economics of Worldwide Stagflation*, Cambridge, Mass.: Harvard University Press.

Calmfors, L. and Driffill, J. (1988), 'Bargaining structure, corporatism and macroeconomic performance', *Economic Policy*, no. 6, April: 14–61.

Cameron, D.R. (1984), 'Social democracy, corporatism, labour quiescence and the representation of economic interest in advanced capitalist society', in J.H. Goldthorpe (ed.), *Order and Conflict in Contemporary Capitalism*, Oxford: Oxford University Press.

Crouch, C. (1992), 'Trade unions in the exposed sector: their influences on neo-corporatist behaviour', in R. Brunetta, and C. Dell'Aringa (eds), *Labour Relations and Economic Performance*, London: Macmillan.

Danthine, J.-P. and Hunt, J. (1994), 'Wage bargaining structure, employment and economic integration', *Economic Journal*, **104**: 528–41.

Flanagan, R. (1987), 'Efficiency and equality in Swedish labor markets', in B. Bosworth, and A. Rivlin (eds), *The Swedish Economy*, Washington, DC: Brookings Institution.

Flanagan, R.J., Soskice, D. and Ulman, L. (1983), *Unionism, Economic Stabilization, and Income Policies: European Experience*. Washington, DC: Brookings Institution.

Franz, W. (1995), *Die Lohnfindung in Deutschland in einer internationalen Perspektive: Ist das deutsche System ein Auslaufmodell?*, Diskussionspapier 24–1995, Centre for International Labour Economics, Universität Konstanz.

Freeman, R. (1988), 'Labour market institutions and economic performance', *Economic Policy*, no. 6: 63–80.

Freeman, R. (1996), 'The new inequality and what we might do about it', Harvard University, ms.

Friedman, M. (1962), *Price Theory: A Provisional Text*, Chicago: Aldine Press.

Glyn, A. (1992), 'Corporatism, patterns of employment, and access to consumption', in L. Calmfors (ed.), *Wage Formation and Macroeconomic Policy in Nordic Countries*, Oxford: Oxford University Press.

Guger, A. (1992), 'Corporatism: success or failure? Austrian experiences', in J. Pekkarinen, M. Pohjola and R.E. Rowthorne (eds) (1992), *Social Corporatism: A Superior Economic System*, Oxford: Clarendon Press.

Hartog, J. and Theeuwes, J. (1993), *Labour Market Contracts and Institutions: A Cross-national Comparison*, Amsterdam: North-Holland.

Kaldor, N. (1987), *Causes of the Slow Rate of Economic Growth of the UK*, Cambridge: Cambridge University Press.

Layard, R., Nickell, S. and Jackman, R. (1991), *Unemployment. Macroeconomic Performance and the Labour Market*, Oxford: Oxford University Press.

Lehmbruch, G. (1984), 'Concertation and the structure of corporatist networks', in J.H. Goldthorpe (ed.), *Order and Conflict in Contemporary Capitalism*, Oxford: Oxford University Press.

Lijphart, A. and Crepaz, M.L. (1991), 'Corporatism and consensus democracy in eighteen countries: conceptual and empirical linkages', *British Journal of Political Science*, **21**: 235–56.

Meidner, R. and Hedborg, A. (1984), *Modell Schweden. Erfahrungen einer Wohlfahrtsgesellschaft*, Frankfurt am Main and New York: Campus.

Meyer, W. (1990), *Bestimmungsfaktoren der Tariflohnbeweung. Eine empirische, mikroökonomische Untersuchung für die Bundesrepublik*, Frankfurt am Main and New York: Campus.

Nickell, S. (1988), 'Discussion of Calmfors/ Driffill', *Economic Policy*, **52**: 55–60.

OECD (1994), 'Collective bargaining: levels and coverage', *Employment Outlook 1994*, Paris: OECD.

OECD (1996), *Employment Outlook 1996*, Paris: OECD.

Olson, M. (1982), *The Rise and Decline of Nations: Economic Growth, Stagflation, and Social Rigidities*, New Haven, Conn., and London: Yale University Press.

Rowthorn, R.E. (1992), 'Centralisation, employment and wage dispersion', *Economic Journal*, **102**: May: 506–23.

Salter, W. (1960), *Productivity and Technical Change*, Cambridge: Cambridge University Press.

Scharpf, F.W. (1990), 'Structures of post-industrial society, or, does mass unemployment disappear in the service and information economy?', in E. Appelbaum, and R. Schettkat (eds), *Labor Market Adjustments to Structural Change and Technological Progress*, New York, Westport, Conn., and London: Praeger, pp. 17–35.

Schettkat, R. (1995a), 'The macroperformance of the German labor market', in F. Buttler, W. Franz, R. Schettkat and D. Soskice (eds), *Institutional Frameworks and Labour Market Performance: Comparative Views on the German and US Economies*, London and New York: Routledge, pp. 316–42.

Schettkat, R. (1995b), 'Behind the U-shape: wage bargaining systems and economic performance', paper prepared for OECD.

Soskice, D. (1990), 'Wage determination: the changing role of institutions in advanced industrialized countries', *Oxford Review of Economic Policy*, **6** (4): 36–61.

Tarantelli, E. (1986), 'The regulation of inflation and unemployment', *Industrial Relations*, **25** (1), 1–15.

Therborn, G. (1992), 'Lessons from "corporatist theorization"', in J. Pekkarinen, M. Pohjola and R.E. Rowthorne (eds), *Social Corporatism. A Superior Economic System*, Oxford: Clarendon Press.

Visser, J. (1991), 'On union density', in OECD, *Employment Outlook*, 97–134.

PART II

The Role of Technology and Innovation

5. The present technological change: growth and employment perspectives

Angelo Reati*

INTRODUCTION

The purpose of this chapter is to summarize the results of recent theoretical investigations and present some empirical evidence on the relationship between radical technical change, growth and employment in order to detect the most likely future trend for employment in western countries.

With this aim, I shall first present the economic analysis of the effects of technological revolutions on growth and employment. To identify the driving forces at work I shall focus on the 'pure' case, assuming that no micro, macro or social factors will prevent the full operation of the basic mechanisms that appear, particularly the links between productivity and (relative) prices, between prices and demand, as well as between productivity and wages. Then, I shall assess the current situation, which is characterized by the diffusion of a new 'paradigm' based on computer and information technologies. It will become evident that, in the medium to long term, the employment trend will be one of stagnation or even decline. Finally, I shall briefly address the policy challenge of such an unfavourable trend, emphasizing the necessity for a reduction in working hours in order to solve the unemployment problem.

RADICAL TECHNICAL CHANGE, GROWTH AND EMPLOYMENT: GENERAL ASPECTS

To prepare the ground for understanding the present situation, the following analysis focuses on *radical* innovations, that is, innovations which produce a technological revolution (see Box 5.1). According to historical

* I thank E. Screpanti and T. Vissol for commenting on a previous draft of this chapter. However, the opinions expressed here are the sole responsibility of the author.

Box 5.1 A typology of innovations

Two distinctions are important :

1. between process and product innovations:

   process innovations aim at improving production costs and the competitive position of the innovator, while product innovations intend
   to increase the demand for a final commodity accruing to a firm;

2. between radical and incremental innovations:

   radical innovations imply a fundamental change in the prevalent
   method of producing (process innovations) or a completely new
   final commodity (product innovation). Incremental innovations
   refer to improvements in the existing technological base, which
   fundamentally remains the same, or to product differentiation of
   final commodities.

experience, such fundamental changes in the technical base of the economy are at the origin of long waves (the so-called Kondratieff cycles) of
capitalist economies.

The economic analysis of technical change will be carried out here in
two stages: first, the individual sector in which the innovation is introduced will be examined; then, in order to show the macro-economic
outlook, the progressive inter-sectoral spread of the new technological
paradigm will be reviewed.

Sectoral Analysis: Process Innovations

Demand and output
Figure 5.1 shows the mechanism generated by radical process innovation,
relating to a sector producing a final commodity (sector i).[1]

To begin with there is a radical technical change which entails, for the
individual innovator, a sudden and large increase in its productivity level
(for example, a 30–50 per cent increase). The innovation is then progressively adopted by the other enterprises in the given sector; according to
empirical experience, the usual form of the diffusion function is a logistic
curve (S-shaped).[2] The pattern of diffusion determines the productivity
function of the sector: with an S-shaped diffusion curve, the productivity
level of the sector will also be S-shaped.

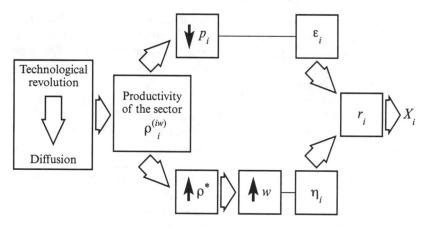

Notes

$\rho_i^{(iw)}$ = percentage rate of change in productivity of the sector involved with the technological revolution

p_i = price of final commodity i

ε_i = price elasticity of demand for final commodity i

ρ^* = percentage rate of change in productivity of total economy

w = wage rate

η_i = income elasticity of demand for final commodity i

r_i = percentage rate of change in demand for final commodity i

X_i = output of final commodity i.

Figure 5.1 From the technological revolution to demand and output

The productivity of the sector has a twofold effect on the demand for commodity i (which in Figure 5.1 is represented by its rate of change r_i):

- a *specific*, or price, effect (upper part of Figure 5.1): when productivity in sector i grows more than the average productivity of the system (ρ^*), the relative price of commodity i (p_i) will decline and this will produce an increase in the demand for the commodity in question (r_i).[3] The price elasticity of demand for commodity i (ε_i) plays a crucial role, because it reduces (when ε_i is less than one), increases (when ε_i is bigger than one) or does not affect (when ε_i is equal to unity) the stimulus to demand as a result of the price decrease;

- a *general*, or income, effect (lower part of Figure 5.1): the increase in productivity of the sector in which there is a technological revolution pushes the average rate of change of productivity of the system upwards and, if wages are indexed to this average productivity, incomes and consumption rise. Each commodity will benefit from the increased purchasing power in a different way, according to an Engel curve path (represented by the income elasticity of demand

η_j).[4,5] Obviously, the importance of the income effect depends on the share of total output taken by the sector in question. If this share is small (because the technological revolution involves only a few sectors), then the income effect will play a secondary role and the price effect will dominate.

The evolution of *output* is straightforward because it is determined by changes in demand resulting from the above endogenous mechanism produced by technical change. Thus the output of the sector in which there is a radical technical change grows much faster than the average. More precisely, the analysis carried out by Reati (1995) shows that physical output in the final sectors follows a long-wave (S-shaped) profile, while in the capital goods sectors it describes a cyclical pattern around the long-wave path displayed by the corresponding final sector.

Employment
Employment is the result of two factors acting in opposite ways:

- the rate of increase of productivity in the sector producing the final commodity *i*, which reduces employment;
- the rate of growth of demand for commodity *i*, which increases employment – the compensation effect.

The net result is crucially dependent on the price elasticity of demand (and, to a much lesser extent, the income elasticity[6]). Thus, abstracting for a moment from the income effect:

- if the price elasticity of demand is equal to one, the sectoral employment will remain constant, because the rate of change in demand (and its job-expanding effect) is exactly offset by the rate of growth of productivity;
- if the price elasticity of demand is higher than unity, the sectoral employment will grow;
- if the price elasticity of demand is less than one, employment will decline.

Sectoral Analysis: Product Innovations

A completely new commodity
A radical product innovation means that the (completely) new commodity is either a response to an entirely new need or a commodity which replaces another commodity in satisfying a perceived consumer need.

The demand for these new commodities results essentially from changes in consumer preferences. In the literature on long waves and marketing the usual reference is to the product life-cycle, in which demand passes through four stages: (a) market development (introduction); (b) growth, when demand begins to accelerate; (c) maturity, when demand levels off; (d) decline.

The length of the diffusion period, that is, the number of years taken to move from the introduction stage to the maturity stage, varies a great deal from one product to another and no general indications are available. Historical experience shows that, for many products, the diffusion period was longer than the diffusion period of several major process innovations. It also seems that, at present, there is a shortening of the diffusion period for both product and process innovations (Marchetti, 1980).

New products can be manufactured by using an existing technique or a completely new technique. In the first case, which will be referred to as the 'pure' case, only incremental process innovations take place and the rate of increase in productivity is small. Alternatively, when the technology which is becoming dominant is pervasive in nature, the manufacture of the new product will also be affected by radical process innovations.

Output and employment
In the 'pure' case, the physical output of the new commodity follows an S-shaped path, similar to the profile of the diffusion function. Employment also grows, because the rate of increase of demand is much larger than the growth of productivity resulting from incremental process innovations.

In the 'mixed' case (in which product innovations are coupled with radical process innovations), physical output grows more than in the pure case, since demand benefits from two positive influences: (a) the 'exogenous' component, resulting from changes in consumer preferences (as in the pure case); (b) the endogenous component, due to the price and income effects resulting from the process innovation.

With regard to employment, the analysis above concerning process innovations applies *mutatis mutandis*. The only difference is that, in the present case, the rate of change of demand is higher, and the employment perspectives are accordingly better. This is for two reasons: there is, first of all, the exogenous component of demand (that we have just seen); secondly, because the diffusion period of the new commodity could be longer than the time span required by the diffusion of process innovations, when the technological revolution in process has come to an end the demand for the new product could continue to grow substantially under the influence of the exogenous component.

Outline of the Macro-economic Trends

Innovations and long waves
The historical experience of the four long waves of capitalist economies shows that, during the depression phase of the long wave, the major innovations tend to appear in existing industries and relate to processes as well as to products. During the recovery phase, the number of major process innovations in existing industries falls sharply, while the flow of product innovations continues. However, the dominant feature of this phase is the appearance of radical product innovations leading to the creation of new industries. The propensity to innovate, therefore, seems to change as described in Table 5.1 (Van Duijn, 1983). This process will probably replicate itself during the subsequent decades, the major difference being represented by the *pervasive* character of the technological revolution which is under way.

Process innovations
Starting with process innovations, the first element which characterizes the overall dynamic is the growing number of sectors affected by the technological revolution (see Table 5.1). If the new technology is pervasive, a substantial part of the economy (including services) will operate on the new technical base by the end of the long stagnation period.

Table 5.1 Propensity to innovate during the phases of the long wave

| | Stagnation | | Expansion | |
	Depression	Recovery	Prosperity	Recession
1. Process innovations (existing industries)	***	*	**	**
2. Product innovations (existing industries)	***	***	*	*
3. Product innovations (new industries)	*	****	**	*
4. Process innovations (basic sectors)	*	**	***	**

Note: Increasing number of asterisks indicates greater propensity to innovate.
Source: Van Duijn (1983, p. 137).

The consequence of the inter-sectoral diffusion of the technological revolution is an acceleration in the average growth rate of productivity. With respect to the previous analysis this implies that:

- the price effect of the demand functions is reduced. In fact, since the average rate of change of productivity is now larger than before, the decline in the *relative* prices of the commodities affected by the technological revolution is less marked;
- the income effect is magnified and becomes increasingly important as the technological revolution extends to other sectors of the economy.

As a matter of fact, process innovations occur throughout the entire long wave (Table 5.1). This means that the two effects arising from the increase in the average rate of growth of productivity are constantly being fuelled. During the first phase of long stagnation (the depression) the stimulus comes from existing industries; when the number of innovations from these sectors falls, there is a wave of innovations from 'basic' sectors, intensifying in the first phase of the long expansion, and so on (Table 5.1).

The other major effect of the inter-sectoral diffusion of the technological revolution is on physical output. We have seen that, when a sector is affected by such technological change, its output follows a long-wave path. The multiplication of this phenomenon during the long stagnation sets in motion a cumulative process of growth which is then further sustained by process innovations in 'basic' sectors during the prosperity phase of the long expansion.

To this should be added the general growth in demand associated with the link between wages and the average growth rate of productivity, which should be considered as an equilibrium condition for the system. This effect operates throughout the long wave and becomes stronger when radical technical change intensifies.

Being the aggregation of all sectoral outputs, aggregate output will exhibit the familiar S-shaped profile. The capital goods sectors add a rolling component to the basic trend set by the final commodities sectors.

Product innovations

Product innovations strongly reinforce the tendencies outlined above, particularly during the long stagnation because, as Table 5.1 shows, it is in this phase of the long wave that the propensity for such innovations to materialize is greater.

To appreciate their overall impact, it is essential to distinguish between product innovations in existing industries and product innovations that give rise to new industries. In fact, in the former case a (completely) new

product satisfies a need which was already being met by another commodity. Enterprises in this sector thus progressively substitute the old
commodity with the new one. The contribution of the sector to aggregate
output in the economy is the difference between the expanding output of
the new commodity and the declining output of the old commodity.

Product innovations which coincide with the creation of new industries
satisfy a new need: their output therefore represents a net addition to
aggregate output. Since such innovations are more frequent during the
recovery phase of the long stagnation, their contribution to the incipient
process of growth could be appreciable.

Total employment

Total employment is influenced by countervailing and uncertain factors
which prevent firm conclusions being obtained from a general analysis. A
precise assessment can only be obtained with some prior knowledge of
the structure of a specific economy, of the characteristics that technical
change assumes in such an economy, and taking into account the values
assumed by some parameters, such as the price and income elasticities of
demand. This will be done in the next section.

Let us start with process innovations and consider the realistic case in
which the new technology is pervasive (that is, it concerns both final commodities and capital goods sectors as well as a large part of the
economy). This technological revolution has two effects on the level of
employment in the economic system: a general effect, with positive repercussions on employment, and a specific effect, which could have neutral
or negative repercussions. Let us first consider the latter.

The sectoral analysis has shown that total employment displays a long-
term positive trend only when the price and income elasticities of demand
are high (greater than one). If empirical evidence shows that such high
values of the elasticities appear only in a few cases, it can be expected
that, for the whole economic system, the trend will be flat or at best
slightly positive, with a more or less pronounced cycle due to the capital
goods sector.

The general effect stems from the increase in aggregate demand resulting from the positive influence of the technological revolution on the
average growth rate of productivity and on wages. In such circumstances,
total employment will be underpinned by the sectors not concerned by
radical technical change. In fact, their demand will increase, but this will
not be offset by an analogous increase in productivity, which continues to
grow at a low rate (resulting from incremental innovations). The magnitude of this effect depends on the relative importance of the sectors in
question with respect to the total economy.

For product innovations the outcome is well defined, in the sense that, even when process innovations also extend to the manufacture of new products, we can expect a positive effect on employment.

THE PRESENT SITUATION

Two elements explain the likely long-term future trend for output and employment: the progressive diffusion of a new technological paradigm and its pervasive nature.

A New Paradigm

The innovations in the field of computer and information technology which developed in the 1970s in connection with the large-scale application of micro-electronics present the characteristics of a technological revolution. They are, in fact, innovations that radically change production methods in an increasing number of industries and services, making the existing plant and equipment obsolete and requiring profound organizational change in firms and institutions.

Computer and information technology was accompanied, in the 1980s, by a cluster of radical innovations. They started with the introduction of new materials (optical fibres) and products (lasers), developed independently of the computer innovation, and we are now witnessing an interesting and promising combination with the computer (telematics, bio-informatics, sensors and switches). Also, the establishment of networks between information technology-based equipment is leading to a wide creation of knowledge and know-how in the economy which encourages the cumulative adoption of many small innovations.[7] The present technological paradigm[8] of information and communication technologies is arising from the convergence of information and computer technologies.

One of the main features of information and communication technologies is that they entail a substantial increase in the level of productivity of the innovator. According to recent micro-economic evidence concerning a representative sample of US large firms, for instance, the leap in the productivity level associated with the use of computer capital is more than 50 per cent (Brynjolfsson and Hitt, 1993).

In terms of the theory of production, this means that information and communication technologies are 'dominant techniques', that is, techniques that, compared with all the other alternative techniques to produce a given commodity, yield a higher rate of profit for any level of the wage rate

(Pasinetti, 1977, ch. 6).[9] This is illustrated in Figure 5.2, which refers to the case in which three alternatives techniques (A, B and C) are available to produce the same commodity. Each technique is associated with a wage rate/rate of profit curve indicating the rate of profit (π) which it is (technically) possible to obtain for any level of the wage rate (w).[10] Let us first consider techniques B and C. When the wage rate is situated between w_1 and w_2, technique B is preferred because it yields a higher rate of profit with respect to technique C. When the wage rate diminishes from w_2 to w_3, technique C is superior to technique B; but when the wage rate drops further, at levels below w_3, technique B becomes superior again to technique C. If we now consider technique A, we can see that, because of the higher productivity which is associated with it, this technique is superior to the other two for the entire range of variation of the wage rate.

Adequate empirical evidence relating to the present technological revolution would provide information on the development of the main 'carrier branches', on induced growth sectors as well as on the infrastructures which facilitate the use of new processes and products everywhere and create appropriate externalities. This would cover:

- main branches: computers, software, electronic capital goods;
- induced growth sectors: advanced machine tools, measuring, precision and control instruments, industrial robotics and flexible manufacturing systems, avionics,[11] telecommunication equipment, databanks, information services;

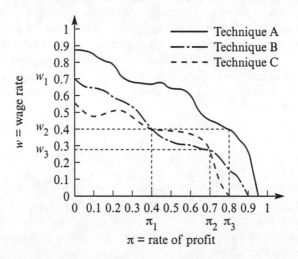

Figure 5.2 The dominant technique

- infrastructure: digital telecommunications networks, satellites;
- other radical innovations: optical fibres, new ceramics, fine chemicals.

However, the available data are far from being exhaustive: new products and activities do not fit into the old statistical classifications and, moreover, they are lumped together with other traditional items. The branches of national accounts which cover quite closely the sectors at the core of the technological revolution are: office and electronic data-processing machines, precision and optical instruments (NACE 33,37) and electrical equipment for industry (NACE 341, 342, 343, 344, 347). Taken together, they cover the main branches and part of the induced growth sectors, since telecommunications equipment is included in the electrical goods branch. As a rough proxy of information services based on the new technologies we can take the communication services (NACE 79).

Table 5.2 indicates that, in the European Union, the 'new technological paradigm' is clearly under way. In fact, if the growth of output in the main branches is compared with that in manufacturing, we can see that these branches were much more dynamic than the average. Concerning the advanced machine tools (not reported separately in the above data), we should note that in 1978 they represented in the European Union less than 10 per cent of the sectors' production value, whereas by 1988 this share amounted to 40 per cent and it is expected that in the second half of the 1990s it will level out at 65 per cent (Atkins, 1990, pp. 41–3).

Table 5.2 Recent trends and medium-term perspectives for the sectors involved in the technological revolution: average annual growth rate at constant prices, EUR-14

Sector	1983–89	1989–95	1995–99
Office and electronic data-processing equipment	12.0	7.5	7.1
Precision instruments	7.0	3.1	0.6
Electrical equipment for industry	4.1	2.3	3.2
Communication services	5.6	4.9	4.1
For comparison:			
Manufacturing	2.9	1.2	2.6
Market services	3.7	2.9	2.9

Source: DRI/McGraw-Hill (1996).

Sustained Growth . . .

In my view, one point is clear: the present technological revolution will produce growth. This assessment is based on the results of Reati (1992, 1995). In Reati (1992), I pointed out that the technological revolution in computer and information technologies initiated in the 1970s reproduces the long-waves mechanism, in which a cumulative process of expansion is originated by massive investment in radically new plant and equipment. Thus, most probably, we are at the eve of a new long-term expansion induced by technological change. This conclusion found theoretical support in Reati (1995), in which I introduced long waves into Pasinetti's model of structural change. Figure 5.3 provides the results of a numerical simulation.[12]

But will a new long-term expansion solve the problem of unemployment? A careful examination of the information and communication technologies paradigm suggests a negative answer.

. . . and High Unemployment

In fact, the information and communication technologies paradigm has a historically unique characteristic which differentiates it from the technological revolutions of the past: *pervasiveness*. Indeed, information and communication technologies are not only transforming all manufacturing sectors but are also diffusing into a substantial and growing share of services (OECD, 1996). Finance, insurance, real estate, wholesale and retail trade, communications and business services now depend crucially on information and communication technologies and account, on average, for about 40 per cent of market services in the EU economy. This movement strongly departs from the features of the technological revolutions of the past, which affected only some segments of industry and excluded services. The Fordist way of producing which characterized the postwar long expansion provides a good example of this fairly limited scope of radical technical change.

The pervasive character of information and communication technologies implies that, in the medium to long term, the service sector (or, at least, a substantial part of it) will be in a similar situation to present-day manufacturing which, as a whole, no longer offers a positive contribution to employment growth. In other words, the peculiarities of the present technological revolution exclude the possibility of finding analogies with the historical experience, in which the 'rising levels of output have gone hand in hand with rising employment levels and with rising productivity, whose growth is largely attributable to technological change' (OECD,

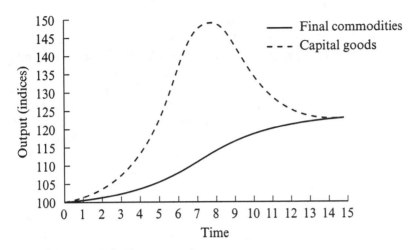

Note: Price and income elasticities of demand = 0.5; technical change in both sectors (pervasive technical change).

Source: Reati (1995, p. 52).

Figure 5.3 Physical output

1994, part I, p. 164). Leontief (1983) was one of the first to draw attention to this novel feature of technical change and its consequences in terms of employment, and this awareness is now gaining ground among scholars.

We have seen that, for process innovations, the employment perspectives are favourable only when the price and income elasticity of demand are high, that is, more than one. The crucial question is thus to know the likely values of such elasticities in real economic systems. The most comprehensive study that I know of is a survey of empirical research concerning five countries (Belgium, France, Italy, the UK and the USA) for the 1960s, 1970s and early 1980s sponsored by the OECD (Bosworth, 1987). It appears that price and income elasticity of demand are usually quite low, that is, less than one. More precisely, classifying final commodities into five broad categories (food, clothing, rent, consumer durables, and 'other goods and services'[13]), we notice (ibid., pp. 141–2) that:

- in all countries the *price* elasticity of demand is less than one for almost every type of commodity. The only exceptions are: clothing and consumer durables in Belgium (where the price elasticities were respectively –1.36 and –1.07); consumer durables in the UK (elasticity –2.93). For the USA, the item 'other goods and services' has an elasticity with the wrong sign (1.45);

- the *income* elasticity of demand is less than one in the majority of cases. For food, it ranges from 0.12 in the USA to 0.87 in Belgium. For clothing, the elasticity in question is less than one in three countries (Belgium, Italy and the USA), while it ranges from 1.09 to 1.53 in France and from 1.17 to 1.28 in the UK. For rent, the income elasticity is usually less than one, except in France (1.19) and in the USA (1.54 to 1.63). For the group 'other goods and services' the elasticity is slightly higher than one in the majority of cases (with a minimum level of 0.87 in the UK and a maximum of 1.75 for the USA). It is only for consumer durables that income elasticity attains very high levels: from 2.5 to 3.3 in most cases.

Of course, price and income elasticity of demand are not constant over time but they change according to the level of income and modifications in consumers' tastes. However, taking into consideration the above results, we can realistically expect that on a global level the 'compensation effect' (the increase in demand resulting from the decrease in price of the commodity involved with process innovations) will be reduced and the long-term employment trend will stagnate or even go into decline.

Considering that the sectors involved with the technical revolution employ a large share of skilled labour, *this unfavourable employment perspective also applies to qualified workers*, and not only to unskilled people who are usually regarded as the losers in the current changes..

Figure 5.4 illustrates the typical situation when radical technical change is pervasive and price and income elasticities of demand are relatively low (0.5). The cyclical pattern shown by the capital goods sector fits quite well with data relative to the 1980s, in which the sectors producing information and communication technologies equipment expanded their output and employment. It should be noted that this numerical simulation is at 'meso' level because the capital goods sector is not an 'industry' in the input–output tables sense but rather a vertically integrated sector (Pasinetti, 1973), which encompasses what is directly and *indirectly* necessary in the whole economic system to produce the final commodity considered.[14]

The theoretical analysis above has shown that product innovations generate the best perspectives for employment. What characterizes the present technological revolution is that the number of process innovations clearly outweighs the number of (entirely) new products (Muldur, 1991). Up to now, the experience of the last long wave – in which a product innovation (the automobile) shaped not only production and consumption structures but also cities, infrastructures and dwellings – has not repeated itself. Of course, many potentialities exist (the multi-media

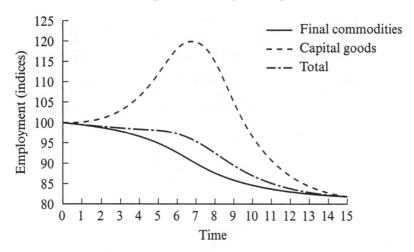

Note: Price and income elasticities of demand = 0.5.

Source: Reati (1995).

Figure 5.4 Pervasive technical change and employment

industry is one of the most important), but the perspectives remain uncertain, in the sense that process innovations could continue to dominate the scene for the next five to ten years. Moreover, the pervasive nature of information and communication technologies implies that new products will be manufactured on the basis of new techniques, with resulting poor employment performances.

The diffusion of information and communication technologies is accompanied by a movement to privatization which has important job-reducing effects. Since we are in a period of poor medium- to long-term employment perspectives, these redundancies will not be temporary (as is usually maintained) but will permanently increase the unemployment level.

A recent study by ERECO (1994)[15] has identified over 120 companies in the European Union and EFTA which are candidates for privatization, and quantifies the potential job losses in the 1990s of more than 800,000. This represents over 20 per cent of the current employment level of the companies concerned. The greater part of such jobs cuts (627,000 units) will derive from the privatization of four sectors (energy, transport, telecommuications, banking and insurance), while privatization in steel, chemicals, engineering, food, forestry and aerospace will add a further 220,000 job reductions.

Most of the potential employment losses will be in three countries: France (290,000 units), Italy (180,000) and Germany (140,000). Some of these have already taken place, but the majority have yet to come.

> If restructuring is especially severe, especially in telecoms and energy . . ., then over 1.1m jobs could be lost . . . If output growth is particularly strong in newly privatised industries, or if governments do not allow these employment implications to follow through in full, then perhaps only 500,000 jobs will be shed. (ERECO, 1994, p. 81)

The aggregate effects on employment of present technical change have been assessed in a number of simulations with econometric models (see Box 5.2). A number of these 'macro' studies employ the input–output technique, which is the most appropriate way of assessing the overall effects of technological change. New sectors are explicitly introduced in the input–output tables and some coefficients are modified on the basis of expert advice. Other studies, on the contrary, rely on the usual aggregate models and are therefore less suitable for the exercise in question. Of course, the findings of these econometric models should be taken with caution, especially when they are issued from aggregate models (such as Interlink), because they are not conceived to take full account of structural change. The general conclusion which emerges is none the less interesting because it shows that, *at the very best*, technical change will have a rather neutral effect on the medium- to long-term level of unemployment.

Two points deserve comment: the US case and the 'productivity paradox'.

Box 5.2 *The impact of technical change measured by econometric models*

These are four studies which are worthy of note:

1. The most interesting and sophisticated input–output study is by Leontief and Duchin (1986), concerning the diffusion of computer technologies in the American economy. The authors present several scenarios for the period 1980–2000: all of them show important losses in employment for the whole economy. For instance, with an hypothesis of moderate diffusion of computer technologies, the unemployment rate in 2000 will be 8.2 points higher than that which would result if the occupational structure in 1978 prevailed (reference scenario).

2. The 'Meta-Studie' (Meyer-Krahmer, 1989), concerning the introduction of robots in the German economy, also relies on
input–output relations and considers the 1980–95 period. The
main conclusion is that an overall positive impact of industrial
robots on employment is very unlikely. As a matter of fact,
around two-thirds of the initial job losses will be compensated by
direct job creation in the manufacturing of robots and by indirect
price and income effects (De Wit, 1991, p. 34).

3. The employment effects of the diffusion of information technologies in the EC were assessed in 1991 in the MERIT-IFO study
sponsored by the Commission services (Gerstenberger *et al.*,
1991; Van Zon, 1991). The methodology is less sophisticated than
in Leontief and Duchin's study in the sense that, instead of
employing a detailed input–output table, the MERIT-IFO team
relied on the HERMES model, in which the economy is disaggregated at the nine sectors level. Also in this case the results in terms
of employment are not encouraging. In fact, under the most
favourable scenario (relatively slow diffusion of information technologies and an improvement in the external competitiveness of
the information technologies industries) the level of unemployment in 2005 will be as high as it was in 1990.

4. OECD (1996) report gives the outcome of eight simulations with
the Interlink model for the G7 countries (ibid., p. 31). The basic
assumption is a moderate increase in the trend of productivity
growth rate (a permanent 0.5 per cent increase in the annual
growth rate) due to technical change; the simulations are performed on alternative hypotheses on the evolution of real
exchange rates and nominal interest rates as well as on some vari-
ants for productivity growth.

   The results for unemployment are similar to those of the
MERIT-IFO study. Over the next five years the unemployment
rate in the G7 countries will decrease by 0.4 per cent with respect
to baseline projection in the most favourable case, and increase by
0.1 per cent in the worst case.* Over a ten-year period the best
outcome would be –0.6 per cent, and the worst an increase of
0.1 per cent.

---

* The baseline projection already foresees a substantial reduction in the unemployment
rate for the year 2000. The figures for G7 are: 6.1 per cent in 2000, as against 6.6 per cent
in 1996, and 8.2 per cent for EUR-4 in 2000, as against 9.6 per cent in 1996. (OCDE,
Perspectives économiques de l'OCDE, no. 57, June 1995, p. 12). The analysis presented in
this chapter casts doubts on the plausibility of such a trend reduction in unemployment.

Discussion

The US employment 'miracle': a mystification?
The US experience, with a relatively low level of unemployment and substantial growth of employment in services, is usually presented as a
success story for labour market flexibility. However, it would be superfi-
cial to extrapolate this model to the European Union without a
preliminary analysis of what such a model means for the persons involved
and for the whole society. Since such an analysis falls outside the purpose
of this chapter, I shall just indicate the direction of the enquiry.

First, it would be interesting to split the growth of employment in services into the shares accounted for by high-tech services and by low-tech
services. Moreover, it would be useful to know how many new jobs in services are precarious, part-time and low-paid jobs and how many are
'normal' jobs.

Next comes the question of the medium- to long-term perspective:
how long can the US service sector continue to be an employment reser-
voir? The 1980s were characterized by a tremendous increase in
inequality in the USA.[16] Inequality has not only evident human rights
and social justice dimensions, but, as recent research suggests (Perrson
and Tabellini, 1994), it is also harmful for growth.

Furthermore, we should consider that the employment growth in the
USA went hand in hand with an appreciable increase of the 'working
poors'. In fact, a study by the US Bureau of Census quoted by OECD
(1994, p. 22) indicates that the incidence of full-time workers with earnings *less than the poverty level*[17] has risen substantially, from around
12 per cent of all workers in 1979 to 18 per cent in 1990.[18]

Finally, I would like to mention that the level of unemployment which
appears in official statistics (a little more than 5 per cent) is very doubt-
ful. Rifkin (1995, p. 11) has estimated the 'true' rate of unemployment
taking into account the 'discouraged' workers (that is, those who are not
actively seeking a job because they have no hope of obtaining one) and
the involuntary part-time workers; the figure he obtains is a rate of unemployment as high as 13 per cent in 1993.[19]

The 'productivity paradox'
The 'productivity paradox' refers to the fact that, in spite of common
knowledge that information and communication technologies are more
pervasive than ever before, data on productivity display a slow trend since
1973 in all western countries.[20] More precisely, we are observing a rapid
increase in productivity in the sectors developing information and communication technologies (computers, electronics) and a much slower rate

of productivity increase in the sectors using it. The explanation of this paradox raised a lively debate, which is summarized in OECD (1991).

Two explanations seem the most important. There is, first of all, a serious mismeasurement of productivity, which has increased over time. The second, and most important, explanation is a mismatch between old institutions and new technological opportunities. In fact, the efficient implementation of information and communication technologies requires a profound organizational change in the innovating enterprise, which is not readily performed: mastering a radically new technology is a long process. Complementary technologies are needed (for example, software), workers must be trained and so sometimes must customers and suppliers: 'the presence of a powerful computer does not suffice to improve productivity' (OECD, 1996, vol. 2, p. 47).

However, the 'productivity paradox' cannot continue for ever, and we can expect that in a few years time the potentialities of information and communication technologies in terms of productivity and job curtailment will become reality.

THE POLICY RESPONSE

The analysis carried out in this chapter has at least two implications for economic policy: (a) the actions on the employment front; (b) the guiding role of public authorities in meeting the equilibrium condition for wages.

Employment policy has two main aspects:

- the measures necessitated in the normal course of events by structural change;
- the specific measures imposed by the pervasive nature of the present technological revolution.

The diversified impact of technical change entails a permanent shift in the structure of employment which calls for a continuous flow of workers from contracting to expanding sectors. There is considerable scope for government action in this field. The first task is to foster the sectoral shifts in the labour force: besides disseminating appropriate information on labour market opportunities, the public authorities must provide constant retraining and skill development for the population.

Of course, these measures are not sufficient to achieve full employment because we are starting from a situation of high unemployment; the most likely outcome is a further deterioration due to pervasive radical technical change. In this context, the only solution that could strengthen social cohesion in the European Union and present it as a desirable model for its citizens is a reduction in the overall labour supply by acting on two parameters: the share of the labour force in the total population and the share of working time in total time.

As for the first parameter, the public authorities could lengthen the period of compulsory education, encourage people to take early retirement, promote part-time work, and so on. However, this would only provide us with a partial solution to the problem. More radical measures are needed on the other front.

The second parameter can be influenced by a reduction in annual working time, mainly through a reduction in weekly working hours. This has actually been happening for a long time: over the last 200 years, we have moved from the 80-hour week (or more) common in the nineteenth century to the present 40-hour week. It was precisely this reduction in working time which rendered compatible the long-term productivity growth with the increase in employment.

Finally, it is important to stress the importance of the equilibrium condition which links wage dynamics to average productivity growth in the system. This element is particularly important in the recovery phase of the long stagnation period and becomes crucial in the long expansion period because it is the way to provide the demand for growing output.

CONCLUSIONS

In this chapter I have attempted to discover the medium- to long-term perspective for employment in western countries by studying the relationship between technical change, growth and employment. Two distinctions are important: (a) process and product innovations; (b) radical and incremental innovations. To understand the present situation, attention should be focused on radical innovations.

Assuming that the basic mechanism put in motion by technical change is not subverted by some factors operating at micro or macro level (the 'pure' case), the *economic analysis* of process innovation shows that two conflicting forces are at work: (a) the productivity effect, which reduces employment; (b) the compensation effect (that is, the increase in demand resulting from the decrease in price of the commodity involved), which expands employment. Which of the two effects will prevail depends crucially on the level of price and income elasticities of demand.

By contrast, the case of product innovation is more clear cut, in the sense that we can expect a growing employment trend both at sectoral and at aggregate level. This positive outcome is nevertheless reduced when radical process innovations also extend to the manufacture of new products.

An examination of the current situation, which is characterized by the diffusion of information and communication technologies, suggests that, in the medium to long term, the *employment trend* will be one of stagnation or will even be in decline, for three reasons:

1. Information and communication technologies have an historically unique characteristic, which distinguishes them from the technological revolutions of the past: pervasiveness. Information and communication technologies now cover a substantial and increasing part of services and, when their diffusion becomes more advanced, the service sector will no longer be able to offer a positive contribution to employment growth.
2. Available empirical evidence shows that the price elasticity of demand is usually less than unity. Thus, in most cases, the net effect of process innovations will be to reduce jobs.
3. Until now, the number of (radical) process innovations clearly outweighs the number of (entirely) new products. Many potentialities exist (for example, the multi-media industry) but the perspectives remain uncertain, in the sense that process innovations could continue to dominate the scene for the next five to ten years.

Since the sectors involved with the technological revolution are skill-intensive, this unfavourable employment trend will also affect qualified workers, and not only unskilled people.

Employment policy has two main aspects:

1. the measures necessitated in the normal course of events by structural change. This implies, in particular, fostering the sectoral shifts of the labour force from contracting to expanding sectors;
2. the specific measures imposed by the pervasive nature of the present technological revolution. Because we are starting off with a high unemployment situation, and the likely outcome is a further deterioration due to technical change, it seems inevitable to envisage a reduction in the overall labour supply, mainly through shorter working time.

NOTES

1. For the capital goods sector the reasoning is similar.
2. The length of the diffusion period varies greatly from one commodity to another; most frequently it takes about 15 years to arrive at a complete intra-sectoral diffusion of new technology.

3. As noted above, this basic relation between productivity and prices relies on the hypothesis that there are no monopolistic market structures and practices preventing the downward price change. Similarly, for demand I assume that the impulse coming from prices is not annihilated by an unfavourable macro-economic environment (restrictive monetary and fiscal policies, stagnating international trade, depressed 'animal spirits' of capitalists, etc.).

4. The Engel curve describes the evolution of the per capita expenditure on a particular commodity in response to an increase in real per capita income. The relationship is not linear: for the majority of commodities it follows a logistic path; for physical subsistence commodities (for example, food), after a sharp increase in expenditure in connection with the lowest levels of income, the curve becomes flat (saturation level).

5. To be complete, we should consider that the rate of change in demand is also influenced by the rate of growth of the population, which increases the demand for each commodity in a uniform way. To simplify, in what follows this element is not included, because the European Union population is roughly stable.

6. In this sectoral analysis, the income effect has little importance because I assume that the weight of the sector in which there is a technical revolution is small and, consequently, the average productivity of the system is only slightly influenced by the faster productivity growth of the sector in question. We shall see later, when assessing the overall dynamic of the system, that the income effect becomes dominant when the number of sectors involved with the technological revolution is growing.

7. Biotechnology is at least as revolutionary as the computer and micro-processors. Its potential impact in agriculture is enormous, as genetically transformed plants could solve the famine problem of the Third World. In industry, the scope for biotechnology is more restricted, even though production methods in a wide range of sectors, such as pharmaceuticals, chemicals, food and drink, will change drastically and it could also be possible to apply biotechnology to mineral extraction. However, it is quite unlikely that biotechnology could be the basis for a technological revolution to put the economy on a new long-term growth path because it is not yet perfected. For industry and services in the industrialized countries, most of the far-reaching innovations derived from biotechnology will probably be implemented at the beginning of the next century, when the microelectronics paradigm will have become established and produced its economic effects.

8. 'Technological paradigm' is defined here by analogy with the scientific paradigm in the Kuhn sense, 'as a model and a pattern of solution of selected technological problems, based on selected principles derived from natural sciences and on selected material technologies' (Dosi, 1984, p. 83). In other words, the technological paradigm refers to 'the prevailing engineering and managerial common sense for best productivity and most profitable practice, which is applicable in almost any industry' (Freeman and Perez, 1988, p. 48).

9. Or a higher wage rate for any level of the rate of profit.

10. The wage rate/rate of profit curve is quite irregular because it is derived from a polynomial expression of degree n, where n is the number of industries in the economic system. See Pasinetti (1977, pp. 87–9).

11. This term refers to all the electronic systems used in aircraft engines, missiles and spacecraft.

12. The simulation is based on the following assumptions:
    1. Radical innovations appear in the final sector i as well as in the capital goods sector k_i.
    2. The technological revolution materializes in a one-shot increase of 30 per cent of the productivity level of the innovator; after this leap, the enterprise in question implements only incremental innovations, entailing a 1 per cent increase in productivity per year.
    3. The diffusion function is a logistic and the diffusion of innovations within a sector takes 15 years to be complete.
    4. The price and income elasticities of demand for the final commodity are 0.5.
    5. The degree of mechanization of the final sector is 'medium', in the sense that the share of direct labour incorporated into commodity i is 40 per cent.

13. In the European Union (EUR-12), in 1992 the percentage share of these groups in respect of total final consumption of households was:

food	19.1
clothing	7.4
rent	13.6
consumer durables (furniture and household equipment)	7.9

Among the other commodities and services which are relevant for the question of income and prices elasticities, the percentage share of total consumption of households was:

recreation, entertainment, education and culture	8.7
transport and communication	15.2
miscellaneous goods and services	15.4

This group includes expenditure in restaurants, cafés and hotels for about 30–40 per cent of total; other items are, in decreasing order of importance: miscellaneous services and commodities, personal care, financial services, package tours.
14. Figure 5.4 is based on the same assumption as Figure 5.3 regarding technical change and its diffusion. See note 12.
15. I. Moore, 'Privatisation in Europe', in ERECO (1994, ch. 6).
16. See OECD (1994, p. 19) for some comparative figures.
17. In 1990, the poverty threshold of $12,195 represented around 44 per cent of median earnings of civilian male, year-round, full-time workers ($27,866) (OECD, 1994, p. 57).
18. In the USA, real earnings for the lowest decile of earners fell by more than 10 per cent over the 1980s (ibid., p. 21).
19. The statistical source used by Rifkin is the US Bureau of Labor Statistics. However, OECD (1995, p. 77) gives a lower figure (10.2 per cent).
20. 'You can see the computer age everywhere but in the productivity statistics' (R. Solow).

REFERENCES

Atkins (1990), *Strategic Study on the EC Machine Tool Sector*, study made for the Commission of the European Communities, Brussels: European Commission, May.

Bosworth, D. (1987), 'Prices, costs and elasticity of demand', in OECD, *Information Computer Communications Policy, Information Technology and Economic Prospects*, no. 12, Paris: OECD, pp. 127–73.

Brynjolfsson, E. and Hitt, L. (1993) 'Is information system spending productive? New evidence and new results', *Communications of the ACM*, **36** (12): 47–64.

De Wit, R. (1991), 'A review of the literature on technological change and employment', paper presented at the EEC Conference on 'Macro-economic and Sectoral Analysis of Future Employment and Training Perspectives in the New Information Technologies in the EC', Brussels, 17–18 October.

Dosi, G. (1984), 'Technological paradigms and technological trajectories: the determinants and directions of technical change and the transformation of the economy', in C. Freeman (ed.), *Long Waves in the World Economy*, London: Frances Pinter.

DRI/McGraw-Hill (1996), *Europe in 1999: Economic Analysis and Forecasts*, Brussels: DRI Europe,

ERECO (1994), *Europe in 1998: Economic Analysis and Forecasts*, Brussels: ERECO (May).

Freeman, C. and Perez, C. (1988), 'Structural crises of adjustment, business cycles and investment behaviour', in G. Dosi, C. Freeman, R. Nelson, G. Silverberg and L. Soete (eds), *Technical Change and Economic Theory*, London: Frances Pinter, pp. 38–66.

Gerstenberger, W., Golinelli, R. and Vogler-Ludwig, K. (1991), 'Impact of information technologies on future employment in the EC', paper presented at the EEC conference on 'Macro-economic and Sectoral Analysis of Future Employment and Training Perspectives in the New Information Technologies in the EC', Brussels, 17–18 October.

Leontief, W. (1983), 'Technological advance, economic growth, and the distribution of income, *Population and Development Review*, **19** (3), 403–10.

Leontief, W. and Duchin, F. (1986), *The Future Impact of Automation on Workers*, Oxford: Oxford University Press.

Marchetti, C. (1980), 'Society as a learning system: discovery, invention, and innovation cycles revisited', *Technological Forecasting and Social Change*, **18** (4): 267–82.

Meyer-Krahmer, F. (ed.) (1989), *Sektorale und gesamtwirtschaftliche Auswirkungen moderner Technologien*, Berlin: DIW.

Muldur, U. (1991), *Le Financement de la R&D au croisement des logiques industrielles, financières et politiques*, CCE, FAST/Monitor, dossier prospectif no. 2, November.

OECD (1991), *Technology and Productivity: The Challenge for Economic Policy*, Paris: OECD.

OECD (1994), *The OECD Jobs Study. Evidence and Explanations*, Paris: OECD.

OECD (1995), *Employment Outlook*, Paris: OECD.

OECD (1996), *The OECD Jobs Strategy: Technology, Productivity and Job Creation*, vol. 1: *Highlights*; vol. 2: *Analytical Report*, Paris: OECD.

Pasinetti, L.L. (1973), 'The notion of vertical integration in economic analysis', *Metroeconomica*; reprinted in L.L. Pasinetti (ed.), *Essays on the Theory of Joint Production*, New York: Columbia University Press, 1980, pp. 16–43.

Pasinetti, L.L. (1977), *Lectures on the Theory of Production*, London: Macmillan.

Persson, T. and Tabellini, G. (1994) 'Is inequality harmful for growth?', *American Economic Review*, **84**: 600–21.

Reati, A. (1992), 'Are we at the eve of a new long-term expansion induced by technological change?', *International Review of Applied Economics*, **6** (3): 249–85.

Reati, A. (1995), *Radical Innovations and Long Waves in Pasinetti's Model of Structural Change: Output and Employment*, Economic Papers, no. 109, Brussels: European Commission, Directorate-General for Economic Affairs, March.

Rifkin, J. (1995), *The End of Work: The Decline of the Global Labor Force and the Dawn of the Post-market Era*, New York: G.P. Putnam's Sons.

Van Duijn, J.J. (1983), *The Long Wave in Economic Life*, London: Allen Unwin.

Van Zon, A. (1991), 'Hermit', paper presented at the EEC Conference on 'Macro-economic and Sectoral Analysis of Future Employment and Training Perspectives in the New Information Technologies in the EC', Brussels, 17–18 October.

6. A micro–macro view of the causes of and remedies for unemployment in an integrating Europe

Andrew Tylecote

INTRODUCTION

The Nature of the Problem

This chapter is concerned with the causes of the current high level of unemployment in the advanced countries in general and the European Community in particular. It is important to begin by stressing the general nature of the problem. Virtually every country in continental Europe now has a rate of registered unemployment considerably higher than at any time since the 1930s (or immediate postwar dislocation). This is not quite true for the UK, whose rate has been falling since 1993 and is now somewhat lower than the average of the 1980s. However, there have been increasing incentives in the UK for those with poor prospects of getting back into work to take 'early retirement' or 'invalidity benefit' instead of registering for unemployment.

The US position is rather similar to the British: the decade averages of registered unemployment were 4.5 per cent for the 1950s, 4.8 per cent for the 1960s, 6.2 per cent for the 1970s, and 7.3 per cent for the 1980s (Rifkin, 1995); but after half a decade of continuous expansion, the 1995 rate (on standardized definitions) was 5.5 per cent, well below that of any major European country. However, the social security system for unemployed people in the USA is so limited in its scope and duration that registered unemployment is highly unreliable as a guide to the extent of long-term unemployment in particular. Surveys which seek to measure all those who would take a job if one were available uncover rates of unemployment there, at least for men, which are similar to European levels. (see Table 6.1).

The role of technology and innovation

Table 6.1 Unemployment rates, real and registered (%)

	Real (1): BLS 'U7' type measure[a]		Real (2): Men aged 25–55 not in work	Registered Standardized unemployment rates				
	1983	1993	1989–94	1974	1990	1991	1992	1995
United States	9.8	6.9	14.0	5.5	5.6	6.8	7.5	5.5
Men	10.1	7.2						
Women	9.3	6.6						
Japan	2.7	2.6		1.4	2.1	2.1	2.2	3.1
Men	2.6	2.5						
Women	2.8	2.8						
Germany	6.9	7.7	15.0	1.6	4.8	4.2	4.6	8.2
Men	5.9	6.5						
Women	8.5	9.4						
France	8.0	11.4	11.0	2.8	8.9	9.4	10.3	11.6
Men	6.1	9.7						
Women	10.5	13.5						
Italy	8.4	10.2		5.3	10.3	9.9	10.5	12.2
Men	5.5	6.8						
Women	14.0	15.8						
UK	11.2	10.3	13.0	2.9	6.9	8.8	10.1	8.7
Men	12.1	12.5						
Women	9.9	7.6						
Spain	20.8	22.4		2.6	15.9	16.0	18.1	22.7
Men	17.2	18.7						
Women	28.3	28.8						
Netherlands	9.7	7.2		2.7	7.5	7.0	5.6	6.5
Men	7.3	5.5						
Women	13.8	9.8						
Sweden	2.0	5.3		2.0	1.8	3.3	5.8	9.2
Men	2.1	6.3						
Women	1.9	4.2						

Note: [a] BLS 'U7' type measure denotes: unemployment rate + discouraged workers as percentage of labour force + involuntary part-time workers as percentage of labour force.

Sources: 'Real 1': OECD *Employment Outlook*, July 1995, pp. 76–7, Table 2.18; 'Real 2': Richard Layard, 'Clues to prosperity', *The Financial Times*, 17 Feb. 1997; 'Registered': John Philpott, 'Anglo-Saxon economics and jobs', *Employment Policy Institute Economic Report*, **11** (1), 1997

Keynesians versus Monetarists

Economists are deeply divided as to how to explain such mass unemployment. Those in the Keynesian tradition emphasize the role of aggregate demand in the determination of employment. In the short run this is taken to work through capacity utilization; in the long run by its effect on capacity-widening investment. Fiscal and monetary policy are both seen as important determinants of demand. There is, however, a new neoclassical orthodoxy which is expressed, for example, in the reports of the IMF and (less reliably) the OECD and the pronouncements of *The Economist*, which has reversed the innovations of Keynes. No longer does the sequence of causation lead from demand to investment to saving, but (as before Keynes) from saving to investment. Once again, as before Keynes, the economy is seen as self-adjusting in its natural tendency, so as to eliminate unemployment unless interfered with by regulation, social security and trade unions. Fiscal reflation (through a public sector deficit) is seen as self-defeating, through various mechanisms. For example, households, observing the deficit, increase their own saving, counterbalancing the reduction in public sector saving, in order to provide for the greater tax burden on them (and their heirs) in future. Monetary reflation, on the other hand, is seen as effective in an immediate sense: it increases demand. However, this merely leads, perhaps after a lag, to a rise in the price level, since there is some kind of vertical supply curve with which an aggregate demand curve intersects. In consequence it is the responsibility of the monetary authorities to restrict the money supply whenever inflation is at whatever are regarded at unacceptable levels or is increasing.

A KEYNESIAN APPROACH

The Effects of Monetary Policy

I have no space in this chapter to discuss the merits of the opposing views. I have set them out merely to clarify my own, which is essentially Keynesian in the senses indicated above. A Keynesian approach can go a long way to explain the present situation. First, we can consider the effects of monetary policy, whose stance for a Keynesian is sufficiently indicated by the rate of interest (unless the authorities maintain tight direct control over the supply of credit, which over the last 20 years has been rare). For the last 15 years the real rate of interest in most countries has been high by historical standards – except for the United States over the last eight or so years, particularly the short rate. That can be expected to reduce the rate of investment in capacity-widening (and other) investment, in housing and in consumer durables, and thereby to reduce demand and employment. (It also has an effect on fiscal policy, as we shall see.) Accordingly, a high average real rate of interest depresses aggregate demand in the world economy on average.

Equally, variations among countries in the money rate of interest can be expected to have a pronounced effect on the distribution of demand. It is open to one country's monetary authorities to reduce their short rate below the average so long as they are prepared to accept the consequences, which will certainly include (*ceteris paribus*) a fall in their exchange rate. The devaluation, among other factors, will make for an increase in the inflation rate, which will reduce the real rate of interest even further than the money rate. So long as the effect of the devaluation has not been cancelled out by domestic inflation, it will combine with the fall in interest rates to increase demand. At the same time, of course, the corresponding *re*valuation of the currencies with higher interest rates will tend, directly and indirectly, to reduce demand in those economies. The reflationary effect of devaluation is most to be relied upon in the largest economies, thus most of all in the United States, since there is least chance there that the acceleration of inflation, and the anticipation of more, will start to get out of hand and force the authorities to intervene with a tightening of policy.

Fiscal Policy and the Effect of Public Sector Deficits

The Keynesian verdict on European monetary policy over the last 15 years is then quite simple: we needed cheap money, and we got dear money. On fiscal policy the verdict cannot be quite so simple. Keynesians certainly see any fiscal deficit as expansionary in its tendency, particularly if it arises from an increase in expenditure (aside from transfer payments), since the expenditure multiplier is higher than the tax multiplier. That is, however, a direct and short-run effect. The higher the deficit now, the higher the debt later, which has to be serviced if not repaid, and any tax revenue which has to be raised to pay interest is likely to depress demand more than the receipt of those interest payments will increase it. (See the discussion of marginal propensity to consume, below.) Reduction in 'primary' public expenditure will have a still more deflationary effect. In fact, this gloomy conclusion about the long run does not automatically follow. The initial deficit may pay for itself in the long run if it leads to higher national income and thus higher tax revenue. This happy result could arise in one or both of two ways. First, the deficit could 'prime the pump', as the phrase once was, that is, lead through higher aggregate demand to greater consumer and business confidence, higher private investment and so on. Secondly, (the rise in) the deficit could consist of public investment of one sort or another – infrastructure, say, or education – which improves the productive capacity of the economy in the long run, and thus (again) increases tax revenues without any rise in rates.

It is unfortunately clear that we have, instead, had the worst of all possible worlds. In the short run, instead of the fiscal deficit 'priming the pump', it was given little chance to do so because the monetary authorities usually compensated for whatever expansionary effect it seemed to be having by a tightening in their own policy. This was, or seemed, necessary in order to hit their targets in terms of inflation and to prevent a loss of confidence in and thus devaluation of their currency. In the longer run there was little benefit to the productive capacity of the economy because the extra expenditure was not concentrated on the productive areas, but went to satisfy powerful lobbies (military in the USA in the 1980s, agribusiness generally, pensioners except in Britain) and, ironically, to pay for the mounting costs of unemployment. Latterly, much of the deficit is accounted for by the costs of servicing the debt. Indeed, as shown in Wolf (1996), in an extreme case such as Italy's, by 1995 the debt burden was such that the public sector was running a primary surplus so large as to be deflationary (>3 per cent of GDP), while it continued to have an overall deficit well above the Maastricht ceiling (>7 per cent of GDP) and such as to increase the debt burden in future.

Inequality Within a Keynesian Framework

From a Keynesian standpoint, there is a further factor which can be expected to have a depressing effect on aggregate demand, at least in the United States and the UK: the rise in inequality of income and wealth. Keynesian analysis makes much of variations in the marginal (and average) propensity to consume. If wealth is taken from those with a high marginal propensity to consume and given to those with a lower one, then *ceteris paribus* there will be a net reduction in aggregate demand. It seems likely that this is what is involved when, for example, the Italian state raises taxes in order to pay interest on its debt, because the recipients of the interest will be relatively wealthy and the relatively wealthy have a relatively low marginal propensity to consume.[1] It is only in the USA and UK that there has been a pronounced increase in inequality over the last 15 years or so, and there a deflationary effect from it could therefore be expected. However, in the USA we have to take account of a demographic effect in the other direction. As shown in *The Economist* (1996), the shift over the last decade towards a larger proportion of retired people in the population, a large fraction of whom depend largely on accumulated assets, has increased the average propensity to consume. (Ironically the possibility of an expansionary effect was the last thing on the mind of the (neoclassical) writer who believed that the reduction in saving was to blame for the low levels of investment in the USA.) There is reason to expect a smaller effect in continental Europe, because of the heavy dependence of retired people on generous pay-as-you-go pensions, paid for simultaneously by the employed. In Britain, where funded pensions are important, a similar effect is conceivable, but it may be outweighed by the 'immaturity' of the system: that is, a large fraction of the (better-paid) working population are saving towards a funded pension, but a much smaller proportion of the retired population are spending out of one (see Tylecote, 1992, ch. 5).

BEYOND KEYNESIANISM

Innovation, Investment and Demand

Investment has a key, active role in any Keynesian model. Any increase in it increases income by more than that, depending on the income multiplier, up to full employment. Since investment itself is a function of income, or more directly of capacity utilization, the sensitivity of income to an initial rise in investment is further magnified. (For an individual economy the multiplier is reduced by the extent of 'leakage' of demand into imports, but that does not hold for the world as a whole, or even for the North as a whole, to the extent that the rest of the world is balance-of-payments-constrained.) What else besides a fall in interest rate could cause such an initial rise? Clearly, one factor would be an increase in the extent of profitable investment opportunities, due to an improvement in the climate for technological innovation or the adoption of others' innovations. Following Perez (1983), I have argued (for example, Tylecote, 1995) that the present period is one in which a new 'technological style' or 'techno-economic paradigm' has recently 'crystallized' and is beginning to diffuse and take over from its predecessor. The new paradigm is (at least mainly) based on information and communication technology (ICT); the old one was/is 'Fordism'. (A 'style' is not so much a set of technologies as a pattern within which technologies change. Thus a Fordist assembly line *circa* 1970 was vastly different from one *circa* 1920, but certain aspects remained unchanged – for example, the inflexibility of the equipment.) It seems probable that the slowdown in growth in the 1970s owed much to the progressive exhaustion of opportunities for innovation within the old Fordist style (Reati, 1996).

In principle the arrival of a new 'style' should improve the opportunities for a broad range of innovations, but there is a catch: these will be inhibited until the 'socio-institutional framework' is well matched with the new style. Unfortunately, to begin with this is certainly not the case. If the socio-institutional framework is well matched to any style it is to the old one. Thus it has been shown, notably by the 'regulation' school, that certain institutions which were general in the advanced north by the 1960s – for instance, the welfare state, mass trade unions, and so on – corresponded quite well to certain requirements of Fordism. For example, the trade unions were able to secure for the workers a large share of productivity gains, correcting a failure which through underconsumption could be blamed for the slump. However, the very success of the expansion under the old style caused changes which spoilt the old 'match': for example, workers during the 1960s began to reject the deal which had given union officials a share of power over them rather than increase their own autonomy (Screpanti, 1984). Thus while societies should have been considering how they might adapt their institutions to the demands of the new style, they were riven by conflict over issues thrown up by the twilight of the old one.

How to Release the Potential of the 'Post-Fordist' Technological Style

Let us consider more specifically what is inhibiting the diffusion of the new style. First, there is education and training. It is clear that the new style puts a higher premium on skill and education than before – and it requires different skills to a large extent. Robert Reich (1996) quotes a US study as showing for the 1980s that raising the average educational level of a company's workers by one year boosts business productivity by about 10 per cent; another study shows for the late 1980s that companies which introduced formal employee training programmes saw their productivity rise 19 per cent more than companies which did not train their workers. Yet other data quoted by Reich showed that US business spending on training per employee *fell* in real terms between 1983 and 1995. It looks as though not only is the level of education and training seriously deficient with respect to the needs of the new style, but there is something about the socio-institutional framework which – in the USA at least – inhibits the actions needed to put this right. We return to this below.

Secondly, there is organizational inertia of some kind: the failure to make the necessary changes to management methods or working practices at some level. This may be due to resistance by unions or middle management or to simple ignorance. Both are likely to decline over time, given learning processes and the weakening of unions. It is certainly increasingly recognized in Europe and the USA that organizational change is necessary for the effective use of ICT (Andreasen *et al.*, 1995). Inappropriate organization, combined with lack of skill, may well account for the 'productivity paradox' observed during the late 1970s and

1980s, in which a slowdown in growth of total factor productivity contrasted with the great expectations of productivity increases arising from the introduction of IT; and the slowdown was most marked among 'information workers' (Cabello, 1996).

We have now moved on: a recent study quoted by Cabello finds that since the mid-1980s IT investments in both manufacturing and services have been yielding high returns. There is, however, no sign of the upsurge in investment and productivity that might be expected to follow. Reich (1996) found an increase in labour productivity in the USA of only 0.8 per cent between the second quarters of 1995 and 1996, and the European rates of increase are also low. It is argued that there are serious deficiencies in the measurement of product quality which depress the figures; but it is hard to believe that they are large enough to conceal the major acceleration in productivity that ought to be happening. However, it seems likely that this will come through within a decade, as we move up the steepening part of the logistic curve which characterizes most diffusion. The more that firms within an industry or an economy have successfully adapted their organization and production methods to ICT, and thus made it pay, the easier it is for the rest to follow suit.

Unfortunately, the gains to be expected in productivity growth will not automatically be matched by gains in employment. The effect on employment will depend, first, on how the gains come about. If (*per impossibile*) the main driving or facilitating factor were the raising up of the tail of under-educated and under-skilled workers (and unemployed), then a levelling-up of productivity across each economy could be expected to follow. This would sharply increase the competitiveness of small firms and thus reduce inflation, probably to the point of eliminating it. (As Reich argues, a plausible explanation for the decline in inflation already witnessed is the increased competitiveness of small firms through ICT.) This would in turn get rid of any excuse for 'tight money' and allow nominal interest rates to fall to the very low levels characteristic of the 1930s and 1940s. If, at the other extreme, the gains were concentrated among the firms which have already made highly profitable returns from ICT investments, the benefits would go more to profits and less to reduced inflation. No doubt the outcome in fact will be somewhere between. The consequences for employment will also depend on whether we see it as constrained by supply-side or demand-side factors. If, following my broadly Keynesian approach, the demand side is emphasized, the job-destroying capability of process improvements must be taken into account. Other things being equal, a process improvement which raises labour productivity (as ICT does) will reduce employment. The other things which are, in the long run, not equal include demand for products – but that does not *automatically* rise to fill the gap.

What is required to match the progress and diffusion of process innovation is an upsurge of product innovations using the new processes. The process of product innovation involves investment expenditure; the tooling up for the production of the new product requires more investment; the offering of the new, attractive product raises consumer demand. At some point in the diffusion of a new style, it appears that an upsurge of product innovation takes place (see, for example, Freeman *et al.*, 1982; Tylecote, 1992). But not at once: and it appears that the conditions required for such an upsurge are more extensive and difficult to satisfy than those required for a leap forward in process innovation and diffusion.

The Specific Impediments to Product Innovation

First, let us consider the problem of depressed and uncertain demand. The adoption of a process innovation may well pay even if demand is static, particularly if the firm waits until existing equipment is near the end of its life. The rate of return expected on the development of a product innovation, on the other hand, is likely to be highly sensitive to demand conditions. It is well known that in periods of slow growth of real take-home pay and of insecure employment consumers are less adventurous in terms not only of total spending but also in terms of the nature of purchases. The problem of uncertainty is even more serious. There are uncertainties attaching to new product development which are absent from process change. With a new process the doubts are essentially technological and organizational: can we get it to work as it is supposed to? With a new product there are similar doubts *plus* market doubts: will it sell? The market doubts are not only additional, they relate to a longer term, after the technological doubts have been resolved. The further ahead the firm is looking, the more the uncertainties about future demand are likely to inhibit it.

There is a more fundamental difficulty in product (and to a lesser extent process) innovation: the relationships with those who finance the innovation and control the innovating firm. I have argued (Tylecote, 1997) that there are three sources of difficulty in this relationship:

- the *visibility* of innovation: how easy is it for someone who is not closely involved in managing the development of a new product or process, to judge what resources are being devoted to it and how well they are being spent?
- the *novelty* of innovation: how far does a product or process innovation involve – or need – radically new ways of organizing its development or production, radically new technologies, and/or radically new markets or selling methods?

- the *appropriability* of innovation: can the firm ensure in a straight-forward way (for example, by patents) that the bulk of the returns on it do accrue to the shareholders; or does innovation in the industry naturally tend to involve large spillovers to other stakeholders?

Visibility, novelty and appropriability have always put strain on these relationships, and, as technological change speeds up, the strain increases. There are ways of coping: low-visibility innovation requires 'firm-specific perceptiveness' on the part of lenders and shareholders; high-novelty innovation requires 'industry-specific expertise' on their part; low-appropriability innovation requires a close, co-operative relationship with the stakeholders (employees and other firms) who share in the returns – in a word, their 'enfranchisement'. I have argued (Tylecote, 1997) that there are economies which have enfranchised stakeholders and developed high firm-specific perceptiveness among lenders and shareholders – notably, Germany and Japan. These economies are accordingly well arranged to encourage technological innovation in those industries which demand such characteristics – engineering, in particular. Neither country has, however, developed to a high level the industry-specific expertise among financiers which is indispensable in the very highest-technology industries: biotechnology and science-based information and communication technology. This has been achieved only in the United States, through venture capital (Bank of England, 1996); but the USA lacks the German and Japanese advantages. Many other advanced countries, such as the UK, are deficient in all three respects. There is no reason in principle why a country – any or all – should not develop all three of these favourable institutional characteristics; they are not in principle mutually exclusive. Until they have diffused widely throughout the advanced countries, the innovative potential of the new style will remain considerably under-exploited. Such diffusion will require a range of legislation which there is no space to discuss here.

The Influence of Factor Costs

Every technological style, diverse though its possibilities may be, has a general direction of development in terms of the factors of production it *uses* and the factors it *saves*. Fordism's thrust is towards saving labour – specifically, low-skilled labour – at the cost of extravagant use of raw materials and energy, while producing much pollution. It also makes heavy use of physical capital. If we treat information and communication technology (ICT), new materials and biotechnology as the key components of the new style (Tylecote, 1995), then it is capable of further large savings of labour and at the same time making great savings in raw materials and energy, while reducing pollution. The key factors of production are 'machine intelligence' and 'human capital': the former, used more and more lavishly to operate existing technology; the latter, used more and more lavishly to develop new technology. Clearly, the incentive to innovate within a given style will be a function of factor prices: the dearer the factors it saves and the cheaper the factors it uses, the better. Fordism thrived on the high wages and the cheap raw materials of the United States; the last nail in its coffin, so far as the advanced countries were concerned, was the rise in energy and materials prices in the mid-1970s. In developing countries like India and China it is now diffusing rapidly (without further major innovations) with the encouragement of the current trough in energy and materials prices. By the same token, what would particularly encourage innovation within the new style is a sharp rise in the price of energy, materials and pollution – which is in any case required to avert ecological disaster (Hinterberger and Seifert, 1998) and a fall in the relative cost of labour with the appropriate skills for the new style. In the next subsection we consider the policies needed to bring these changes about.

The Shift from Natural Capital to Human Capital

It is easy to show that the only quick way to make pollution and the use of natural resources more expensive is a new regime of 'eco-taxation'. (Quite apart from the beneficial effects arising from the taxes themselves, it will need considerable innovative effort within the new style to develop the monitoring system: pollution meters, road pricing equipment, and so on) The revenue benefits for governments may stiffen their resolve against the inevitable onslaught by the lobbies of those who will lose. Extra taxes, post-Maastricht, are naturally attractive to governments; the extra spending needed to increase the rate of accumulation of human capital will not be. Happily, there is a way of reducing the fiscal burden. Higher education, which yields substantial private benefits to those who receive it, is currently massively subsidized by the taxpayer. It need not and should not be. The general principle should be that the recipients borrow to pay for their tuition and subsistence and repay during their working lives. Government subsidies should be directed to specific categories of student – the poor, and the mature – to favoured areas of study and to those who turn out *ex post* to earn too little to afford full repayment. To make the scheme work well, low general interest rates would be required – as already advocated – and the linking of the repayments system to the income tax machinery. Governments would need to collect repayments for each other. Government education spending could then be concentrated on nursery, primary and secondary education where the whole population, rather than a privileged minority, benefit and the social returns are higher. Those social returns do, however, depend on the condition of those who receive the education: the generous provision of education to children (and adults) who are demoralized by poverty and unemployment is unlikely to be sufficient to make them an economic asset to their community. Again, this directs us to the damaging effects of inequality.

Once the recipients of higher education were the purchasers of it, the grip of the state on the university systems could be loosened. Universities could acquire the autonomous status that British universities already have, and compete with one another – within and across borders – on cost and quality. (Such a regime would, incidentally, stimulate process and product innovation within education: including educational software, which would itself generate significant employment.)

CONCLUSION

In order to restore employment and growth, it is necessary to focus on investment and innovation. Physical and human capital should be accumulated as quickly as possible, natural capital depleted as slowly as possible. The crucial responsibilities of government are:

1. *to insist on low real rates of interest* It is a monetarist error to suppose that, whenever there is any threat of inflation, interest rates must be raised. Inflation can and should be held down by ensuring lively competition in product markets and an abundance of the key factors of production. Low interest rates contribute to creating these conditions. Market forces can do the rest, as long as there is no excess aggregate demand. If there is, *fiscal* policy should be tightened – with a welcome reduction in the public sector deficit – until the necessary reduction in demand is achieved;

2. *to adjust the relative prices of factors of production to suit the new technological style* As we have seen, this requires a new regime of eco-taxation, on the one hand, and the rapid accumulation of needed skills and capabilities in the labour force. The latter will involve targeting extra government expenditure on the deprived sections of the population and a new system of funding for higher education which frees the state of most of this burden;

3. *to encourage institutional changes in industry and finance which adapt the system of financing of innovation to the characteristics of the new technological style* We have seen that different countries already have elements of the required institutions. They need to be diffused and brought together.

NOTE

1. There is in fact little direct empirical support for this latter statement, because the empirical work has not been done. However, there is evidence that at least the poorest quarter of the population here have very low levels of assets and poor access to credit. it is thus difficult to see how their marginal propensity to consume over any significant range and period of time can be far from 1.

REFERENCES

Andreasen L.E., Coriat, B., Den Hertog, F. and Kaplinsky, R. (eds) (1995), *Europe's Next Step: Organisational Innovation, Competition and Employment*, London: Frank Cass.
Bank of England (1996), *The Financing of Technology-based Small Firms*, London: Bank of England.
Cabello, C. (1996), 'Returns on IT investment: the end of the productivity paradox?', *IPTS Report*, no. 3: 10–13.
The Economist (1996), 'Growing old expensively: are old people responsible for America's falling savings rate?', *The Economist*, 7 September: 94.
Freeman, C., Clark, J. and Soete, L. (1982), *Unemployment and Technical Innovation: A Study of Long Waves and Economic Development*, London: Frances Pinter.
Hinterberger F. and Seifert, E. (1998), 'Reducing materials throughput: a contribution to the measurement of dematerialisation and sustainable human development', in A. Tylecote and J. van der Straaten (eds), *Environment, Technology and Economic Growth: The Challenge to Sustainable Development*, Cheltenham: Edward Elgar.
Morgan, J. (1996), 'What do comparisons of the last two recoveries tell us about the UK labour market?', *National Institute Economic Review*, May: 80–93.
Perez, C. (1983), 'Structural change and assimilation of new technologies in the economic and social systems', *Futures*, October: 357–75.
Reati, A. (1996), 'The present technological change: growth and employment perspectives', paper presented to EAEPE conference, Antwerp, 7–9 November; reprinted as Chapter 5 in this volume.
Reich, R. (1996), 'Casualties of the inflation war', *The Financial Times*, 24 September: 16.
Rifkin, J. (1995), *The End of Work*, New York: G.P. Putnam's Sons.
Screpanti, E. (1984), 'Long economic cycles and recurring proletarian insurgencies', *Review*, **VII** (2): 509–48.
Tylecote, A. (1992), *The Long Wave in the World Economy: The Present Crisis in Historical Perspective*, London: Routledge.
Tylecote, A. (1995), 'Technological and economic long waves and their implications for employment', *New Technology, Work and Employment*, **10** (1): 3–18.
Tylecote, A. (1997), *Corporate Governance, Financial Systems and Innovation*, CRITEC Paper no. 16, Sheffield: Sheffield University Management School.
Wolf, M. (1996), 'To seize the moment', *The Financial Times*, 24 September: 16.

7. Product versus process innovation: implications for employment

Charles Edquist, Leif Hommen and Maureen McKelvey*

INTRODUCTION

The OECD *Jobs Study* (1994a) argues that it is necessary to develop a more detailed and differentiated understanding of the relation between 'growth' and employment, since some kinds of growth destroy jobs while others create jobs. At the same time, the Commission of the European Communities (1994, pp. 57–60) suggests the 'employment intensity of growth' differs between various kinds of productivity and economic growth, and the source and content of growth has significant employment implications. At the core of these studies is the crucial question: Which kinds of growth lead to more jobs and which do not?

The effects of innovations on the generation and destruction of jobs form an especially complicated part of the relations between growth and employment. The relationships between innovation and employment are seldom direct and are usually mediated by a number of offsetting factors (Vivarelli, 1995, ch. 4). These include 'multiplier' effects on demand in other industries and sectors, 'real income' effects influencing the level of demand and 'adjustment' effects in labour markets (wage movements) that partly compensate for the substitution of labour by other factors – all of which are affected by macro-economic conditions and institutional characteristics. Thus unemployment rates have been shown to differ substantially across countries which share similar levels of technological development and similar rates of growth. For example, the OECD

* This chapter is based on work in the project 'Innovation Systems and European Integration (ISE)', funded by Targeted Socio-economic Research, DG XII, European Commission, contract no. SOE1-CT95-1004 (DG 12-SOLS). The subproject associated with this chapter, 'Innovations, Growth and Employment', aims to increase our understanding of the sources of growth and employment as perceived by the systems-of-innovation approach in contrast to traditional approaches.

(1994b, pp. 53–5) reports that during the most recent recession member countries commonly experiencing an initially 'weak rebound' in output growth performed very differently in terms of employment growth.[1] In Europe unemployment is much higher (12 per cent) than in Japan (3 per cent) and the USA (5 per cent).

On the basis of recent work within the so-called systems-of-innovation approach, this chapter proposes an analytical framework for the study of the relationships between innovations and employment.[2] The systems-of-innovation approach is mainly about the determinants of innovation and technical change (Edquist, 1997a). As such, it informs the key distinctions we make between product and process innovations, and, with respect to the latter, between technological and organizational innovations. The first distinction is well-established in the literature, having originated with Joseph Schumpeter, who defined product innovation as 'the introduction of a new good . . . or a new quality of a good' and process innovation as 'the introduction of a new method of production . . . [or] a new way of handling a commodity commercially' (Schumpeter, 1911; compare Archibugi *et al.*, 1994, p. 7). The second distinction, which points to the difference between technological and organizational process innovations, is a more recent development but flows naturally from the first. Utterback and Abernathy (1975), in their studies of the product life-cycle, demonstrate this continuity with a model of development in which transformations in a firm's organizational structure are related to the changing emphasis a firm places on product and process innovation.

Taking our point of entry to be the distinction between product and process innovations and the identification of organizational innovations as an important class of process innovations, we shall deal not only with the production of industrial goods but also with the production of services. The theoretical discussion will be of an 'appreciative' kind (Nelson, 1994, pp. 292–3): that is, we shall try to stay relatively close to empirical substance and shall argue in verbal terms. This discussion will lead to three summarizing propositions that can be tested or answered only through empirical work. Specific hypotheses, questions and systematic analyses of existing empirical studies have been more fully developed elsewhere (Edquist *et al.*, 1997).[3] Where possible in this brief chapter, we shall indicate whether existing empirical work provides a basis for answering the questions raised and give some illustrative empirical examples. Beyond that, we have no systematic empirical ambitions here. Rather, this chapter is a conceptually orientated review of existing theory and research conducted with the aim of developing a framework for assessing the employment effects of different types of innovations.

SPECIFICATION OF BASIC CONCEPTS

Many economists argue that it would be highly advantageous to deal with the employment impact of innovation in a general equilibrium framework. That would mean looking at an economic system as a whole and dealing with the simultaneous determination of all prices and quantities of all goods and services, including the consequences of innovation for employment. To our knowledge, no one has ever attempted to conduct such an analysis, and it seems that a general equilibrium analysis of innovations and employment is not possible to carry out for the time being. One reason is that mainstream economic models have problems in dealing with product innovation (Lundvall, 1985; Pasinetti, 1981; Vivarelli, 1995): in that framework the terms 'innovation' or 'technical change' normally refer only to technological process innovations. Another reason is that technical change and innovation are evolutionary processes which tend to preclude equilibrium situations (Dosi, 1982, 1988).

In contrast, the systems-of-innovation approach can include product innovations as well as technological and organizational process innovations. Moreover, this chapter will discuss material goods as well as intangible services. Ideally, the analysis would identify not only the most important (direct) consequences of innovation for employment but also second- and third-order effects. Our attempt to do this will gradually take us closer to what the term 'general' in 'general equilibrium analysis' essentially means: an approach acknowledging that everything is tied together with everything. This, however, has nothing to do with the term 'equilibrium', since innovation is its opposite.

Product innovations are *what* is produced and sold in terms of new, or better, products (or product varieties). The products may be brand new to the world, or they may be new to a firm or country, that is, diffused to these units. In his original definition Schumpeter (1911) referred to goods or qualities of goods 'with which consumers are not familiar'. The category of product innovations, however, can include both new goods and new services. While new goods are product innovations in manufacturing and the primary sectors, new services are intangible, often consumed simultaneously to their production, and capable of creating values that satisfy non-physical needs of the user (Hauknes, 1994, pp. 8–9).[4] Examples of product innovations in goods include the automobile at the turn of the century, industrial robots in the 1960s and high-definition television (HDTV) in the 1990s. In services, product innovations include the (first) offer of a curly hairstyle, heart transplants in the 1960s, a new insurance payment plan for drivers who lose their licences, video-on-demand over the telecom network, education with regard to the European Union legal system, and the design and maintenance of computer systems in firms.

Process innovations are new ways of producing goods and services; they are defined by *how* existing products are produced. Schumpeter's (1911) original definition referred to a 'method of production' or 'way of handling a commodity' that is 'not yet tested by experience in the branch of manufacture concerned'. In that we are discussing methods, process innovations may be technological or organizational.

Technological process innovations are units of real capital (material goods) that have been improved through technical change and that lead to productivity growth in their use. Some of these goods may once have been product innovations that were sold as commodities to other firms.[5] In other words, they can appear in two 'incarnations' in the economic system, where an industrial robot is a product innovation when produced by ABB in Västerås and a process technology when used by Volvo in Göteborg.

In addition to this relation between material product and process innovations at different stages, other important kinds of relationships exist within the sphere of production. Generally, empirical studies have shown a strong interrelation between product and process innovation at the firm level (Archibugi *et al.*, 1987; Kraft, 1990; Lunn, 1986). However, this relationship is neither simple nor deterministic (Rosenberg, 1976, ch. 8), and requires clear specification. In some cases the production of new products requires the modification of process technologies. In other cases, product innovations do not require new process technologies. A third case is when the same – or a very similar – product is produced with radically different process technologies. An example is human growth hormone, which was previously extracted from human pituitary glands and is now produced through genetically engineered cells.[6]

Organizational process innovations are more productive ways to organize work; a new organizational form is introduced. These innovations are intangibles, that is, they are non-material. Examples are just-in-time production, total quality management (TQM) and lean production. Organizational changes are normally developed through processes of trial-and-error and learning-by-doing within the innovating firms; they are not based on formal R&D activities.[7] Other firms generally copy the vanguard firms; this means of diffusion is facilitated by there normally being no property rights associated with organizational innovations. This differs considerably from the legal environment of most technological innovations. None the less, the process of copying is sometimes facilitated by organization consultants, who act as 'social carriers' of organizational knowledge. Thus the knowledge basis of organizational innovations may sometimes be sold as consultancy *services*, in which case organizational innovations are commodified.

There can be a link between services and organizational process innovations, but it is probably weak.[8] Only a tiny share of all service products become organizational innovations, and conversely, most organizational innovations are not services in that they are not products sold on markets.[9] In other words, the categories of services and organizational innovations are fairly independent of each other, although they have some similar characteristics.

While organizational innovations are not always included in discussions of product versus process innovations, there are at least three important reasons for doing so. First, organizational changes are important sources of productivity growth and competitiveness which may also strongly influence employment.[10] Secondly, organizational and technological changes are closely related and intertwined, with organizational change often being a requirement for successful technological process innovation (Nyholm, 1995). Thirdly, as all technologies are created by human beings, they are 'socially shaped', and this is achieved within a framework of specific organizational forms (Edquist, 1997a).

RELATIONSHIPS BETWEEN INNOVATIONS AND EMPLOYMENT

In order to analyse the different consequences that different types of innovations have for employment and growth, we propose six arguments for distinguishing between product and process innovations and between technological and organizational process innovations. The rather complex relationships between productivity growth, economic growth and (un)employment are addressed and later delineated as three propositions. The six arguments and the evidence adduced to support them are as follows:

1. Different types of innovations exist, with potentially different effects on productivity and employment. Process innovations may be technological as well as organizational, while product innovations may be goods or services.
2. The patterns of diffusion of technological product and process innovations are very different. For example, Swedish industry does well at diffusing process innovations but poorly at diffusing product innovations. The pattern is the reverse of the USA, while Japan is good at both product and process diffusion (Edquist, 1989; Edquist and Jacobsson, 1988).
3. The determinants that explain the differing patterns of diffusion are radically different for technological process and product innovations (Edquist and McKelvey, 1992, 1998). Determinants for diffusing process innovations include industry structure, relative factor prices,

regional wage differentials, rate of unemployment and union attitudes (Edquist, 1989, pp. 4–5). Determinants for diffusing product innovations include the propensity of firms to stay locked into 'core business' activities and the orientation of government policies (Edquist and McKelvey, 1992, pp. 52–63). Thus any action or policy to influence innovations must be based on a more detailed understanding of how and why different categories of innovations are made and diffused.

4. Some product innovations become process innovations at a later stage of the economic cycle. More specifically, consumer products only take the form of product innovations, whereas investment goods can change over time from being product innovations (when sold) to being process innovations (when used). This holds for some goods products which become technological process innovations and for some service products which become organizational process innovations. This dynamic is important because product innovations that become process innovations have second-order effects which can reduce the overall positive employment consequences of product innovations.

5. The consequences for productivity of the various kinds of innovations differ and work through different mechanisms. While process innovations tend to enhance productivity by reducing labour inputs (Vivarelli, 1995), some organizational process innovations are an exception (Dreher, 1996; Nyholm, 1995). In contrast to process innovations, the increased productivity growth associated with new products (particularly new goods) has to do with changes in labour productivity – the nominator of the ratio (Assarsson, 1991; Hansson, 1991). In this sense, the productivity increase (associated with new goods) is not 'real' in the sense of physical output but is rather an increase in productivity 'as measured'.[11] (See, 'Conclusions and policy implications', pp. 142–5.)

6. An analytical distinction between product and process innovation is necessary to make possible the study of the relations between the two. The tendency of mainstream economic theory to assume that all innovations are forms of process innovation ignores product innovations as the main mechanism behind structural economic change (Pasinetti, 1981). While technological process innovation normally has the net effect of reducing employment (Vivarelli, 1995), 'If we abstract from product innovation, we abstract from the most important of factors counteracting stagnation and unemployment' (Lundvall, 1985). This reasoning draws attention to the special character of product innovation as a 'differentiating mechanism' (Katsoulacos, 1984) and to the argument that 'in determining the effect of product innovation on the level of employment, the primary factor involved is the "welfare effect" implying generation of employment' (ibid., p. 83).

These six points clearly indicate that analysis of the relations between innovations, employment and growth depends on a more nuanced discussion of different types of innovations. Our conceptual framework helps to identify which types of innovations, sectors and industries may be more beneficial for employment than others. It suggests that the type and locality of economic and productivity growth is vital for understanding the pattern of employment generation and destruction. Clearly, the consequences of product and process innovations for employment differ sharply between these two major categories and between our three subcategories of (a) technological and organizational process innovations; (b) product innovations in services and goods; and (c) investment, intermediate and consumer products. With these distinctions made, blanket statements such as 'technology destroys jobs' are nonsense.

Our main arguments and observations about the relationships between different types of innovations and employment can now be summarized in the form of three general propositions.

Propositions

Proposition 1 The balance between product and process innovation differs sharply between industrial sectors and also between different service sectors.[12]

Technological process innovations can cumulatively lead to 'technological trajectories' or 'growth patterns' that are either labour-saving or employment-generating (Freeman and Soete, 1987, p. 46). National growth patterns with a relatively low employment intensity reflect the predominance of industrial sectors characterized by a labour-saving technological trajectory in which there is a primary concentration on process, rather than product, innovations (Pianta *et al.*, 1996, p. 13). The evidence comes from a variety of sources. Both comparative studies of national technology specialization (Pianta, 1996; Pianta and Meliciana, 1994) and national studies of sectors of employment growth and decline (Edquist and Texier, 1996; Greenan and Guellec, 1996; Meyer-Krahmer, 1992, 1996) indicate that R&D-intensive manufacturing sectors with high levels of product innovation have also experienced net employment growth. In broad terms, there is greater emphasis on developing new products in the more R&D-intensive industries while there is greater emphasis on process improvements in the less R&D-intensive industries, largely through the acquisition of investment products (Calvert *et al.*, 1996; Papaconstantinou *et al.*, 1995; Pollack, 1991). Within the manufacturing sector, a clear division has thus emerged between the 'high-tech' (R&D-intensive) industries and 'traditional' manufacturing industries (OECD, 1996b, pp. 64–71).

Similar national and international evidence supports similar patterns of employment growth and decline in the service sector (Denmark Ministry of Business and Industry and OECD, 1996; McKinsey Global Institute, 1994). However, it is much harder to identify service industries with a high level of R&D. Because formal R&D is less important for the development of new services, conventional measures of R&D intensity are less applicable within the service sector (Lee and Has, 1995). Moreover, it is more difficult to distinguish between product and process innovation in the service industries. Nevertheless, on the basis of trial survey results, Evangelista and Sirilli (1995) have argued that 'the distinction between product (service) and process innovations (including delivery innovations), even if less clear-cut compared to the manufacturing sector, is still useful in identifying different firms' innovative objectives and strategies'. We have adopted a similar position. Given these analytical difficulties, we treat the introduction of new process technologies in service industries as an indicator of both process innovation and (possible) product innovation (Barass, 1986, 1990).

Just as there is diversity within different industrial sectors, so too there is diversity within service sectors; and just as there are R&D-intensive and low R&D-intensive industrial sectors, so too there are 'dynamic' and 'traditional' services (Economic Council of Canada, 1991, p. 93). Traditional services have a primary focus on incremental product innovation based on improvements to human capital, while dynamic services exhibit a stronger emphasis on the development of new products based on 'enhancements to all the factors of production' (Baldwin, 1995, p. 23). In 'dynamic' services, therefore, the pattern of product innovation is based on quality-enhancing and diversifying uses of new process technology combined with complementary improvements to human capital. This has been the case, for example, in the financial, insurance, real estate and business services industries (Fincham *et al.*, 1994), the second most important segment of services in terms of employment creation for OECD countries (OECD, 1996b, pp. 73–5, 88–91; Sakurai, 1995).

Despite this close relation between process and product in the service sector, there are also segments of services where product and process innovations are not as closely related as first thought. On the one hand, there appears to have been extensive product innovation which has not relied primarily on technological process innovations. For example, the community, social and personal services sector has been a primary source of employment growth throughout OECD countries (OECD, 1996b, p. 73) but most of this growth cannot be attributed to technological change: rather, it is due to increases in final demand (Sakurai, 1995).

Further, there is much evidence to link these increases in demand to extensive product innovation (Illeris, 1996, ch. 4). This indicates a primary emphasis on investment in human capital, rather than capital equipment, as a basis for product innovations. To the extent that these product innovations involve, or are related to, 'process innovation', this may be predominantly 'organizational innovation', which can have capital-saving and neutral employment effects (Dreher, 1996; Nyholm, 1995). On the other hand, some service sectors concentrate more exclusively on process innovation without a complementary emphasis on product innovation. This appears to be the case in high-productivity service industries that are strong consumers of new process technologies, and which have expanding markets but stable or declining levels of employment. An example is the transportation, communication and storage sector in services, which has been a heavy investor in new process technology (Papaconstantinou *et al.*, 1995, table 5), yet has not made any large contribution to employment growth in services (OECD, 1994b, p. 159).

Significantly, the service sector, where the great bulk of employment and job creation in OECD countries has been located for several decades (OECD, 1996a, 1996b, p. 73), has few industries based on investment products. Thus negative employment effects of the 'second incarnation' are less likely to characterize the development of new services. Instead, the positive, first-order effects tend to remain at full strength. In addition, because new services are more likely to complement than to compete with new goods, this relationship between goods and services will have positive effects on employment. The case of (non-public) community, social and personal services is instructive. This sector accounted for 30 per cent of all OECD employment in 1991 and its rate of employment growth was ranked among the top five employment sectors in nine out of ten OECD countries (Sakurai, 1995). It has been demonstrated empirically that its growth has been due to the development of services that cannot be replaced by goods (Illeris, 1996, ch. 4).

Proposition 2 The employment effects of innovation differ between sectors.[13]

As argued above, in both manufacturing and services, sectors in which there is a strong emphasis on process innovation tend to be characterized by labour-saving trajectories, while sectors with high levels of product innovation tend to have employment-generating trajectories. The relative mix of sectors of these two types will have a major effect on the overall national pattern of employment creation and destruction.

In manufacturing across the OECD world, there has been a growing divergence between industries with high levels of product innovation and those concentrating on process innovation. The former industries, which are the most R&D intensive, are clearly the 'growth industries', and have experienced net gains in employment; the latter, which are not R&D intensive, tend to be 'declining' industries with net employment losses (Pianta *et al.*, 1996). Recent German research (Meyer-Krahmer, 1992) reviewed in Meyer-Krahmer (1996) offers some particularly illuminating results. This research found that R&D-intensive sectors of West German industry enjoyed 'outstanding growth' during the 1980s, increasing their share in industrial employment from 39.5 per cent to 44 per cent by 1990. Since 1984, moreover, the net additional jobs created in industry were all in the R&D-intensive sector. Despite a slight reversal of this dynamic suffered in the early 1990s, these industries continued to expand while others contracted. 'The non-R&D-intensive sectors stagnated in comparison at the shrunken level reached during the recession' (Meyer-Krahmer, 1996, p. 217).

The body of argument and evidence indicating that there is a strong positive association between product innovation and employment growth provides the basis for a more complete explanation of why the labour-saving effects of technological process innovations tend to vary widely between sectors and within both goods-producing and services-producing sectors. Process innovations generally have a net negative effect on employment. Although compensation effects exist, such as increased demand resulting from lower production costs or from rising incomes and consumption – which may result from productivity-enhancing process innovations – these are not normally large enough to make the net employment effect of process innovation positive (Johnson, 1995, p. 56). In this connection, the most crucial issue for employment is generally the size of price elasticities, which is usually not large enough to compensate for the immediate decreases in employment caused by process innovation (Bosworth, 1987).

None the less, there has been extremely wide variation in the pattern of employment growth, or decline, among sectors that have experienced comparable levels of productivity improvement due to labour-saving process innovations (Blazecjak, 1991; Freeman and Soete, 1987; Johnson, 1995; Levy *et al.*, 1984). This variation cannot be explained solely in terms of the compensation mechanisms linked to process innovation, but must also take into consideration the positive employment effects of product innovation.

In the services sector, the pattern is similar to manufacturing, although it is much less clearly defined. For manufacturing, product innovation is positively associated with R&D intensity (Calvert *et al.*, 1996, p. 8;

Papaconstantinou *et al.*, 1995, p. 3). There is a similar positive relationship between employment growth and product innovation (Edquist and Texier, 1996). For services, 'formal R&D' is less important to product innovation (Baldwin, 1995), and alternative measures of 'R&D intensity' such as education of employees are necessary (Lee and Has, 1995). Even when reviewing research using such proxy measures, it has remained more difficult to establish clear linkages between R&D intensity, product innovation and employment growth for the services sector.

Against this background, we have observed that both a (knowledge-intensive) R&D-intensive segment (finance, insurance, real estate and business services) and a relatively non-R&D-intensive segment (community, social and personal services) have acted as the main engines of employment growth (OECD, 1996b, p. 73). However, it must also be recognized that one of the most R&D-intensive industries within the community, social and personal services sector – health care – has been this segment's main force of employment growth (OECD, 1994b, p. 52). Therefore, if R&D intensity is correlated with a higher performance of product innovation, it is possible to discern in the services a pattern somewhat similar to that observed for manufacturing, although differences are less easily identified.

Moreover, our proposed proxy of a high proportion of highly educated people as a measure of R&D intensity in services may require further specification in terms of how these human resources are actually employed. Their work might involve creating new products with positive effects on employment, but conceivably they could be engaged in forms of technological process innovation whose overall effects on employment are negative. Examples of this labour-saving trajectory in service sectors with relatively high R&D intensity are found in the air, rail and pipeline transportation, communication and utilities industries which have always been among the most capital-intensive sectors (Quinn, 1987), but have not been leaders in the creation of service employment (OECD, 1994b, p. 159). In other instances, a dual focus on process and product innovation might have mixed employment effects, as appears to be the case in the finance, insurance, real estate and business services sector (Barass, 1990). The pattern of innovation underpinning this sector's rise as a leading generator of employment has been one in which labour-saving process technologies have eliminated many 'back-office' jobs while later expanding 'front-office' employment based on product innovation, namely the development of 'new services and operations' (Fincham *et al.*, 1994, p. 7).

The community, social and personal services sector has been a leading source of job creation throughout OECD countries, both within services and among all sectors of the economy (Sakurai, 1995). The focus of innovation in this sector has been on the development of new products that are primarily, if not exclusively, consumer products with the least potential for reducing employment through a 'second incarnation' as process innovations. They are also, contrary to the 'self-service society' thesis, resilient to the employment-reducing effects of replacement by new consumer goods (Gershuny and Miles, 1983; Illeris, 1996, ch. 4). Many of these service products have been developed to complement goods innovations that originally threatened to replace them, and this complementarity often involves the creation of highly skilled employment (Gadrey, 1988, 1992). For these reasons, the type of 'final demand' involved in product innovations should be taken into account in analyses of their employment effects. For both manufacturing and services, products that do not replace existing ones have a larger effect on employment creation than those that do, and consumer and intermediate products can have a larger overall positive effect than investment products.

Proposition 3 It is too blunt to argue that industrial employment is decreasing and that only 'the service sector' can save the world from massive unemployment.[14]

Certain service and manufacturing sectors will be of far greater strategic importance to job creation than others. These sectors are R&D intensive and engage most heavily in product innovation. Knowledge-intensive industries, in both manufacturing and services, have dramatically higher rates of employment growth and have made a disproportionately large contribution to total employment growth (Department of Finance, 1992; OECD, 1994b, pp. 152–4). Our findings also point to the importance of interactions between R&D- (or knowledge-) intensive goods and services-producing sectors for employment growth. In other words, goods-producing and services-producing sectors have become increasingly interlinked.[15]

The sectors most important for the creation of employment are those engaged in the creation of new products and new markets. This has been shown most recently in an analysis of employment changes in the manufacturing sectors of the six largest OECD countries, where it was found that innovation, production and employment opportunities are concentrated in a few highly R&D-intensive industries (Pianta *et al.*, 1996). From a more detailed analysis of the dynamics of employment growth by sector in one country, the same study concluded that '[a] labour increasing pattern has been found only in sectors characterized by higher design and engineering expenditure and higher shares of product innovations' (Pianta *et al.*, 1996, p. 13). With respect to service industries, the most innovative and rapidly growing ones are those where there is a close correlation between manufacturing and services (OECD, 1996b, p. 77). Since service industries in general will continue to be the main source of employment growth in the OECD world, it is appropriate to dwell briefly on the importance of the interaction between new goods and new services for the development of new jobs.

We have shown that the community, social and personal services segment has been a main source of new employment in services throughout the OECD. Further, we have argued that employment growth in this segment has greatly depended on the development of new service products and, in turn, on complex interactions between consumer goods and consumer services. These interactions have predominantly taken the form of complementarity, rather than competition, between goods and services (Gadrey, 1988, 1992).

New service products are also based on the acquisition of new process technologies, particularly equipment incorporating information and communications technology, which are produced in the capital goods sector. This type of product innovation has been pronounced in the financial, insurance, real estate and banking services sector (Fincham *et al.*, 1994), which is the second main area of service employment growth in OECD countries (OECD, 1996b, p. 73). As argued above, much of the employment growth in this sector can be attributed to the employment-generating effects of product innovation which counteracts the normally employment-reducing effects of process innovation. However, this type of product innovation would not have been possible without the initial process innovations. There can thus be a dynamic of 'virtuous interaction' between R&D-intensive manufacturing and service sectors, even when it is based on the initial application of labour-saving investment goods in services (OECD, 1996b, ch. 2).

The development of the mobile telecommunications industry is an example of a virtuous interaction between new consumer goods and new consumer services (Miles, 1996). With over 44 million subscribers within OECD countries at the end of 1994, and with more than 1.2 million subscribers being added per month, its rate of growth in 1994 was double that of 1992 (OECD/ICCP, 1996). The innovation profile for mobile communications, as for the communication industry in general, is also extremely high (Kelly, 1995; Mercer Management Consultants, 1994). The country of Finland provides further indications of this segment's rapid growth. The Finnish telecommunications sector is the first major knowledge-based industrial development block in Finland and the fastest growing, expected to become soon the second most important block (after the historically dominant 'forest' block) in that country's economy (Rouvinen, 1996, pp. 39–40).[16] Finland is a major telecommunications equipment exporter, and its most significant products in this sector – in terms of export value, share of total exports and share of OECD markets – are mobile and fixed networks as well as mobile telephones. Mobile telephones, moreover, have experienced particularly rapid growth during the 1990s (ibid., pp. 84–9).

Moreover, the development of communication infrastructures has been identified as one of the most strategically important bases for job creation in several OECD countries – notably, the USA and Japan (Imai, 1996). For example, Japanese authorities estimate that 2.43 million jobs can be created in network-based service employment in the multi-media market by 2010 (Ministry of Posts and Telecommunications, 1994). Similarly, estimates in France project an increase in this type of employ-ment between 2.5 and 5 times the 1993 level (OECD, 1996b, p. 110). In addition to its potential for explosive growth, this indicates that the growth in communication service employment will be closely tied to growth in the infrastructure of telecommunications goods.

As this example suggests, it is necessary to develop a more discriminat-ing analysis of innovation–employment dynamics in particular sectors and industries than available data now permit. In some manufacturing sectors employment increases rapidly. In some service sectors, employ-ment is decreasing. For empirical research and analysis to be fruitful, manufacturing as well as service production will have to be disaggregated. This crucial point raises two questions to be addressed in later empirical research, before we summarize our arguments:

1. In which disaggregated goods and service sectors does employment decrease or increase? What is the relation to productivity growth and various kinds of innovation?
2. What are the immediate as well as the indirect effects of various kinds of innovation for employment at a disaggregated level?

To summarize, this section has concentrated on refining a conceptual framework for the type of disaggregated empirical analysis recommended above. The distinctions between process and product innovations and between three subcategories of innovation – (a) technological and organi-zational process innovations; (b) product innovations in services and goods; and (c) investment, intermediary and consumer products – have been posed here, although more conceptual specification could be done. These categories have been quite useful for analysing the effects of differ-ent types of innovations on productivity growth and on employment, enabling us to make some observations about which types of manufactur-ing and service sectors will tend to lead national growth patterns into either labour-saving or employment-generating trajectories. These observations will now be used in the final section of this chapter to draw conclusions and policy implications.

CONCLUSIONS AND POLICY IMPLICATIONS

Politicians and mainstream economists often argue that 'more rapid growth' would solve or mitigate the unemployment problem. However, the relation between 'growth' and 'employment' is by no means simple and mechanical. Some kinds of growth create jobs, other kinds destroy jobs, and there is the phenomenon of 'jobless growth'. Economic growth and productivity growth do not automatically or always lead to employment growth. Therefore a general policy of growth will not necessarily create more jobs. Moreover, specialization at the firm, industry and national levels will influence future ability either to continue along or to shift between labour-saving and employment-generating trajectories. On the basis of arguments presented here, this concluding section will try to outline a more detailed and differentiated understanding of the relations between 'growth' and 'employment' with reference to innovations.

There are many problems associated with measuring productivity growth. Analytically it is important to distinguish between quality changes in products and increased output, and determine which is associated with demand growth. The importance of these differences has led us to try to further clarify and distinguish productivity and economic growth and their relationships to employment, as summarized in the following points.

First, productivity growth which is associated with more of the *same* kind of output and produced by the same amount of input leads to a reduction in the number of jobs (per unit of output). Labour productivity is the ratio between production value (value added) and amount of employment. Thus if output (production value) is constant, this kind of productivity growth means that the *denominator* (amount of employment) in this ratio decreases. The most important source of this kind of productivity growth are technological or organizational *process innovations*. While compensation mechanisms can mitigate job losses, they can promote net employment gains only when growth in production (that is, demand) outstrips productivity growth.

If the general level of demand is kept constant and if the price elasticity of demand for the product is below 1, jobs (in the world economy as a whole, that is, in a closed economy) will be lost in the sector of production where the process innovation occurred. If the elasticity is above 1, the number of jobs will increase in that sector (in the world economy as a whole) in spite of the process innovation. The price elasticity is, however, normally below 1. Thus, on the whole, labour productivity growth associated with process innovations is labour saving. If there is an exogenous demand increase for the product, jobs are of course created.[17] However, this is not the result of productivity growth but of economic growth, that is, increased output. Output and the number of jobs are increasing, but the number of jobs *per unit of output* is not increasing.

Secondly, productivity growth which is associated with *new* kinds of output leads to job creation.[18] This is the case of *product innovation*. Productivity growth of this kind reflects the quality improvements of output as well as the monopolism often associated with new products. It influences the *nominator* in the ratio between production value (value added) and amount of employment (that is, labour productivity), resulting in a higher price paid for the new products.[19] The denominator (employment), however, is not directly influenced by productivity growth associated with product innovations. In other words, the amount of labour needed per unit of output does not decrease; labour is not saved through product innovation.

Instead, the production of new products influences production value (value added). Product innovations often lead to the establishment of new units of production, which means new investments and structural change, and possibly more jobs *as well as* higher productivity. The new product which satisfies a completely new kind of demand or serves a new function contributes most to increased employment.[20] This statement holds whether the product is new to the world, or new to a country, region or company, that is, if the production of a product diffuses. Thus the 'immediate' effect of a product innovation is to increase employment.

However, employment generation caused by product innovation can be counteracted through (a) substitution between old and new products, and (b) new products that become process innovations in a later incarnation. If the new product functionally replaces an old one, either increased or decreased employment may result. The net employment effect depends on whether demand for satisfying the function changes when the new product replaces the old one, and whether there are changes in the labour intensity of the process used to produce the new product.

Some new products are transformed into process innovations in a second incarnation. These products generally lead to a net reduction in the number of jobs in the economy as a whole. However, only investment products can play this double role over time. Therefore, the net employment-generating effect of consumer products and intermediate products is larger than that of investment products. Because the proportion of investment products is smaller in services than in goods, the production of services destroys jobs to a lesser extent than goods production. Product innovation in services is, in this respect, more employment-generating than product innovation in goods production.

Thus, productivity growth associated with product innovations is not, on the whole, labour saving. On the contrary, new jobs are created, mostly through the development, production and use of new products which satisfy new needs and wants. Moreover, the demand for new products often grows more rapidly than for old products. This implies an increase in (production and) employment in some industrial sectors as well as in (some) service sectors.

On average, technological process innovations seems to increase labour productivity faster in goods production than in service production. Therefore process-related job destruction seems to be larger in manufacturing than in services. In both cases, however, the variation between subsectors is large. A net increase in employment can be expected in some industrial sectors and in some service sectors (due to product innovation).

The implications of these arguments are that the firms, regions and countries producing new products do so for markets that are often growing rapidly. Growing markets mean an increase in output (demand) which reinforces the intrinsic employment-creation effect of product innovations. Again, this effect is not associated with productivity growth, but with economic growth.

In summary, firms, industries and national economies that specialize in product innovations generally create more employment than those that specialize in process innovations. The overall extent of employment creation or destruction depends on factors such as changes in market growth and in demand (price elasticity) as well as dynamic effects within the economic system. Product innovations which neither substitute for an existing product nor are later used as process innovations have the greatest positive effect on employment creation. Both manufacturing and service sectors can be roughly divided into those that are more R&D-(knowledge-) intensive and product-innovation-orientated and those that concentrate less on R&D and are more process-innovation-orientated. The links between dynamic manufacturing and service sectors seem to offer the greatest potentials for employment growth.

The implications for government policy can be summarized in the following points:

1. Employment policies need to reflect the differences between sectors highly concentrated on process or product innovations. If a country (time period, firm or region) is characterized mainly by process innovations (technological or organizational) this constitutes a tendency to decrease employment. If product innovations dominate, there is an opposite tendency of increasing employment.[21]

2. A reallocation of resources from process to product innovation will have positive employment effects. An example is policy which identifies and strengthens those manufacturing and service sectors where product innovation dominates over process innovations, namely those with a high R&D (knowledge) intensity.[22] Such a policy would support structural change in the economy in the direction of new sectors.[23] Such a policy of structural change would increase employment in the long run.
3. However, technological and organizational process innovations should not be stopped or hindered in any firm, region or country. While employment problems can be solved by decreasing productivity in the short term, in the longer run such a policy would have devastating consequences. Productivity is the main source of increased material welfare, and competitiveness (of the firm, region or country) depends on productivity growth. Those that attempt to avoid process innovations will end up lagging behind, with worsened prospects for gaining material welfare.
4. Any policy that gives priority to employment generation over productivity growth by preventing process innovation will fail, partly because competition normally requires that potential increases in labour productivity be exploited in the long run.
5. Policies for increased employment should support more capital-saving types of organizational process innovations than labour-saving ones.

As Europe seems to have become locked into a technological trajectory or growth pattern that is predominantly labour saving, the employment intensity of growth is relatively low. For this reason, policy supporting structural change in the direction of more R&D-intensive and less process-innovation-orientated sectors is called for to a greater extent in Europe than in the USA and Japan. The present European trajectory will lead to an increasing competition with eastern Europe and advanced developing countries. This trend has continued for at least two decades without being corrected by market forces. There is thus a strong justification for considering policy intervention.

Discussions with colleagues in ISE provided valuable input into this chapter, which also benefited from editorial assistance by Dawn House.

APPENDIX: TWENTY HYPOTHESES

Hypothesis 1 The labour-saving effects of technological process innovations vary widely between sectors – in manufacturing as well as in service production.

Hypothesis 2 The variation in labour saving caused by technological process innovations is larger between service sectors than between manufacturing sectors.

Hypothesis 3 In some service sectors labour saving attributed to technological process innovations leads to very large productivity increases.

Hypothesis 4 There are different kinds of organizational process innovations; one category is similar to technological process innovations with regard to the factor-saving bias; another class is capital saving without direct effects on employment levels.

Hypothesis 5 Organizational process innovations require different kinds of investment than technological ones, and more directly affect the type of employment created.

Hypothesis 6 New goods originate more often from R&D-intensive manufacturing sectors than from other sectors.

Hypothesis 7 The pattern of diffusion of product innovations is different from that of process innovations, and so are the determinants.

Hypothesis 8 There is a strong association between the production of R&D-intensive goods and new goods, on the one hand, and high labour productivity, high productivity growth and rapid market growth, on the other.

Hypothesis 9 Employment grows faster in R&D-intensive industrial sectors than in other sectors.

Hypothesis 10 The increased productivity (growth) associated with new goods does not mean decreased employment (per unit of output), but relates to changes in labour productivity – the nominator of the ratio.

Hypothesis 11 The productivity increase related to goods innovation is not 'real' but matters to the welfare of the members of the unit producing the innovation.

Hypothesis 12 The production of new goods might lead to more jobs as well as higher productivity (as measured).

Hypothesis 13 Service sectors with a large proportion of highly educated people can be classified as 'R&D intensive'.

Hypothesis 14 Formal R&D is not important for the development of new services.

Hypothesis 15 There is a correlation between 'R&D-intensive' service sectors and service sectors with high levels of product innovation.

Hypothesis 16 Service sectors characterized by high levels of product innovation are also characterized by rapid market growth.

Hypothesis 17 The service sectors where there is a close relation between a new good and a new service are, generally speaking, more innovative and growing faster than others.

Hypothesis 18 There is also rapid growth and a high level of innovation in service sectors where there is a close relation between new process technologies and new service products.

Hypothesis 19 Only a small part of the services produced are investment products.

Hypothesis 20 Product innovation generates more employment in the service sector on the whole than in the manufacturing sector. Moreover, service industries are less susceptible to employment-reducing substitution effects than are manufacturing industries.

NOTES

1. These differences are described in OECD, (1994b) ch. 2.
2. This framework is partly based upon Edquist (1997b).
3. The hypotheses are listed in the appendix.
4. Because the focus of this chapter is on employment in the sense of wage labour, only products produced for the market (commodities) are addressed here, excluding goods and services produced for direct use by the producer (within the household or the internal market of the firm).
5. For reasons of simplification we are including only material elements in the concept of technological process innovation, thereby obviously excluding services. When the conceptual basis of technological process innovations has become more solid, non-material elements (like skills and knowledge) might also be introduced – although they may fit best in the category of organizational process innovations.
6. The growth hormone example is analysed in detail in McKelvey (1996).
7. Hence original organizational process innovations normally emerge within the using firm; unlike technological process innovations, they are seldom sold and bought on the market.
8. More research should be done to establish empirically the strength of this link, and whether or how it grows stronger under different circumstances.
9. Nevertheless, these innovations may have important effects on both production costs and the delivery of products, and so may have a significant impact on products and product markets.
10. Thus 're-engineering' techniques have been shown to result in significant productivity increases and reductions in employment. See the example in Hammer and Champy (1993, pp. 36–9).
11. The usual convention of national accounting is to split the output at current prices of a new product into two components: a volume effect, which reflects the improved quality, and the price effect (the residual).

12. Evidence and arguments supporting proposition 1 can be found in hypotheses 3–6, 8, 9, 12–18 and 20 in Edquist *et al.* (1997).
13. Evidence and arguments supporting proposition 2 can be found in hypotheses 1–3, 6–16 and 18–20 in Edquist *et al.* (1997).
14. Evidence and arguments supporting proposition 3 can be found in hypotheses 6–12 and 15–20 in Edquist *et al.* (1997).
15. Thus the future development of business services is, to a large extent, dependent on the further 'unbundling' of vertically integrated firms, particularly in the manufacturing sector. 'Outsourcing' could proceed along either a low-skill or a high-skill path, with important consequences for both manufacturing and service industries, not only in terms of the quality of employment, but also in terms of its quality (Abraham and Taylor, 1993).
16. The term development block refers to a set of enterprises and industries coupled together by strong quantitative and qualitative linkages of interactive learning and commodities flows (McKelvey, 1994).
17. The case of increases in exogenous demand points to the crucial importance of co-ordination between innovation policies and macro-economic policies, including fiscal, monetary and exchange rate policies. A reasonable degree of macro-economic stability is important for innovation processes and for investment more generally – and therefore for economic growth and employment creation. However, it seems extremely difficult to solve the problems of low growth and high unemployment in western Europe through innovation policy if macro-economic policies remain excessively strict. Fiscal and monetary policies in Europe might become less restrictive once the European Monetary Union has been established – and national governments may thereby avoid the contractionist grip of the Maastricht convergence criteria (of low public debt, low government deficit, low inflation, low interest rates and a stable exchange rate).
18. This refers to productivity growth as it is measured. See note 11.
19. This kind of productivity growth (measured at constant prices) is not 'real' (in physical terms), but it matters to the welfare of the members of the unit producing the innovation.
20. The size of employment generation is related to the size and growth of demand.
21. Although there are counteracting forces.
22. However, this does not mean that it is easy to start new sectors within a country. McKelvey (1996) and references discussed there analyse the importance of trajectories which tend to lock firms into a set of technological choices whereas the systems-of-innovation literature argues for national specialization trajectories.
23. On the whole, these sectors are characterized by higher productivity and higher productivity growth, and therefore can carry higher wages and profits. They are also characterized by more rapid market growth than other products.

REFERENCES

Abraham, K.G., and Taylor, S.K. (1993), *Firms' Use of Outside Contractors: Theory and Evidence*, NBER working paper no. 4468, Cambridge, Mass.: NBER.
Archibugi, D., Casaratto, S. and Sirilli G. (1987), 'Innovative activity, R&D and patenting: the evidence of the survey on innovation diffusion in Italy', *Science, Technology and Industry Review*, **2**: 135–50.
Archibugi, D., Evangelista, R. and Simonetti, R., (1994), 'On the definition and measurement of product and process innovations', in Y. Shinonoya and M. Perlman (eds), *Technology, Industries and Institutions: Studies in Schumpeterian Perspectives*, Ann Arbor, Mich.: University of Michigan Press.
Assarsson, B. (1991), 'Kvalitetsförändringar och produktivitetsmåatt', in K. Eklund (ed.), *Hur mäta produktivitet? Expertrapport nr. 1 till Produktivitetsdelegationen*, Stockholm: Allmänna Förlaget.

Baldwin, J. (1995), 'Human capital development and innovation: a sectoral analysis', paper read at conference on 'Implications of Knowledge-based Growth for Micro-economic policies', Ottawa, 30-31 March.

Barass, R. (1986), 'Towards a theory of innovation in services', *Research Policy*, **15**: 161–73.

Barass, R. (1990), 'Interactive innovation in financial and business services: the vanguard of the service revolution', *Research Policy*, **19**: 215–37.

Blazecjak, J. (1991), 'Evaluation of the long-term effects of technological trends on the structure of employment', *Futures*, July–August: 594–604.

Bosworth, D. (1987), 'Prices, costs and elasticities of demand', in OECD (eds), *Information Technology and Economic Prospects no. 12*, Paris: OECD.

Calvert, J., Ibarra, C., Patel, P. and Pavitt, K. (1996), *Innovation Outputs in European Industry: Analysis from CIS*, Report to DG XIII (EIMS 93/52), Brighton, Sussex: Science Policy Research Unit, University of Sussex.

Commission of the European Communities (1994), *Growth, Competitiveness, Employment: The Challenges and Ways Forward into the 21st Century*, White Paper, Luxembourg: Office for Official Publications of the European Communities.

Denmark. Ministry of Business and Industry and OECD (1996), *Technological and Organisational Change: Implications for Labour Demand, Enterprise Performance and Industrial Policy. Country Report: Denmark*, Copenhagen: Danish State Information Service.

Department of Finance, Canada (1992), *Employment Growth in High-tech and High-knowledge Industries*, ed. Economic Analysis and Forecasting Division, Ottawa: Department of Finance, Canada.

Dosi, G. (1982), 'Technological paradigms and technological trajectories', *Research Policy*, **11**: 147–63.

Dosi, G. (1988), 'The nature of the innovative process', in G. Dosi, C. Freeman, R. Nelson, G. Silverberg and L. Soete (eds), *Technical Change and Economic Theory*, London: Pinter Publishers.

Dreher, C. (1996), 'Measuring innovations in manufacturing: diffusion, adopter potentials and characteristics of technical and organisational process innovations', paper read at 'Innovation Measurement and Policies', International Conference of the European Commission (Eurostat DG XII), Luxembourg, 20–21 May.

Economic Council of Canada (1991), *Employment in the Service Economy*, Ottawa: Economic Council of Canada.

Edquist, C. (1989), 'Empirical differences between OECD countries in the diffusion of new product and process technologies', paper read at international conference on 'Diffusion of Technologies and Social Behaviour: Theories, Case Studies and Policy Applications', International Institute for Systems Analysis, Vienna, 14–16 June.

Edquist, C. (1997a), 'Introduction', in C. Edquist (ed.), *Systems of Innovation: Technologies, Organizations and Institutions*, London: Pinter Publishers/Cassell Academic.

Edquist, C. (1997b), 'Product versus process innovation: a conceptual framework for assessing employment impacts', in *Creativity, Innovation and Job Creation*, Paris: OECD.

Edquist, C., Hommen, L. and McKelvey, M. (1997), *Innovations and Employment in a Systems of Innovation Perspective*, ISE (Innovation Systems and European Integration) report, subproject 3.1.2: 'Innovations, growth and employment', Brussels: European Commission.

150   *The role of technology and innovation*

Edquist, C. and Jacobsson, S. (1988), *Flexible Automation. The Global Diffusion of New Technology in the Engineering Industry*, Oxford: Basil Blackwell.

Edquist, C. and McKelvey, M. (1992), *The Diffusion of New Product Technologies and Productivity Growth in Swedish Industry*, Consortium on Competitiveness and Cooperation working paper, no. 91-15. Berkeley, Cal.: Center for Research in Management, University of California at Berkeley.

Edquist, C. and McKelvey, M. (1998), 'The Swedish paradox: high R&D intensity without high-tech products', in K. Nielsen and B. Johnson (eds), *Evolution of Institutions, Organizations and Technology*, Aldershot, Hants: Edward Elgar.

Edquist, C. and Texier, F. (1996), 'The perverted growth pattern of Swedish industry: current situation and policy implications', Linköping, Sweden: Department of Technology and Social Change, Linköping University, mimeo.

Evangelista, R. and Sirilli, G. (1995), 'Measuring innovation in services', *Research Evaluation*, **5** (3): 207–15.

Fincham, R., Fleck, J., Procter, R., Scarborough, H., Tierney, M. and Williams, R. (1994), *Expertise and Innovation: Information Technology Strategies in the Financial Services Sector*, Oxford: Oxford University Press.

Freeman, C. and Soete, L. (1987), *Technical Change and Full Employment*, Oxford: Basil Blackwell.

Gadrey, J. (1988), 'Des facteurs de croissance des services aux rapports sociaux de service', *Revue d'economie industrielle*, **43**: 34–48.

Gadrey, J. (1992), *L'Economie des services*, Paris: La Découverte.

Gershuny, J. and Miles, I. (1983), *The New Service Economy: The Transformation of Employment in Industrial Societies*, London: Frances Pinter.

Greenan, N. and Guellec, D. (1996), *Technological Innovation and Employment Reallocation*, Paris: Institut National de la Statistique et des Etudes Economiques (INSEE).

Hammer, M. and Champy, J. (1993), *Re-engineering the Corporation: A Manifesto for Business Revolution*, New York: Harper Collins.

Hansson, B. (1991), *Measuring and Modelling Technical Change*, Doktorsavhandling, Nationalekonomiska Institutionen, Uppsala Universitet, Uppsala.

Hauknes, J. (1994), *Tjenesteyende næringer: Ökonomi og teknologi*, STEP report no. 13, Oslo: Studies in Technology, Innovation and Economic Policy.

Illeris, S. (1996), *The Service Economy: A Geographical Approach*, Chichester, Sussex: John Wiley.

Imai, K.-I. (1996), 'Information infrastructures and the creation of new markets: Japan's perspective', in D. Foray and B.-Å. Lundvall (eds), *Employment and Growth in the Knowledge-based Economy*, Paris: OECD.

Johnson, K. (1995), 'Productivity and unemployment: review of the evidence', in *The OECD Jobs Study: Investment, Productivity and Employment*, Paris: OECD.

Katsoulacos, Y. (1984), 'Product innovation and employment', *European Economic Review*, **26**: 83–108.

Kelly, D. (1995), 'Service sector productivity growth and growth in living standards', *Service Economy*, **9** (4): 9–15.

Kraft, K. (1990), 'Are product and process innovations independent of each other?', *Applied Economics*, **22**: 1029–38.

Lee, F.C. and Has, H. (1995), *A Quantitative Assessment of High-knowledge versus Low-knowledge Industries*, Ottawa: Industry Canada.

Levy, R., Bowes, M. and Jondrow, J. (1984), 'Technical advance and other sources of employment change in basic industry', in E. Collings and L. Tanner (eds), *American Jobs and the Changing Industrial Base*, Cambridge, Mass.: Ballinger.

Lundvall, B.-Å. (1985), *Product Innovation and User–Producer Interaction*, Industrial Development Research Series no. 31, Aalborg: Aalborg University Press.

Lunn, J. (1986), 'An empirical analysis of process and product patenting: a simultaneous equation framework', *Journal of Industrial Economics*, **34**: 319–29.

McKelvey, M. (1994), 'National systems of innovation', in G. Hodgson, W. Samuels and M. Tool (eds), *The Elgar Companion to Institutional and Evolutionary Economics*, Aldershot, Hants: Edward Elgar.

McKelvey, M. (1996), *Evolutionary Innovations: The Business of Biotechnology*, Oxford: Oxford University Press.

McKinsey Global Institute (1994), *Employment Performance*, Washington, D.C.: McKinsey Global Institute.

Mercer Management Consultants (1994), *Future Policy for Telecommunications Infrastructure and Cable TV Networks: Study for the European Commission*, Boston, Mass.: Mercer Management Consultants.

Meyer-Krahmer, F. (1992), 'The effects of new technology on employment', *Economics of Innovation and Technical Change*, **2**.

Meyer-Krahmer, F. (1996), 'Dynamics of R&D-intensive sectors and science and technology policy', in D. Foray and B.-Å. Lundvall (eds), *Employment and Growth in the Knowledge-based Economy*, Paris: OECD.

Miles, I. (1996), 'Infrastructure and the delivery of new services', in D. Foray and B.-Å. Lundvall (eds), *Employment and Growth in the Knowledge-based Economy*, Paris: OECD.

Ministry of Posts and Telecommunications, Japan (1994), *Reform Toward the Intellectual, Creative Society of the 21st Century: Programme for Establishment of High-performance Info-communications Structures*, Tokyo: Ministry of Posts and Telecommunications, Japan.

Nelson, R. (1994), 'What has been the matter with neoclassical growth theory?', in G. Silverberg and L. Soete (eds), *The Economics of Growth and Technical Change: Technologies, Nations, Agents*, Aldershot, Hants: Edward Elgar.

Nyholm, J. (1995), 'Information technology, organizational changes and productivity in Danish manufacturing', paper read at the conference on 'Effects of Advanced Technologies and Innovation Practices on Firm Performance: Evidence from Establishment and Firm Data', Washington, D.C., 1–2 May.

OECD (1994a), *The OECD Jobs Study: Facts, Analysis, Strategies*, Paris: OECD.

OECD (1994b), *The OECD Jobs Study: Evidence and Explanations*, Part I: *Labour Market Trends and the Underlying Forces of Change*, Paris: OECD.

OECD (1996a), *Technology, Productivity and Job Creation*, Vol. 1: *Highlights, the OECD Jobs Strategy*, Paris: OECD.

OECD (1996b), *Technology, Productivity and Job Creation*, Vol. 2: *Analytical Report, the OECD Jobs Strategy*, Paris: OECD.

OECD and ICCP (1996), *Mobile Cellular Communications: Pricing Strategies and Competition*, ICCP report no. 39, Paris: OECD.

Papaconstantinou, G., Sakurai, N. and Wyckoff, A. (1995), *Technology Diffusion, Productivity and Competitiveness: An Empirical Analysis for Ten Countries*, Part 1: *Technology Diffusion Patterns*, EIMS publication no. 13: European Innovation Monitoring System (EIMS).

Pasinetti, L. (1981), *Structural Change and Economic Growth*, Cambridge: Cambridge University Press.

Pianta, M. (1996), 'S&T specialization and employment patterns', paper read at conference on 'Creativity, Innovation and Job Creation' organized by OECD and the Norwegian Ministry of Education, Research and Church Affairs, Oslo, 11–12 January.

Pianta, M., Evangelista, R. and Perani, G. (1996), 'The dynamics of innovation and employment: an international comparison', paper read at the expert workshop on 'Technology, Productivity and Employment: Macro-economic and Sectoral Evidence', organized by OECD, Paris, 19–20 June.

Pianta, M. and Meliciana, V. (1994), 'Technological specialization and national performances', paper read at the conference on 'Technological Performances and Economic Performances', organized by GREGI, BETA and CERETIM, Le Mans, 14 October.

Pollack, M. (1991), 'Research and development in the service sector', *Service Economy*, July.

Quinn, J.B. (1987), 'The impacts of technology in the service sector', in B. Guile and H. Brooks (eds), *Technology and Global Industry*, Washington, D.C.: National Academy Press.

Rosenberg, N. (1976), *Perspectives on Technology*, Cambridge: Cambridge University Press.

Rouvinen, P. (1996), *The Comparative Advantage of Finland*, Helsinki: Research Institute of the Finnish Economy (ETLA).

Sakurai, N. (1995), 'Structural change and employment: empirical evidence for eight OECD countries', *STI Review*, (15): 133–76.

Schumpeter, J. ([1911] 1934), *The Theory of Economic Development*, Cambridge, Mass.: Harvard University Press.

Utterback, J. and Abernathy, W. (1975), 'A dynamic model of process and product innovation', *OMEGA*, **3** (6): 639–56.

Vivarelli, M. (1995), *The Economics of Technology and Employment: Theory and Empirical Evidence*, Aldershot, Hants: Edward Elgar.

8. Regional innovation strategies: can they combat regional unemployment?

Sara Davies and Kevin Morgan

INTRODUCTION

Regional economic disparities within the European Union remain stubbornly wide, with spatial concentrations of high levels of long-term unemployment a seemingly permanent feature of the landscape. This situation is most dramatic in regions affected by structural decline: so-called 'old industrialized regions', or 'Objective 2 regions' in EU terms. Policymakers often attempt to address these deep-rooted problems by creating spatially targeted policies which aim to increase the competitiveness and innovativeness of indigenous companies, in the hope that new jobs may be created and existing jobs secured. But the poor track record of traditional regional policies has led some policy actors to focus on more fundamental issues underlying regional economic disparities, namely the lack of endogenous capacities for action. While these new policies are not, in themselves, sufficient to combat regional concentrations of unemployment, we argue that the type of capacities which they aim to stimulate are necessary preconditions for structural change.

In the next section, we examine the conceptual foundations and implications of these policies, within the context of the debate on territorial institutions and innovation. In the following two sections, we assess a number of policy initiatives in two regions: Wales in the UK and the Ruhr area of North-Rhine Westphalia (NRW) in Germany. Finally, we analyse the capacity of initiatives to promote co-operation and trust, on the one hand, and to combat unemployment on the other.

INNOVATION AND INSTITUTIONS

Policy actors choose to prioritize initiatives aimed at stimulating innovation because the capacity to innovate, change and learn is key to corporate competitiveness and, therefore, to safeguarding and creating employment. Technological change acts as the dynamo of capitalist economies, driving them forwards by means of the continual emergence and exhaustion of new possibilities, ideas and 'combinations' (Schumpeter, 1934). Yet technological change does not take place in a vacuum, nor can it be seen as the result of a flash of individual inspiration by the heroic Schumpeterian entrepreneur. Innovations result from webs of interrelations, not only in terms of the co-evolution of technological opportunities and specific forms of market demand (Arthur, 1989; Bijker *et al.*, 1987), but also in regard to the range of technical, socio-institutional, individual, natural and other actors involved in any innovation process (Callon, 1991). We focus here on the relations between specific forms of technological change and the socio-institutional frameworks within which they are located. 'Institutions', or collective behavioural and conceptual regularities located at a societal level, may either be formal (such as legislative frameworks and codified rules and contracts) or informal (such as cultural norms and conventions). Because they persist through time and are slow to change, institutions have traditionally been perceived as inhibiting or impeding innovation. Yet change is usually generated within existing institutional contexts (Hodgson, 1988) and stable patterns of thought and behaviour can stimulate innovation in a variety of ways, particularly by reducing uncertainty, managing conflict and providing incentives for innovation (Edquist and Johnson, 1996).

Institutions are specific to particular societies and territories. Recent literature, particularly on national innovation systems (Lundvall, 1992; Nelson, 1993; Freeman, 1995) and on national institutional frameworks (Zysman, 1994), has emphasized the role of institutional factors specific to particular nation states in causing differentials in innovation processes. Yet certain institutions which affect innovation are clearly supranational in character, such as regulatory and legislative mechanisms within the European Union. Similarly, institutions may be located at a subnational or regional level. Formal institutions at a regional level have become increasingly important in many European countries in recent years yet, in many cases, have little impact on actual processes of technological change. There is, however, one dimension in which regionally specific institutions can be of particular importance in promoting innovation: namely, by creating conditions which are conducive to the development of trust. Trust plays an important role in many economic processes; indeed, without a minimum level of trust in the honesty of others, trading and interaction between economic agents would be impossible. Trust can promote innovation by reducing uncertainty and making it unnecessary for actors to attempt to calculate the potential risks and costs of opportunism within given circumstances. Trust, which is generated via co-operation, facilitates conflict management and resolution, which are critical capacities for actors in the innovation process. Not only can trust reduce transaction costs incurred by risk, but agents will be able to act and react more rapidly if detailed, formal contracts are less necessary. Moreover, levels of knowledge shared will be deeper and more extensive, and will include tacit forms of knowledge which can only be exchanged via the labour market or interactive learning processes. Trust and spatial and cultural proximity can promote the use and transmission of tacit knowledge.

Whereas 'generalized trust' (Sako, 1992) tends, by definition, to be pervasive, more specific forms of trust are likely to be spatially rooted. Zucker (1986) differentiates between three sources of trust, arguing that it may be 'process-based' if it is generated by prolonged personal experience; 'characteristic-based' when founded on particular family, ethnic or cultural commonalities; or 'institutionally-based' where it derives from specific social structures. All three types are linked to spatial proximity; even process-based trust accrues more quickly where repeated interaction between agents is facilitated by territorial and cognitive closeness. Informal or formal institutions can encourage agents to conform to non-opportunistic behavioural patterns, and can also embody channels carrying relevant technological and organizational knowledge – as well as information about agents breaking rules that govern co-operation. Institutions can also promote a 'sense of groupness' (Miller, 1995) which is essential to the development of trust and which stems from interconnectedness among people and organizations and from sharing common activities and goals. All these factors contribute to the reduction of uncertainty and assist firms to manage conflict.

These trust-generating institutions can, however, lead to territorial 'lock-in' (Arthur, 1989) to a particular developmental path. Institutions are characterized by their resistance to change because they are rooted in social and political processes, and represent a balance between many differing and potentially conflicting interests. Particularly in times of radical paradigmatic change, the stability of institutions can mean that some regions fail to adapt rapidly enough. If sufficient political and economic power is located within the region, processes of change may be resisted or ignored for some time, so that traditional modes of behaviour and perception are maintained and new actors and strategies are excluded. Resisting change, however, tends to mean that its effects, when they do arrive, are even harsher, because they are sudden and the region's actors are unprepared. Institutions embodying co-operation and interaction, as well as routines for knowledge production and transmission, tend to be centred around dominant companies, so that their disappearance can mean the loss of a region's capacities to react positively to changing circumstances. Particularly in regions where the dominant companies have been set up with non-indigenous or externally controlled capital, there tends to be a lack of institutions which promote entrepreneurship and risk-taking. Other regional companies often lack innovative and strategic capabilities because they have grown up around the dominant corporations and have focused on meeting their supply needs.

Institutional set-ups in old industrialized regions tend to be characterized by strong intra-regional linkages and by a lack of openness to external forces. Yet, while economic restructuring implicitly involves the development of new institutions linked to new forms of innovation and co-operation, strong institutions can prove to be a resource for regeneration if the wealth of tradition which they encapsulate can be mobilized and transformed. Regeneration in regions where formal and informal institutional frameworks are dismantled rapidly and indiscriminately is likely to be more problematical because the foundations for creating new forms of action and co-operation will have been lost. None the less, institutions do not change because they have outlived their usefulness but rather as a result of conscious or unconscious individual action (Granovetter, 1985), although this may be stimulated by a sense of identity and culture in some regions, based on a shared traumatic history of industrialization. Although dynamic private sector capacities may be lost, public or quasi-public actors can stimulate collaborative action and generate new forward-looking strategies. The effective implementation of novel responses to specific problems depends on the existence of capacities for dealing with conflict, crisis and uncertainty (Coriat and Dosi, 1994). The irony, however, is that regeneration strategies are generally implemented by those individuals, groups and organizations with vested interests in the status quo and who may oppose change either because it brings loss of power and prestige or because the regional consensus is such that they do not perceive external or internal crises (Grabher, 1993). The generation and implementation of effective strategies for action therefore depends on the extent to which actors are willing to come together to develop mutually coherent sets of expectations (Storper, 1995).

The particular configuration of institutions within a region can determine not only whether trust is generated but also the extent to which it is conducive to innovation, for example by influencing the range and type of agents who participate in collaborative and knowledge-transmitting mechanisms, and by conditioning those mechanisms' openness and capacity to discriminate among external sources of information. In the next sections, we examine the experiences of two old industrialized regions, Wales and the Ruhr area, where policy-makers have introduced initiatives aimed at stimulating regeneration by building trust-promoting mechanisms. On the one hand, attempts are made to promote innovation by encouraging inter-firm co-operation while, on the other hand, wide-ranging regional discussions have been developed which aim to address future economic strategies and policy action.

WALES

Industrial and Institutional Legacies

The Welsh economy has declined more or less continuously since the 1930s, with coal and steel receiving their most decisive blow in the 1980s; only two steel plants and one deep coal-mine now remain. While the Welsh unemployment rate was extremely high in the 1980s, it is no longer way out of line with the UK average (7.4 per cent in December 1996, compared to 6.7 per cent in the UK: DoE, 1997). None the less, unemployment – much of it long term – is far higher in some areas, as are rates of people excluded from official statistics on grounds of sickness. Wales also lags behind the UK average on a number of key indicators, such as GDP per capita, income and activity rates, and continues to lie at the bottom of British league tables for a range of indicators of social deprivation (CSO, 1995).

Yet, since the 1980s, economic regeneration in some areas has occurred in tandem with social dislocation brought about by structural decline. New development has been based in particular on the attraction of inward investment; in the early 1990s, Wales, with just 5 per cent of the UK population, was 'the number one performing region, attracting around 20 per cent of total new foreign projects entering the UK annually' (Hill and Munday, 1994). By 1996, foreign-owned companies accounted for some 74,000 employees, equivalent to 33 per cent of all manufacturing jobs in Wales, nearly twice the foreign share of total UK manufacturing. Although such plants are often dismissed as low-pay, low-skill operations with few multiplier effects, this stereotype is not entirely confirmed by the Welsh case. Low Welsh pay levels are due to low wages in service sectors rather than in branch plants, as manual wages in manufacturing are slightly higher in Wales than in Britain as a whole (United Kingdom Office of National Statistics, 1996). Employment growth among managers and professional engineers, scientists and technologists in electronics, for example, has recently been significantly higher than in the UK as a whole, albeit from a very low base (Lawson and Morgan, 1991). Foreign plants are no longer so impervious to local suppliers, providing they can meet exacting standards for quality, cost and delivery. The strength of foreign direct investment (FDI) in Wales is, moreover, one reason why, in the decade to 1995, manufacturing output in Wales grew by over 40 per cent, more than double the UK rate, and why manufacturing employment in Wales grew by over 5 per cent, while it declined by over 15 per cent in the UK as a whole. The combination of higher productivity and lower wages means that Wales now has significantly lower unit labour costs than the UK as a whole.

Although the strategy of attracting FDI has been perceived as a means of overcoming structural decline and generating employment, it has also consolidated Wales's traditional dependency on external actors. Policy-makers in Wales are have been criticized for focusing on inward investors rather than providing assistance to indigenous small and medium-sized enterprises (SMEs) to become more innovative and competitive. The problems of such firms are compounded by the UK's anti-industrial syndrome, which is composed of a complex set of problems, particularly the lack of 'patient money', a low commitment to R&D, an inadequate system of skills provision, weak inter-firm networks, ineffective professional associations and a centralized state system that fails to provide a stable and stimulating regulatory framework. Some of these problems are less severe in Wales, particularly due to the region's governance structures such as the Welsh Office and the Welsh Development Agency, which embody a capacity to use local knowledge for policy-making which does not exist in the English regions.

The Welsh Development Agency's 'Source Wales'

The Welsh Development Agency (WDA) has recently attempted to address the over-reliance of the Welsh economy on external actors by extending its traditional focus on land reclamation, factory building and inward investment to include business support services, technology transfer and skills development. The Source Wales programme, set up in 1991, aims to promote linkages between branch plants and indigenous firms, particularly by using the supply chain to promote learning among both customers and suppliers. A high-quality local supply base is seen not only as a key factor in attracting more sophisticated inward investors, but also as a means of boosting local multiplier effects and of supporting indigenous SMEs. The WDA attempts to do this by acting as an intermediary in the supply chain, seeking to build and develop long-term, high-trust partnerships between major corporate buyers and Welsh-based suppliers (Hines, 1992). In a major departure from traditional enterprise support thinking, the WDA aims to design business support initiatives with, rather than for, firms.

On the one hand, Source Wales's sourcing activities involve the identification of suitable suppliers via a database of original equipment manufacturers in the electronics, automotive, IT sectors and other major purchasers. Since 1991, the number of sourcing projects has been running at around 120 per annum, with some 50 per cent of these yielding deals for Welsh companies. On the other hand, the programme's development-side activities involve the provision of different services offered to different firms, depending on their size and ability. Companies can, for example, access programmes which are designed to help them attain global 'best practice'. These include:

- the Time to Market Programme, which aims to improve the product development process so that firms bring products to market more quickly and efficiently;
- the Supplier Association Programme, or *Kyoryoku Kai*, which aims to build long-term, high-trust relationships between client companies and their key suppliers in order to raise performance through the supply chain;
- the Materials Management Network Programme, which aims to disseminate 'best practice' in materials management by forming regional networks.

Welsh Regional Technology Plan

Although co-operation between policy actors tends to be more effective in Wales than in the UK generally, there are key structural constraints, particularly the region's dependence on central government via the Welsh Office, which perceives partnership in terms of control rather than empowerment. The Regional Technology Plan (RTP), financed by the Commission of the European Communities (CEC), has been used as a means of building a strategy for the future on the basis of co-operation among a wide range of regional actors (CEC, 1994). The RTP programme breaks with the supply-side emphasis of past EU regional policies and is predicated on the notion that the impetus for renewal must come from within the region (Morgan, 1997). This emphasis on generating a consensus-based strategy for endogenous development has been particularly important in Wales because in the past actors have had to respond to initiatives from central government or to economic processes outside their control, rather than having the resources to generate medium- to long-term strategies.

The RTP in Wales has therefore been used as an opportunity to consult and involve as many relevant groups of interests as possible, including the regional state, private firms, public agencies, social partners and organizations spanning education, training and technology transfer. This two-year consultation process has given many actors their first chance to voice their views formally and with some prospect of their being taken seriously. The RTP Action Plan, officially launched in June 1996, provides a coherent framework for strategic policy action, so that resources may be channelled and projects designed to complement rather than conflict with one another. Problems remain, however, particularly the lack of a central strategic actor which has the political and financial power to coerce or encourage actors to implement projects effectively and to continue to make good their commitments with actual investments. None the less, this weakness appears to be offset by the success of the consultation process in promoting co-operation, and the actors' recognition of the need for collaboration. The adoption of the RTP Action Plan also suggests that the regional authorities have begun to acknowledge the need for a strategy which is not imposed from above but which harnesses the skills and resources of a wide and varied constituency. In this sense, the RTP has met one of its principal aims of providing an opportunity 'to break old habits and to create new openings' (Shotton and Miege, 1994).

THE RUHR AREA OF NORTH-RHINE WESTPHALIA

Industrial and Institutional Legacies

Structural decline of coal and steel in the Ruhr area since the 1970s has led to long-term high levels of unemployment (standing at 13.3 per cent in December 1995, compared with 9.7 per cent in the old Federal Republic of Germany: KVR, 1996), even though social dislocation has been minimized by concerted public and private sector action. The most powerful actor in economic development policy has been the NRW *Land* government, initially via large-scale overarching programmes such as the *Entwicklungsprogramm Ruhr* and the *Aktionsprogramm Ruhr*, which financed improvements in traditional locational factors and provided subsidies for process developments in traditional sectors. Since the mid-1980s, however, the *Land* has shifted towards the provision of information and advice for SMEs and the creation of decentralized policy mechanisms (Heinze and Voelzkow, 1991), partly due to increasing financial restraints and partly because of the perceived need to mobilize regional and local capacities for action.

Innovation Support Policy

NRW has many innovation support organizations, such as Higher Education Institute technology transfer stations, technology advisers in the chambers, and R&D centres, which aim to assist SMEs to become more innovative and competitive. There are, none the less, concerns that these agencies are used by only a very small percentage of firms (Staudt *et al.*, 1991; Widmaier, 1991), and that the quality of their services is variable. This has led the *Land* to attempt to develop more flexible innovation policy mechanisms via the Technology Initiatives. Rather than setting up further formal organizations, the Initiatives bring together companies, academic researchers and industry representatives with interests in a specific theme, in order to generate specific activities. The Initiatives are largely financed by the *Land*, although participating companies also pay a fee and attempts are made to sell services to other companies. Most Initiatives are in new growth areas, such as fuzzy technology, microstructural technologies, telematics and software, although some address more traditional sectors, such as coal-mining or automotive suppliers. The Initiatives emphasize specific collaborative projects which can increase firms' access to markets and improve their competitiveness. This type of mechanism aims to be more efficient and less bureaucratic than traditional forms of innovation support. By establishing patterns of active and practical interaction and co-operation, the Initiatives can also build trust and reciprocity among the actors involved. They appear, however, to have been most successful in emerging fields, largely because there is more scope for co-operation where firms do not compete directly with one another (Hafner, 1996). If projects involve market- orientated product development, competition between companies is likely to be acute, so co-operation is more likely to be successful in areas such as pre-competitive research or vocational training. The use of subsidies as a means of promoting co-operation is also problematic because firms may focus primarily on the subsidies rather than on co-operation or innovation. In the Automotive Suppliers Initiative, for example, very few instances of co-operation have continued since project funding has ended (Matrix, 1995). The Technology Initiatives are, however, an advance on more traditional forms of innovation support because they move away from building sophisticated supply-side mechanisms and attempt instead to discover ways in which demand among firms may be addressed and stimulated.

NRW's Regional Conferences

The strength of NRW *Land* has tended to lead to a highly centralized and top-down approach to policy-making which, along with the lack of mechanisms promoting communication and co-operation across existing boundaries between local actors, has undermined effective decentralized action in the field of economic development. Since the late 1980s, however, attempts have been made to mobilize expertise at the regional level, particularly via the *Regionalkonferenzen*, which are regional policy networks set up at a level between the metropolitan authorities and the *Land*. NRW's 15 regional conferences are made up of representatives from local authorities, the *Land*, chambers, professional associations, trade unions and voluntary bodies. While statutory powers remain with the *Land* and local authorities, the conferences draw up regional development strategies (*Regionale Entwicklungskonzepte* – REKs), which analyse regional strengths and weaknesses, recommend projects to the *Land* for finance, and inform the *Land*'s policy-making. The initial REKs focus on themes such as improvements to basic infrastructure, technology transfer and training provision, business parks, image-related factors, and the need for regional co-operation (Ache, 1994). The conferences aim to stimulate collaborative activity by increasing the intensity of contacts between actors at the regional level, by creating structures which provide opportunities for concrete co-operation, and by promoting consensus-building, in order to construct a basis for effective policy action.

There are, none the less, tensions between the conferences' roles of generating regional co-operation on the one hand and channelling *Land* subsidies on the other; lip-service may be paid to consensus and co-operation as a pragmatic means of obtaining finance. The conferences' capacities for building trust and for instigating radical new ideas and strategies may also be undermined by the need to legitimize the REKs and to ensure that public finance is gained; for example, potential areas of conflict may not be addressed for fear of alienating traditionally powerful actors. More fundamentally, despite the conferences' aim of developing regional capacities, they remain dependent on the central *Land* government which retains the power to allocate funding (Fürst and Kilper, 1995). None the less, if the regional conferences succeed in stimulating regional co-operation and consensus-building, they may have an important impact on policy-making and on economic development processes in in the longer term.

CONCLUSIONS AND IMPLICATIONS

In this chapter, we have argued that, while institutions allow uncertainty and conflict to be managed and can provide incentives for innovation, they can also block change and the introduction of new ideas. While institutions which generate trust are likely to be located at a regional level, regions affected by structural decline may find that traditional forms of trust and co-operation actually exacerbate inertia. Policy strategies, such as the Regional Technology Plan in Wales or the Regional Conferences in North-Rhine Westphalia, can begin to break down institutions which prevent change, while simultaneously building new institutions on the basis of co-operation by consciously aiming to build capacities for action. More important than specific results is the development of a cultural disposition which sets a premium on finding joint solutions to shared problems.

We have also argued that policy strategies can promote innovation among existing firms by constructing collaborative networks. The examples discussed here within the Source Wales programme and NRW's Technology Initiatives have thus far had a modest effect and are confined to a small number of sectors. While such strategies have been criticized for offering little prospect of alleviating the key problems of structural decline, namely mass unemployment and social exclusion (Lovering, 1996), this has never been, and can never be, their aim. Although developing firms' ability to co-operate and to tap into the knowledge of other actors is likely to increase their competitiveness, it is highly unlikely that this will lead directly to large increases in employment; nor can other short-term policies, such as attracting foreign direct investment, achieve this goal. Moreover, the benefits of such strategies are likely to be distributed highly unevenly in spatial and social terms – a trend which may be seen in both the regions studied here, although more vividly in Wales, due to the greater level of centralization and spatial inequality in the UK compared to Germany. However, if we are serious about addressing unemployment and social exclusion, we need to recognize that conventional economic growth no longer offers a credible solution for the long-term unemployed. Indeed, this problem requires more innovative labour market policies, like the 'socially useful third sector' (Lipietz, 1992; Rifkin, 1995), the 'sheltered economy' (Freeman and Soete, 1994) and the 'intermediate labour market' (WISE Group, 1994). The common thread running through these new labour market concepts is the idea of marrying idle hands with unmet social needs, an idea which is now being explored by the European Commission (CEC, 1995). If it is to operate on an EU-wide basis, however, this third-sector strategy must combine local knowledge of supply and demand with national and supra-national political support, because it presupposes radical reform of the current tax and benefit systems (Gregg, 1996).

None the less, the actual rationale for the regional innovation strategies discussed in this chapter is sound, and we would argue that they are necessary for two reasons. First, increasing the innovativeness of indigenous companies is of critical importance for safeguarding the future of existing jobs and companies. Moreover, innovating in declining regions means working with what exists, however inauspicious. This may mean assisting companies in low-quality saturated product markets where competition is harsh to diversify into more specialized high-quality product markets. If they do not do so, they may not survive and further jobs will therefore be lost. Policy action to stimulate organizational and technological change in existing companies – as well as to encourage the growth of new companies – is necessary if levels of unemployment are not to increase further. Secondly, it should be recognized that building long-term competitiveness and the level of economic dynamism and prosperity which allows unemployment to be minimized are long-term objectives and therefore require strategic action over an extended period of time.

Yet decades of economic decline cannot be reversed overnight. The first step in regions which have long been dominated by exogenous economic and political forces must be to mobilize endogenous capacities – hence initiatives such as the Welsh Regional Technology Plan and NRW's Regional Conferences. The process of developing consensus around a future strategy for action can lead to the growth of patterns of interaction, co-operation and knowledge exchange which, if they persist in the longer term, can crystallize into institutions which generate trust. While such an objective may appear trivial in the face of large-scale unemployment and may lead to accusations of 'all talk and no action', it should be seen as the first step towards breaking the cycle of structural decline, joblessness and poverty. In the absence of endogenously based strategic action, the status of old industrialized regions as victims of global economic change will continue to be exacerbated. By acting, on the basis of co-operation, a region can minimize its liability to be acted upon.

REFERENCES

Ache, P. (1994), *Wirtschaft im Ruhrgebiet*, Dortmund: University of Dortmund.
Arthur, W.B. (1989), 'Competing technologies, increasing returns, and lock-in by historical events', *Economic Journal*, **99**: 116–31.

Bijker, W., Hughes, T. and Pinch, T. (eds) (1987), *The Social Construction of Technological Systems: New Directions in the Sociology and History of Technology*, Cambridge, Mass., and London: MIT Press.

Callon, M. (1991), 'Techno-economic networks and irreversibility', in L. Law (ed.), *A Sociology of Monsters: Essays on Power, Technology and Domination*, London and New York: Routledge.

Central Statistical Office (CSO) (1995), *Regional Trends*, London: HMSO.

Commission of the European Communities (CEC) (1994), *The Regional Technology Plan Guidebook*, Brussels: CEC.

Commission of the European Communities (CEC) (1995), *Local Development and Employment Initiatives*, Brussels: CEC.

Coriat, B. and Dosi, G. (1994) 'Learning how to govern and learning how to solve problems: on the co-evolution of competences, conflicts and organizational routines', paper to Prince Bertil Symposium, Stockholm.

Department of Employment (DOE) (1997), *Regional Unemployment Statistics*, London: HMSO.

Edquist, C. and Johnson, B. (1996), 'Institutions and organizations in systems of innovation', in C. Edquist (ed.), *Systems of Innovation: Technologies, Institutions and Organizations*, London: Pinter Publishers and Cassell.

Freeman, C. (1995), 'The "national system of innovation" in historical perspective', *Cambridge Journal of Economics*, **19**: 5–24.

Freeman, C.L. and Soete, L. (1994), *Work for All or Mass Unemployment*, London: Pinter Publishers.

Fürst, D. and Kilper, H. (1995), 'The innovative power of regional policy networks: a comparison of two approaches to political modernisation in North-Rhine Westphalia', *European Planning Studies*, **3**: 287–304.

Grabher, G. (1993), *The Embedded Firm: On the Socioeconomics of Industrial Networks*, London and New York: Routledge.

Granovetter, M. (1985), 'Economic action and social structure: the problem of embeddedness', *American Journal of Sociology*, **91**: 481–510.

Gregg, P. (1996), *Jobs, Wages and Poverty*, London: London School of Economics.

Hafner, S.A. (1996), 'Wege aus der Wirtschaftskrise: Unternehmensnetzwerke als Instrument zur Gestaltung des regionalen Strukturwandels? Erfahrungen bei der Implementierung des "Programms für Industrieregionen im Strukturwandel" in *NRW*' Masters dissertation, Munich: Technische Universität München.

Heinze, R.G. and Voelzkow, H. (1991), 'Neue Politikmuster in der nordrhein-westfälischen Strukturpolitik: Regionalisierung und Korporatismus', in Institut für Landes- und Stadtentwicklungsforschung des Landes NRW, *Regionale Politik und regionales Handeln*, Duisburg: WAZ.

Hill, S. and Munday, M. (1994), *The Regional Distribution of Foreign Manufacturing Investment in the United Kingdom,* London: Macmillan.

Hines, P. (1992), *Creating World Class Suppliers*, London: Pitman.

Hodgson, G.M. (1988), *Economics and Institutions: A Manifesto for a Modern Institutional Economics,* Cambridge: Polity Press, and Ann Arbor, Mich.: University of Michigan Press.

Kommunalverband Ruhrgebiet (KVR) (1996), *Regionalinformation Ruhrgebiet, Jahresübersicht: Überblick der im Jahr 1995 erschienenen Beiträge*, Essen: Kommunalverband Ruhrgebiet.

Lawson, G. and Morgan, K. (1991), *Employment Trends in the British Engineering Industry*, Watford, Herts: Engineering Industry Training Board.

Lipietz, A. (1992), *Towards a New Economic Order: PostFordism, Ecology and Democracy*, Cambridge: Polity Press.

Lovering, J. (1996), 'New myths of the Welsh economy', *Planet*, **116**: 491–503.

Lundvall, B.-A. (ed.) (1992), *National Systems of Innovation: Towards a Theory of Innovation and Interactive Learning*, London: Frances Pinter.

Matrix (ed.) (1995), *Kooperationen mittelständischer Unternehmen*, Düsseldorf: Matrix.

Miller, L. (1995), Packaging Networks: The Institutional Foundations of an Industry, PhD dissertation, New Haven, Conn.: Yale University.

Morgan, K. (1997), 'The learning region: institutions, innovation and regional renewal', *Regional Studies*, **31** (5): 491–503.

Nelson, R.R. (ed.) (1993), *National Innovation Systems: A Comparative Analysis*, Oxford: Oxford University Press

Nordrhein-Westfalens (NRW) (1992), *Regionalisierung: Neue Wege in der Strukturpolitik Nordrhein-Westfalens*, Düsseldorf: Ministerium für Wirtschaft, Mittelstand und Technologie des Landes.

Rifkin, J. (1995), *The End of Work*, New York: G.P. Putnam's Sons.

Sako, M. (1992), *Prices, Quality and Trust*, Cambridge: Cambridge University Press.

Schumpeter, J.A (1934), *The Theory of Economic Development*, Cambridge, Mass.: Harvard University Press.

Shotton, R. and Miege, R. (1994), *The Regional Technology Plan: Why and How*, RTP Newsletter no.1, Brussels: Commission of the European Communities.

Staudt, E., Bock J. and Mühlemeyer, P. (1991), *Die Rolle von Technologie-transferstellen zwischen dem Wissenschaftssystem und der mittelständischen Industrie: Makler oder Kompetenzzentren?*, (Bochum: Institut für angewandte Innovation.

Storper, M. (1995), 'The resurgence of regional economies, ten years later: the region as a nexus of untraded interdependencies', *European Journal of Urban and Regional Development*, **2**: 191–221.

United Kingdom Office of National Statistics (1996), *New Earnings Survey*, London: UK Office of National Statistics.

Widmaier, B. (1991), *Marktstrategien, Produkt- und Verfahrensinnovationen im Verarbeitenden Gewerbe Nordrhein-Westfalen*, Gelsenkirchen: Institut Arbeit und Technik.

WISE Group (1994), *Annual Review*, Glasgow: WISE Group.

Zucker, L.G. (1986), 'Production of trust: institutional sources of economic structures, 1840–1920', *Research in Organizational Behavior*, **8**: 53–111.

Zysman, J. (1994), 'How institutions create historically rooted trajectories of growth', *Industrial and Corporate Change*, **3**: 243–83.

PART III

The World of Work

9. The employment relationship in transition

Eugenio Benedetti and Marco Rangone

INTRODUCTION

When looking at how the employment relationship has recently been transformed, it can be seen that the way in which working conditions, economic and political relationships, and welfare arrangements were bargained over and developed during the postwar period has undergone a process of continuous minor revisions – sometimes punctuated with major symbolic fractures. In fact, the sum total of such changes is challenging the general framework of rules that protect labour from the oddities of business activity – the basic goal of the twentieth-century working-class movement.

Nowadays, the place of labour – as income generator and provider of social identity – is quite different in the popular perception from only twenty years ago; on the other hand, the social value attached to economic efficiency as opposed to the right to labour has also increased dramatically. It is widely acknowledged, and almost as equally accepted, that firms need even more drastic changes in the degree of labour 'usability', in relation to performance requirements; many legally protected labour rights are under reform by governments which think that the prosperity of firms automatically means collective welfare.

In this chapter, we put forward the argument that the transformations which employment relations are undergoing also have far-reaching consequences for the welfare prospects of individuals and families. The behaviour of labour and of firms is closely linked to the social and

* This is a revised version of the paper presented at the Twentieth EAEPE Annual Conference, held in Antwerp, 7–9 November 1996. We would like to thank Toni Calafati, Stefano Solari, Paolo Ramazzotti and many people at the 1996 EAEPE Summer School for useful comments and suggestions (special thanks to Pat Northover); of course, they cannot be considered responsible for anything written here.

Although it should be considered the outcome of a joint effort, the chapter was written separately; hence the first four sections can be attributed to Eugenio Benedetti, while the following eight sections are the contribution of Marco Rangone.

economic regulatory setting. Micro-behaviour must find a consistent counterpart in the macro-social setting, which provides the general framework in which stable micro-relations can be developed. When the terms of the micro-relation are disputed, consistency might come to an end; some form of conflict is likely to arise, if widely diffused norms of behaviour contrast with the emerging properties of the evolving environment.

We believe that welfare concerns should play a greater role in designing the regulatory setting in the future. Hence this framework is used to debate some policy implications. There is a growing dissatisfaction with current economic policy; what we face, in fact, is a world where known policy approaches and instruments, whether neoclassical or Keynesian, prove highly inefficient in coping with unemployment, fiscal crises and external constraints at the same time. Unfortunately, harshly conflicting interests reinforce the negative effects of policy measures that do not pay much attention to the complexity of the economic and social system.

POST-FORDISM AND THE TRANSITION OF THE EMPLOYMENT RELATIONSHIP

In this chapter, we try to set out an interpretative framework to understand the present phase of transition away from that specific industrial system and regulatory setting known as 'Fordism'. To mark the difference, the new phase is commonly named 'post-Fordism'. This negative definition, however, makes it apparent that its nature and character are still uncertain (see Table 9.1). None the less, some basic features may be singled out.

In general, post-Fordist organizations are expected to show productive and organizational flexibility, a perpetual search for quality, the capability to modify products at the right time, a reduced time from conception to marketing, a continuous need to act in an ever-changing environment, an ability to respond to widespread competition, and an increasing responsibility for individuals at all levels.

Microelectronic technologies have definitely helped this process. Technological progress formalizes procedures, leaving the co-ordination and control activities of processes to labour. Work activity is now losing most of its physical nature and is becoming abstract; individual task boundaries tend to become fuzzier, and are increasingly defined alongside the production process. A single worker may integrate the functioning of larger parts of the technological and organizational system by the control of variances, and this requires a greater understanding of the system as a whole. An individual's responsibility is enhanced because tasks are virtual *ex ante*. To single out events and make them meaningful is a crucial and

Table 9.1 Fordism and post-Fordism compared: main features

	Fordism	Post-Fordism
Tasks	Fixed roles	Flexibility
Job duration	Legally protected lifelong jobs	Temporary and uncertain
Renumeration	Bargained fixed wage	Dependent on firm's performance
Relation	Labour vs. capital	Total quality
Basic concept	Labour as a right	Freedom of enterprise

tricky capability, that requires both a grasp of the technical and cultural codes of the organization and a large degree of empathy with it.

All these traits need widespread consensus, shared objectives and identification with the firm. People are now persuaded to accept and service all the requirements of a free market and of the firm's system, even when these clash with their own interests. A new set of values and norms is required, as post-Fordism becomes dominant. Adopting Dopfer's (1994) definition, we argue that people should move from one pattern of behaviour to another, that is, they should conform to a different norm.

The analysis of this cultural change points in two directions: the selection of norms, on one hand, and its diffusion on the other (Figure 9.1).

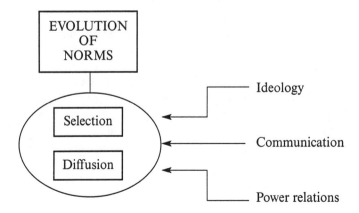

Figure 9.1 Evolution of norms

From a general point of view, three aspects are involved in both processes: ideology (the structure of interpretative models of reality), communication and power relations. However, as all these analytically distinct characteristics work side by side, we may distinguish between an artificial evolution – directly influenced by individual and collective pur-posive action – and a spontaneous evolution, developed in the daily interaction between agents.

We shall focus only on the implementation of normative changes. In the next section we set forward a consideration of the firm's purposive action first towards its internal 'equilibrium', and then in the social envi-ronment. In the following sections we move our attention to the 'spontaneous' interaction in the firm, and then to the discussion about the conditions to be fulfilled in order to pursue changes successfully.

THE FIRM'S ACTION AND THE NEW RULES OF THE GAME

The creation of a co-operative environment is a tricky operation indeed. Workers face various – and sometimes conflicting – stimuli which lead them to select among patterns of co-operation. At the firm level, actions are pursued daily to make sure that employees do the right things in the right way. Workers are especially motivated by means of cultural involve-ment and effective incentives structures; socialization to the specific *corporate culture* may begin as early as the hiring stage, when people may be chosen according to their ability to fit into the organizational network of roles and relations that any position implies, rather than according to their absolute abilities and competencies.

While it cannot categorically be said that individual firms have played an explicit role in putting in place the existing system of rules which govern employment relations, it is plausible to state that some larger firms felt so constrained by the conflictual attitude of workers towards industrial relations, that they directed their search for new technology towards labour-saving methods. This reaction was sometimes used specif-ically to rid the firm of less co-operative workers. In fact, when changing the attitudes of employees proves too difficult – because of inflexible atti-tudes to innovation or due to ideological opposition – resocialization may be replaced by direct substitution of people. The experience of Japanese transplants in the USA (Mazda) and the UK (Nissan), as reported by Boyer and Orleon (1992), supports the argument. Similar results were obtained from plant closures and delocalization.

Here we see how micro-behaviour links to cultural evolution. At the societal level, socialization is needed to build shared values and to maintain social cohesion. Generally speaking, we may say that this kind of socialization, as well as the design of the regulatory system, is outside the firm's direct control; social participation and involvement would typically be the object of political confrontation, both in the struggle over ideas and in the polity. Yet we may see that firms trying to cope with globalization and change do not limit themselves by accepting the constraints of the environment, but rather they choose to act at both levels: the more general economic and cultural level as well as the organizational one.

In fact, the firm–environment interaction is more complex, and we may assume that the firm is 'socially constructing' its reality. Whereas an *adaptive* firm strives to make internal strengths and weaknesses compatible with external pressures, the management of an *interpretative* firm tries to shape the collective perception of the environment, enlarged to include the macro-social habitat, through the control of the production process of symbols and meaning, values and beliefs. An interpretative strategy is devoted to enacting reality, its goal is to influence the external environment or even to create a new one. In a complex environment, a key to success is to become an architect of the system of cultural beliefs (Steidlmeier, 1993).

Here we may find the theoretical justification of the increasing role played by firms in many spheres of social life:

- they own all kinds of media, from television and radio channels, to newspapers and magazines, at national as well as local levels;
- their advertising campaigns are often centred on lifestyles rather than products;
- many big cultural events are heavily sponsored by them;
- even the educational system is increasingly denoted by firm-based action, whether directly – through financial aid to research – or indirectly, by encouraging economic thinking in schools.

Hence a changing environment cannot be regarded as independent of the firm's actions. This represents a turning point in our discussion; what is happening (or will happen) in the firm is likely to influence the external context – both economic and social – and strictly interacts with it. In the following sections, we shall focus on the links between the firm's action and social evolution, by first exploring the micro- and macro-conditions for economic co-operation.

Social cohesion usually implies the acceptance of the existing regulatory setting by the great majority of the community, although cultural ties may sometimes prove even more effective. We will therefore suggest that, as far as economic relations – such as the employment relation – are concerned, one essential condition is the equivalence between the two sides of the exchange process. We will try to show that this *equivalence principle* is valid in the micro-economic environment of the firm as well as in the macro-economic setting. The strict interrelation between the two will help us to understand the limits of economic policy for labour, and to suggest alternative measures; this will be the concern of the final sections.

THE FIRM AS A SOCIAL SYSTEM

In their seminal work, Nelson and Winter (1982) suggested that the set of routines in a firm is a 'truce'[1] in the organizational struggle over scarce resources among individual members or groups (for example, lines of production, divisions). The argument – deeply rooted in the behavioural tradition (Cyert and March, 1963) – views 'strategic' agents holding preferences and behaving according to their relative role or position in the organization, while the firm tries to develop cognitive and economic devices in order to keep the conflict latent and obtain efficiency through the co-operation of workers. Any implementation process is shaped by the pattern of existing core and complementary competencies, and the internal network of relations and relative power;[2] people in the organization might be able to influence the process while pursuing their own interests, thereby leading to unwanted (from the firm's viewpoint) outcomes (March, 1981; Harrison and March, 1984).

While standard economics focuses on the direct control of agents who perform badly, and searches for the optimal design of structures, evolutionary theorizing stresses that in the real world people do in fact achieve some sort of accommodation over organizational rules (which brings with it the additional feature that members come to define a smooth symbolic arrangement which is peculiar to the firm, comprising linguistic and other active signals; we may understand it as the *corporate culture* of a firm[3]). Apart from the information problems created by specialization and separation in the workplace, the unavoidable *incompleteness of the employment contract* appears to be the most remarkable source of 'inefficient' behaviour. The point was brilliantly singled out by scholars such as Herbert Simon (1951) and Harvey Leibenstein (1978).

However, what we want to stress here is that the internal political equilibrium of the firm comprises the terms of the labour exchange, as it evolved through bargaining, persuasion, inertness, authority and even guile. After all, what the accommodation will turn out to be depends heavily on cultural (and apparently external) factors:[4] workers bring to the firm an indistinguishable core of beliefs, values, social norms and habits that contribute to the definition of the firm's structure and behaviour; this, in turn, impinges upon an individual's personality and overall attitudes. Especially in highly regulated countries, the core of the employment relation – customs relative to wages, working hours, tasks, career ladders – springs up and develops in the social arena. On the other hand, the final outcome will also reflect the internal evolution of power relations, possibly related to information asymmetries and group cohesion.

However, a basic point is that the specific terms of the relation must be accepted by the parties: we do not refer to non-democratic systems. We shall see in which sense this statement is acceptable.

THE BASIS OF SOCIAL AGREEMENT IN ECONOMIC RELATIONS

As time passes, labour standards become institutionalized; that is to say, the diffusion of labour standards in the economy is such as to become accepted as the basis of the employment relation. To explain this, we may assume the existence of an *equivalence principle* in the employment relation. The fictitious commodity called the 'labour force' is exchanged on the market at a price that reflects the correspondence of services given and salary paid. This principle is indeed generally accommodated in modern economic theorizing about exchange-based economies; neoclassical theory proposes the notion of marginal productivity to define what is a *just* salary: an employee should receive as much as her/his contribution to production. In contrast,[5] the evolutionary approach need not refer to external and – allegedly – objective parameters; correspondence is an outcome of the daily process of social interaction. As such, it may have very little to do with ethical equivalence; the reference is rather to existing customary practices and habits, possibly normatively fixed in collective contracts or laws (Hodgson, 1988). It is worth spending a few more words on this.

Let us use Simon's concept of the area of acceptance, used to describe the indeterminacy of work rules governing the employment relationship; by applying it to, say, salary, it is possible to define a (socially) acceptable wage as any wage that is higher than a minimum threshold, in relation to the job accomplished (a fair day's pay for a fair day's work):

$$w_i \geq \bar{w}_i$$

where $i = 1, 2, ..., n$ are the labour services. In fact, there is a whole set of wage levels compatible with the same labour service, according to the degree of diffusion of the social norm. (So we can understand the process of diffusion of a norm about wages as the definition of the threshold level, at an early stage, and the subsequent calibration of wages over the threshold.)

Furthermore we may extend the argument to other characteristics of the employment relation, such as working hours, number of pieces, or whatever; then the formulation becomes:

$$W^* \subset W \text{ such that } w_{ij} \geq \bar{w}_{ij}, \forall w_{ij} \in W^*,$$

where $i = 1, 2 .. n$ are the labour services;
        $j = 1, 2 .. m$ are the characteristics of the employment relation.

Of course, the organization's internal co-operation is a complex combination of trust, social control and incentives, depending on the cultural and social attitudes of participants; we should therefore understand that the acceptance of the terms of the relationship and the *evaluation* of equivalence cannot be located in the working sphere alone.

As far as exchange relations (*vis-à-vis* tight communitarian relations such as those in clans or ideological groups) are concerned, co-operation means above all sharing the general framework within which people recognize available resources and mutually acknowledge identity. A necessary condition for any stable equilibrium is that both sides recognize the counterpart as such, and take the opponent's reasons as part of the basic platform of agreement. In this simple theory of social production,[6] the reciprocal acknowledgement of agents' *identity*,[7] as well as the criteria for product distribution, is derived from the position in the social production (both material and symbolic); these relations permit exchange between actors, which is hampered (or even interrupted) when mutual recognition is disputed. Figure 9.2 shows a possible representation. Therefore we suggest that, for an economic system to work smoothly, the terms of the employment relationship must be accepted both privately and socially. The problem is to define the specific reference system of

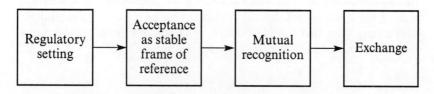

Figure 9.2 Necessary steps for the exchange process

each actor (either individual or collective) as well as the general, common one, towards which there is competition side by side with sharing.

CHANGE AND CONFLICT

From the labour economics standpoint, routines have the nature of an accommodation over members' task discretion, balancing the requirements of the on-going organization with the (possibly conflicting) motivations of its members. The resulting compromise takes the form of a *de facto* contract, the terms of which are implicitly agreed by the parties by not turning to any disruptive form of conflict, on the one side, and not appealing to any definitive sanction, on the other. In such a context, members are rarely surprised by each other's behaviour, and people continue to do their jobs in the usual way, that is, according to the usual standards. Some degree of conflict may persist, but it shows in stable and predictable ways.

However, we may expect the internal equilibrium marked by established routines to be threatened by changes that may arise within or from outside the firm.

There will be heavy costs in breaking the truce: we should expect co-operation to decrease dramatically and internal co-ordination to become looser. The difficulty of implementing decisions involving change adds up to the problem of finding a workable equilibrium between constraints and opportunities created by the existence (lack) and acquisition (loss) of internal and external capabilities. Even strategic decisions that are passed down by the top management, if they involve major changes, will probably encounter some problems of implementation: they must be accepted by all members of the organization, who must also make the effort to give concrete form to them.

Customs and habits are particularly important within organizations: they reinforce the self-control of individuals' innate tendency to behave impulsively (for example, to be irrational, short-sighted, time-inconsistent); habits do so by excluding free choice and reinforcing initial disadvantageous behaviour (Postrel and Rumelt, 1992). Moreover, habits are basically learned through a reward-and-sanction process, and correct timing is often crucial in determining the effectiveness of the structure of incentives and sanctions. Accordingly, to teach habits is quite a difficult task, particularly if existing habits must be replaced by the new ones.[8]

Older customs, in fact, stabilize into 'commitment positions': that is, the standard behaviour that members of the organization define contextually around their interpretation of other members' behaviour, requests and pressures.[9] These are influenced by the costs of abandoning the present position plus the costs to start and stabilize the new position. Whenever such influences are weak (for example, if the current procedures are enjoyed and there is no search for change) the costs of moving from one 'commitment position' to another are higher and the benefits are lower, and behaviour is restrained to a limited number of 'commitment points', defining an *area of inertia*.

It is worth recalling that, where a norm already exists, its replacement requires breaking the equilibria previously formed and the forced resocialization of the agents involved. When such a norm is shared, we should expect co-operative action, while breaking the settled terms of exchange may originate conflict, which may be deviant, competitive or antagonistic (Melucci, 1991; Hirschmann, 1982).

To take further the simple theory of action sketched in the previous section, we shall try to decontextualize antagonistic relations by explaining conflict in terms of generally defined social relations. While contradiction and conflict are rooted in the structural functioning (synchronic: Kay, 1984) of the system, they only emerge from diachronic evolution; we therefore need a theory of action. This means that we try to define the link between the 'investment', that is, the *expected* effects of action, and the reward obtained.[10] In our simple model, action – whether conflictual or co-operative – stems from the confrontation between the two terms, though the outcome is not deterministic; for example, aggression is a plausible response to equivalence breaks, but not the only one: restructuring the means and/or ends of action, depression, sublimation, political action, forced indifference, exit, are some other possible replies (the researcher can probably only collect good answers through case-studies).

However, the social outcome will also depend on the relative power of the actors. It may be suggested that breaking the equilibrium leads to a period of 'confusion', when the structure of power relations is crucial to establish new rules of the game; although conflict may well characterize social relations in the first place, it is plausible that sooner or later the losing actors accept – *malgré lui* – the new terms that define the relation: such terms allow social life to continue and are the basis of future bargaining.

We found it useful to draw on Thompson's (1981, p. 33) description of how working-time customs changed and developed during the Industrial Revolution. He says that while the first generation of factory workers was educated by their masters about the value of time, the second generation fought to reduce working time by ten hours; the third generation went on strike to claim 50 per cent overtime payment. The moral is that the work-

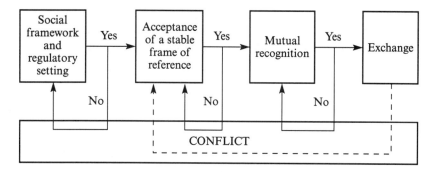

Figure 9.3 Steps for the exchange process: where conflict may arise

ers had accepted capitalists' categories and had learned to struggle within them; they learned the lesson that time is money quite well (see also Hobsbawm, 1972).

Conflict is the likely outcome when steps between stages are hampered, though other behaviour is possible. Moreover, the possibility to move the conflict to the previous stage, as shown by the dotted relation in Figure 9.3, is possible when expectations are greatly disappointed for a prolonged period.

THE MICRO AND THE MACRO

So far we have tried to describe how the firm's action may influence the propagation of a new norm about labour standards, as a result of postfordism. Hence we showed that previously settled norms, marking the internal equilibrium of the organization, also reflect the basis of mutual recognition and co-operative exchange. The evolution of some (not necessarily external) conditions may lead to changes of the terms of such equilibrium, thereby leading to conflict.

We would hence advocate the idea that people move from their acquired positions only if the rewards are sufficiently high. The following proposition therefore is suggested: individuals and groups would accept procedures that might juxtapose different subjects, and they would be willing to transform them into common, shared and stable knowledge, only inasmuch as the level and the kind of expected rewards maintain a fair labour exchange relation.

However, the terms of exchange mirror social identity and the relative position of people in society. We may hence expect consistency between actors' behaviour in daily life and the general framework into which their behaviour is going to fit. Expectations and claims are not relegated to the realm of labour matters. Let the individual willingness to change be:

$$d = f(R_m^a, R_m^r, R_e^r, \Delta, c, o)$$
$$\quad\; +\quad +\quad +\quad -\quad +\quad -$$

where: R_m^a are the absolute internal rewards

R_m^r are the internal rewards relative to other members

R_e^r are the internal rewards relative to non-members

Δ is the degree of change requested

c is her/his attitude towards conflict (for example, subculture, personality)

o is the probability of taking up new opportunities

and plus and minus are the usual sign of derivatives.

Not satisfying expectations in the labour sphere can be compensated at the collective level, and vice versa (though in this latter case, total satisfaction is going to depend much more on the individual attitude). It remains true, however, that when actual rewards – whether individualistically or collectively supplied – do not correspond to expectations (or when the 'match' is very loose) some sort of frustration or conflict is likely to arise.

An interesting story dating back to the first Industrial Revolution helps us to see how the organization's internal equilibrium relates to the dominant norm in the broader society. This story, concerning the 'insensitive' behaviour of eighteenth-century English workers facing the newly created factory system, has been cited by Postrel and Rumelt (1992) and by Thompson (1981) with completely different emphases.

As in many important business stories,[11] the charisma of the entrepreneur – Josiah Wedgwood, in this case – was crucial, according to Postrel and Rumelt. He was apparently successful in controlling quarrelsome and uncommitted people and in urging them to comply with the needs of the new system of production. However, the story was not so straightforward.

Thompson (1981, p. 37) notes that the same previously independent potters as are cited by Postrel and Rumelt, who went to work as wage earners in Josiah Wedgwood's plant in Staffordshire, were in fact 'educated' to worktime discipline using all possible means: the division of labour and direct surveillance of the workforce; the use of fines, bells and watches, along with monetary incentives; sermons and education accompanied by the suppression of local festivity and amusements. Unfortunately, one generation was not enough, Thompson reminds us; at that time, the 'educators' in the potteries could not yet rely on the formidable help of machinery; In fact, when the charismatic Josiah died, the hopeless potters reverted to many well rooted – though 'insane' – habits (ibid., p. 30)[12].

It is instructive to compare this story with other examples of resocialization within firms (as those reported by Postrel and Rumelt; see note 10). Whenever a radical change is needed in organizations, there is a problem of cultural change to pursue; however, in the pottery story employees not only had to be socialized to the new, firm-specific culture claimed by Josiah Wedgwood: they were also to be 'educated' to a generic industrial culture, involving a completely different set of rules: that of the factory system in a capitalist world. This kind of socialization, obviously enough, takes place first: before you learn how to work better or fairly or whatever, you must learn to work (with the scientifically artificial regularity of the machinery, for that matter).

To put it another way, we can distinguish a systemic socialization, embracing widespread and general categories and culture, from the – essentially micro-economic – socialization which involves the direct interactions of specific actors in idiosyncratic organizations. Both processes involve the propagation of a norm to a given population (for example, the labour force). In Figure 9.4 are shown the forces acting upon this process, as described so far.

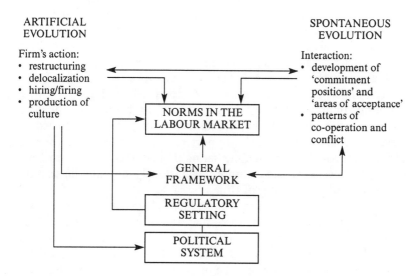

Figure 9.4 Norms in the labour market: spontaneous evolution and purposive action

STRUCTURAL CHANGE IN EXCHANGE RELATIONS

Socialization, therefore, must occur both at the micro-level – the firm, for instance – and at the macro-level, that is, society at large, when drastic changes are under way. The latter in particular, which may well take much longer, is crucial when coping with historical changes; unfortunately, its necessity is often neglected.

We currently face a structural change in the economic relations implied by the labour market; this change is causing a dramatic fall-out in the general economic social system, because the dynamics in the structure of labour demand and supply directly affect families' patterns of consumption and the welfare system.

From a social viewpoint, the restructuring process has incurred a high cost: above all, the dismantling of the collective identity of millions of workers for whom labour and its ethics represented the main expression of the self; the reduction of safety controls, perceived as unacceptable constraints by smaller and larger firms; the increasing number of individuals and families who have approached or even crossed the poverty threshold.

For decades, stable workplaces, regardless of prestige, had been the basic goal of millions, who for the first time could rely on remarkable purchasing power. In the 1970s, after a long period of impressive economic growth, the trade unions achieved sufficient numeric strength and bargaining power to impose their view on economic facts; this happened all over Europe. The egemonic viewpoint, for that matter, was that jobs were the inalienable appurtenances of individuals, and that wages had to guarantee people's economic stability (wages were, it was usual to say, the 'independent variable' in any economic contingency).

By the end of the decade that shared view was being smashed by both objective crisis and active behaviour. A 'compatibility logic' (that is, say, the subordination of bargaining to firms' problems) was becoming accepted even by the major unions, and diffused into society. Governmental action strongly supported such change during the whole decade, directing rather than mediating industrial conflicts through the adoption of wage-cutting measures (against inflation) and the search for greater flexibility (in favour of firms).

Labouring rights have since become increasingly ancillary to industrial restructuring. They have been somewhat transformed: they maintain legitimacy *within* the system of legal norms, of course, but they have been losing their character of *natural rights* – as they had been perceived to be in the previous decade. The change of perspective is all but negligible: the former are subject to modification merely through legislative action, while the latter can rely on the inherent stickiness of political processes.

This could be seen as a further step in the capitalistic domination of production and exchange relations. It has been achieved by emphasizing the centrality of economic aspects, both through the breaking up of technological and organizational limits to creation and the satisfaction of material needs, and through the action of the media and scholars who throughout the 1980s put the emphasis on consumption and hedonistic behaviour, thereby reversing the productive stress on work posed by the 'labour ethic' in the industrial era: the stock exchange, not the factory, has become the symbol of the wealth of nations, where dozens of trades based on little competence and much invention have proved to be noteworthy sources of conspicuous and sometimes transient money.

It appears now that the individual stability granted by lifetime jobs is being replaced by much more uncertain (as to place, time, mode) flexible activity; the safety of a lifelong stable income (wage plus public pension scheme) is being replaced by variable-with-business-conditions wages and private self-funded pensions; the collective representation of interests and the basic equality principle (equal wage for equal work) are disputed in favour of individualistic and 'political' bargaining.[13] However, it is by no means clear how people can adapt themselves to the required changes, if no 'reward' is given for this effort.

ECONOMIC POLICY IN TRANSITION

We have to couple the emerging needs of the dominant subsystem (the labour market, on the demand side) with the permanence of cultural perspectives and material needs in the larger social dimension.

Unfortunately, economists usually fail to take into account that any process of change, to proceed smoothly, should show consistency between individual expectations from her/his own social investment and the evaluation of actual rewards. It is becoming apparent that firms accepting the challenge of globalization may adopt strategies which conflict with individual plans for consumption patterns, working aspirations, even lifestyles. Delocalization, frequent layoffs and evolving competence are some of the pressures individuals will have to face in the labour market; they also have to cope with the internal push towards flexible and relational skills, variable working hours and total commitment to the firm's goals. Although the rhetoric of media and speakers tends to stress the cultural aspects involved in such widespread changes, there also exists precise welfare concerns, because families and individuals can hardly predict their employment prospects and therefore cannot plan consumption, let alone investments or their lives.

It seems to economists that the problem is to mobilize the labour market. They suggest measures that make use of concepts such as incentives, insurance and the like, that are valid within the established social collection of rules and behaviours. Unfortunately, when this social arrangement is under structural modification, as it appears to be in this phase, parameters are no longer invariable, and subsystems and individuals will probably respond in unusual and – what is worse – unwelcome ways. Economic policy should first address the problem of supplying a stable reference framework for agents' behaviour.

Let us explain the argument by discussing customary labour policy analysis. In mainstream economics, whenever the standard market mechanism:

$$\text{unemployment} \rightarrow \text{lower wages} \rightarrow \text{increase employment}$$

does not work well, the distortionary effects of policy intervention (usually those passive policies protecting income) are assumed to be responsible. For instance, subsidies and unemployment benefits bear the negative consequences of lengthening people's search period: without them, if people cannot find a suitable job they will reduce their requirements, accept lower-paid jobs and thus shorten their unemployment spell. Such benefits impair adjustment towards equilibrium, displace less-qualified jobs and favour the informal economy.

Similar freezing effects on the labour supply would also be the consequence of worktime reductions and early retirement schemes; moreover, collective bargaining reduces wage differentials and hampers regional and job mobility by raising the costs of requalification, when coupled with hiring and firing costs. As an unhappy finale, rigidities make capital-intensive technologies cheaper, thereby reinforcing unemployment. Welfare policies can only relieve unemployment flows in the short term, but they would undermine the system's efficiency properties, and hence long-term equity.

At the same time, proposals are advanced to deregulate the labour market by making it more flexible; suggested medium- and long-term policies are intended to support self-employment creation, on the one hand, and qualification and retraining on the other. In the past few years, the policy-makers have become firmly convinced that people's active participation in ongoing change is enhanced by better qualifications. Human capital seems to be the strategic goal of active labour market policies.[14]

If skill obsolescence, associated with a too-relaxed search behaviour, were the structural cause of current unemployment, we might even agree that passive policies could eventually increase that same unemployment which they are devised to relieve.

Unfortunately, the picture is far from being so simple; by changing the framework we may easily obtain quite different outcomes. The present market conditions are critical for labour because the technical coefficients are being reduced (Vivarelli, 1995) and growth is hindered by widespread fiscal troubles and harsh competition. It would make sense, hence, to raise the embarrassing question: why bring everybody up to high qualification levels, so as to compete effectively on the market? We in fact risk recreating unemployment through the competitive mechanism even if the qualitative gap between demand and supply were to be overcome.

Let us recall first that if the *absolute* level of qualification is crucial for society as a whole, this is not true for individuals: they must compare their own competence with that held by any other competitor. It is the *relative* level of the individual's qualification that allows her/him to be successful on the market (at the expense of someone else, of course). To explain this, let us describe a production function as the relation between output and the ratio of skilled labour L_s to unskilled labour L_u (for our purpose, we may leave out other variables, for example, capital):

$$y = \left(\frac{L_s}{L_u}, \bullet \right)$$

Let us set the output to be produced at 1,000; assume also that this level may be reached with a new technology, for which $L_s = 30$ and $L_u = 80$, and an old technology, which uses $L_s = 10$ and $L_u = 100$. Both technologies, therefore, use the same total inputs (110 workers) to produce a given amount of output ($y = 1,000$).

The basic argument of those advocating generalized training activities goes as follows. Suppose that the production function takes the specific form $y = \min (L_s, L_u, \bullet)$. We should make sure that $L_s^d = 30 \le L_s^s$, that is, supply of skilled labour must be (at least, if we allow for some informational or other frictional problems) equal to the level of its demand. *In fact*, if it was $L_s^s = 10 < L_s^d$ as in the older technology, we would verify:

$$L_u^d = \frac{L_u}{L_s} \cdot L_s^s \approx 67$$

with vacancies (20) and unemployment of unskilled labour (33). We therefore need to overcome the constraint by training people and providing a sufficient pool of available (qualified) workers so as to absorb overall unemployment.

However, the picture changes radically if new techniques save a lot of 'unskilled labour'; if, for instance, the same output ($y = 1,000$) can be obtained with $L_s = 30$ and $L_u = 40$, we find that, even if we fill in the supply of skilled labour, unemployment persists:

$$L_{tot}^s = 110 > 80 = L_{tot}^d$$

It is apparent, then, that training policy should not be considered separately from labour demand concerns (the more labour-saving the new techniques, the more new firms have to ensure increasing labour demand), or from output demand (as greater labour demand is only possible for increased production levels).[15]

Such concerns become even more important as we account for technical innovation or new firms displacing existing firms which are more labour-intensive. Furthermore, we ought to remember that constraints act on both skilled *and* unskilled labour; if, for instance:

$$L_u^s < L_u^d,$$

L_s^s cannot be fully utilized.

This is not unusual in the more industrialized countries; we may understand it by referring to the diffusion process of norms of behaviour, as outlined above. First of all, as shown by Calafati (Chapter 1 in this book), unemployment should be considered as the outcome of the family process of allocation of time (given some chosen consumption pattern). In the short period, the unemployment (or under-employment) of some members might be sustained by the family as a whole, with the expectation that future rewards will be higher. None the less this 'strategy' may prove (*ex post*) rational even in the longer term, if choosing a low-skill job means forgoing future opportunities of a better occupation. So we may face the contemporaneous presence of a net flow of immigrants employed in less-skilled jobs with a large stock of more skilled indigenous 'unemployed'. This, however, may not be a disequilibrium in a strict sense, as it reflects a historical structure of preference over the family's time-use.

The economist's standard reluctance notwithstanding, it remains true that the economic system can only work properly if a large set of legal and social norms and of organizations – the *regulation system*[16] – make capitalist production of commodities coherent in all its relevant dimensions (industrial relations, technological regime, organization of work, welfare mechanisms and so on). These institutional constraints protect individuals from the distortions and excesses of market functioning, permitting a general consensus to be built and diffuse in society.

However, the social regulatory setting cannot be regarded as immutable over time: its definition and evolution is a long-lasting bargaining process (whether internal or external to the specific institution); hence the degree of systemic cohesion assured by social institutions is variable through space and time. These institutions are shared and accepted inasmuch as they comply with the multifaceted interests and aspirations of the vast majority of the population. Conflict, or its concrete possibility at least, is always present; nevertheless it reveals itself basically within limits that are compatible with the system: for instance, in the political arena when competing for resources.

Nowadays, the old regulation system proves unable to cope with inflated debt, growing unemployment, increasing regional divergence, vested interests, or firms' claims for extended flexibility. The mismatch can be solved by designing a new set of relationships, values and norms that support the economic system.

INDIVIDUAL COSTS OF SOCIAL AND ECONOMIC EVOLUTION

In principle, a sound design might come about as the outcome of people's daily interactions (with its assortment of ability, irrationality, power); or it might be publicly devised by discussion and the evaluation of available options. Although the latter case seems most appropriate for democracies, analysts and politicians seem to rely on the system's capacity to adjust as time passes; it is likely to be so, as a matter of fact, if they do not care whether 'way A' is better than 'way B' according to some value systems.

From a standpoint that attaches a high value to individual well-being, however, this is going to be a ruinous process. To make this clear, let us recall what Polanyi (1974, p. 51) said: that if the immediate effect of some change is harmful, then so also will the final effect be, because any long-term consideration refers to the *net* effect: not the only effect of some importance, but only the one that is visible and noticeable after a period of time conventionally set. Consequently, both the duration and the tempo of adaptation should rather be taken into account by institutional analysts, who would find highly unsatisfactory the idea that – sooner or later – things will go straight. No one should ever forget that a job loss produces unfortunate consequences for the person involved, who may feel them to be so definitive as to influence her/his pattern of behaviour and social interaction.[17] Hence, these considerations suggest that policymakers should try to govern change so as to reduce these negative effects.

Training policy does not represent a panacea. (Re)training activities (as well as any part of the general education system that provides support to the productive system) are probably useless in that they inevitably *follow* technological evolution: the goal of reducing the time lag between innovation and the diffusion of relative knowledge by making university, vocational training and firms interact with one another, bears the heavy risk of overspecialization (as knowledge requires specific investments of time and money, decisions about which are made in advance and rarely reversible). It may, therefore, be that training programmes will not solve the unemployment crisis, even when they respond to real needs. On the other hand, selecting people for training raises many problems: of efficiency, of democracy, and of equity, at least.

Similar arguments may be put forward with regard to job creation policies such as self-employment schemes. When competition is tightened on the supply side, there is little room for new entrants because margins are low. If new firms are supported by public help of any kind, they are going to displace existing firms; inasmuch as intervention is not limited to very innovative high-tech firms, but rather is spread over all sectors (otherwise wide unemployment rates would scarcely be reduced even in a few years' time), there is little hope that they would operate at higher efficiency levels than existing firms on the fringe. It is instead quite possible that at least some of the new ones will be more efficient *because of* the public support.

The discussion so far has none the less shed a different light on Keynesian, *passive* measures: they are both income policies and are instruments of a wider, social regulatory action. During the harsh transformation phase, transition is not harmless; change itself calls for steps that reduce negative effects, possibly substituting one source of income with another – though, for many, subsidies do not have the same meaning as wages. Moreover, support measures could also have the effect of favouring change, because too rapid modification may be devastating and provoke hostile and incompatible reactions. We may possibly learn something from Karl Polanyi's discussion of the two Poor Laws in early eighteenth-century England; the first was devised when the market system was still in its infancy: it made the problem of enclosures somehow less dramatic for people who were deprived of their customary source of subsistence. The second, adopted when the market mechanisms were developed and needed a further boost, had the effect of slowing down the process of creating an effective labour market, biasing the incentive structure and making worse off many of those who were excluded by production.

THE LABOUR MARKET AND THE POLICY-MAKER

In the previous two sections we have tried to show how the customary reasoning on labour policy may be misleading when structural change is under way.

There is another justification for adopting a different framework of analysis: we think that the personal capability to identify new prospects in life, to create new opportunities, to avoid the vicious cycles of poverty and depression cannot be left to standard labour policies. Labour is an inalienable human urge (Veblen, 1914); it is an activity which takes up most of the time, energy and expectations of individuals. By simply sustaining the systemic requirements of work specialization within the economy, whether by supporting self-employment or through training processes, we are going to overlook these features of labour. We also risk ending up with a dramatic segmentation of the labour supply: a minority of skilled people with high incomes who are a constituent part of the value chain, and a second larger layer of less-qualified people whose social role is to supply the former with a growing range of personal services, and firms with a pool of freely disposable manpower. This is indeed a pessimistic view, but it is based firmly on a realistic (micro) view of what labour markets are and how they work (Rangone, 1997).

To an institutionalist, labour markets look rather peculiar, and s/he can easily find that non-market factors will probably explain social positions better than standard variables such as mobility, investment in education or even competence.

The probability of an individual getting a job is usually described as a function of the search effort and the information available, given the level of education and competence achieved (Figure 9.5). Yet we have to distinguish between the macro-economic problem of unemployment, and the micro-economic status of unemployed people. The problem, in this latter case, is not strictly the number of available jobs, but the relation between a person and the job position(s) s/he can achieve. An important question to raise when looking at the labour market from this perspective

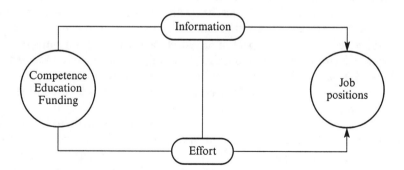

Figure 9.5 Standard view of job search

is:[18] how is it that some people are less hit by prolonged periods of scarce labour demand (such as in downturns or during structural changes)?

The first answer we suggest is that standard economics neglects important issues of labour marketing functioning, such as the creation of future opportunities, social mobility, continuity and change in economic and social reproduction. Most of these characteristics filter the search process; to put it another way, an individual's *search technology* is not purely constrained by the intensity s/he puts into it, nor is it limited by the information available about job opportunities. Though important, the former is just a proxy of an individual's motivation to get a job; its analysis is somewhat trivial, as we consider the relevant labour supply as the amount of time offered when labour market constraints are internalized in the family's preference function over consumption bundles. The latter is more crucial, the more the labour market *works as a market*; in other words, the less are personal ties and social networks relevant in getting a job. In fact, we propose the following formulation for the matching process of person *i*:

$$S_i: (C, F, N; I, E) \rightarrow L_j$$

where S is the search function that maps a set of individual resources on to a set of attainable job positions L_j, denoted by some characteristics as to the qualification and education required on the demand side. C denotes the resources with which an individual is endowed, the set of educational levels and the professional skills achieved; F the amount of funding (necessary for example for starting a business, if we consider self-employment too); and N the set of all personal and social traits which are of some relevance for matching demand requirements; this endowment relates to the standard parameters: the information on labour demand I, and the effort made to get the desired job L_j. Along with personal attributes such as age, sex and race, typically accommodated in standard empirical analysis, we stress the network of relations into which a person is embedded. Typically, a person (a) develops her/his relationships in the working environment; (b) maintains the family's contacts, ties and friendships; (c) establishes new links with other persons. Moreover, the individual's *curriculum vitae* is related to choices made with the influence and the support of the family, so even in labour affairs *history matters*.

The set of personal ties and social relationships is likely to influence directly both the access to relevant information that is not widely publicized through newspaper advertising or employment agencies and the amount of effort made (it may become unrelated to the opportunities open). We may also claim that, in many cases, information and effort are so negligible as to suggest a direct link from resources to jobs; this extreme case is depicted by the bold line in Figure 9.6. It is obvious enough that the range of opportunities created due to the family background or to autonomously developed ties is far from being the same for everyone; on the contrary, it is probably a major source of segmentation of the labour supply, and operates against the equalizing dynamics of *both* market *and* redistributional mechanisms.

In fact, we can see that the labour market works *as a market* as it overcomes the lock-in effects of path-dependent social reproduction. Following Granovetter (1991), the stronger the ties influencing an individual's choice of job opportunities and prospects, the less efficient are the market and the re-equilibrating dynamics of structural changes, which affect most those who cannot rely on private channels of communication and matching.

This framework has important implications for the policy measures which should be used to help labour market difficulties.

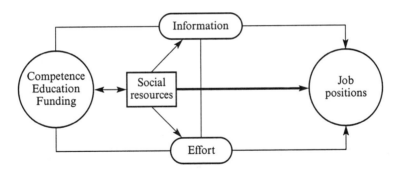

Figure 9.6 Resource-enhanced view of job search process

UNEMPLOYMENT AND THE FUTURE OF LABOUR

In the previous section we suggested that the labour market should be thought of as the place where the search for jobs is directed by historical facts; some of them may be incorporated into the analysis, while others – though often crucial when looking at personal stories – are too specific for a theorist (think of attitudes towards parental authority, which may lead the offspring to deviate from the expected path).

But if we take the set of the individual's resources as an analytical category, we may understand better why some policy schemes fail. For instance, regional measures typically address job creation: often new jobs designed for local unemployed people are instead taken up either by people already employed (in the region or outside) or by new entrants to the labour force (West, 1994). This is likely to happen because some unemployed people actually lack many of the resources listed above; not only competence, but also the right personal connections.

People who can put in the labour 'market' no other resources than their obsolete labour skills have little hope of competing successfully with others. The only possible solution for them is the growth in the number of jobs offered, up to a level at which they can be absorbed. Unfortunately, for a number of reasons growth is far from being a straightforward option. First of all, industrialized countries face increasing problems of pollution. Secondly, there is the problem of technical coefficients, with the continuous displacement of workers; although we may rely on ever-increasing consumption, based on the emergence of new products, we should expect even product innovation continuously to displace activities – and workers. Thirdly, where job creation is boosted is crucial; even by supporting quality activities, such as better product services, we increase intermediation and – in the short term at least – the inflationary bias of a superspecialized economy. Fourthly, there are issues of efficiency when job creation is artificially protected. Finally, increasing demand will raise prices if innovation is slow. The problem is that activity rates have never been so high in capitalism and unemployment so widespread. On the other hand, it cannot sensibly be said that at the turn of the century there still exists a problem of *creating* resources. This has been the economic problem in the past; now industrialized countries are, no doubt, rich, and their wealth has been spread over a number of other countries (despite the myriad contradictions that are present in the world economy). The economic problem of the twenty-first century can only be that of distribution of the social product, either in the form of rearrangement of income (or of time used to produce income), or through a different use of time. Perhaps new ways of policy-making should be sought, as increasing wealth seems to be detached from employment growth. There are two possible ways to break down the embarrassing dependence on growth: the first is to provide sufficient income for those families whose activity has that goal; the second is to redistribute labour (time) to favour activity. In all cases, the redistribution issue is ineluctable and overrides efficiency concerns.

The idea is not new to institutional theory, as Marc Tool's (1994, p.12) analysis of social costs of unemployment ends up with the indication of government as the employer of last resort. Our suggestion is that policy-makers should not provide a list of 'jobs', but rather the means for activity with income; satisfaction may be found in *labour as activity* freed from strict productive co-ordination when this proves too difficult. Admittedly, efficiency is not the crucial end, in our view, but this in an unavoidable issue if we want to counteract the sad fact that not everybody can be employed in market activities. What has to be guaranteed is the widest participation in social production. Moreover, we would be in favour of policy-making with the micro-economic stress on personal attitudes and skills (which would partly readdress matters of inefficiency).

The growth of a non-profit sector in most industrialized countries possibly reflects the spontaneous (un)consciousness of a non-market solution to unemployment. Though no general theory of non-profit activities is available, these 'firms' appear to be much more concerned with employment and satisfaction than with economic efficiency; on the other hand, such firms continuously relate to the market, occupying niches for which the market supply seems insufficient or mobilizing resources that the private sector prefers to 'save'.

For these activities, an adequate structure of incentives should be designed, facilitating their survival without subsidizing them. For instance, monetary incentives that decrease over time, as activities settle down; easier and larger access to credit for start-up and innovation, as riskiness should be reduced; monetary support for individual training and retraining, so as to facilitate change and the creation of new opportunities for work and life. The perspective of labour policy is changed under this view. Job creation via new firms may be a sensible scheme if we want to revive disappearing crafts, but it might be counterproductive if we simply enhance market competition.

Other ways are being suggested, apart from leaving it all to the market: the provision of basic income or a reduction of working time and its redistribution over a larger number of employees. In a way, such options imply a modification of how unemployment is viewed socially. A cultural change is needed, similar to that in the 1930s when the Keynesian solution radically changed our understanding.

CONCLUSIONS

The transition out of Fordism is bringing about many changes in the nature of the employment relation. Some of these changes are dramatic for individuals and families who must abandon their well-rooted cultural background (which views labour as a crucial expression of human activity and think of jobs as lifelong commitments). However, we have shown that the required new attitude is not just a matter of cultural adaptation – a demanding task in itself; it also involves a material – that is, economic –

evaluation of changes: of the final outcome as opposed to the older situation, as well as of the transition implied. In other words, the welfare implications of this regulatory transformation must be taken into account.

The comparison of the economic characteristics of the two settings is not necessarily positive; on the contrary, for many it will turn out to be negative. This is true if we look at employment relations at the firm level: for example, from the workers' viewpoint flexibility may mean loss of job and salary, at least for a period, the length of which may depend on individual capacity to compete effectively on the labour 'market'. We have suggested that a person's willingness to accept change from her/his acquired position depends on whether the expected rewards in the future situation will be high enough compared to the expected rewards from maintaining the present position.

However, the process of valuation may not be limited to the internal structure of losses and gains. We have argued that change is more acceptable, the more that possible internal losses are compensated at the higher level of regulatory setting. Unfortunately, macro-economic constraints seem to make this opportunity occasional rather than strategic. In this framework, social conflict is an outcome that cannot be excluded *a priori*. Hence in this chapter we have emphasized that there is a need for social regulatory system design.

Measures for combating unemployment devised by policy-makers tend to rely upon market mechanisms which, when structural change is under way, are unlikely to work. Our final suggestion is to think of a new social and economic regulatory setting that would allow for non-market solutions to the welfare problems due to structural un(der)employment.

The right to labour, according to attitudes and aspirations, should not, at the turn of the century, be regarded as Utopian. We do not want to deny 'realist' considerations of system requirements and the necessity to cope with domestic and international constraints. Therefore, let the discussion on the technical details of a new labour and welfare system start soon.

NOTES

1. The idea of routines as truce has been somehow neglected, perhaps because of the industrialist tradition of the evolutionary stream.
2. Some personal interaction is implicit in any step of the decision-making process, from the identification of the problem and its context, to the choice of the decision rule and its implementation, to the possible adoption of adjustments. Skills, information networks, and the technology adopted constrain the strategy that management is willing to pursue; following Lazonick (1991), it is possible to use this evolutionary model to explain technology adoption that mirrors the distribution of internal comparative advantages to a segmented labour force. However, in the Fordist enterprise – but to a

lesser extent in other organizational settings, such as the J-firm – some levels can generally play a smaller role in defining the organizational adaptation of strategic and structural aspects through interaction. That someone has the power to take the final decision is also recognized by some careful standard economists; see Hart and Moore (1990) and Moore (1992).

3. Indeed, the adoption of a shared symbolic reference probably has a number of positive effects on the functioning of the organization: first, it permits only a limited amount of initial information to be exchanged (in a structure, and thus valuable, form), while reducing the processing and storing capability constraints of individuals; secondly, it provides a social norm which strengthens the integration of the structure by inducing a sense of belonging to the firm; thirdly, it reduces semantic ambiguity by inducing a collaborative spirit among people, which itself makes mutual understanding easier. On the other hand, organizational cultures and structures which are too sharply defined may hamper firms' capability to seize new opportunities; in fact, rigidity and incapabilities litter the story of business evolution (Lorsch, 1986).

4. See Nelson and Winter (1982). See also March (1981, p. 181): 'The mix of organizational foolishness and rationality is deeply embedded in rules, incentives and beliefs of society and the organization'. Even effective 'control methods' other than neoclassical direct monitoring (Alchian and Demsetz, 1972) – from peer control and reputation effects, to the design of a delayed incentive structure (as is the case of internal labour markets) and the losses connected to being fired by a specific firm (as in efficiency wage theories) – usually prove very effective. However, control as well as the design of an effective incentive/sanction structure are a constituent part of the routinization process. Their relative importance and effectiveness are likely to vary among tasks, depending on their specific characteristics; further, they also depend on members' cultures and subcultures, which equip people with 'different attitudes towards the responsibilities and rewards of organizational membership' (Nelson and Winter, 1982, p. 110).

5. Certainly the two approaches differ in many respects. Factor remuneration ($w/p = mpl$), according to standard economics, claims to be simultaneously fair and efficient; whenever this principle is invalidated, the reason can be traced to peculiar power positions (such as monopoly, ownership of specific goods, asymmetric information) that originate quasi-rents – as insiders oppose to outsiders in internal labour markets – and to second-best situations. Optimality, however, is at hand and is not reached only for some 'political' reasons. Any *best* is instead kept out in the evolutionary approach, as it may occur only by chance.

6. We refer to the non-formalized version proposed by the Italian sociologist Alberto Melucci (1991): he defines social production as the transformation activity of human environment.

7. The necessary conditions for which are the continuity of actors over time, through comparison of expected rewards in the different periods $[E_t(x) \leq E_{t+1}(x)]$; the social acknowledgement and identification of the counterpart's reasons according to the reference terms of the actor; perception of belonging of the 'product'.

8. In the few examples they quote, managers were concerned with changing attitudes of the organization (that is, of the staff in it); the greatest difficulty was to dissuade staff from inappropriate behaviour and to make them start thinking in terms of trust and fairness. In one case, the argument had extreme implications: in a steel plant, restructuring required the replacement of most personnel at various levels of hierarchy.

9. The choice of any 'commitment position' is based on some compromise between the behaviour one wishes to have, if free from any constraints, and the behaviour that s/he feels obliged to following according to pressures from moral feelings and interpersonal relationships: it reflects one's awareness of constraints. In fact, Leibenstein tries to sketch out a psychoanalytical theory of human behaviour, where the interiorized control that causes individuals to accomplish role obligations counters their instinctive craving for pleasure.

10. This is the level of distributive justice and of political action around it.

11. In the tradition of Chandler (1962, 1977, 1990).

12. For instance, while acknowledging the crucial role played by Ohno in triggering the success of Toyotism, Coriat (1991) recalls that from a social point of view it was necessary to defeat on several occasions during the 1950s the strong classist trade unions. Without such victories, it would probably not have been possible to reformulate successfully the terms of the value system, or to achieve wide consensus and co-operation through a *mix* of cultural elements (Morishima, 1984) and economic incentives (Koike, 1990; Aoki, 1984).

13. This aspect is highlighted by the growing non-material character of production, which excludes an objective evaluation of the product of work in favour of an ambiguous ability to *sell* one's competence; presentation of effort and results may override the 'real' terms, inhibiting incentive alignment. Bargaining over compensation and work practices becomes an action between persuasion and mediation (as it is for political action, indeed).

14. Garonna (1994) lists the following: vocational training and retraining programmes; supporting schemes for employment in the private sector and incentives for self-employment; general public services (employment agencies, counselling, mobility, and so on); direct employment in the public sector. In Europe, but not in Italy, demand-side policies are also implemented: in fact, they are industrial policies acting on local labour market characteristics.

15. We may stand for an increase of product-related services for customers, as is happening with some high-quality products; however, it is far from clear if this solution could apply to a wide range of medium-class commodities without boosting inflation.

16. We take the term from the French 'regulation school' (Aglietta, 1979; Boyer, 1985), though our use of the notion is possibly looser.

17. For instance, their purchasing capacity is reduced, leisure prospects will change, social appreciation and willingness to co-operate may be altered; see for instance Gallie *et al.* (1994).

18. This line of reasoning is an attempt to follow Sen's (1981) analysis of famines.

REFERENCES

Aglietta, M. (1979), *A Theory of Capitalist Regulation*, London: New Left Books.

Alchian, A. and Demsetz, H. (1972), 'Production, information costs, and economic organization', *American Economic Review*, **62**: 777–95.

Aoki, M. (ed.) (1984), *The Economic Analysis of the Japanese Firm*, Amsterdam: North-Holland.

Aoki, M. (1986), 'Horizontal vs. vertical information structure of the firm', *American Economic Review P&P*, **76**: 971–83.

Boyer, R. (1985), *Les Approches en termes de régulation: présentation et problèmes de méthode*, Paris: CEPREMAP.

Boyer, R. and Orleon, A. (1992), 'How do conventions evolve?', *Journal of Evolutionary Economics*, **2**, October: 165–77.

Chandler, A.D. (1962), *Strategy and Structure*, New York: Doubleday.

Chandler, A.D. (1977), *The Visible Hand*, Cambridge, Mass.: Harvard University Press.

Chandler, A.D. (1990), *Scale and Scope*, Cambridge, Mass.: Harvard University Press.

Coriat, B. (1991), *Ripensare l'organizzazione*, Bari: Dedalo.

Cyert, R. and March, J. (1963), *A Behavioural Theory of the Firm*, Englewood Cliffs, N.J.: Prentice-Hall.

Dopfer, K. (1994), 'How economic institutions emerge: institutional entrepreneurs and behavioural seeds', in Y. Shionoya and M. Perlman (eds), *Innovation, Technology and Institutions*, Ann Arbor, Mich.: University of Michigan Press.

Gallie, D., Marsh, C. and Vogler, C. (1994), *Social Change and the Experience of Unemployment*, Oxford: Oxford University Press.

Garonna, P. (1994), 'Introduction', in ISFOL (ed.), *Le prospettive OCSE per l'occupazione*, Milan: Angeli.

Granovetter, M. (1991), 'Economic institutions as social construct: a framework for analysis', paper presented to CREA Conference on 'Economics of Conventions', Paris, 27–28 March.

Harrison, J.R. and March, J.G. (1984), 'Decision-making and postdecision surprises', *Administrative Science Quarterly*, **29**: 26–42.

Hart, O. and Moore, J. (1990), 'Property rights and the nature of the firm', *Journal of Political Economy*, **6**: 1119–58.

Hendricks, K. (1991), 'Waste not, want not', interview by G. Gendron and B. Burlingham, *INC*, March: 33–42.

Hirschman, A.O. (1982), *Lealtà, defezione, protesta*, Milan: Bompiani, first published 1969.

Hobsbawm, E.J. (1972), *Studi di storia del movimento operaio*, Turin: Einaudi; Italian trans. of *Labouring Man* (1964).

Hodgson, G.M. (1988), *Economics and Institutions*, Oxford: Basil Blackwell; published in Italian as *Economia e istituzioni*, Ancona: Otium, 1991.

Kay, N.M. (1984), *The Emergent Firm*, London: Macmillan.

Koike, K. (1990), 'Intellectual skill and the role of employees as constituent members of large firms in contemporary Japan', in M. Aoki, B. Gustafsson and O.E. Williamson (eds), *The Firm as a Nexus of Treaties*, London: Sage, pp. 185–208.

Lazonick, W. (1991), *Competitive Advantage on the Shop Floor*, Cambridge, Mass.: Harvard University Press.

Le Goff, G. (1977), *Tempo della chiesa, tempo del mercante*, Turin: Einaudi.

Leibenstein, H. (1978), *Teoria Generale dell'Efficienza-X*, Turin: Rosenberg & Sellier.

Lorsch, J.W. (1986), 'Managing culture: the invisible barrier to strategic changes', in P.E. Earl (ed.), *Behavioural Economics*, Aldershot, Hants: Edward Elgar, pp. 419–33.

March, J.G. (1962), 'The business firm as a political coalition', *Journal of Politics*, **24**: 662–78.

March, J.G. (1981), 'Footnotes to organizational change', *Administrative Science Quarterly*, **26**: 563–77.

Melucci, A. (1991), *L'invenzione del presente*, Bologna: Il Mulino.

Moore, J. (1992), 'The firm as a collection of assets', *European Economic Review*, **36**, April: 493–507.

Morishima, M. (1984), *Cultura e tecnologia nel 'successo' giapponese*, Bologna: Il Mulino.

Nelson, R.R. and Winter, S.G. (1982), *An Evolutionary Theory of Economic Change*, Cambridge, Mass.: Harvard University Press.

Polanyi, K. (1974), *La grande trasformazione*, Turin: Einaudi.

Postrel, S. and Rumelt, R.P. (1992), 'Incentives, routines and self-command', *Industrial and Corporate Change*, **1** (3): 397–425.

Prahalad, C.K. and Hamel, G. (1990), 'The core competence of the corporation', *Harvard Business Review*, **68** (3): 79–91.

Rangone, M. (1997), 'An institutional theory of individual labour supply', University of Padua, mimeo.

Sen, A. (1981), *Poverty and Famines: An Essay on Entitlements and Deprivation*, Oxford: Clarendon Press.

Simon, H.A. (1951), 'A formal theory of the employment relationship', *Econometrica*, **19**: 293–305.

Steidlmeier, P. (1993), 'Institutional approaches in strategic management', *Journal of Economic Issues*, **27** (1): 189–211.

Thompson, E.P. (1981), *Società patrizia, cultura plebea*, Turin: Einaudi original version: 'Time, work-discipline, and industrial capitalism', *Past and Present*, **38** [1967]).

Tool, M.R. (1994), 'Social cost and social values', paper presented at the EAEPE conference, Copenhagen, 27–29 October.

Veblen, T. (1914), *The Instinct of Workmanship and the State of Industrial Arts*, New York: Macmillan.

Vivarelli, M. (1995), *The Economics of Technology and Employment*, Aldershot, Hants: Edward Elgar.

West, C.T. (1994), 'The problem of unemployment in the United States: a survey of 60 years of national and state policy initiatives', *International Regional Science Review*, **16** (1–2): 17–47.

10. Creating your own job: the behaviour of micro-business households in the risk society

Jane Wheelock and Susan Baines

Home is the place where, when you have to go there,
They have to take you in.
Robert Frost 'The Death of the Hired Man'

INTRODUCTION: CREATING A LIVELIHOOD

Strong political and economic forces are at work to expand the number of households dependent – entirely or in part – on small business activity. These include the changes towards more 'flexible' labour markets (with poorer pay and conditions for those at the lower end of the income scale), organizational changes in large businesses with downsizing and the 'hollowing out of the corporation', and the cutting back and restructuring of the welfare state. As we approach the end of the millennium, more and more productive work is being undertaken in the 'new' and 'less encumbered' organizational form of micro-businesses.[1] Under these conditions it is increasingly the household which manages business organization risk. This chapter is about the ways in which these structural changes are played out in the daily lives of a group of British households in which people have taken the risks involved in starting micro-businesses. They are people who have, as exhorted by government, created their own jobs and, sometimes, employed others as well.

The analysis is based on a 32-month study of micro-businesses in the business services sector in two contrasting enterprise environments in Britain.[2] We examine the survival, maintenance and growth of the micro-business, and argue that these cannot be understood without developing an understanding of the relationship with the household (or households) in which the business person is based. In focusing on business behaviour in this context, we are going to the heart of a key aspect of the evolution of organizational change taking place in the 'risk society' (Beck, 1992): the growth of micro-businesses as a source of livelihood against a background of insecurity in employment and of unemployment.

Undertaking research at the level of the household and its members provides an essential counterweight to ideas that the household (or the micro-business) can be modelled as though a single economically rational individual were acting as proxy for all (for example, Becker, 1993). Individual behaviour is, rather, the outcome of complex processes of interaction within both household and micro-business depending upon social relations and the status of gender, generation, business ownership and earning capacity in the labour market, for example. In addition, an economically rational behaviour will be complemented and modified by other concerns. Actions may be based on traditional or patriarchal reasoning, people have a need for dignity and self-respect, a need to care and nurture (see Wheelock and Oughton, 1996). There is a further analytical significance in starting from the household. It is particularly by examining the economic character of the household that we can investigate the borderline between the formal and the complementary (or informal) economy, the latter comprising unmeasured economic activity (Wheelock, 1992a). The changing nature of this borderline lies at the heart of household business interaction in handling risk.

Drawing on a regulationist framework, we start by placing the forces that underlie the growth in the number of micro-businesses – economic restructuring, ideological support for the market as a mechanism for distributing resources, and policies to promote an enterprise culture based on small business – into a thumbnail macro-level analysis of economic change. Economists have usually focused on the importance of incentives to the functioning of the capitalist economic system. They have tended to ignore the other side of that coin: the effects of the insecurity that a system built on market-based incentives inevitably induces. In focusing on the experience of households gaining their livelihoods from micro-business, the rewards for risks taken may be finely balanced against experiences of insecurity. The first section outlines the empirical study of micro-businesses which forms the basis of the argument. It illustrates – mainly from questionnaire data – some of the ways in which new micro-businesses in Britain show continuities with old ways of working, under pressure from the labour market and responding to the risks and opportunities provided by a restructuring economy.

In the following section Beck's (1992) analysis of risk in relation to individual and family behaviour is outlined. Drawing upon detailed in-depth interviews with a subset of questionnaire respondents we indicate that business services micro-businesses can be classified into four different groupings, each of which has developed a particular pattern for handling risk. We provide evidence from each group: survival and security, business intrinsic, creative, and achievement. In doing so, we make use of what Stanfield (drawing on Polanyi) calls a substantive institutionalist methodology, to draw out the economic character of actors in their social context (Stanfield, 1982; Polanyi, 1946). The conclusions draw together suggestions on how the variety of ways in which people reunify their lives and their work allow us to make generalizations about the links between the formal and the informal, or complementary, economy. This provides a perspective on how a regulationist framework can be extended to incorporate the household, by making use of insights from an institutionalist approach.

RISK, INSECURITY AND THE RETURN TO OLD WAYS OF WORKING

The regulationist school contends that the forces of production must be understood in conjunction with the principles by which social relations are regulated. History can then be periodized according to successive 'regimes of accumulation', each underpinned by a set of supporting rules and social practices called a 'mode of regulation'. From this perspective on the contemporary western world, capitalism has been undergoing a complex process of restructuring in which the mass production and consumption which characterized the late 1940s to the early 1970s – 'Fordism' – is now being replaced by a new 'regime of accumulation', sometimes labelled 'neo-' or, more usually, 'post-Fordism'. Faced with declining profitability, Fordist corporations instigated changes in the labour process, in what has been graphically labelled as a process of 'hollowing out'. Relocation of manufacturing activities to Third World countries with a 'new international division of labour', subcontracting to smaller companies, and a variety of forms of flexible working practices were used to help stem the fall in profitability. Characteristic of this regime, then, is increased fragmentation and flexibility in the organization of work, and the production and consumption of goods and services. Hollowed-out corporations have delegated risk further down the line: to subcontractors, to smaller firms, to a more flexible workforce, to the self-employed. Yet although there has been much analysis of management and delegation within large firms as a means of controlling the labour process, and of how this has changed with the fragmentation of large enterprise, there has been much less on the impact on small firms and micro-business, and it is notable that there has been little attempt to extend such concepts and models to the level of the household and the family.

Jessop (1994) argues that the state, in response to this restructuring process, has developed a new set of tactics for securing the regime of accumulation, and the post-Fordist state can be seen as a Schumpeterian workfare one. This means that a hollowing-out of the state parallels that of the corporation, with governments arguing that intervention simply distorts the market mechanism. The economic ideology of the market makes a virtue of insecurity: for markets, so the argument goes, operate best when there are incentives for personal gain or the avoidance of loss. The state now tends to intervene on the supply side, in the interests of promoting a market economy and an enterprise culture.[3] Indeed, throughout the 1980s small business start-up was heavily promoted in the UK as a solution to national economic problems and to individual employment needs. Here, for example, are the words of one typical UK government publication:

> Over 400,000 people a year were prepared to take the risks involved in starting a business, reflecting a real change in attitudes towards the small firms sector and towards enterprise generally. Over the decade there were, in total, just under two million new VAT registrations and a net total increase 370,000. Self-employment rose by over 70% to around 3.25 million. (Department of Employment, 1992, p. 5)

The increase in self-employment in the UK between 1979 and 1989 was more than three times the European Union average. At the beginning of the 1980s one in ten of the UK labour force were self-employed. By the beginning of the 1990s this had risen to one in eight. However, despite hopes that micro-businesses would begin to sweep up large numbers of the unemployed, it was self-employed people without employees whose numbers rose most dramatically (Campbell and Daly, 1992). People were certainly creating their own jobs, but the capacity of the newly self-employed to create jobs for others proved much more limited than had been anticipated. Indeed, research has demonstrated that only a tiny minority of new small businesses ever grow to become significant employers (Storey, 1994). We now overview some of the main characteristics of the livelihoods created by people who were, in the words of the Department of Employment, 'prepared to take the risks involved in starting a business'. We consider their uneven capacities to create employment for others, and we see what the underside of those risks may mean by indicating some of the ways in which these changes confirm old ways of family working.

Families in Business?

The empirical study investigated the characteristics, and the survival, maintenance and growth of business service businesses in two contrasting urban locations: Newcastle upon Tyne in the north-east of England and Milton Keynes in the south-east. A particular concern of the study was to tease out the interaction between businesses and families. An earlier pilot study of small businesses, conducted by one of the authors, Jane Wheelock, had found that business survival appeared to be associated with a very specific kind of competitive advantage based on the presence of the family (Wheelock, 1992b). That study was conducted in Wearside in the north-east of England. It seemed possible that the resort to proto-typically pre-modern practices in order to survive in a modern economy might have been specific to a locality characterized by the severe decline of traditional industries and by lack of employment opportunity. Very little evidence was available from other research with which to make comparisons across different kinds of location, for it is rare for academic or policy-orientated enquiries into small businesses in industrialized urban settings to concentrate on, or even to notice, the household and family. The locations of Newcastle upon Tyne and Milton Keynes, therefore, were chosen for their contrasting socio-economic environments.[4]

Businesses interviewed had all been trading for at least two years. It must be stressed that the businesses in this study were a representative sample of *surviving* businesses in the selected locations, size band and sector. New firms which die in the first two years of life were not included. The average size (by employment) of businesses interviewed was 3.5 (including owners), and the sample included 30 per cent that consisted only of one owner without employees or partners. The average age of the businesses was 7.24 years in 1994: as many as two-thirds (66.3 per cent) were founded between 1980 and 1989, in the political and economic climate of the 1980s with its pressures on individuals to create their own jobs.

A telephone survey delineated the broad contours of formal family involvement in micro-businesses in each location. The hypothesis that familial involvement would be most characteristic of the less-advantaged location was not confirmed. Numbers of businesses formally involving husband and wife in some way (either as co-owners or employees) proved to be extremely similar across locations, at 30 per cent in Milton Keynes and 33 per cent in Newcastle. Businesses formally involving *any* family member were also similarly represented in each location (39 per cent in Milton Keynes and 41 per cent in Newcastle). Thus a significant minority (40 per cent) of the micro-businesses in both locations were 'family businesses' in the sense that they formally involved family members as co-owners or employees, and by far the most common family relationship in business was husband and wife.[5] For most of the rest of the analysis reported in this chapter the two locations are treated together.

The other results we draw upon for the analysis in the rest of the chapter are based on the more detailed and context-sensitive information obtained from the two stages of face-to-face interviews which were conducted with subsets of the 200 telephone respondents. The first of these stages was an interviewer-administered questionnaire with 104 owner-managers. In this, details of employment background, household situation and reasons for business start-up as well as extensive information on divisions of labour and sources of help and support in business and domestic life were collected. Although the questionnaire was mainly in multiple-choice format, open-ended questions were also asked about attitudes to business growth and to support networks. The final stage was designed to extend and deepen understanding at these more difficult and sensitive levels. It consisted of in-depth interviews with owner-managers (and where possible another significant person in the business) of 34 of the businesses already interviewed. People were invited to talk in detail through critical incidents in the recent life of their families and their businesses (Chell, forthcoming), and from the taped interview transcripts obtained it was possible to uncover motives and values, and relate these to family interaction and to business survival, maintenance and growth.

The background to business start-up for business owners in each location is given in Figure 10.1. Unemployment of founders[6] prior to start-up was, unsurprisingly given the relative prosperity of the two locations,

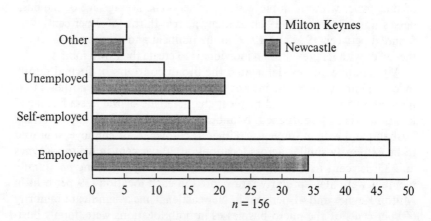

Figure 10.1 Employment status prior to start-up (all owners)

more prevalent in the Newcastle sample. However, when respondents were asked to indicate their reasons for start-up, the locational difference almost disappears. By far the most popular stated reason for business start-up in both locations was 'to be my own boss' (Table 10.1). Respondents were also asked to sum up their reasons for business start-up using one of three broad motivations: 'business positive', 'employment negative' or 'domestic'. Factors pulling people into business – both positive attitudes to business and the more positive circumstances of starting up from some other job – appear to predominate. Yet in terms of employment creation, business owners who said they had started their businesses for employment negative reasons were only slightly less likely than the 'business positive' to have become employers of others (Table 10.2).

Out of the sample of 104, 40 micro-businesses had no employees at the time of the interview. Of these, just over a quarter (11) had employed at least one person in the past. Some had employed considerably more. Movement between the employing and non-employing categories was frequent in both directions. General insecurity in the labour market appears to be reflected in the employing patterns of micro-businesses. The 104

Table 10.1 Reasons for business start-up, by location

Reason for start-up	Milton Keynes n = 50	Newcastle n = 54	All n = 104
Be my own boss	33 (66.0%)	33 (61.0%)	66 (63.5%)
Increase earnings	19 (38.0%)	15 (27.85)	34 (32.7%)
Develop business idea	14 (28.0%)	18 (33.3%)	32 (30.8%)
Dissatisfaction with job	17 (34.0%)	16 (29.6%)	33 (31.7%)
Unemployment	11 (22.0%)	12 (22.2%)	23 (22.1 %)
Job insecure	6 (12.0%)	5 (9.3%)	11 (10.6 %)
Domestic/personal	12 (24.0%)	7 (13.0%)	19 (18.3 %)
Other	4 (8.0%)	6 (11.1%)	10 (9.6 %)

Table 10.2 Creation of jobs, by reasons for business start-up

No. currently employed by business	Business-positive n = 58	Employment-negative n = 25
None	19 (32.8%)	10 (40.0%)
At least one	39 (67.2%)	15 (60.0%)

The world of work

questionnaire respondents were invited to talk in their own words about plans and opportunities for the growth of their businesses in the immediate future. Business owners' 'intentions to grow', in order of prevalence, were: 'growth rejecting' (39 per cent) who do not intend to grow at all; 'growth ambivalent' (29 per cent) who may grow in the longer term; and 'growth enthusiastic' (25 per cent) who are actively pursuing some employment growth. Finally, a small group (8 per cent) intend to expand their sales but emphatically without more direct employment (Baines *et al.*, 1997). Yes, those setting up micro-businesses were prepared to take the risk themselves, but they had very limited intentions with regard to the employment of others.

This contrasts with the work that micro-businesses provide for family members: 40 respondents (representing 46 per cent of those with domestic partners) reported what we describe as 'very high' involvement of that partner in the business. These 40 out of 104 businesses are husband/wife businesses in the sense of either being co-owned by husband and wife (21) or employing the owner's spouse (13) or having very substantial unpaid *daily* practical input from a spouse (6). When the cases reporting some form of unpaid contribution to the business by an owner's spouse are added to these cases of 'very high' involvement, as many as three-quarters of the businesses in which the respondent lived with a spouse may be described as, in some way, husband/wife businesses.

The division of labour in business between family members tended to follow traditional gender lines. Of 21 spouse-owned businesses, there were only four cases in which both owners were full-time and working in a professional or management role. Much more typical were instances of co-owning wives working in a clerical or administrative capacity. There were 13 instances of wives employed in businesses owned by their husbands, but none of husbands employed by their wives. The roles of employed wives were even more gender stereotypical than those of co-owning wives. Unpaid support for the business by spouses also tended to follow traditional gender roles, but less straightforwardly than more formal involvement. Male domestic partners of female sole traders were found to be supportive of their wives.

Overall, then, the division of business tasks between husband and wife was traditional, with wives, whether co-owners, employees or unpaid helpers, characteristically performing the support and service roles associated with women in the labour force as a whole. Cases reflecting recently popularized, idealistic images of 'co-preneurial' couples (Barnett and Barnett, 1988) in business partnership were rare. Businesses owned by spouses, or in which spouses were highly involved, were by no means trivial enterprises but they were, overall, less likely to be growth-enthusiastic than other businesses (see Table 10.3).

Table 10.3 Spouse involvement, by attitudes to business growth

Spouse involvement	Growth rejecting $n = 40$	Growth ambivalent $n = 30$	Non-employment growth $n = 8$	Growth enthusiastic $n = 26$
Very high	18 (45.0%)	10 (33.3%)	5 (62.5%)	7 (26.9%)
Moderate or none	22 (55.0%)	20 (66.7%)	3 (37.5%)	19 (73.1%)

The common practice of working long and inconvenient hours further underlines micro-business activity as a return to old ways of working, rather than as the dawn of any new set of entrepreneurial values. Hours worked were generally long and flexible. Respondents were asked to indicate the weekly hours worked by them and their business partners in a 'typical' and a 'busy' week. Many insisted that there was no such thing as a 'typical' week and the figure given was an estimated average which inevitably masks the unevenness of the workload. Nearly half (47 per cent) report working 48 hours or more in a typical week. In a busy week 69 per cent of owners worked 48 hours or more. Hours could be unsocial as well as long, with 60 per cent reporting working evenings and 55 per cent weekends on a frequent and regular basis.

Let us now put some flesh on the bones of these figures by drawing upon two case studies from the in-depth interviews to bring together the themes of employment opportunities (or lack of them) and, very centrally, the ways in which the marital relationship and the development of a business can be intimately interrelated. To make this point most strongly, we have selected one case of a joint husband and wife business, and one in which support for the business by the owner's spouse is relatively limited. We shall take the latter first.

One of the starkest statements of how hard the pressures can be comes from Pauline, sole owner of a Milton Keynes home-based secretarial business, and mother of a one-year-old son:

> If I've got the work, I have to do it, and that could mean working through until 4 o'clock in the morning, if necessary. You can't afford to turn work away, to cover a lean time, so in a lot of cases that can mean really long hours for me, and fitting it round Danny and the family and the house can be a stress and my husband can get fed up with me sometimes, and Danny does as well [long pause]   I don't feel power from it, I don't feel proud, I don't feel anything. It's just a vehicle for me being able to have money. If we didn't need the income I wouldn't be doing it.

The urgency for Pauline to earn money had recently been intensified when Jack, her husband, was suddenly made redundant and was only able to earn a very modest wage from temporary work. Pauline's narrative focuses upon a series of stresses around the combination of income earning and caring work. She had originally set up the business in the hope that it would offer her flexibility to work from home while caring for the baby. Pauline's words above demonstrate that this hope had not been fulfilled. The unpredictability of her clients' requirements and the desperate need to bring money into the household meant that Pauline felt obliged to take on any work offered to her.

A range of options were discussed between Pauline and Jack including the possibility of Jack giving up his poorly paid work and looking after the child full-time while Pauline concentrated on the business. To an outsider such a strategy would appear to be the rational choice in the light of the income earning opportunities of each of the couple. Yet it was not the path chosen:

> My husband was under stress because he wasn't earning money, so here was I doing really well, having to maintain all our expenditure and him feeling . . . [pause]   He's an old fashioned sort of guy. He feels that as a man he should be the bread winner, and I was earning a hell of a lot more than he was. It put a strain on us and that.

Pauline was working for the survival of her business and her family's livelihood under very difficult conditions, with extremely high monthly outgoings as a result of an old business debt. In the longer term she plans for her business to grow and to employ others. The first employee will be her sister-in-law, whose hard work and conscientiousness she knows she can trust. Pauline's story captures how intimately the lives and livelihoods of husband and wife can be entwined in the business venture of one partner, even in a case in which levels of direct support for the business by the owner's partner are low.

Let us now look at the differences and similarities in a husband and wife co-owned business. Tom founded the marketing and design business after his redundancy, but in common with others who set up in business following unemployment, he stressed some of the positive motivations for business ownership in his answers to the questionnaire survey. His words in the in-depth interview a year later are sadder and more pessimistic:

> TOM: If I had known then [at start-up] what I know now, I might, the chances are I wouldn't have gone down that route, I would have gone back into the market place, looked, to see what er [pause]
> INTERVIEWER: Right, and why is that, is it because of the stress and the struggle of having to find new clients to replace old ones?

Tom: Well, I think it's been, you know, you, you sort of get built up and knocked down, and you build yourself up and get knocked down, and build yourself up and get knocked down –

Marie: And you sometimes think – like when you're not well – and you think, yeah, well if I worked somewhere I'd just report in sick, but when it's your own company you have to keep going.

Marie is co-owner, but speaks of their business as Tom's. She has worked in the business and in the labour market and sometimes both at once, according to business and household needs. We saw from the survey work that, overall, wives who participate in business alongside their husbands typically play a supporting role to the husband's professional or craft skills. Marie follows this pattern. She has taken on business tasks for which she had no taste, aptitude or prior training. Marie is responsible for learning and using the new technology which the business acquired. This is arduous and frustrating for her, yet without the new technology she and her husband are sure that the business could not have continued to compete in a rapidly changing business environment.

In Marie's story we once again see tension between the needs of a business and of a spouse, this time with a different resolution:

Interviewer: What about you, Marie, I mean did you always want to be part of a small business?

Marie: No, not at all. I was perfectly happy working where I worked, but it's just that Tom couldn't do it on his own. [pause] If I'd have remained in full-time employment I would probably have a much better job than I've got now, working part-time, erm, but, that's the commitment we took on, and just continue.

Tom: Yes.

Marie: I mean one of us can't pack up without the other, so –

Tom: I mean had, had Marie not have done that then I would've been forced to consider employing somebody if only part-time, which would have been –

Marie: Which wouldn't have worked out, employing somebody working from here, working from home.

Together: Which wouldn't have worked .[7]

The balance between Marie's own needs and those of the business is difficult and clearly she feels on one level that she has made personal sacrifices. On another level her words convey the conviction that it is inappropriate to view the situation from her individual career perspective because the business *is* herself and Tom.

Overall then, both from the questionnaire data and from the personal narratives, the importance of the husband and wife 'team' to the survival and maintenance of the micro-business is apparent. When a spouse does not support a business, or does so only half-heartedly, the result can be distressing in the extreme. At the same time, employment growth is actively pursued only by a minority of all the micro-businesses interviewed.

It is apparent that the exhilarating rhetoric of the Department of Employment quoted above describes only very partially the actual experiences of individuals and their families, as more and more households become reliant upon micro-business activity for all or part of their income. An alternative characterization of the same changes would be that the buck stops with the vastly increased numbers of those who are made redundant or unemployed. Economic and political change have restructured the incidence of risk towards the individual within the household as an institution. Micro-business activity frequently relies on a return to distinctly old ways of working: traditional gender roles, long hours of work with low monetary returns (see also Wheelock, 1992b).

THE RISK SOCIETY IN MICROCOSM: SMALL BUSINESS HOUSEHOLD BEHAVIOUR

Ulrich Beck, from his perspective as an industrial and a family sociologist, drew together his ideas in *The Risk Society* in 1992. There is much in his discussion of 'the new modernity' that can be used to illuminate the variety of solutions which we found micro-businesses adapting in the face of risk and insecurity. Beck argues that the contemporary logic of risk production and its distribution can be contrasted with the production and distribution of wealth. The social production of wealth is nowadays systematically accompanied by that of risks. As people are 'set free' from the certainties and modes of living of the industrial epoch, individuals can reflexively construct their own identities. There is much that is familiar here from the themes of the small-business literature which emphasizes 'being your own boss' as an important factor for many setting up in business. The analysis of our in-depth interviews shows that this is only one part of a much more complex story.

Indeed, as we hope to demonstrate in this section, many of the stories which arise from the patterns of interaction between small business and the household seem more concerned with overcoming the individualization of social insecurity that Beck highlights so much in his work. Beck redefines what he see as an old-fashioned idea of inequality in terms of the individualization of social risks. He talks of the individual mobility and the mobile individual required by the modern labour market. This means that a spiral of individualization takes hold inside the family as the demands of the labour market, education and mobility are felt by individual members of households: 'There is a hidden contradiction between the mobility demands of the labour market and social bonds' (Beck, 1992, p. 94). The problems of the system, argues Beck, become understood in terms of personal failures. Thus, 'total industrialisation, total commercialisation and families in the traditional role are mutually exclusive'. We now show how a variety of adaptations by micro-business owners and their households to the 'old ways of working' can provide opportunities for overcoming such contradictions. On the other hand, argues Beck, continuing mass unemployment and the limited capabilities of the labour market conserve and restabilize the traditional roles and responsibilities of men and women. As already suggested, this is certainly one of the forms that returning to old ways of working takes within the micro-business household.

For Marx, writing in the middle of the nineteenth century, the individual was cushioned by his or her collective experience. The first section has documented that, in the case of micro-business households, it is usually the domestic partnership of husband and wife which provides the collectivity. As we shall see in a moment, in some circumstances we can perhaps argue that spouses are reflexively constructing their own biographies; in others the risk produced in modern society is distributed so unevenly that there is a much more passive relation with biography. We have already caught sight of some of these struggles in the lives of Pauline and Tom. So to what extent are people able to reunify life and work in micro-business households, and how do they do it?

In-depth interviews with owners of a subset of 34 of the original businesses enabled us to pursue the interaction between businesses and families in daily life. At this level of enquiry it is clearly demonstrated that household and business are often economically and functionally interconnected by the need to prioritize the use of limited material, but particularly human, resources. The extent to which this necessity is welcomed or resisted by business owners and their families varies greatly, however.

Many and varied experiences were described to us but for the purposes of analysis they can be grouped into four sets of overriding concerns and priorities. These are: 'survival and security', where satisfactions beyond providing or contributing to a living for the owner/s and family are barely in evidence; 'business intrinsic', where satisfaction in the ownership and running of a business is associated with personal independence, producing good work and serving clients' needs; 'intrinsic creative', where there is a creative output and very strong emphasis on and pride in creativity; and, finally, 'achievement', where there is an expressed and demonstrated capacity to seek out and face business challenges.

The survival and security group (with 8 out of 34 businesses: see Table 10.4) experience relentless pressure to offer 'flexibility' in the form of long

Table 10.4 *Characteristic behaviour of micro-business owners*

Priorities and concerns	Family	Employment / partnerships	Networking	Growth
Survival/security (8 businesses)	The labour of family members is used. Family members earn income outside to keep up household needs. There may be tension between these and domestic and caring needs which is difficult to manage. There can be stress on traditional gender roles.	The main resource is the labour of the owner and sometimes the spouse. When there is a 'feast' of work, working longer hours is usual. Where there are employees there is much informality.	Some complain of loneliness and seek support of 'work like' organizations; otherwise there is relatively low network activity.	Opportunities are limited. Where domestic responsibilities are a barrier to business development the situation is usually seen as temporary and there can be well thought out long-term future plans.
Intrinsic business (11 businesses)	There is a tendency to seek physical and emotional separation between business and family.	This is the most successful of groups in establishing smooth employment relations.	Some networking is practised for business development and personal support.	Some have grown to the level the owners want. Others seek some growth, but usually quite limited.
Intrinsic creative (8 businesses)	Respondents report, more commonly than in any other group, a harmonious integration between business and personal and family life.	Owners' self-worth is so involved in the business activity that it can be very difficult to incorporate others.	Networks within a specific subsector are most likely to be valued.	Business development and creativity can sit uneasily together. Some have growth potential which is not being fulfilled because of problems encountered or feared around bringing new people into the business.
Achievement (7 businesses)	Family and business are more detached than for any other group. In extreme cases there is conflict between business and family with painful consequences.	Owners recognize a need to employ and sometimes bring in partners but these processes are often fraught with conflict over responsibilities, roles and demands.	Network very energetically and proactively.	Owners are willing to sacrifice independence by seeking outside expertise but difficulty in managing relationships with business partners and employees prevents smooth path to growth.

hours of work with precarious financial rewards. For these business owners there can be uncomfortable tensions between business and family life, yet the support of their spouses, and more rarely other family members, often makes such flexibility sustainable. A few hope for some growth in employment in the longer term, but it is rarely an immediate objective. They do not court risk. On the contrary, their behaviour is devoted to minimizing so far as possible the extreme riskiness of their circumstances. At the other end of the scale, businesses in the achievement group (comprising seven businesses) usually express enthusiasm for growth which, in a few instances, is growth without direct employment. Achievement-orientated business owners are least likely to call upon family support and most likely to take financial and other risks willingly, even in some cases describing risk as exhilarating and enjoyable.

Enthusiasm for growth is rarer but not entirely absent from the business-intrinsic (11 businesses) and the creative groups (8). The business-intrinsic tend to strive for, and may attain, a separation of family and business. It is characteristic of the creative to express a very positive attitude to integrating their personal relationships and their work, but to recount extreme difficulty with incorporating other people outside their family into the objectives and values of their business. Neither of these groups relishes risk, but they do enjoy the independence of the way they earn their livelihoods.

Survival and Security Group

The main resource for these businesses is the owner/s' own labour, sometimes supplemented by that of his or her spouse and, more rarely, other family members and one or two employees. Owners are beset by 'feast and famine' in terms of workload. Self-exploitation in the form of extremely long and often inconvenient hours of work is characteristically practised to compete in business. The experiences already reported by Tom and Marie and by Pauline are characteristic of this group.

In Don's story very similar pressure is resolved rather differently in that he describes making a choice to prioritize his wife's career. Nevertheless, his narrative brings out the reactive way in which he constructs his own and his family's biography. We see him searching for a way of providing meaning in difficult circumstances. Don started his training and consultancy business because he was made redundant when the voluntary organization which had employed him underwent rationalization. His former employer then bought in his services on a contract basis – a classic case of a 'hollowed-out' organization. Don has begun to build up a clientele through his extensive local networks. He knows that there are opportunities to develop his business further, but to seize them would involve financial risks which he is unwilling to take. He offers two explanations for his aversion to risk-taking: one is his working-class family background – 'I was brought up to go down the pit, basically, and not to be entrepreneurial', the other is his commitment to the needs of his wife and child.

Don's wife was pursuing a separate career plan by taking a degree course and, after the birth of their baby, he gave up his office premises and moved the business into the family home in order to save money to pay for child-care. Don feels very keenly his wife's lack of engagement with his business. His distress at this and his perception that a different response to the business on the part of his wife could have promoted a much more successful enterprise are brought into sharp relief in the following speech in which he talks of a competitor who was once a friend and confidant:

> But one of the key differences, advantages that they've got, is that his partner is his partner in the business, and they've got no children. So they have got between them about 80/90 hours a week that they invest in the business, person hours, you know. They do two 40 hour weeks, and the rest probably, because they don't go home. They work over the weekend. If they're not actually physically working for a customer, they're thinking about the business. I've got – me. I haven't got anyone else helping and erm, er, and I've got other responsibilities to this because [my wife] isn't involved in it. When I'm with [my wife] we have to talk about other things, you know.

Don now accepts that he does not aspire to employ people. Here he talks of the personal experiences which led him to reject employment growth as an objective:

> I'm retreating from the notion of a very ambitious three-year plan and, you know, targets about doubling turnover and employing people. I've definitely retreated from that. Again that, that model was driven by my experience with [the husband and wife business owners referred to above]. It was their model. Erm, and it would be lovely in many ways but it would be very difficult. It would be hard, it would be stressful. [pause] Actually, I want to be home with the baby now, you know.

Don has found from experience with his family and his business that his own values, abilities and ambitions do not fit what he has been *told by others* is an appropriate model for a new small business. He cites as endorsement of his changed ideas, not an individual known to him personally, but the popular management writer Charles Handy: 'It's like the Charles Handy model of the future. I'm quite impressed. I read that, I thought, Christ I'm already that!'. He now feels that he has the confidence to pursue his business livelihood in a way which is home-based and family-centred.

Note how it is the stress of having to rely on themselves alone, not the freedom of independence, of which Don, Pauline and Tom and Marie speak. Although the bitter disillusion with business life expressed by Tom and Marie is extreme, it is characteristic of the survival and security group to emphasize relentless pressure to offer 'flexibility' in the form of long hours with precarious financial rewards. The owners in our study whose business lives were dominated by the quest for survival and security have self-employed status which, as some commentators have noted, suggests personal autonomy which is not real (Jones *et al.*, 1994). Nevertheless, respondents were often resolutely optimistic about the future. They commonly observed that business, with all its struggles, was preferable to unemployment and to poorly paid, insecure, stressful employment.

Business intrinsic group

Let us now hear from an owner who certainly wants a livelihood and security but for whom, in contrast to Pauline, Tom and Marie, and Don, there are also definite rewards intrinsic to the ownership and running of a business:

> Out of the business, well personally I want a job until I retire, which [pause] – that's what everybody wants – even if they're working for someone else [pause] and I also get a lot of satisfaction out of working for myself. If anything went wrong tomorrow I think I, I would be able to get a job back in the industry but I'm not sure how happy I'd be getting a job back in industry. Working for somebody else. I've worked for myself for about ten years now. (Guy, Newcastle printer, sole trader employing two)

For Guy there is much satisfaction in the independence of the kind summed up in the well-worn phrase 'being my own boss'. A few business owners also articulate a related but stronger pleasure which cannot quite adequately be conveyed in such terms. The business is valued as something they themselves created. Vic not only expresses this feeling for himself but is also sure, from his interaction with other business owners, that it is a value he holds in common with many of them:

> It's not just economics. Nobody in their right mind would run small businesses! But there's just something else. [pause] It's this idea that [pause] I don't want to earn a lot of money but you might just do so bloody well that we, you know, that we get really rich. I mean there's that element in the background. It doesn't preoccupy it. I'm sure it does preoccupy people for a time [long pause] but it's also the fact that if you do it you'll have done it yourself, and it's you, it's your mind and your ability to do things, the ability to sort of create it. (Vic, Newcastle printer employing five)

The words of Guy and Vic are illustrative of the much-celebrated 'independence' of business owners. A theme running throughout the literature on small firms is the overwhelming desire of business owners for 'independence'. The priority placed upon independence is called upon in explanation of business owners' relationships (or lack of them) with other business owners and organizations (Curran and Blackburn, 1994), of their reluctance to seek growth (Gray, 1995) and, indeed, of their very propensity to become business owners (Stanworth *et al.*, 1989). From the accounts we have collected from business service businesses, it is not micro-businesses as a whole but the distinctive subgroup whose motivations and values are 'business intrinsic' who overwhelmingly articulate their 'independence'.

An aspect of business owners' independence emphasized by Curran and Blackburn (1994) is their extreme reluctance to seek any form of support or help from outside agencies. According to evidence presented by those authors, such reluctance extends also to involving families in business. As we have seen, this is not a useful way to describe the relationship of business and family for the business owners we interviewed who were dominated by survival and security. Their businesses and families were so interconnected that it is almost impossible to talk about them as separate entities. There is evidence from our interviews, however, that the owners for whom the pleasures and satisfactions in business life are 'business intrinsic' do behave in ways more like those described by Curran and Blackburn. These owners often strive for, and may achieve, a separation of family and business.

The businesses in the business-intrinsic group are characteristically small employers and their employment relations are generally smoother than for any other group. They do indeed create their own jobs, and the value they place on their independence fits in with the policy rhetoric, but their lack of any dynamic growth contradicts policy objectives that small business can take any economic lead in revitalizing local economies.

Creative Group

Independence is important to the creative business owners, as it is for the 'business intrinsic' group, but it is most characteristically a very different form of independence associated with the freedom to do their best creative work. The spirit of business as a vehicle for creativity is well expressed in this longish extract from an interview with Gerry, a specialist design artist,[8] and his wife Judy, who is company secretary:

> GERRY: It's not just to make lots of money. I mean there's more money to be made in other areas. I could do something else to make more money, but, erm, I just want, you know, a bit, I want to be recognized as, you know,

being a – being part of the British design industry and doing good work. I mean British [design in my specialist area] is respected worldwide and, you know, I think I'm capable of doing [pause]

JUDY: I don't – I would feel that money's not been Gerry's driving – . If, if, you know, if it was, I think he would have given up a long, long time ago. That's my feeling. Gerry's driving force is to be seen to be good at what he does and for the right kind of people, because he won't just deal with anybody.

GERRY: No.

JUDY: He doesn't deal with everybody. I mean, if he could, there's lots of things he could have taken that would have compromised [pause]

We see from this extract how closely husband and wife are together engaged in the business's aims and ideals (although Judy herself has a separate career). These ideals include a desire for growth, but only if this is compatible with creativity recognized by his peers. Although he employs three people, Gerry rather incongruously speaks of himself as a 'one-man band'. He has recently extricated himself from a business partnership with a former friend which ended in much bitterness, and he has extreme difficulty in delegating any responsibility for creative work to his employees.

The difficulty of employing others was even more fraught for the husband and wife design partnership run by Isobel and Tony. They have employed three people during the short life of their business. They dismissed one employee for unsatisfactory work after hesitating for nearly a year. Another left soon after that incident with many recriminations and bitter words. A temporary employee had then been reasonably satisfactory, but 'not right for the company', according to Tony. Here the couple talk of the time, soon after the departure of the temporary employee, when they moved to a new office:

ISOBEL: At first we didn't know whether we'd manage when we came here. There was just the two of us. But now it's just so wonderful just to concentrate on the work and we work together very, very well, and we don't have to spend all that time trying to brief people and make them understand the objectives. And basically there's so much time investment in people and not just time. It's just [long pause] being just the two of us we can just be ourselves as well and just get on with things and, and, and –

TONY: Not be on show [pause] and I know it's quite difficult to explain.

It is indeed not easy for Tony and Isobel to find words for their feelings about their experience as employers. What is very clear from their long and convoluted narrative, however, is that despite their expressed desire to train and help their former employees, they cannot readily fit others into the world of their business. Tony's complaint that he and Isobel were 'on show' when they had employees is, as he seems to be aware, a very peculiar way indeed to talk about an employer–employee relationship. Tony's words make sense only if his pleasure in the integration of his creative business and his personal life are understood.

It is characteristic of the 'creative' group, as the above extracts illustrate, to show a much more positive attitude than any other business owners to involving the people with whom they share their lives in their businesses. At the same time, the creative owners often have difficulty when they try to include other people as employees. For the creative group, forming a business is a means to an end: a means of integrating income-earning with creative activity. Integrating life and livelihood also seems to extend to spouse involvement in the creative business. Husbands and wives each construct a biography which has their joint interest in creative endeavour at its heart.

Achievement Group

The achievement group strive for all or some of the following: wealth, the recognition of others, the opportunity to have influence and change things. There are fewer instances of close involvement of family members in these businesses than for any of the other groups. All these businesses seek growth of some kind yet their relationships with employees and business partners are particularly fraught with conflict. They characteristically are willing to sacrifice independence for the benefit of gaining outside expertise, but this can be a risky strategy and some have suffered emotionally and economically as a consequence. Individuals in this group tend to have much in common with what Elizabeth Chell and colleagues (1991) define as an entrepreneurial personality.

Nicholas is sole owner of the youngest business in the sample, a public relations business in Newcastle employing two at the time of the critical incident interview. He explained that he started his own business because only by working for himself could he hope to earn as much as he believed himself to be worth. As the interview progressed it became clear that Nicholas's drive to achieve goes far beyond a desire to make money. As the following speech conveys, it is not easy for him to articulate what that is:

> You know, if I made a million quid, I'd probably still be working because there would always be [pause]. Well, maybe it doesn't then become a point of making money because it's just a point of doing something creative, constructive. [pause] I've always thought if I die tomorrow I'd like to think that my existence had been of benefit to the world, to people, to nature, to anything, than not. And [pause] I'd like to think I made a difference in some small way. So, you know, it's a funny sort of thing but whether you're a priest and you convert people and just do good work, or whether you're a businessman who creates jobs, I don't see any difference. I think if you're contributing something to society, that's important.

Nicholas presents an unusual case of an individual for whom the family is inspirational as an ideal but of only minor significance as a reality:

> If there's one overriding feeling that I have, it is in a belief that members of our family have been able to be very, very successful in the past, and maybe I cling to it as a justification of what I'm trying to do, but because they, some people have been successful in the family, or that they've lost everything in the war, tried and picked themselves up again and again, erm, I think if they could do it, I'll bloody well try and do it myself.

Nicholas lives alone and works hours which preclude almost any social life. When he had a choice between spending a small sum of money on a deposit on a new flat, which he would dearly like, or leaflets to promote his business, it was the latter he chose. Although he has few material comforts he would restrict these even more for the sake of the business: 'I'll go down to living on tins of baked beans to keep the business going', he declared. Despite his lonely lifestyle, he recounted using an enormous range of individuals and organizations in very opportunistic ways for practical help, new business ideas and making contact with potential clients and collaborators.

Nicholas's long narrative sometimes reads like an adventure story, with him as the hero striving in a hostile world. For example, he recounted that in his first 'entrepreneurial venture', when working in France at a ski resort, he and a friend spotted a chance to make money selling bread and cakes to tourists and persisted in that activity despite threats of violence from rival traders. Now he knows that decisions taken in board rooms in Europe and the USA could scupper his new small business's hard-won contracts with multinationals. At one point he speaks within a few sentences of being endangered by 'thunder clouds', 'a watershed' and 'a time bomb'. Nicholas's use of such heightened language to convey the excitement and fear of business risk-taking is unusual but not unique. Here, for example, are the words of Cherrie, one of two women who together founded a training and consultancy business with an unusually ambitious goal: 'What we were going to do was change how people thought about organizations. We were quite clear that's what we were about you know. And it was terrifying.'

The realistic possibility of very high earnings as a reward for the hard work and risk-taking involved in founding and managing a small business is expressed unequivocally by Janet, co-owner with Claire of one of the largest and fastest-growing micro-businesses in the study. Here she talks of the achievement of her former employers, now competitors:

> I think the fact that you see them driving around in a very great expensive car
> and from what they've done and what they've achieved and – it's achievable.
> And they've started off in exactly the same position. It's operating at a desk or
> working for a high street [employment] agency and they've gone on to literally,
> erm, you know, take Milton Keynes. And they've obviously had all the fences
> and [pause] It's achievable.

Claire and Janet are both married although without dependent children,
and insist that they separate business and family life. They acknowledge
that long hours intrude upon social time somewhat, but this is noted in a
matter-of-fact way, with none of the distress apparent in so many other
interviews. In the following extract, Janet makes a rare reference to family
in response to the interviewer's line of questioning, but jumps in mid-sen-
tence to talk about her responsibility to her staff:

> INTERVIEWER: What are your ambitions?
> CLAIRE: Definitely to be the number one in Milton Keynes looking at the long
>   term.
> JANET: I think both Claire and I have, erm, found it very draining, erm, and
>   the stress levels are very high, erm, because you've no longer got your own
>   income and we both are the major income earners in our respective families,
>   but we've got staff to consider as well.

Feelings of unsatisfied need for a domestic partner's approval, interest
and support are not uncommon, as we have already seen. There are particularly intense cases in the achievement group. Here Charles tells us
how painful such feelings may be:

> You take your problems, just as you take your triumphs home, you take your
> problems home, and the person with whom you're sharing your life has to be
> ready for that and, erm, and if that person isn't ready for that, it can be very
> difficult, well it was very difficult. And, erm, the person I was with at that time
> needed to perceive me as being a success. What really affected my life at that
> time was, er, the feeling that I wasn't being the success that I'd promoted
> myself as being. So that was difficult.

There is, in stark contrast, one outstanding case of a business in which a
quest for business achievement is combined with an overwhelming commitment to integrate the business and family in a harmonious way. The
emphasis on home and family is similar to that we observed in the survival and security case of Don, but here there is none of Don's sense of
having lowered his sights as a businessman. Bernard is, as he said, a 'per-
former', and throughout his speeches he conveyed energy, vision and a
capacity for hard work as pronounced as the young and ambitious
Nicholas. To impart some of the flavour of his taste for new and exciting
business challenges, here is what he said when he had just related how he

pitched for and won a very large contract for his new, home-based and extremely small business from a major multinational company:

> That's risk, you know. I mean I suppose I got quite a kick from it actually. 'Cos that's the challenge, you see. That's then somebody laying it down and saying, well, you know, can you really do this? Course I can. And if somebody said, you know, do you want to do brain surgery? I'd do it.

Fighting words, certainly, and the story of Bernard and Linda's various businesses ventures is indeed eventful. They had until two years prior to the interview employed 50 people in a very different business. There was a series of misadventures including fraud by some of their employees. This was particularly hard to bear as it happened with the collusion of a former colleague of Bernard's who had been brought into the business by the couple as a partner. Their response was to radically rethink how yet another new business could be organized and managed. Bernard described how he and his wife sat down together with a list of their objectives, with 'no employees' at the top:

> When Linda and I sat down we said right, no employees, no leasehold properties ever again, no banks, 'cos we never trusted them. [pause] So, let's cut all that lot off, we don't want to know about all that. And what we will do is actually develop something, organically, cottage industry, but with people that we know and we trust, and we'll do it via technology.

Bernard and Linda see themselves as pioneers in their way of working and are keen to recommend their home-based business organization to others. For them, despite their many misfortunes, the conditions of economic restructuring do indeed represent a form of personal freedom. As Linda expressed it:

> If it had been you know 50 years ago when you had to go and work for the railways all your life, you would have driven everybody mad.
> BERNARD: I would, wouldn't I?

Overall, it is harder to identify patterns of household and family interaction for the achievement-motivated businesses owners than for any of the others. Only in the one case described above is there an intimate relationship between business and family, and more typically there is tension or outright conflict. Without exception, the business owners in the achievement group are energetic users of non-family networks for business development. They have a much more positive attitude to risk than the other business owners. Rarely do they describe reckless risk-taking but there is a characteristic narrative pattern in their sometimes heady stories of old risks confronted and new risks yet to be faced.

OVERCOMING FRAGMENTATION? REWARDS AND CONTROLS IN THE MICRO-BUSINESS HOUSEHOLD

Karl Polanyi (1946) recognized that an economy cannot prosper in the long term without being embedded in the society of which it is a part. Yet the logic of the market is to destroy the stability of forms of livelihood, and with it the humanity of its less powerful participants. This contradiction lies at the heart of economic ideology too. For the economic ideology of the market makes an inadvertent virtue of insecurity. Markets, so the argument goes, operate best when there are incentives for personal gain or the avoidance of loss. At the lower end of the income scale in labour markets, these negative incentives take the form of the threat of unemployment or redundancy. It was under just such a threat that a substantial proportion of the business owners whom we interviewed started up.

Economists talk about risk and about uncertainty: they are interested in how business people respond to these challenges thanks to the possibility of reaping rewards. Post-Keynesians draw out the distinctions between risk and uncertainty (Skuse, 1994). In the case of risk, probability can be attached to the range of possible outcomes: it is businesses based on speculation that rely on such calculations. Short-term decisions about whether to expand or contract output from a given plant may also be based on specific calculations of risk. In the case of uncertainty even the outcomes are unknown, so Shackle often preferred to use the term 'unknowledge' instead (Loasby, 1996). Businesses undertaking investment will inevitably do so on the basis of uncertainty, of partial ignorance. Both risk and uncertainty, then, are analysed by economists from the perspective of their impact on capital. But what of the uncertainty experienced by labour?

Very few economists have concerned themselves with the other side of the coin of the profit incentives seen as essential to induce firms and entrepreneurs to undertake risky or uncertain ventures in a market economy. There is no coherent modern analysis of the impact of insecurity on labour as a factor of production, and the ways in which it might promote or hinder economic efficiency. Yet three of the greatest political economists, Karl Marx, Karl Polanyi and J.A. Hobson, were tireless in pointing to the negative impact of insecurity on that other set of economic actors, employees. 'Constant revolutionising of production, uninterrupted disturbance of all social continuities, everlasting uncertainty and agitation', wrote Marx and Engels in *The Communist Manifesto*, 'mean that everything that is solid melts into air' (Marx and Engels, n.d., pp. 53–4). As Polanyi (1946, p. 77) sees it: 'Labour ... [is] no other than the human beings themselves of which every society consists ... To include them in the market mechanism means to subordinate the substance of society itself to the laws of the market', and he goes on to argue that we cannot allow the market mechanism to be the sole director of the fate of human beings, for they would perish from social exposure. Instability in standards of living, argues Hobson, 'robs labour of the primary condition of progress in civilised life', making it into a 'commodity', a non-human factor of production. 'Unsettled standards of living ... stop those gradual processes of improvement' in the efficiency of labour (Hobson, 1922, pp. 89–90).

Small business has been identified as an 'uneasy stratum' (Bechhofer and Elliot, 1981). The behaviour of the petty capitalist owners of micro-businesses can best be understood as encompassing aspects of the economic character of both labour and capital as economic agents. In creating their own jobs, our study shows micro-business owners and their families responding to, and attempting to control, the insecurity arising from the threat of unemployment. As business people, they are at the same time responding to the risk and uncertainty which are also the concern of larger businesses. Given the duality of their economic character, it is not surprising that the analysis of micro-business behaviour presented in this chapter indicates a range of responses to risk and insecurity, with only one group out of four showing typically entrepreneurial behaviour.

The empirical work reported on here suggests that the economists' lack of interest in the impact of insecurity on labour may derive from their assumptions about the factors underlying people's economic behaviour. On the whole, economists hold to a set of simplistic psychological presuppositions: that of maximizing individuals, who need incentives to drive and force them to do things (Wheelock and Oughton, 1998). In a recent scrupulously researched investigation of economic psychology, Robert Lane highlights the importance of intrinsic rewards for work: 'People do not work for "nothing", but what they do work for is often not just the pay they receive'. Indeed, the pleasure in working activities can be much greater than it is in leisure: 'Whatever their motives may be, people evade the market's focus on exchange, for these motives are satisfied by internal rewards that do not depend on exchanging money for work' (Lane, 1991, p. 337). The cardboard-cut-out nature of economic agents in the conventional model is reinforced by the fact that such people are without identity when they operate in markets (Ben-Porath, 1980), and the formation and moulding of character is not an issue (Loasby, 1996).

Such presuppositions can lead to serious contradictions in the real world. Economic principles of rational choice and the response to rewards in the market tend to undermine and destroy other values: co-operation, reciprocity, trust (Kohn, 1993). Yet markets rely on trust as well as regulation to ensure that people don't just rip each other off to make a quick buck. Institutionalists argue that it is the whole organizational structure of the economy that allocates resources. Insecurity can break up the social relations so essential to the functioning of a market system. The existence of institutions and of the conventions which they embody enable economic agents to form expectations in conditions of uncertainty and insecurity. The New Institutionalist analysis of transaction costs can be used to go some way to providing a more realistic analysis of how the firm and the family can help to preserve trust in a market economy (see Pollak, 1985). Our study of micro-businesses shows how the reinstatement of aspects of old ways of working, particularly the greater dependence on the family, can help to maintain those social relations. But at what expense?

Widespread deregulation in the post-Fordist economy, the fragmentation of economic institutions, the ever-increasing flexibility demanded of those in (and out of) the labour market create costs which it seems that few firms, or economists, care to look at. The first set of costs are those which fall on individual small business people and their families. Self-exploitation may appear less undesirable than being exploited by others, but working punishingly long hours for poor rewards is as likely to be destructive of health and life in the dying breaths of the twentieth century as at any other time in history (Rainbird, 1991; Wheelock, 1994). Self-exploitation within the family is an element in transaction costs that can bring dangers of pressures on personal relations and, ultimately, of family breakdown (Pollak, 1985).

The second set of costs are those to the long-term health of the economy. They cannot be clearly separated from the first, in that individual and family costs soon become a macro-cost, even though they may not be measured as such (see Waring, 1989). The costs of workforce exploitation during the first half of the nineteenth century were clearly recognized (even by most political economists, with the exception of Nassau Senior) and resulted in factories legislation that limited hours of work. The costs of family instability, and the contribution that this makes to macro-economic instability, is only beginning to be recognized (O'Hara, 1995). Yet small business in general, and micro-business in particular, is generally excluded from regulations covering conditions and hours of work. For example, Joseph Steindl, back in 1945, was withering about the role that small businesses play, especially in conditions of high unemployment, when small firms make it easy to pass price pressure on to wages, with little incentive for technical advance. Setting up a small business has the immediate advantage of giving the individual self-employment, along, perhaps, with members of his or her family. They can reduce their wage rate by any amount, something that would not provide wage-earners with employment: 'The survival of small firms is thus dependent on a series of factors not very creditable to our economic system' (Steindl, 1945, p. 61). Historical and contemporary research confirms the possibility that small firm growth in times of economic recession may best be seen as a symptom of economic decline (Foreman-Peck, 1985; Storey and Johnson, 1987).

How does this fragmentation, typified by the growth of small and micro-business, affect the way in which the post-Fordist economy is regulated? Modernity is not just defined by systematic instruments of regulation: there is a constant ebb and flow, posits Smith (1994), going on to argue that the regulationist school looks too much at the institutional features of regulation and not enough at intersubjective norms and interiorized rules. This leads to a view that informal economies are unregulated, and to ignoring the role of the household in the mode of regulation. While the formal, Fordist economy has management as its dominant function, with supervision and delegation as contradictory poles, this is reformulated in the complementary economy of the small business household where people have to claim and counterclaim in the ideology of a shared identity (see also Wheelock and Mariussen, 1997).

As Beck (1992) anticipates, the limited capacity of the post-Fordist labour market to provide employment tends to restabilize the traditional roles and responsibilities of men and women in micro-business households. In addition, those households forming the creative group of micro-businesses show evidence of reflexively constructing their own biographies, in the way that Beck sees as typical of a post-modern risk society, and this is also the case for the business-intrinsic group. However, neither of these groups shows the 'real change in attitudes towards the small firms sector and towards enterprise generally' as asserted by the Department of Employment. For the survival and security group there is a much more passive relation with biography, and substantial role strain is evident for both men and women. It is only the achievement group who fulfil both the criteria for modernity, in constructing their own biographies, and the enterprise criteria of small business policy-makers. It is only this group whose personal values also approximate to those assumed to be universal by economists. It is interesting that this is also the group least likely to embed their economic behaviour in social relations with their immediate family. For the rest, it is indeed the case that:

> Home is the place where, when you have to go there,
> They have to take you in.

It would be to the long-term competitive health of the economy, however, if micro-businesses were not driven into the bosom of their families by insecurity. Joseph Steindl's (1945, p. 66) comment remains as valid as ever: 'There is one condition which must be fulfilled if small business is to make the best of its situation: it is a high and stable level of employment.

NOTES

1. Meaning businesses employing between zero and ten employees.
2. J. Wheelock and E. Chell, *The Business Owner-managed family Unit: An Inter-regional Comparison of Behavioural Dynamics*, ESRC Award no. R 000 23 4402.
3. Some have argued that the British state has taken the lead in demonstrating to the private sector how large-scale organizations can be hollowed out and operated more flexibly (see, for example, Pollert, 1991).
4. The work of Champion and Green (1992) on so-called 'booming towns' identifies Milton Keynes as exceptionally strongly performing on a range of prosperity indicators. Milton Keynes was ranked third out of 280 UK towns and cities. Newcastle upon Tyne, although not quite as disadvantaged as Wearside, was ranked a poor 210th.
5. A recent survey suggests similar figures for family businesses (Poutziouris and Chittenden, 1996).
6. Including people reported unemployed or on sickness benefit, but not including any others not in employment, such as full-time housewives or the early retired.
7. Other business owners do manage to employ others while working from home, however.
8. The description of Gerry's business activity has been deliberately left vague. This is because, in common with some other creative and specialist businesses, his field is quite unusual and more precise description could make him identifiable.

REFERENCES

Baines, S., Wheelock, J. and Abrams A. (1997), 'Micro-business owner-managers in social context', in D. Deakin, P. Jennings and C. Mason (eds), *Entrepreneurship in the Nineties*, London: Paul Chapman, pp. 47–60.

Barnett, F. and Barnett, S. (1988), *Working Together: Entrepreneurial Couples*, Berkeley, Cal.: Ten Speed Press.

Bechhofer F. and Elliott, B. (eds) (1981), *Comparative Studies of an Uneasy Stratum*, London: Macmillan.

Beck, U. (1992), *The Risk Society: Towards a New Modernity*, London: Sage.

Becker, G. (1993), *Treatise on the Family*, enlarged edn, Cambridge, Mass: Harvard University Press.

Ben-Porath, Y. (1980), 'The F-connection: families, friends and firms and the organization of exchange', *Population and Development Review*, 6: 1–30.

Campbell, M. and Daly, M. (1992), 'Self-employment into the 1990s', *Employment Gazette*, June: 269–92.

Champion, A.G. and Green, A.E. (1992), 'Local economic performance in Britain during the late 1980s: the results of the third booming towns study', *Environment and Planning A*, **24** (2): 243–72.

Chell, E. (forthcoming), 'Critical incident technique', in G. Simon and C. Cassell (eds.), *Qualitative Methods in Organizational Research: A Practical Guide*, London: Sage.

Chell, E., Haworth, J. and Brearley, S. (1991), *The Entrepreneurial Personality: Concepts, Cases and Categories*, London: Routledge.

Curran, J. and Blackburn R.A. (1994), *Small Firms and Local Economic Networks: The Death of the Local Economy*, London: Paul Chapman.

Department of Employment (1992), *Enterprise in Action: Small Firms in Britain Report*, London: HMSO.

Foreman-Peck, J. (1985), 'Seed corn or chaff? New firm formation and the performance of the interwar economy', *Economic History Review*, **38** (3): 402–22.

Gray, C. (1995), 'Managing entrepreneurial growth: a question of control?', paper presented to the Eighteenth Institute of Small Business Affairs National Small Firms Conference, University of Paisley, Scotland.

Hobson, J.A. (1922), *The Economics of Unemployment*, London: Allen & Unwin.

Jessop, B. (1994), 'The transition to post-Fordism and the Schumpeterian workfare state', in R. Burrows and B. Loader (eds), *Towards a Post-Fordist Welfare State?*, London: Routledge, pp. 14–37.

Jones, T., McEvoy, D. and Barrett, G. (1994), 'Labour intensive practices in the ethnic minority firm', in J. Atkinson and D. Storey (eds) *Employment, the Small Firm and the Labour Market*, London: Routledge, pp. 172–205.

Kohn, A. (1993), *Punished by Rewards: The Trouble with Gold Stars – and Other Bribes*, Boston and New York: Houghton Mifflin.

Lane, R.E. (1991), *The Market Experience*, Cambridge: Cambridge University Press.

Loasby, B.J. (1996), 'Uncertainty, intelligence and imagination: George Shackle's guide to human progress', paper presented to the European Association for Evolutionary Political Economy, University of Antwerp, November.

Marx, K. and Engels, F. (n.d.), *Manifesto of the Communist Party*, Moscow: Foreign Language Press.

O'Hara, P.A. (1995), 'Household labour, the family and macroeconomic stability in the US, 1940s–1990s', *Review of Social Economy*, **53** (1): 89–120.

Polanyi, K. (1946), *Origins of our Time: The Great Transformation*, London: Victor Gallancz.

Pollak, R.A. (1985), 'A transaction cost approach to families and households', *Journal of Economic Literature*, **23** June: 581–608.

Pollert, A. (ed.) (1991), *Farewell to Flexibility?*, Oxford: Basil Blackwell.

Poutziouris, P. and Chittenden, F. (1996), *Family Businesses or Business Families?*, Leeds: Institute for Small Business Affairs Monograph, in association with National Westminster Bank.

Rainbird, H. (1991), 'The self-employed: small entrepreneurs or disguised wage labourers?', in A. Pollert (ed.), *Farewell to Flexibility?*, Oxford: Basil Blackwell, pp. 200–13.

Skuse, F. (1994), 'Decision making', in P. Arestis and M. Sawyer (eds), *The Elgar Companion to Radical Political Economy*, Aldershot, Hants and Vermont: Edward Elgar.

Smith, G. (1994), 'Western European informal economies in historical perspective', in H. Lustiger-Thaler and D. Saleé (eds), *Artful Practices: The Political Economy of Everyday Life*, Montreal, New York and London: Black Rose Books, pp. 11–12.

Stanfield, J.R. (1982), 'Towards a new value standard in economics', *Economic Forum*, **13**, Fall: 67–85.

Stanworth, J., Stanworth, C., Granger, B. and Blyth, S. (1989), 'Who becomes an entrepreneur?', *International Small Business Journal*, **8** (1): 11–22.

Steindl, J. (1945), *Small and Big Business: Economic Problems of the Size of Firms*, Oxford: Basil Blackwell.

Storey, D. (1994), *Understanding the Small Business Sector*, London: Routledge.

Storey, D. and Johnson, S. (1987), *Job Generation and the Labour Market*, London: Macmillan.

Waring, M. (1989), *If Women Counted*, London: Macmillan.

Wheelock, J. (1992a), 'The household in the total economy', in P. Ekins and M. Max Neef (eds), *Seeing the Whole Economy*, London: Routledge, pp. 124–36.

Wheelock, J. (1992b), 'The flexibility of small business family work strategies', in K. Caley, F. Chittenden, E. Chell and C. Mason (eds), *Small Enterprise Development: Policy and Practice*, London: Paul Chapman, pp. 151–65.

Wheelock, J. (1994), 'Survival strategies for small business families in a peripheral local economy: a contribution to institutional value theory', in H. Lustiger-Thaler and D. Saleé (eds), *Artful Practices: The Political Economy of Everyday Life*, Montreal, New York and London: Black Rose Books, pp. 21–40.

Wheelock, J. and Mariussen, A. (eds) (1997), *Households, Work and Economic Change: A Comparative Institutional Perspective*, Boston: Kluwer.

Wheelock, J. and Oughton, E.A. (1996), 'The household as a focus for research', *Journal of Economic Issues*, **30** (1): 143–59.

Wheelock, J. and Oughton, E.A. (1998), 'The household as a producing unit', in S. Himmelweit *et al.* (eds), *Firms, Households and Markets*, Milton Keynes: Open University pp. 147–80.

11. In search of employment creation via environmental valorization: towards an eco-Keynesian mode of regulation and a sustainable regime of accumulation for Europe

Ray Hudson*

There is no shortage of work; only a shortage of jobs.
F.E.K. Britton, *Rethinking Work*

INTRODUCTION

For about two decades following the Second World War, over much of the advanced capitalist world, rapid economic growth, profitable production, rising material living standards and full employment appeared to be simultaneously attainable objectives. This can be reasonably characterized as an era of a Fordist regime of accumulation and mode of regulation and its main features are well known. Mildly progressive income redistribution encouraged growing private consumption. Growing public expenditure on the welfare state led to rising levels of collective consumption. 'Full employment' was predominantly defined in terms of full-time jobs for life for male industrial workers. The male 'family wage' plus the 'social wage' delivered via the welfare state, perhaps supplemented by the wages of married women working part-time, were seen as assuring continuing increases in material living standards for nuclear families, regarded as the normal form of household unit. Growing mass production validated by expanding mass consumption as the route to 'full employment' was unavoidably dependent upon the natural environment

---

* This chapter draws heavily on joint work with Paul Weaver, though the usual disclaimer applies.

in various ways, but this grounding of economy and society in nature was not generally seen as problematic. There were apparently no ecological limits to growth while growing state involvement along Keynesian lines was seen as central to facilitating and managing macro-economic growth and guaranteeing social justice within a 'full employment' economy. It is important, however, to remember that there were certainly national variations around the basic themes (for example, see Hudson and Williams, 1995; Lash and Urry, 1987; Lipietz, 1987), in part linked to the extent to which centre-left or centre-right politics were dominant and in part as a consequence of the inheritance of uneven development, so that Fordism diffused unevenly over space and through time within Europe and this had important implications for the trajectory and character of development in different places.

From the mid-1960s, however, this model of growth became increasingly fragile. This was partly because of the maturing contradictions of mass production at the micro-scale within workplaces. One consequence of this was accelerating deindustrialization as companies closed capacity or switched production abroad. The associated decline of full-time male industrial jobs for life and the further growth of paid work for women (largely in the services sector and much of it part-time) called into question the notion of the male 'family wage' as central to household living standards. The changing gender composition of the labour force, and the growing variety of forms of labour contract, increasingly problematized the conception of 'full employment'. In many ways, the apparently relict forms of the household economy and informal sector of southern Mediterranean Europe seemed to offer a vision of the future. At a macro-scale, the mode of regulation was becoming increasingly and visibly crisis prone. National states could no longer seek to maintain full employment via Keynesian demand management policies, continue to expand public sector provision of services such as health and education or, increasingly, even maintain a floor level to living standards via the safety net of a welfare state. As the goal of 'full employment' was abandoned, the workfare state increasingly replaced the welfare state. Neo-liberalism increasingly dominated the policy agenda in other advanced capitalist states as they searched for a new post-Fordist growth model and mode of regulation. State involvement was increasingly seen as the proximate cause of, rather than part of the solution to, the problem of poor national economic performance. Renewed national economic growth, stimulated by a resurgence of enterprise released via deregulation and increasingly flexible and segmented labour markets, was seen as the solution to problems of unemployment. A concern with social justice was pushed down the policy agenda in an increasingly and multiply divided society. There was a greater awareness of environmental constraints and impacts but the dominant motives informing a neo-liberal national economic policy were those of increased GNP growth rates. The transition to neo-liberal approaches was not uncontested, however. There was variable national resistance to the adoption of neo-liberal strategies and therefore an uneven diffusion of the transition to neo-liberal modes of regulation and growth models. By the mid-1990s it had made its mark upon modes of regulation throughout Europe, not least in the east. At the same time, however, it became increasingly recognized that mass production and consumption as the route to 'full employment', underpinned by Keynesian state policies, had severe and unsustainable ecological impacts. Simply returning to past practices and policies could, therefore, at best provide a short-term solution to problems of unemployment (see Hudson, 1995).

As a result, European states currently face an interrelated set of difficult and apparently irreconcilable social, environmental and economic dilemmas. They encompass issues of social cohesion, environmental quality and stability, international competitiveness and economic sustainability. Challenges arise: to social cohesion, particularly from high and persistent levels of unemployment/underemployment and the associated polarization of wealth; to environmental sustainability, from materials-intensive patterns of production and consumption; and to international competitiveness and economic sustainability, from comparatively high (direct and indirect) production costs, technological backwardness, mature markets and oligopolistic supply structures. Globalization and liberalization of global markets expose industry to competition from emerging market economies and/or developing countries with lower production costs, growing markets and fewer regulatory constraints and to technologically more sophisticated advanced capitalist economies (notably Japan and the USA) and newly industrializing countries' (NICS') economies.

There is a pressing need to tackle all these problems in order to secure high and continuing levels of welfare and 'quality of life', to discover a new model of development and mode of regulation within which this will be possible. Unemployment undoubtedly poses the most serious challenge, however, because of its immediacy, its human consequences and its political significance. Unemployment and related problems of social exclusion have pushed concern about environmental sustainability down the political agenda. This demotion might be seen as damaging both for the environment and for those campaigning for greater environmental protection. While these risks should not be underestimated, this situation also presents an opportunity. The crux of the matter is the way in which these problems are seen or are not seen as systemically related. Regarding them as unrelated leads to a prioritization of problems and trade-offs

between policy goals. Keynesian economic management *de facto* traded
off the pursuit of full employment against environmental damage and
pollution, albeit unintentionally. Contemporary neo-liberal policy is less
concerned with restoring fuller employment than it is with boosting profitability and growth rates but remains largely insensitive to the
environmental consequences of implementing such a policy approach.
Seeing these problems as systemically related, in contrast, allows for a
model of development in which the challenges to employment creation
and social cohesion, economic performance and the environment can be
addressed simultaneously. This new approach can be characterized as an
eco-Keynesian mode of regulation through which to discover a sustainable regime of accumulation. This eco-Keynesian approach seeks to
create a different regulatory regime and a return to fuller employment
and a more egalitarian distribution of work (defined to include both
unwaged work as well as waged work in the formal and informal sectors)
through the pursuit of enhanced environmental quality and environmentally sustainable patterns of production and consumption. It seeks to
return to the commitment of a social democratic centre-left politics to
greater social justice, inclusion and equality, while combining this with a
recognition that economy and society must respect the relationships that
they have with the natural environment.

Development is, however, to a considerable extent, path dependent
(Nelson and Winter, 1982). Consequently, in the absence of radical
change in the processes that shape the trajectory of change, future development will be strongly autocorrelated with past trends. Restructuring on
to a new trajectory therefore requires fundamental change in those for-
mative processes. It remains an open question as to whether a
revolutionary shift can be achieved via incremental change and evolutionary reformist modifications to the existing developmental trajectory, or
whether it requires a rapid quantum leap from one trajectory to a qualitatively different one. The former is the more feasible option, however. It is
difficult, for example, to conceive of the structuring principles of capitalism and (socially constructed) markets being replaced by those of some
alternative principles of political economy, such as those of the centrally
planned economy, in the foreseeable future. On the other hand, while capitalism will remain the dominant developmental model, there are
distinctive varieties of capitalism, and different trajectories of change,
within a variety of regulatory and political frameworks (for example, see
Albert, 1993; Lash and Urry, 1987).

The key issue, then, is to *envision* how the economy might be restructured (acknowledging that this is a multidimensional process: Simonis,
1994) on to the path of a sustainable regime of accumulation, how a new

distribution of work and employment might emerge within a new mode of regulation, and to *conceptualize* models of transition processes that specify the conditions under which desired changes might be realized. While environmental sustainability is a contested concept, moving towards sustainability will certainly involve patterns of production and consumption that are much less materials-intensive – with a need for perhaps a tenfold increase in resource productivities in the advanced industrialized countries over the next 50 years (Wuppertal Institute for Climate, Environment and Energy: Factor 10 Club, 1994). This will have profound implications for lifestyles and ways of living. In short, we must address normative and ultimately moral questions about the sort of society in which we wish to live and about the mechanisms through which desired societal goals such as social cohesion, improved economic performance and environmental sustainability might be achieved.

The remainder of this chapter is organized as follows. First, the nature of the unemployment problem is examined and current approaches to job creation are evaluated. Then an alternative approach, based upon a transition to a different development trajectory, to a more sustainable regime of accumulation and enabling eco-Keynesian mode of regulation that might deliver higher levels of social cohesion and environmental protection, is outlined. Rather than seek to specify instruments and mechanisms to produce desired changes (which are discussed at length in Weaver, 1995a), the focus here is upon identifying and conceptualizing linkages between these desired goals both in restructuring processes and in outcomes from them.

THE CURRENT IMPASSE: CLUES ABOUT POSSIBLE FUTURES FROM THE PARADOXES OF HIGH UNEMPLOYMENT

The persistence of permanent high unemployment in Europe reflects a deep paradox. On the one hand, unemployment can be seen as an outcome of one of late modern societies' greatest achievements: the capacity to produce so efficiently that the socially necessary labour time 'formally' required (that is, in remunerated employment involving formalized and legally recognized relationships between an employer and an employee) absorbs only around 20 per cent of the potentially available working time. On the other hand, unemployment simultaneously reflects one of late modern societies' greatest failures: the absence of necessary corresponding adjustments in systems for redefining and allocating work and income across society – hence Britton's (1994) view that there is no shortage of work, only one of jobs. Although much useful and welfare-enhancing work is done informally or outside the wage relationship (for example, within households), the polarization of wealth and income results in a lack of effective demand for much welfare-enhancing work, which consequently remains undone. The welfare state system is in large part financed through taxes on employment. These discourage job creation. Equally, the benefits system provides disincentives and barriers to working for a wage. While the welfare and benefits systems have been eroded in the advanced capitalist countries in recent years, these disincentives remain within societies that have become more polarized, with significant groups of people marginalized and excluded.

Clearly, there are several facets to the problem, all of which revolve around notions of economic democracy and citizens' entitlements, expectations and responsibilities. The first concerns allocation of work and income. Paid employment is 'needed' – and unemployment is currently considered a problem – because the employment system and the wage relation are the major mechanism for allocating entitlement to a share of GNP, directly through income and indirectly through related welfare benefits. There is, however, no necessary correspondence between either useful (welfare-enhancing) work and the availability of paid employment (jobs) or between the contribution an individual makes to society through his/her work and his/her income and status. The second facet is that necessary welfare-enhancing 'work' remains undone because the work is not underwritten by 'effective demand' or is bureaucratically barred to the unemployed by threat of benefit withdrawal. A third facet is that, as a consequence of exclusion from employment, individuals rapidly become 'unemployable'. They lose touch with the skills and contacts needed for gaining or 'creating' a job (Britton, 1994).

The social costs of unemployment are therefore highly significant. Unemployment can lead to marginalization or exclusion beyond the immediate realms of the economy. The social, economic and political costs of this disenfranchisement are growing and are evidenced in phenomena as wide-ranging as growing criminality, violence, vandalism, drug abuse, fear and ill health (Schmidt-Bleek, 1994). Those in employment experience intensification of the labour process because of economic pressures for greater productivity and performance underpinned by fear of job loss. While there have been some changes (such as the growth of part-time work) that have increased labour market flexibility, for many people the rigidities of the job market continue to present stark choices: an all-or-nothing commitment to full-time long-term paid employment, full-time long-term unemployment, a life in the 'grey/black' areas of the labour market, or even, for some, criminality as a survival strategy. Much of the 'flexibilization' of the labour market and labour process that has occurred has been on terms that have simply emphasized the need for strong progressive and egalitarian regulatory regimes if the restructuring of work is to be compatible with enhanced levels of social inclusion (Hudson, 1989). Other aspects relate to the opportunity costs of leaving people 'jobless' in terms of welfare-enhancing work that remains 'undone' and 'lost' human potential associated with long-term unemployment.

THE LIMITS TO CONTEMPORARY POLICY APPROACHES

With the demise of state socialism, capitalism is now virtually unopposed as the dominant political and economic philosophy within Europe. There has been a widespread diffusion of neo-liberal policy approaches. The latter presume that prosperity is to be achieved through GNP growth based on productivity gains, investment in new technologies and free trade. The focus is upon the production and consumption of material commodities (which are appropriable and can be exchanged), driven by competition. The need for profitability results in incessant pressure for total factor productivity gains, but relative factor prices have strongly focused attention on increasing labour productivity linked to greater mechanization and automation as a result of increased fixed capital investment. Profits depend on simply the units of output sold, rather than on these as the first element in a more comprehensive package of end-user services that extend over the life of the product. This leads to a 'throughput' economy rather than an economy orientated towards conservation and the efficient delivery of end-user services. Patterns of production and consumption are materials-intensive and 'leaky' (see Weaver, 1995b). Although there has been considerable apparent business service sector growth, much of this reflects a changing social division of labour and increasing out-sourcing and subcontracting (Sayer and Walker, 1992). Consumption of labour-intensive personal services is discouraged relative to consumption of material goods and such employment growth in these activities as has occurred has often been of low-skill, poorly paid jobs in minimally regulated labour markets.

This developmental model is open to severe criticism on two grounds *inter alia*. First, it is by no means obvious that it results in the enhancement of welfare. There is mounting evidence that further growth in GDP does not necessarily increase welfare. Adjusting GDP to give a more broadly based measure of economic progress, Jackson and Marks (1994) argue that growth in production has not delivered additional welfare, for example. Indeed, their 'Index of Sustainable Welfare' shows a negative correlation with GDP growth since 1974 (see also Nordhaus and Tobin, 1972). There are clear signs that 'wage-working' and 'consumerism' (Robertson, 1995) are no longer welfare-enhancing and are not what many people want (Lenk, 1994; Kistler and Strech, 1992).

Secondly, there are also severe limitations to job-creation policies cast in the current dominant policy mould. Growth in output will not necessarily translate into employment growth (Fontela, 1994; United Nations Development Programme, 1993). Since part-time working has recently increased significantly, this almost certainly represents a decrease in employment-hours. This phenomenon of jobless or 'job-shedding' growth is generally observable to a greater or lesser extent in all OECD countries.

Economic growth (if sufficiently rapid) can temporarily create new jobs at a faster rate than others are destroyed by labour-saving innovations, but the constant drive for efficiency (or 'technological rents', as Mandel, 1975, puts it) under a competitive, profit-driven market system constitutes a compelling imperative to increase labour productivity. This will be the case irrespective of existing levels of labour productivity and labour cost. By implication, under a system that treats all inputs as scarce, there are only limited opportunities to create 'conventional' jobs directly in activities that produce traded goods and services. Furthermore, such jobs may be precarious and poorly paid. Even without gains in labour productivity, no realistic rate of growth could deliver an increased number of conventional jobs sufficient to return to anything resembling 'full employment' and to secure social cohesion. Growth in conventional formal sectors and activities can be, at best, a temporary panacea to unemployment problems.

There are likely to be limits also to the extent to which unemployment can be reduced by changes in relative factor costs. The job-creation potential of changes in the relative direct cost of labour depends upon the degree to which labour can substitute for other factors. As a result of technological and market changes, however, labour is far less substitutable than it once was in conventional manufacturing activities. Many of today's products and services simply could not be delivered to the same standards of quality and complexity or within the same time-frame using human labour rather than machines (see Ayres, 1991). Consequently, there is a ratchet effect in much (though admittedly not all) of the labour market rather than the often-supposed reversibility in choice of production technique. While higher direct and indirect labour costs reduce manufacturing and traded-service sector employment, lower labour costs will not necessarily increase employment. Lower indirect costs could contribute to greater flexibility in working arrangements, however.

Therefore, a reduction in unemployment within the prevailing policy framework and economic paradigm, including via downward currency adjustments and competitive devaluations, would be necessarily partial, painful and further damaging to social cohesion. Several analysts (such as Fontela, 1994) have observed that extrapolations based upon current pathways all suggest outcomes characterized by the emergence or strengthening of dual societies, involving either a coexistence of workers and unemployed (the continental west European model), increases in precarious and low-paid employment (the US model), or a combination of the two (the UK 'Two Nations' model and the model increasingly observable over much of eastern Europe). Indeed, the processes of labour market segmentation are more complex as factors such as age, ethnicity and gender interact to influence the distribution of employment and unemployment (Hudson and Williams, 1995). In addition, these scenarios imply continuing high levels of environmental impact. In practice, the most likely effect would be to stymie further an already inadequate pace of progress towards sustainable development. New government policies are urgently needed to limit the extent of dualistic processes and to move towards a new model of structural change (Fontela, 1994). For this, the scope of policy discussion needs to be broadened, *a fortiori* once one recognizes that the complexities extend beyond simple dualisms.

SEARCHING FOR A SUSTAINABLE REGIME OF ACCUMULATION: IN PURSUIT OF ENVIRONMENTAL VALORIZATION AND A NEW DISTRIBUTION OF WORK AND EMPLOYMENT

A key issue in this search for a new sustainable regime of accumulation is to create links between economic restructuring to resolve unemployment problems and economic restructuring to address challenges to environmental sustainability and to competitiveness. The striking feature is the overlap between policy measures needed to address both challenges. Shifts to sustainability will involve vastly increasing materials productivity, perhaps by a factor of ten (Wuppertal Institute for Climate, Environment and Energy: Factor 10 Club, 1994). Such a shift has two components. One is to increase the materials productivity of goods and services and deliver useful end-services more efficiently. The other is to change the mix of the goods, services and technologies to favour those with lower environmental impact potentials. Both components imply changes in the sectoral structure of the economy, of output and of work and employment.

Addressing problems of competitiveness and economic efficiency, unemployment and environmental sustainability could be systemically interlinked through incentive and disincentive structures defined by regulatory and governance frameworks and the implications of these linkages for choice of technologies, patterns of resource use and patterns of production and consumption. Simultaneously achieving the goals of social, environmental and economic sustainability requires a systemic approach, harmonizing changes, especially to taxation and benefits systems. The challenge is to show how synergies and 'virtuous cycles' can be sustainably developed via policies which shape the restructuring process.

Reconceptualizing employment and work and changing the ways in which they are distributed between people would clearly involve a rethinking of both demand- and supply-side approaches to the organization of work and remuneration. Waged work in the formal sector and welfare-enhancing unwaged work outside of that sector need to be linked through transfer payments to ensure 'effective demand' for the latter. Efficiency and effectiveness in both sectors in the performance of welfare-enhancing work depends upon loosening the rigidities that currently prohibit or discourage flexible working arrangements and which deter employers from providing employment, workers from working and individuals from choosing how best to allocate their time between work (paid and unpaid) and leisure. Ensuring that welfare-enhancing work is efficiently and effectively accomplished and that a balance is struck between work and leisure that maximizes individual and social benefits implies a major shift in consumption profiles and in approaches to meeting end-use demands. It implies a new focus on the performance of individually organized work, particularly in the non-traded personal services sector. Welfare-enhancing and labour-intensive activities currently precluded from the formal economy (though perhaps already part of an informal economy) would be recognized and encouraged but within a regulatory framework that guaranteed labour market conditions and standards and enhanced social inclusion. Lipietz (1992) refers to the need for the emergence of a 'socially useful third sector' as one mechanism for ensuring that such work gets done while providing work and incomes for those currently unemployed.

The transition to a new sustainable regime of accumulation will require the creation of an enabling regulatory framework by a strong state. It will require appropriate state policy measures to encourage this desired pattern of change, many of which would call for new regulatory mechanisms and revised patterns of public expenditure. The most important of these state policy changes would undoubtedly be a gradual but comprehensive and systematic root and branch revision of the tax and benefits system to one based ultimately on the taxation of environmental resources used (virgin materials, energy, land and pollution) with the revenues raised forming the basis for a citizen's income and public expenditure. The idea of a citizen's income is not new (see, for example, Friedman and Friedman, 1980), although linking this with a system for revenue-raising based upon eco-taxes is more recent but is gaining increasing support in both the academic (for example, von Weizsäcker, 1994) and the business (Business Council for Sustainable Development, 1994) communities. The gains from such a shift in the basis of taxation could be widespread and considerable. For example, Repetto (1992, cited in Robertson, 1995) reports significant possible economies from shifting the tax burden from incomes, employment and profits to environmental charges on waste collection and pollution in the USA. Gains come, *inter alia*, in the form of higher environmental quality, reduced infrastructure needs and increased employment.

Other policy changes would also be needed to facilitate the transition towards sustainability. Public policy initiatives to help identify and support R&D on technologies to increase the materials efficiencies of end-service delivery would be important, especially in growth sectors with potential applications in process/product redesign and with export potential, such as materials science, electronics and biotechnologies. Infrastructure investment to underpin the new information- and knowledge-based economy would also be critical. Policy innovations to legitimize and strengthen the 'grey' and informal economy to ensure performance of welfare-enhancing work and maximize the multiplier effect of state transfer payments through the development of voucher or credit systems (local 'shadow' currencies) for trading community services could play a key role. So too could information exchanges and 'job' centres for the organization of community, voluntary and personal work. A further set of policy changes might reduce the cost (financial and environmental) of comfortable living; in particular, measures to reduce unnecessary travel, improve energy productivities in the housing sector, encourage heat-recovery from waste materials, reuse or recycle waste materials, increase the longevity of products and structures through repair and maintenance, and increase food self-sufficiency would all have a role to play. Such changes in ways of living and working imply significant changes in individual and community attitudes. A further important area of policy innovation, therefore, would be investment in educational and information facilities for self-development (with both leisure and commercial applications) and for societal ends (to encourage shifts towards socially responsible behaviours, to develop social solidarity and to encourage shifts in consumption profiles).

In summary, the elements of a sustainable new regime of accumulation are a highly competitive and efficient industrial and service economy in the traded sectors, a new regulatory regime embodying a revised system of taxes and benefits that penalizes value-diminishing activities and rewards value-adding activities, and mechanisms that maximize the local and regional economic, social and environmental benefits accruing from transfer payments. The last of these depends upon maximizing the multiplier effects of transfers and public expenditures and so involves a significant reorientation of territorially defined economies towards greater self-sufficiency.

WHAT WOULD BE AN APPROPRIATE TERRITORIAL LEVEL OF STATE INVOLVEMENT IN AN ECO-KEYNESIAN MODE OF REGULATION IN EUROPE?

The transition to a new sustainable regime of accumulation will require the creation of an enabling regulatory framework by a strong and socially progressive state. While recognizing that there are tendencies to redistribute state power upwards to the supranational level (notably, in Europe, to the EU) and downwards to cities and regions, for the foreseeable future this implies a central role for national states. Appropriate national measures will be needed to encourage this desired pattern of change, many of which will call for new regulatory mechanisms and revised patterns of public expenditure. It may seem perverse that in the context of debates about the increasingly global character of competition and economic relationships, emphasis should be placed upon the possibilities for policy innovation at the national level: even more so, as there is some evidence of political authority being recast at the supranational level in the evolution of organizations such as the EU, which is both widening its spatial reach within Europe and deepening the degree of integration amongst its member states. The relationship of the EU to globalization processes is, however, ambiguous. From one point of view, it can be seen as facilitating globalization. From another point of view, however, it can be seen as a barrier, a site of resistance, to it.

There are certainly themes in recent EU policy documents which resonate with arguments advanced in the previous section, making clear that any supranational regulatory framework would need to incorporate the sort of incentives and disincentives outlined above (for example, see European Commission, 1993). For example, the need to switch taxation to the use of environmental services (materials and land used, wastes emitted, and so on) is recognized as part of its 'incentive-based' approach to the integration of environmental and economic policies (European Commission, 1994). There is also no doubt that the emergence of a global regulatory authority (or authorities) would greatly ease the widespread diffusion and adoption of more stringent environmental regulation. Again there is some evidence that such international organizations and movements are emerging (Yearley, 1995). It would be naive, however, to believe that considerable variations will not remain at the national, or perhaps macro-regional (for example, the EU or NAFTA), level in environmental standards, permitted pollution levels and regulatory regimes, not least as a result of the past impress of uneven development.

At the same time, there is undoubtedly a general recognition of clear limits to the regulatory capacities of all national states. Recognition of such limits was important in the demise of the Fordist mode of regulation in the advanced capitalist states. A variety of crisis tendencies (Habermas, 1975), in particular those associated with fiscal crisis (O'Connor, 1973), could no longer be contained. As a result, national states could not continue to pursue Keynesian policies to maintain full employment. In their place came neo-liberal policies, led by Thatcherism and Reaganomics. While often represented as deregulatory, as national governments both acknowledged and encouraged the play of global market forces, these were in practice strongly re-regulatory as the relations between economy, society and state were redefined. There is growing evidence that they are subject to the same structural and systemic forces that underlay the demise of the previous Keynesian–Fordist regimes. It is precisely this recognition that is encouraging exploration of supranational approaches to regulation.

Another corollary of the growing recognition of the limits to national state regulation has been the growing pressures from various subnational regionalist movements within Europe. There are undoubtedly some regional economic 'winners' within the EU, and many other cities and regions seek to emulate this success. There is also, however, a growing recognition of the importance of environmental sustainability at the local and regional levels. The transition to a more sustainable regime of accumulation will also necessitate regulatory changes at these territorial levels and a greater emphasis on socio-spatial justice and inclusion. For example, there could be policy changes to promote environmental restoration and improvement, including ways of using the environment and local heritage as a basis for improved recreational and leisure opportunities and, as a result, of generating income and jobs locally. There could also be policies to increase investment in 'soft' and 'electronic' infrastructures that support individual and local economic initiatives for greater economic self-reliance and 'closure' of local and regional economies (while recognizing the difficulties of so doing: see Hudson and Plum, 1986). Without a doubt, however, the transition to a more sustainable regime of accumulation will need to create and guarantee 'room for manoeuvre' at local and regional levels, to allow local knowledge and creativity to be expressed and help shape local policy agendas, and to seek to combine employment creation with environmental valorization in ways that are sensitive to local and regional contexts.

There is therefore no doubt that a restructuring of the territoriality of state power is ongoing and that further changes will be needed as part of the process of facilitating the emergence of a sustainable regime of accumulation. Some see the demise of the national state as state power moves both upwards to emergent supranational states (such as the EU, though it is important to recall that this has evolved as a result of decisions of national states) and downwards to subnational units, representing, respectively, larger or smaller versions of current national state forms. Others caution against a too-ready acceptance of reports of 'the exaggerated death of the nation-state' (Anderson, 1995) and argue that what is emerging is a much more complex form of regulation involving supranational, national and subnational scales. Globalization and regionalism are both powerful, and to a degree related, tendencies but are by no means uncontested ones. While there continues to be a significant degree of unbundling of the relations between national territory and regulation, national states still will remain key actors in this emergent restructured regulatory system.

There are good grounds, therefore, for believing that national states do and will continue to retain important regulatory powers, both directly and indirectly, in so far as they play a key role in the construction of both supranational and subnational regulatory mechanisms. While it remains an open question as to whether they choose to deploy these in pursuit of environmental sustainability, regulatory systems that insist upon high environmental standards may well be compatible with economic success. For example, at regional level the economy of the Ruhr is being successfully restructured around clusters of environmental protection industries while at the national level the German economy has prospered because of, rather than despite, stringent environmental standards. Compliance with these within the national territory has often given German companies a competitive edge via pioneering new environmentally friendly products and processes. At the same time, differences in national environmental standards and regulations have allowed companies to escape strict regulation within their 'home' territories by seeking 'spatial fixes' via 'pollution dumping', particularly to Third World countries in which jobs take precedence over environmental protection (Leonard, 1988). This raises broader questions regarding the transition to 'sustainability' at global scale. Nevertheless, within the First World the transition to 'sustainable production' and employment creation 'at home' via restructuring which focuses on more technologically sophisticated and environmentally friendly products and processes can be compatible with both corporate and territorial competitive advantage. That said, the imperatives of capitalist production will continue to impose limits both on company strategies and on national states' 'room for manoeuvre' in policy formation – with longer-term implications for 'sustainability', a point to which we return in the final section.

SO WHAT MIGHT A SUSTAINABLE ECO-KEYNESIAN FUTURE LOOK LIKE?

There are influential voices which emphasize the conventional job-creation potential associated with the growth of 'green' technologies and environmental protection (for example, see Jenkins and McClaren, 1994). Certainly, an important aspect of the switch in emphasis from increasing labour productivities to increasing materials and energy productivities is that it creates needs for innovative product and process redesign, which generates markets in both private and public sectors for new environmentally improved technologies and for people to design, manage and monitor the eco-transition. Further potential sources of job creation are the new sectors that would emerge or grow in importance, especially those involved with life-time materials management; for instance, jobs associated with organizing product sharing or leasing (that increase intensity of use), in product maintenance and repair (that increase product longevity) and in materials recycling and reuse (that provide for materials cascading). While some of these jobs are locationally 'fixed', those involved in developing, manufacturing and selling environmental technologies are not. The latter, along with the jobs and export revenues they yield, would be located in response to national and local initiatives and policies so that eco-Keynesianism, like Fordism, would have its characteristic geographies of production. Furthermore, ready-made markets for these products would be guaranteed if the tax system became based upon eco-taxes. Consequently, there are real opportunities for governments to steer the transition process in ways that make environmental protection and job creation compatible goals.

However, although jobs may be created in these sectors, this job-supply approach comprises only one element of the needed strategy. The links between economic, social and environmental sustainability must extend beyond job creation and loss in the formal sector (for there will surely also be job losses, especially in the transport and travel, automotive, energy and chemicals sectors). Of greater significance are mechanisms by which the environment might be protected or enhanced in the process of forging and serving a viable future economy and society. Conceptualizing structural change systemically, effective synergies could be harnessed to achieve a broad range of public policy goals linked to the overall aim of enhancing welfare and quality of life rather than of job creation *per se*.

Governments are presently restricted in their capacity to tax profitable enterprises by the mobility of capital and its capacity to switch location increasingly rapidly. This has increased markedly as a result of liberalization and the pace of technological change in the most profitable industries (which contributes to higher depreciation rates and more frequent reviews of location), although it is important not to overgeneralize in this context. While there has been considerable emphasis on capital's growing 'hyper-mobility', there are counterarguments that key activities and sectors are deeply embedded culturally and institutionally in specific places and, hence, are not locationally mobile (for example, see Amin and Thrift, 1994). Much depends upon the activity in question. Shifting taxes from employment, income and profit and on to services received by firms and consumers, including environmental resources consumed (virgin inputs, land-use and environmental sink services), is likely to be one of the few solutions that will allow for income redistribution in a world without borders. Greater levels of recycling, encouraged by such tax reforms, would also help 'hold down' capital and fix it within the markets served, and are reinforcing existing tendencies towards 'glocalization' (see ibid.).

Whatever the nominal purchasing power of future incomes, their real purchasing power in respect of products and services whose consumption involves dissipative loss of materials and energy will decrease. This has several implications for defining 'welfare-enhancing' work. Meeting many *basic* needs, in particular for physical mobility and space conditioning (mostly heating), involves dissipative losses of materials and energy. Current systems for meeting these needs are materials- and energy-inefficient or needlessly profligate (Löfstedt, 1995) while residential-sector energy use is among the highest. These inefficiencies are embedded within present infrastructures and inefficient organizational patterns. These need to be changed. Buildings can be made to be nearly or completely energy self-sufficient (Building Services Research and Information Association, 1994). Transportation can be reduced through tele-applications (such as teleworking) and greater mixing of land uses, and physical transport efficiency improved by modal switches associated with new public and private transport systems. The needed changes all involve 'welfare-enhancing' work in both the private and (especially) public domains, and have strong equity implications since they help decouple the link between comfortable living and high income. They could be integrated into a new mode of regulation via revised systems of transfer payments or public expenditure programmes in ways that would foster nascent 'green' industries (many of which would have considerable export potential, such as construction-materials-embedded photovoltaic cell technologies).

Purchasing power in relation to conventional *status* goods will decrease since these, too, are energy- and/or materials-intensive. In particular, recreational and optional travel and automobility will become relatively more expensive. Reduced physical mobility will put a premium on enhancing local environmental quality and providing leisure and recreational services at the local level. They will also foster greater local self-sufficiency as imported goods (embodying high energy taxes associated with transportation) will become more expensive relative to local produce. *Services* provided at little or no cost to the environment, especially those provided mostly by human work, will become relatively more affordable. Health care and education will increase in importance and contribute to an enhanced quality of life. Education and learning within a 'learning culture' (Lutz, 1994) will become key elements of 'welfare-enhancing' work.

This suggests that the potential for information and communications technologies (ICT) to contribute to local and regional economic revival, support alternatives to conventional employment and provide for environmentally benign development will be realized. Some experiments are already under-way, such as the Strategies for Optimal Strength (SOS) project involving six communes in northern Sweden making extensive use of ICT. Unlocking this potential more generally will require the lifecycle environmental performance of ICT to be enhanced, as the production of electronic-grade silicon, in particular, currently involves high levels of materials loss and toxic wastes such as contaminated solvents (Ayres *et al.*, 1994). Moreover, rapid technological advance leads to equipment soon becoming technologically obsolete although it is important not to confuse technological obsolescence with an inability to allow particular tasks to be undertaken. Others have emphasized ICT as an essential element for enhancing economic competitiveness, especially in respect of the important and growing traded business services sector. The essential element is that commissioner and contractor need never meet as ICT provides the opportunity to market skills worldwide.

The capacity to use ICT to replace travel, especially commuting, and to facilitate decentralized living–working arrangements which might spread the stresses placed upon the environment more thinly both in space and time could also be environmentally beneficial. Teleworking is likely to be encouraged as firms seek to reduce office space, which accounts for an ever-higher proportion of overall costs and represents an increasing liability to many companies (Henkel, 1994). Time–space compression (Harvey, 1989) seemingly paradoxically can enhance the importance of the specificities of *some* (but not *all*) places in a global economy – with a clear resultant risk, therefore, of deepening socio-spatial inequalities which could endanger the achievement of environmental and employment goals if left unchecked. The growth of global 'back offices' clearly illustrates this danger. Henkel (1994), for example, cites the cases of Swissair which has switched its ticketing arrangement for international flights to Bombay and of an American insurance company that employs nurses at home in Ireland to process medical claims 'overnight'. More generally, the new global centres for 'back office' work are Russia, India and China, which offer masses of technologically skilled labour at very low cost. This illustrates the need for global regulation of labour market conditions if employment creation in such places is to avoid the worst excesses of a neo-liberal approach to economic management.

CONCLUSIONS AND IMPLICATIONS

Establishing a new sustainable regime of accumulation will require the realization of a new model of structural economic change. Many of the elements that might form part of a policy package within an eco-Keynesian mode of regulation have already been identified: the need for a facilitating meta-policy framework at international, national, regional and local levels; the identification and removal of barriers to change; and the need to steer and harness technological and cultural developments in ways that support the attainment of economic, social and environmental goals. The development of a new system of transfer payments and public expenditures which, unlike earlier redistribution systems, contributes to rather than detracts from the achievement of economic, social and environmental 'goods' such as efficient production, job creation and the performance of welfare-enhancing work, is central to this approach. The linchpin of the system is its guaranteeing a citizen's income while providing the needed incentives and flexibilities to ensure that welfare-enhancing work is accomplished and a balance struck in personal and societal time allocations between work, education and leisure.

Although some elements of past economic practice may remain in a new environmentally sustainable economy, there is unlikely to be a reversion back towards a system of Keynesian 'full employment'. Nor should we necessarily seek to replicate such a system, which brought misery and suffering to many people, not least because 'full employment' for many years was defined in relation to white men. 'Full employment' in this sense will no longer occupy a pivotal role in the equating of production and consumption as the route to increased economic growth rates. Indeed, increasing growth rates *per se* will no longer be the sole – or even main – goal of state policies. Even if it were the case that making production more environmentally compatible would directly employ more people, this is unlikely to have a major impact on overall unemployment levels. Nevertheless, there are compelling reasons why a switch to a more equitable distribution of work, and to a more environmentally sustainable economy is necessary.

Both unemployment and environmental stress can be related to the current neo-liberal development paradigm. Revision of the policy framework surrounding the market and its operations is needed to tackle these problems, but a return to the Keynesian certainties of 'full employment' is not a feasible option. None the less, it does not follow that a revision intended to internalize environmental costs will *necessarily* and *automatically* also resolve the 'unemployment' problem (and vice versa), although such a revision would undoubtedly have employment implications (both positive and negative). It does follow that the goals and practices of contemporary capitalism need radical review for both employment and environmental reasons, that the urgency for making such a review is all the greater because both problems are products of the same malaise. Such a review should seek to *create* major synergies between the achievement of greater environmental protection, the creation of more equitable and satisfying employment opportunities and the delivery of enhanced individual and collective welfare. Changes should be steered in ways that enhance security, equity and economic performance while reducing the materials-intensiveness of production and economic growth. Complementary measures are needed to enable social inclusion, guarantee minimum living standards and reduce the materials-intensiveness of delivering these. Policy changes should facilitate the welfare-enhancing use of human resources, including 'work' that contributes to welfare by enhancing environmental quality or reducing the stresses that comfortable living place on the environment.

In summary, there is a need for a switch to a sustainable regime of accumulation shaped by an eco-Keynesian mode of regulation. The distribution of, and entitlements to, society's output need to be shifted from their current close relationship to inherited wealth and position in the wage labour market to one which relates more closely to the socially useful work – waged and unwaged – that people carry out and to their rights as citizens. The needed changes could be designed to facilitate greater environmental protection, improved economic performance (through productivity improvements of the currently unemployed) and greater social equity and cohesion. There are opportunities for win–win outcomes *if* the challenges faced are seen as systemically linked and a coherent strategy for economic restructuring is formulated and implemented accordingly. Conversely, a failure to do so could lead to continuing environmental destruction and permanent unemployment for many.

In the final analysis, however, there are unavoidable questions which must be faced about the possibilities for and limits to state involvement in steering the trajectory of economic and social development within capitalism. The win–win scenarios referred to above assume that state regulation and involvement can successfully contain, if not abolish, crisis tendencies that are inherent in a capitalist economy. But there are powerful reasons to believe that an eco-Keynesian approach would be no less susceptible to the forces that drive a capitalist economy than any other mode of regulation and regime of accumulation. The maturing contradictions of state involvement were decisive in bringing about the end of the Fordist regime of accumulation and mode of regulation within the advanced capitalist countries. The emergent crisis of one mode of state regulation spelled the end for Keynesianism and ushered in its neo-liberal successors but these proved to be no more immune to crisis. Similar longer-term dangers may await their eco-Keynesian successor within the parameters of a capitalist economy, with the resultant threat of a future of further environmental destruction and permanent unemployment for many. The best that may be expected – or hoped for – is to contain the problem for a while and buy some time in which more radical solutions may be explored.

REFERENCES

Albert, M. (1993), *Capitalism against Capitalism*, London: Whurr.
Amin, A. and Thrift, N. (eds) (1994), *Globalization, Institutions and Regional Development in Europe*, London: Oxford University Press.
Anderson, J. (1995), 'The exaggerated death of the nation state', in J. Anderson, C. Brook and A. Cochrane (eds), *A Global World?*, Oxford Oxford University Press, pp. 65–112.
Ayres, R.U. (1991), *Computer Integrated Manufacturing: Revolution in Progress*, London: Chapman & Hall.
Ayres, R.U., Frankl, P. and Lee, H. (1994), *Life Cycle Analysis of Semiconductors*, CMER Working Paper, Fontainebleau: European Institute of Administrative Affairs (INSEAD).
Britton, F.E.K. (1994), *Rethinking Work: New Concepts of Work in a Knowledge Society*, Report of the RACE Program, Paris: EcoPlan International.

Building Services Research and Information Association (1994), *Environmental Code of Practice for Buildings and Their Services*, London: BSRIA.

Business Council for Sustainable Development (1994), *Internalising Environmental Costs to Promote Eco-efficiency*, Geneva: BCSD.

European Commission (1993), *Growth, Competitiveness, Employment: The Challenges and Ways Forward into the 21st Century*, Brussels: Commission of the European Communities.

European Commission (1994), *The Potential Benefits of Integration of Environmental and Economic Policies: An Incentive Based Approach*, Brussels: Commission of the European Communities.

Fontela, E. (1994), 'The long-term outlook for growth and employment', in OECD, *Societies in Transition: The Future of Work and Leisure*, Paris: OECD, pp. 25–40.

Friedman, M. and Friedman, R. (1980), *Free to Choose: A Personal Statement*, New York: Harcourt Brace.

Habermas, J. (1975), *Legitimation Crisis*, London: Heinemann.

Harvey, D. (1989), *The Condition of Postmodernity*, Oxford: Basil Blackwell.

Henkel, H.O. (1994), 'Risks and opportunities of telework for the individual, the environment and society at large', in *Proceedings of the European Assembly on Teleworking and New Ways of Working*, Berlin, 3–4 November, pp. 11–17.

Hudson, R. (1989), 'Labour market changes and new forms of work in old industrial regions: maybe flexibility for some but not flexible accumulation', *Society and Space*, 7: 5–30.

Hudson, R. (1995), 'Towards sustainable industrial production: but in what sense sustainable?', in M. Taylor (ed.), *Environmental Change: Industry, Power and Place*, Winchester: Avebury, pp. 37–56.

Hudson, R. and Plum, V. (1986), 'Deconcentration or decentralization? Local government and the possibilities for local control of local economies', in M. Goldsmith, and S. Villadsen (eds), *Urban Political Theory and the Management of Fiscal Stress*, Aldershot, Hants: Gower, pp. 137–60.

Hudson, R. and Williams, A. (1995), *Divided Britain*, 2nd edn, Chichester, Sussex: John Wiley.

Jackson, T. and Marks, N. (1994), *Measuring Sustainable Economic Welfare: A Pilot Index, 1950–1990*, Stockholm: Environment Institute.

Jenkins, T. and McLaren, D. (1994), *Working Future? Jobs and the Environment*, London: Friends of the Earth.

Kistler, E. and Strech, K-D. (1992), 'Die Sonne der Arbeit: Arbeitsein-stellung als Forschungsgegenstand im Transformationsprozess', in D. Jaufmann, E. Kistler, K. Meier, K. and K-D. Strech (eds), *Empirische Sozialforschung im vereinten Deutschland*, Frankfurt: Campus.

Lash, S. and Urry, J. (1987), *Disorganised Capitalism*, Cambridge: Polity Press.

Lenk, H. (1994), 'Value changes and the achieving society: a social-philosophical perspective', in OECD, *Societies in Transition: The Future of Work and Leisure*, Paris: OECD, pp. 81–94.

Leonard H.J. (1988), *Pollution and the Struggle for the World Product: Multinational Corporations, Environment and International Competitive Advantage*, Cambridge: Cambridge University Press.

Lipietz, A. (1987), *Miracles and Mirages*, London: Verso.

Lipietz, A. (1992), *Towards a New Economic Order*, Cambridge: Polity Press.

Löfstedt, R.E. (1995), *The Times Higher Educational Supplement*, 31 March: 18.

Lutz , C. (1994), 'Prospects of social cohesion in OECD countries', in OECD, *Societies in Transition: The Future of Work and Leisure*, Paris: OECD, pp. 95–119.

Mandel, E. (1975), *Late Capitalism*, London: New Left Books.

Nelson, R.R. and Winter, S.G. (1982), *An Evolutionary Theory of Economic Change*, Cambridge, Mass.: Harvard University Press.

Nordhaus, W.D. and Tobin, J. (1972), 'Is growth obsolete?', National Bureau of Economic Research, General Series 9, New York: Columbia University Press.

O'Connor, J. (1973), *The Fiscal Crisis of the State*, New York: St. Martin's Press.

Repetto, R. (1992), *Green Fees: How a Tax Shift Can Work for the Environment and the Economy*, Washington, D.C.: World Resources Institute.

Robertson, J. (1995), *Electronics, Environment and Employment: Harnessing Private Gain to the Common Good*, Oxford: Oxford Green College Centre for Environmental Policy and Understanding.

Sayer, A. and Walker, R. (1992), *The New Social Economy*, Oxford: Basil Blackwell.

Schmidt-Bleek, F. (1994), 'Work in a sustainable economy', in *Proceedings of the European Assembly on Teleworking and New Ways of Working*, Berlin, 3–4 November, pp. 19–34.

Simonis, U.E. (1994), 'Industrial restructuring in industrial countries', in R.U. Ayres and U.E. Simonis (eds), *Industrial Metabolism: Restructuring for Sustainable Development*, Tokyo: United Nations University Press, pp. 31–54.

United Nations Development Program (1993), *Human Development Report 1993*, New York: Oxford University Press.

von Weizsäcker, E.U. (1994), *Earth Politics*, London: Zed Books.

Weaver, P.M. (1995a), *Implementing Change: A Resource Paper for the Factor 10 Club Meeting*, Carnoules, September.

Weaver, P.M. (1995b), 'Steering the Eco-transition: A Materials Accounts Based Approach', University of Durham, mimeo.

Wuppertal Institute for Climate, Environment and Energy: Factor 10 Club (1994), *Carnoules Declaration*, Wuppertal.

Yearley, S. (1995), 'The transnational politics of the environment', in J. Anderson, C. Brook and A. Cochrane (eds), *A Global World?*, Oxford: Oxford University Press, pp. 209–48.

12. Some alternative explanations of Irish unemployment

Charles M.A. Clark and Catherine Kavanagh*

INTRODUCTION

The Irish economy, in terms of GDP growth, has outperformed the rest of Europe over the past five years, leading some to label it the 'Emerald Tiger'. Yet it also has one of the highest unemployment rates. Although this rapid growth in GDP is beginning to produce some job growth, the unemployment rate remains stubbornly high and persists at double-digit levels. The purpose of this chapter is to examine some of the options available to policy-makers in alleviating unemployment, to assess their legitimacy in the light of the causes of Irish unemployment and to evaluate their possibilities for success.

Solutions to economic problems begin with how we understand and explain the problem. This is as true for the issue of unemployment as it is for any other issue. In economics, there are two approaches to the problem of high unemployment. It is perceived to be either a macro-economic issue or a micro-economic issue. Although these two approaches are not mutually exclusive, it is common for analysts to emphasize either macro or micro factors and rarely both. Yet it is quite possible that unemployment, particularly mass unemployment, could be due to both macro and micro factors. Which approach the policy analyst or theorist/consultant takes will greatly determine the advice given to policy-makers. This chapter examines how the macro and micro perspectives explain unemployment in Ireland, and explores the policies which each perspective advocates. It is organized as follows. The next section reviews the problem of unemployment in Ireland. This is followed by an examination of the macro-economic approach to Irish unemployment and the policy recommendations it suggests. The fourth section considers the micro-economic explanations and its policy prescriptions. The subsequent

* The authors gratefully acknowledge financial support for this project from the Arts Faculty Research Fund, University College Cork, Ireland.

section proposes a redefinement of employment to one of social participation which would be aided by the introduction of a basic income. Finally, the chapter concludes with a summary of the main points.

IRELAND'S DUAL UNEMPLOYMENT PROBLEM

The current level of unemployment in Ireland is both the result of the general level of labour slack in the advanced capitalist economies and of factors specific to the Irish economy. To understand the persistently high levels of unemployment and to design policies to fight high unemployment, it is necessary that both sets of factors be addressed.

Table 12.1 illustrates the trends in unemployment rates in Ireland, the EU, and the USA. These figures highlight the rise in Irish and EU unemployment rates over the period. An obvious question arising from Table 12.1 is: Why did Ireland's unemployment rise to such high levels, surpassing all other EU countries (with the exception of Spain)? In fact, Ireland's unemployment and employment experience is unique in many ways. Several reasons have been suggested to explain this. These include the country's failure to create sufficient employment growth, combined with increased labour force growth. The growth in the labour force has gener-

Table 12.1 Unemployment rates for selected years, 1960–96

Year	Ireland	EU	US
1960	5.5	2.5	5.4
1973	5.7	2.6	4.8
1980	7.3	6.4	7.0
1985	17.0	10.5	7.1
1990	13.3	8.1	5.4
1991	14.7	8.2	6.6
1992	15.5	9.3	7.3
1993	15.6	10.9	6.7
1994	14.8	11.3	6.0
1995	13.9	11.1	5.6
1996	13.6	10.9	5.7

Note: The EU figures up to and including 1990 refer to the EU-12, excluding East Germany, while the figures for 1991 onwards relate to the EU-15, including East Germany.

ally outstripped the growth in employment. Kennedy (1998) notes that the total level of employment is not much higher now than it was over 70 years ago at the time independence was achieved. During the 1970s and 1980s, the rate of employment growth in Ireland was one of the slowest recorded among the OECD countries. As shown in Table 12.2, for the countries listed, Ireland is the only country which experienced a decrease in employment in the period 1982–90.

It is not altogether surprising, therefore, that Ireland has had an endemic unemployment problem. In addition, the lack of job opportunities was associated with other problems such as emigration and low participation rates. In the past, emigration acted as a safety valve and was effectively seen as an acceptable alternative to employment. However, this changed during the early 1970s and early 1980s. With depressed labour market conditions abroad, particularly in the UK, and the worldwide rise in unemployment since the first oil crisis of 1973, emigration was no longer a viable option; this resulted in acute problems for Ireland. However, due to expansionary fiscal policies during the latter half of the 1970s, the rise in unemployment was comparatively muted up to 1980, despite reduced emigration and a substantial increase in the labour force. With the introduction of contractionary policies during the early 1980s, and dismal employment growth, unemployment began to soar. The growth in the labour force was stemmed somewhat by emigration which grew rapidly again during the second half of the 1980s. Had it not been for emigration,

Table 12.2 Employment and employment growth in selected OECD countries

Country	1992 (millions)	1982–90 annual % change	1991–95 annual % change
Australia	7.7	2.6	0.5
Belgium	3.8	0.6	−0.3
Denmark	2.5	0.8	0.1
Ireland	**1.1**	**−0.2**	**0.9**
Italy	21.3	0.6	−1.0
Japan	64.4	1.3	0.9
The Netherlands	6.7	1.6	1.1
Spain	12.4	1.4	−1.2
UK	25.3	1.5	−0.9
USA	117.6	2.1	1.0

Source: O'Hagan (1995, p. 37)

unemployment during the 1980s would have been considerably greater. O'Hagan (1995, p. 233) estimated that the growth in the potential labour force would have been 2.3 per cent between 1983 and 1990, a figure that is well above the average growth rate for most OECD countries. However, emigration brings with it its own problems. Since the early 1980s, there has been a change in the composition of emigration from unskilled workers to skilled graduates, raising concerns about the loss of human capital. The combination of poor employment growth, growth in the labour force (which has mainly shown up in higher unemployment), low participation rates and emigration has resulted in relatively higher dependency rates in Ireland compared to other EU countries.

The full impact of worldwide events and domestic influences on Irish unemployment can be seen from Figure 12.1, which illustrates the trend in Irish unemployment over the full period 1973–96. It should also be remembered that these figures mask to some extent the problem of youth unemployment, which is among the highest in the OECD countries, at 25.1 per cent in 1993 for the 15–24-year age group. In addition, long-term unemployment has received much attention in recent years. OECD (1994b) estimated that Ireland's long-term unemployment rate in 1992 was 9.5 per cent, rivalled only by Spain, at 10.6 per cent, among the OECD countries.

During the worldwide economic recovery in the second half of the 1980s, most countries, including Ireland, experienced a moderate fall in unemployment. These gains, however, were largely reversed in the downturn in the 1990s. The recovery since then has brought little reduction in unemployment in the EU as a whole, so that the EU unemployment rate

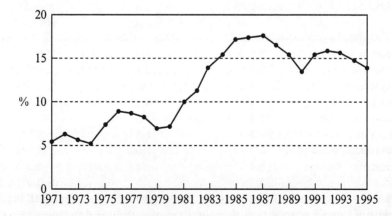

Figure 12.1 Unemployment rate in Ireland, 1971–95

is nearly double that of the US rate, which is back to approximately 5.5 per cent. The improvement in Ireland's unemployment rate has also been somewhat better, although some of this is undoubtedly due to emigration which has continued, albeit at a much slower pace.

Although Table 12.1 suggests that Irish unemployment is now approaching the EU level, it should be noted that the unemployment problem is on an altogether higher scale than in the EU as a whole. In addition, it is not satisfactory merely to reach the EU level, given that this rate is itself unacceptably high. Also, as Kennedy (1998) notes, sustaining progress is not automatic: it will be influenced strongly by the policies and decisions that are followed.

Finally, it is worth mentioning that unemployment as measured by these statistics can considerably underestimate the problem of labour slack, as has been shown in recent work by the OECD (1995a), Eatwell (1995) and Standing (1986). More generalized measures of unemployment seriously challenge the so-called success of the 'deregulated' labour markets (such as the United States), indicating that much of their success is in fact shifting the statistically unemployed to the disguised unemployed (Eatwell, 1995).

The questions now to be addressed are: Is Ireland's unemployment problem being caused by exogenous macro factors in the world economy? Or is Ireland duplicating the micro-economic conditions which are at the root of the rise in world unemployment?

THE MACRO-ECONOMIC EXPLANATION OF IRISH UNEMPLOYMENT

The macro-economic perspective we adopt is that developed in the post-Keynesian tradition. Post-Keynesian economic theory is used because it more consistently follows Keynes's theories and because neoclassical macro-economic theory has abandoned the theory of aggregate demand in favour of 'rigid wages' theories of unemployment, which essentially constitute micro-economic approaches.

The post-Keynesian explanation of unemployment differs from neoclassical economics in two ways. First, post-Keynesians accept the essential message of John Maynard Keynes that the economy has no self-correcting mechanism to bring it to full employment. Secondly, they have a very different view of how labour markets behave. This approach begins with Keynes's proposition that the level of output is determined by the level of aggregate demand, and that there is neither a 'natural' nor 'long-run equilibrium' level of output nor any mechanism to adjust current levels of employment to full employment. The post-Keynesian view of the 'labour market' differs in many ways from neoclassical economic theory. According to post-Keynesian economic theory:

> [t]he labour market is not a 'market' as that term is usually understood, for the labour market does not possess a market-clearing price mechanism. Variations in either money wages or in the real wage rate are unable to assure a zero surplus supply of labour, and thus eliminate unemployment. In the context of (1) an industrial structure that is largely oligopolistic, (2) fixed technical coefficients in production and (3) mark-up pricing, the demand for labour depends on the level of aggregate economic activity. It has little, if anything, to do with the marginal product of labour. The supply of labour, meanwhile, depends largely on demographic and other sociocultural factors, though it is somewhat responsive to changes in employment opportunities. (Appelbaum, 1979, pp. 115–16)

In Keynes's analysis, the problem of a tendency for unemployment (labour slack) stems from the institution of money. It is the essential properties of money, and the workings of the financial system, which keeps the money rate of interest at a level that is too high to promote maximum employment. We shall see below that 'money' is still at the heart of the problem of mass unemployment.

Following Keynes, the post-Keynesian perspective sees the problem of mass unemployment as an aggregate demand problem. This raises the question: Why has the level of aggregate demand been inadequate to sustain full employment? An examination of the decline in the rate of growth of real GDP in the G7 countries (Table 12.3) demonstrates this general fall in aggregate demand.

Table 12.3 Growth rates of real GDP for the G7 countries: 'the slowdown'

Country	1964–73	1983–92	Col. 3/Col 2[a]
West Germany	4.5	2.9	0.64
France	5.3	2.2	0.42
Italy	5.0	2.4	0.48
UK	3.3	2.3	0.69
USA	4.0	2.9	0.72
Canada	5.6	2.8	0.52
Japan	9.6	4.0	0.42

Note: [a]This column represents 'the slowdown' or the difference in the growth rate in the second subperiod relative to the first subperiod. In other words, West Germany's growth rate in the second period was 64 per cent of the growth in the first period.

Source: Eatwell (1994, p. 9).

The decline in aggregate demand can be traced to many factors:

> Put simply, lower wages and greater wage inequality reduce consumption spending, fears of capital flight and trade deficits lead policy-makers to employ restrictive domestic macro-economic policy, inappropriate monetary policy stifles business investment, and fear of government budget deficits prevents fiscal policy from stimulating demand through tax cuts or greater government expenditures. With every component of aggregate spending being reduced, it is no wonder that unemployment has been rising throughout the world. (Pressman *et al.*, 1995, p. 127)

The dominance of restrictive macro-economic policies has been greatly aided by the two most important institutional changes to have taken place in the international economy in the past three decades. These are the break-up of the Bretton Woods system and the increased mobility of capital. These two changes have greatly increased the amount of risk and uncertainty in the international economy, raising real interest rates and thus stifling investment. Furthermore, they have placed strict limits on the ability of governments to initiate stimulative economic policies for at least two reasons. The first is the balance of payments constraint (Glyn and Rowthorn, 1994), which places pressure on the exchange rate when one economy grows faster than its trading partners and thus causes imports to rise and chokes off much of the multiplier effects. The second is due to international investors and speculators who can create a crisis for a nation's currency if they do not agree with the country's policies.

Moreover, it could be argued that the world financial markets have become what Keynes warned us about: casino capitalism. As Eatwell (1994, p. 10) noted:

> Financial markets are today dominated by short-term flows that seek to profit from changes in asset prices; in other words, from speculation. The growth in the scale of speculation, relative to other transactions, has been particularly marked in the foreign exchange markets over the past twenty years. It is estimated that in 1971, just before the collapse of the Bretton Woods fixed-exchange-rate system, about 90 percent of all foreign exchange transactions were for the finance of trade and long-term investment, and only 10 per cent were speculative. Today, those percentages are reversed, with well over 90 percent of all transactions being speculative. Daily speculative flows now regularly exceed the combined foreign exchange reserves of all the G7 governments.

Thus, the financial community's reaction to government policy is crucial for the success of any economic policy. If investors and speculators feel that the policy will lead to inflation (that is, lowering the real value of their assets) they can act in such a way as to counter the government policy. Specifically, a stimulative government policy will cause the financial community to expect higher inflation, or merely a change in currency values, thus causing a fall in the value of the currency. To prevent capital flight, governments and central banks are forced to increase interest rates. Even though economic theories such as monetarism and the natural rate of unemployment hypothesis which lead to the conclusion that stimulative economic policies cause inflation and have no real influence on the level of economic activity do not stand up either to theoretical or to empirical criticism, the belief (based partly on their self-interest) is enough to prevent any government from attempting to increase aggregate demand. Financial markets are led by speculation about where the 'market' opinion feels the average opinion will be in the short-term future. So-called 'economic fundamentals' have very little role to play in what is essentially gambling.

A word which dominates economic policy today is 'credibility', meaning 'market friendly', or in other words, 'a policy that is in accordance with what the markets believe to be "sound"', (Eatwell, 1994, p. 12). Thus, the need to have a credible policy forces governments to lower, or attempt to lower, government spending, deficits and inflation or to pursue a restrictive macro-economic policy. The extent of this restrictiveness for the G7 nations has been shown by Pressman (1995). He demonstrates how the fiscal impulse (a measure of whether a fiscal stance is expansionary or restrictive) has moved from being mostly expansionary in the 1970s to mostly restrictive in the 1980s.

Even without the credibility factor, the new international arrangements have a contractionary affect on macro-economic performance. Under the Bretton Woods system, much of the risk in the international economy was transferred to the international agencies and governments. Pressures on currencies were mediated by the central banks, thus eliminating the risk of a swing in values. This lowered real interest rates by reducing risk. Furthermore, since there was little economic incentive to speculate in currency values, there was much less uncertainty in the Keynesian sense of the word. Thus, interest rates were lowered further by a more certain future. The break-up of the Bretton Woods system, in and of itself as an institutional change, therefore caused a significant rise in real interest rates, which, along with the rise in monetarism and restrictive monetary policy, led to the high real interest rates of the 1980s and 1990s.

The Case of Ireland

Much of the rise in Irish unemployment can be explained by reviewing the changes in aggregate demand. From 1973 to 1979, the average growth in real total domestic demand in Ireland was 5.04 per cent, whereas for 1980–94 it rose at an average rate of 0.63 per cent. In these same periods, Ireland's unemployment rate increased from an average of 7.34 per cent to 15.26 per cent. The fall in investment was particularly striking. According to the OECD (1995b), gross fixed capital formation rose by an average rate of 0.0 per cent from 1984 to 1993, which is to say that during that period, there was no capital accumulation undertaken in Ireland. A recent Forfás report (1996) also notes this disturbing trend. In 1981, Irish non-residential fixed investment as a percentage of GDP was 24.1 per cent. This figure fell steadily during the 1980s to 12.5 per cent in 1992. The most dramatic aspect of this fall is the decline in business investment, which fell from 19.5 per cent in 1981 to 10.3 per cent in 1992. Some of this decrease can be accounted for, according to the report, by the fall in profitability of Irish firms, a clear sign of inadequate aggregate demand, while much is accounted for by the increase in Irish firms acquiring financial assets and investing overseas. This, we argue, is a reflection of the new institutional arrangements of increased capital mobility and the dominance of speculation over productive investment.

Capital formation has been shown to be a major determinant of employment (Rowthorn 1995), a point which is ignored by those who view unemployment as a labour market problem. Only Lee (1988–89), in the studies on Irish unemployment reviewed by McGettigan (1994), mentions capital formation as an important factor in Ireland's increase in unemployment. The lack of capital formation in Ireland, at a time when the EU average of non-residential fixed investment as a percentage of GDP increased marginally, should be seen as one factor in explaining its differentially high unemployment rate.

Similarly, public consumption fell during the 1980s and 1990s, which no doubt contributed to the rise in unemployment. From 1973 to 1979, real public consumption rose at an average annual rate of 5.47 per cent in Ireland, while from 1980 to 1992 its rate of increase fell to 0.92 per cent. This is a much sharper fall than the average for all smaller European countries for the same time periods: from 4.44 per cent to 2.33 per cent. The contractionary effects of the government sector can also be seen in Ireland's fiscal stance, which was generally restrictive during the 1980s and 1990s.

Table 12.4 summarizes the changes in the various components of aggregate demand, as measured by the OECD, from the 1970s to the 1980s and early 1990s. The only aspect of aggregate demand which improved during the 1980s and 1990s was the balance of trade, with the growth rate in exports falling only slightly, while the growth rate in imports fell to 42 per cent of the 1970s rate. This too can be attributed to weak domestic aggregate demand.

In addition to the deficient aggregate demand problem, a large portion of the social surplus, from which societies typically get the funds for capi-

Table 12.4 Changes in aggregate demand in Ireland, 1973–92

Average annual growth rate in:	1973–79	1980–92	Col.3/Col. 2[a]
Real private consumption	4.16	1.74	0.42
Real public consumption	5.47	0.92	0.17
Total gross fixed investment	7.71	–0.40	–0.05
Total domestic demand	**5.04**	**0.34**	**0.07**
Real exports	8.53	8.26	0.97
Real imports	9.16	3.85	0.42
Unemployment rate	7.34	14.57	1.99

Note: [a] This column represents the 'slowdown'.

Source: OECD (1993).

tal accumulation, leaves Ireland for other countries. According to the OECD (1995b, p. 5), from 1988 to 1993 an average of 11.5 per cent of GDP leaked out of the Irish economy in the form of repatriated profits, dividends, royalties and net interest (profits, dividends and royalties accounting for 9.5 per cent and net interest for 1.9 per cent). This far exceeds the amount of foreign investment, and in many years the figure approximates total domestic investment.

From the preceding macro-economic analysis, it seems clear that a portion of Ireland's unemployment problem can be explained by insufficient aggregate demand. This insufficient aggregate demand stems from two sources: (a) the international move towards flexible exchange rates; and (b) the rise in capital mobility which has raised real interest rates for the Irish economy, as elsewhere. Both raised the cost of capital, leading to a fall in the level of investment. The situation was exacerbated by the change in fiscal stance from expansionary to contractionary policies, which was particularly acute in Ireland. Yet the new institutional environment also limits Ireland's macro-economic policy options. For 'credibility' reasons, and because of Maastricht regulations, Ireland is incapable of embarking on an expansionary fiscal or monetary policy. Furthermore, neither interest rates nor exchange rates can be manipulated to stimulate aggregate demand. Moreover, even if fiscal stimulus were an option, the high degree of openness of the Irish economy greatly weakens any multiplier effects associated with any injection into the economy. The lack of effectiveness of this option can be seen by the experience of the late 1970s when the Irish government allowed the government deficit to rise dramatically in order to counteract the effects of the worldwide recession. This conferred only a short-term benefit. Eventually the debt grew at an uncontrollable rate, chiefly because of the lack of any multiplier effects due to the openness of the Irish economy. Lacking any real macro-economic policy options, it is unsurprising that policy has concentrated on micro-economic solutions, to which we now turn.

MICRO-ECONOMIC EXPLANATIONS OF UNEMPLOYMENT

Neoclassical economic theory treats the labour market in the same way as it analyses all markets: as the arena that co-ordinates the rational self-interested actions of individual economic agents. The buying and selling of labour is the same as the buying and selling of any other good or service, with its price being determined by the interaction of supply and demand. If quantity supplied and quantity demanded are not equal (that is, not in equilibrium), then the price of labour (the real wage) will adjust upward (to alleviate a shortage of labour) or downward (to alleviate a surplus) to re-establish the equilibrium market-clearing price. The most important features of this theory are its market-clearing assumption and its determination of factor prices. Market clearing is the process that leads to zero excess supply, which for the labour market means the existence of no involuntary unemployment. This process is worked out through adjustments in relative prices (as described above) which, for the labour market to clear, entails the real wage, the return on capital (profit rate) and the rate of interest.

Any deviation of the level of employment from full employment, if it persists beyond the short run, must be due to some market imperfection, the most common of which are government intervention and the influence of trade unions. The obvious policy implication of this theory is to deregulate labour markets, that is, move them closer to the perfect competition model. Most economists seem to argue that making the labour market more flexible is the primary means by which governments can promote employment.

Given that the neoclassical explanation of unemployment is based on a market-clearing model of the labour market, it is unsurprising that the most common 'causes' of unemployment in neoclassical economics are various forms of market failures or government interventions in the labour market. Of the former category, labour market inflexibility is most frequently seen as the cause of high unemployment, the solution to which is to increase labour market flexibility. The latter set of diagnoses is often also closely related to the labour market inflexibility thesis, with the assumption that government spending on programmes creates inflexibility in the labour market (for example, minimum wage).

Several micro-economic reasons have been put forward as explanations of persistent unemployment in Europe and Ireland. These include real wage rigidity, the wage-bargaining process, labour market rigidity, the structure of the tax and social welfare systems, a mismatch between the skills of the workforce and those being sought by employers, and hysteresis. All of these, it is assumed, introduce inflexibility and prevent labour demand equalling labour supply to clear the market. In the neoclassical analysis, high unemployment should lead to a fall in the real wage rate, encouraging employers to move down their demand-for-labour curves and hire more workers until full employment is restored. Increased inflows into unemployment (caused by increased redundancies) should cause increased outflows as employers recruit more unemployed people. For this to happen, the real wage must fall. The real-wage resistance argument suggests that if reductions in the real wage are resisted, then the larger inflow into unemployment will not be matched by a larger outflow, and a temporary rise in unemployment will be converted into a higher equilibrium rate of unemployment (see Table 12.5).

As this table indicates, there is some evidence to support the argument that real earnings have risen considerably, particularly in the EU and

Table 12.5 Real earnings, employment and unemployment rates

	1960	1990
Real earnings (index)		
USA	100	145
EU-12	100	251
Ireland	100	275
Employment (index)		
USA	100	176
EU-12	100	109
Ireland	100	107
Unemployment (rate)		
USA	5.7	5.5
EU-12	2.5	8.4
Ireland	5.6	13.4

Source: Leddin and Walsh (1995, p. 233).

Ireland, while at the same time unemployment has increased dramatically. However, the rise in Irish unemployment is on an altogether different scale to that in EU countries, and the rise in real earnings alone cannot explain the problem.

The nature of wage-bargaining and the role of trade unions are some of the reasons frequently put forward to explain real-wage resistance. One could argue that trade unions exist in part to ensure that real wages are rigid. For example, in inflationary periods, unions look for indexation of wages. Different approaches have been tried to develop a wage-bargaining process that will reduce real-wage resistance. One approach, developed by Calmfors and Driffill (1988) suggest that co-operation (or corporatism) between the 'social partners' (unions, employers, farmers and government) reduces real-wage resistance. The experience of Sweden was often contrasted with other European countries to support the view that unions and governments can act together and reduce confrontation, ensuring a better outcome. But the sharp rise in unemployment in Sweden and other Scandinavian countries in the 1990s casts doubt on this view.

A number of other factors have been suggested to explain why European employers have been more reluctant to take on workers at the same rate that occurs in the USA. Most of these can be categorized as factors which contribute to labour market inflexibility. For example, employers in many European countries have to offer long-term contracts to their new recruits, and thus find it costly to lay off workers once they are hired. In addition, many unions oppose flexible working arrangements such as part-time working and shift working. As a reaction to this problem, the trend has been towards increasing flexibility in contracts and other aspects of employment in order to encourage the recruitment of job seekers. In fact, the European Commission's (1993) White Paper, *Growth, Competitiveness, Employment*, encourages the move towards a more flexible labour market, and encourages the removal of disincentives to hiring and firing, in an attempt to promote employment. It also promotes flexibility in the form of part-time working, a shorter working week, career breaks and so on.

The structure of the tax and social welfare systems in many European countries is perceived to be yet another factor which inhibits the flexibility of the labour market. Leddin and Walsh (1995) argue that generous social welfare systems tend to support high reservation wages, acting as a minimum wage and prolonging job search. The combined tax and social welfare systems can lead to high replacement ratios and to poverty and unemployment traps. Layard *et al.* (1994) suggest that replacement ratios are relatively higher in European countries than in the USA, Japan and Canada.

Neoclassical analysis proposes that government intervention in the form of income taxes, minimum wages and so on will distort the workings of the labour market. The growth in the tax wedge, the difference between what it costs to hire a worker and the purchasing power of his or her wage, is another reason for high European unemployment rates, according to Layard *et al.* (1994) and Leddin and Walsh (1995). The effect of the wedge is to move the employer back up along the labour demand curves and the worker back up along the supply curve, leading to a reduction in employment. The fall in employment then depends on the elasticity of both the demand and supply curves.

Skill mismatch is also perceived to be a micro-economic cause of high unemployment. The argument is that the long-term unemployed do not possess the necessary skills for the type of work that is available. The rise in the numbers unemployed together with the rise in the number of vacancies in many European countries is frequently suggested as evidence to support this proposition. In view of this, active labour market policies are playing an increasingly important role in the move to fight unemployment in many OECD countries, including Ireland. These policies are aimed at improving labour market efficiency and equity by enhancing labour market mobility, producing a more effective match between the demand and supply of labour, strengthening the job-search process and increasing workers' productivity. This argument is supported by the European Commission (1993) which believes that flexibility in the form of increased mobility of workers will be enhanced with a more adaptable workforce, and hence stress the need for increased education and training. However, there are also negative effects associated with active labour market policies, including crowding-out effects, displacement and deadweight effects, and substitution effects, and these have been well documented by Calmfors and Lang (1995).

Proponents of the natural rate of unemployment hypothesis often resort to the hysteresis argument to explain why the rate of unemployment does not revert to its pre-recession level after adverse shocks. For example, Layard *et al.* (1991) propose that an important possible explanation of hysteresis is that rising unemployment in Europe has been associated with an increase in the proportion of long-term unemployed in the total. In many European countries, unemployment rose not just because of an increased inflow as people lost their jobs, but also because of a reduced outflow as the unemployed found it increasingly difficult to obtain work. The average spell of unemployment had lengthened. This argument is similar to the skill mismatch argument, in the sense that advocates of the hysteresis hypothesis also call for increased education and training to facilitate the match between the demand for and supply of labour. In particular, they propose that programmes should target the disadvantaged, such as early school-leavers, the long-term unemployed and women, who are the most likely to become structurally unemployed.

The shift in emphasis to micro-economic solutions to the problem of high European and Irish unemployment ignores the possibility that unemployment may not be due to an inefficient labour market, but may rather be an aggregate demand problem. Increasing workers' productivity and improving the efficiency of the labour market will have little benefit if jobs are unavailable. Effective labour demand which is determined by aggregate demand will be less than 'notional' labour demand, and involuntary unemployment is an expected outcome. However, Ireland has relied heavily on micro-economic solutions in recent years. It is to this issue that we now turn.

The Case of Ireland

Can micro-economic factors such as labour market inflexibility help in explaining Ireland's unemployment problem? Certainly, policy since the 1970s appears to reflect the change in emphasis from traditional macroeconomic policies to labour market policies which have been varied and broadened to cope with rising unemployment. This was accompanied by the observation that economic growth does not necessarily lead to employment growth, which some interpreted as the failure of traditional macro-economic policies in reducing unemployment (Dineen, 1984).

Wage agreements have been used in Ireland periodically since 1960 in the form of wage agreements, national understandings, and more recently, national programmes. Initially, these agreements were introduced to improve industrial relations, but later the belief was that corporatism would promote wage moderation and prevent unemployment rising. Since 1987, these agreements[1] have set ceilings on wage increases over a three-year period, with the objective of strengthening the economy's potential for sustainable employment and economic growth. In Ireland, the average unionization rate is 56 per cent, which is one of the highest in the EU apart from the Scandinavian countries. In the public sector, up to 76 per cent of the workforce is unionized, whereas in the production sector the figure is lower, at 54 per cent. These agreements are only binding to the extent that they are compulsory in the public sector and are generally adhered to in the private sector, although there are clauses for opt-out if companies are financially unable to award the pay increases.

All such agreements can be criticized on the grounds that they are tailored to the needs of stronger unionized sectors (especially the public sector) rather than to those of small and medium-sized firms facing international competition where a competitive cost structure is essential for success. These agreements have not altered the emphasis of Irish wage bargaining on protecting the after-tax income of those in employment, and there is little evidence of practical concern for the unemployed who are not represented at the bargaining table.[2] In fact, there is much evidence to suggest that the insider–outsider relationship is applicable to the Irish labour market.

Several authors have identified micro-economic factors such as wage rigidity and the structure of tax and social welfare systems as contributing to Irish unemployment. Lee (1988-89) posits the hysteresis hypothesis. Tansey (1991) takes the neoclassical stance and proposes that real wage growth is the primary cause of high unemployment. Leddin and Walsh (1995) propose that the substantial improvement in the social welfare system over the years is likely to have contributed to the upward drift in unemployment. They also note that the tax wedge rose by 30 per cent between 1979 and 1986 which, they argue, may have played an important role in Ireland's poor employment record. Newell and Symons (1990) propose that it is a combination of the high replacement ratios that have reduced labour market incentives and the growth in the tax wedge which has reduced labour demand. Walsh (1987) supports this argument. Barry and Bradley (1991) also hold this view, but also suggest that worldwide factors such as the downturn in world demand, world interest rates and the downturn in the UK labour market also had a role to play.

According to O'Connell and Sexton (1994), structural change may also have contributed to Ireland's rise in unemployment. Although since 1979 total employment has remained almost constant, the structure of employment has undergone change, as illustrated in Table 12.6.

Recent trends from the Labour Force Survey illustrate the continuing fall in the share of agricultural employment, the decline in manufacturing employment and the strong upward trend in the share of service employment since 1979. Furthermore, the performance of total manufacturing masks the trends in various subsectors. Employment in food and in traditional manufacturing has fallen since the 1980s although they still constitute the highest proportion of total employment. In contrast, employment in high-tech manufacturing is volatile and is subject to changing international conditions. Although significant growth occurred in the 1970s, numbers remained more or less static in the first half of the 1980s. Employment recovered quickly in the second half of the 1980s, particularly in the pharmaceutical and computer equipment industries. The majority of firms in this group are foreign-owned multinational companies.

The argument that structural change has contributed to Ireland's unemployment problem is supported by Barry and Hannon (1998). They

Table 12.6 Composition of employment in Ireland (% share of
          total employment)

Sector	1979	1983	1993	
Agriculture	19.3	15.5	12.6	
Industry:	31.9	28.4	27.2	
Manufacturing[a]	23.1	21.7		21.1
Building	8.8	6.7		6.1
Services	48.8	56.1	60.2	
Total	100.0	100.0	100.0	
Total employment (000s)	1145.3	1080.9	1145.0	

Note: [a]Includes Food, High-tech, Traditional and Utilities.

Source: O'Connell and Sexton (1994, p. 38).

note that real wages have increased in Ireland as well as Europe, despite
the large increase in the number of highly educated workers. Industrial
change, they suggest, has reduced the relative demand for unskilled workers, and this has shown up in the form of a dramatic increase in
unemployment while the demand for highly skilled workers has increased.
The OECD (1994b) shares a similar view. Technical change and a growing international division of labour, it argues, has tended to shift the
demand for labour from low-skilled jobs to high-skilled jobs. Hence, they
postulate a growing skills mismatch between labour demand and labour
supply, which is why they recommend active labour market policies to
alleviate the problem.

To some extent, the rise in the share of public expenditure in Ireland
on active labour market policies reflects this view. In fact, Ireland spends
a proportionately higher share of GDP on such policies (as distinct from
passive unemployment compensation) than other OECD countries, at
1.77 per cent of GDP in 1992, rising to 1.81 per cent in 1993. However,
Kavanagh (1998), in a review of the role of active labour market policies
in Ireland, has shown that much of this expenditure has been unsuccess-
ful in generating employment and reintegrating the unemployed into the
labour force. The reasons range from a lack of coherent monitoring of
programmes to insufficient targeting of the disadvantaged who are in
most need of skill enhancement. Additionally, Duggan (1993) has
demonstrated that the skills acquired by participants on programmes are
not necessarily those that are sought by employers. This is not to say that

these policies are altogether ineffective, because effectiveness should not necessarily be judged solely on economic grounds but should also include social considerations and the ability of programmes to act as preventative measures. Certainly, some programmes such as the Part-time Jobs Opportunity (PTJO) scheme and Community Employment (CE) create jobs that the market does not create and employ primarily those who are long-term unemployed. They are therefore more successful at meeting the objectives of social inclusion and equity. Given that some programmes are more successful than others at conferring benefits on their participants, and that Irish public policy has come to rely heavily on these methods in an attempt to combat unemployment, their role needs to be seriously questioned. It should not be assumed that these policies are a quick and easy solution to the problem of unemployment.

BASIC INCOME AND THE PROBLEM OF MASS UNEMPLOYMENT

The overall labour slack in the world economy is not expected to improve in the near future, and probably will never improve under existing institutional arrangements. The problem of mass unemployment is exacerbated by the break-up of the Bretton Woods system, the increase in capital mobility, the almost universal acceptance of restrictive macro-economic policies and the neoclassical ideology which supports it, and the rise in inequality. Yet the existence of a labour surplus is a common feature of all stages of capitalism and is particularly the case in demand-constrained, affluent economies. In the Golden Age of capitalism (from the end of the Second World War to 1971) a host of factors helped to generate demand artificially (the Cold War; the Marshall Plan; the rise of consumerism, conspicuous consumption and advertising; increased state spending from the full development of the welfare state). This served to conceal the fundamental problem, but none of these individually or collectively can permanently conceal the basic contradictions in modern capitalism: the ability of societies to produce more than they need to consume, and the assignment of income based on one's role in the production process.

Such inherent problems will not be addressed by marginal analysis or solely economic policies. Labour market reforms, such as increasing labour market flexibility, will not improve the developed world's obviously inadequate aggregate demand. The recent push for more active labour market policies has as its central tenet that unemployment is caused by rigidities in the labour market. Such policies, when they entail training and education, would probably be of benefit to the long-term unemployed and should be pursued towards this end. However, since they do not address the problem of inadequate aggregate demand, they will at best redistribute jobs but will have little on the overall level of unemployment.

The escape from the old ideas which Keynes advocated would do much to lessen the problem of mass unemployment. Furthermore, enacting policies and institutions to end the 'privatization' of risk, such as a new version of the Bretton Woods system along with restrictions on capital mobility and speculation, would go a long way towards improving the employment situation. We cannot revert to the world of the 1950s and 1960s, but we could enact reforms like the 'Tobin Tax' to reduce some of the incentives for speculation. However, the central problem is that the productive success of capitalism has led to a situation where fewer and fewer workers are needed to generate the already high standard of living in OECD countries. Thus, what is ultimately needed is for us to rethink the nature of work, social participation and the purpose of economics.

The purpose of economics should be the improvement in the quality of life of the inhabitants of a given society, and not merely to increase GDP or other statistical measures of economic well-being. The past 20 years have demonstrated that increases in traditional measures of economic well-being (such as GDP or GNP) do not necessarily entail improvements in the quality of life. Alternative measures of economic and social well-being which adjust for 'green' factors, include social factors and distinguish between production that promotes the quality of life and production that retards the quality of life, show that the last two decades have seen little or no real progress. According to the 'Genuine Progress Indicator' of Redefining Progress (an environmental organization), increases in GDP in the USA over this period are mostly attributable to pollution, the break-up of the family and the rise in social problems. Thus, 'growth [has become] social decline by another name' (Cobb *et al.*, 1995, p. 65).

It is possible to imagine a scenario in which the problem of insufficient aggregate demand is solved and the developed countries return to full, or near full, employment. The Second World War gives us an historical case study. We are now faced with the same problem Keynes faced in the 1930s, yet the world is very different today. Keynes's solution was to generate economic activity artificially. Today, with large government budget deficits the norm, and with advertising and conspicuous consumption keeping consumer indebtedness at record high levels, the ability to increase consumption is quite limited. Certainly, increasing the level of equality in the distribution of income would provide an increase in consumption. However, this would be marginal at best. Unlike the 1930s, the material well-being of the populations of the developed nations is rather high. Poverty that does exist in the developed world is due to the institutions that determine the distribution of income and not to the level of income. It should not be assumed that more economic growth will help the poor in the developed world.

Rising social problems have been a consistently reliable source of increased aggregate demand, the break-up of families being the best example. Yet this is not the type of policy that should be promoted. Increasing the amount of waste is another way to generate aggregate demand, as is war, but these too should not be promoted in a civilized society. In fact, one of the biggest differences between our world and the one in which Keynes wrote is that we know that you just cannot expand the level of economic activity without taking into account the effect on the environment.

What is required is a rethinking of work and welfare. There are many ways to contribute to society and social reproduction, yet society only rewards paid employment and the ownership of capital or natural assets. Certainly, the parent raising a child, the adult caring for an elderly parent, or the volunteer who works for a civic organization, all make a valid and necessary contribution to society. In today's society, we generously reward those who care for our money (financial services) yet we fail to support adequately those who care for our children. All the activities that are necessary for civil society yet are performed outside the market place are as important as those activities which are performed within the market place. In fact, market activities require these non-market activities and institutions in order to exist. No society can exist on market relations alone, a point Adam Smith knew full well but which modern economists seemed to have forgotten.

Providing a basic income to all would recognize that everyone has something to contribute to society, and thus all should benefit. It would allow for greater social participation, while at the same time providing a clear signal from society that all are important contributors to social life. Social participation would be increased in many ways. First, a basic income would increase the income of the poor, allowing them to consume at levels necessary to participate fully in society. Secondly, since a basic income is universal, it substantially eliminates poverty and unemployment traps, removing a barrier many neoclassical economists feel significantly deters the unemployed from taking up work. Thirdly, a basic income would provide a significant boost to the 'social economy', those activities which are aimed at meeting human needs which go unmet in the 'market economy', thus allowing for greater and more varied forms of social participation. A basic income would allow individuals more flexibility in shaping their lives in a rapidly changing world. This would also entail labour flexibility, which is different from labour market flexibility.

By providing income security for unemployed workers who seek paid employment, as well as for those seeking to escape from poverty, a basic income would allow such individuals to experiment with different strategies, including but not limited to education, training and self-employment. It would allow those who work solely to provide an adequate income to reduce their level of market employment and increase their level of non-market production, such as a parent staying at home while children are young. Additionally, a basic income would also allow for more non-traditional forms of working relations, such as shared jobs, and for the necessary reduction in the work week (if we are going to distribute more equally the limited number of paid jobs) without a loss of income. Most importantly, it would allow the benefits of technological change to be more widely shared among all.

A basic income is also a more rational way of distributing society's output and income. By providing for more equality, it would better distribute income to where it is needed. Furthermore, it reflects the fact that much of society's wealth is social wealth, that is, it is due to the legacies of knowledge and social institutions given to us by our ancestors, and not solely to individual contributions at the margin. We are rich principally because we live in rich societies, and not solely because of our individual attributes, skills or talents. Currently, only a minority of the population are engaged in paid employment, and those outside of paid employment (the young, the elderly, the unemployed, those engaged in household production) have their incomes and standard of living determined mostly by their relation to those in paid employment or by their past paid employment history. It would be extremely difficult to find many whose incomes, according to neoclassical economic theory, match their marginal product.

CONCLUSION

Through most of human history, the central economic problem has been how to increase production. When unemployment arose, it brought with it much pain which was shared by all in the form of lost output, but it was not equally shared. Under such a system, it is reasonable to assume that poverty will be tackled through increases in production. Yet, in the developed world, the problem of scarcity has been more or less solved. Furthermore, mindless devotion to increasing GDP at all costs has produced statistical economic growth and declining or stagnant social well-being. John Maynard Keynes was well aware of the limited usefulness of economists' exclusive attention to production and efficiency. He noted that increasing production was necessary at a certain stage of economic progress, and that at such a level of development the institutions which promote production can be justified as being necessary for solving the economic problem of generalized poverty. However, he never lost sight of the real issues. 'Our problem', Keynes wrote, 'is to work out a social organisation which shall be as efficient as possible without offending our notions of a satisfactory way of life' (Keynes, 1963, p. 321). In his essay 'Economic possibilities of our grandchildren', Keynes argued that once the affluent stage of development is reached, society should and will rearrange its economic institutions to promote more laudable goals and aspiration than those that dominate in a society where poverty is the norm:

> When the accumulation of wealth is no longer of high social importance, there will be great changes in the code of morals. We shall be able to rid ourselves of many of the pseudo-moral principles which have hag-ridden us for two hundred years, by which we have exalted some of the most distasteful of human qualities into the position of the highest virtues. We shall be able to afford to dare to assess the money-motive at its true value. The love of money as a possession as distinguished from the love of money as a means to the enjoyments and realities of life will be recognized for what it is, a somewhat disgusting morbidity, one of those semi-criminal, semi-pathological propensities which one hands over with a shudder to the specialists in mental illness. All kinds of social customs and economic practices, affecting the distribution of wealth and of economic rewards and penalties, which we now maintain at all costs, however distasteful and unjust they may be in themselves, because they are tremendously useful in promoting the accumulation of capital, we shall then be free, at last, to discard. (Ibid., p. 369)

One of the social customs and economic practices which must be changed is the linkage between employment and income, between work and welfare. Since it is no longer necessary, or desirable, to pursue economic growth at all costs, there is no longer any need to tie one's economic well-being solely to paid employment. Breaking the link between work and welfare would also legitimate non-market forms of production and social contributions. This would allow for a higher level, and a wider variety, of social participation. Thus, it would address the real problem of mass unemployment in a manner which is sustainable in the long run. Finally, it would also have the effect of changing the 'code of morals' of our society, which currently exalts greed and selfishness as public virtues. With this change, we could then begin the task of addressing the numerous social problems which we have allowed to explode while our attention was fixated on economic growth.

The dilemma of Ireland's unemployment crisis is that conventional policy options which would address the problem, to the extent that they address the actual causes of insufficient aggregate demand, at least in the short run, are for most practical purposes not viable. Maastricht restrictions, the smallness and openness of the Irish economy and the internationalization of capital all conspire to make such traditional macro-economic policies of fiscal or monetary expansion either unavailable or ineffective. Furthermore, the long-run trend of technological unemployment must eventually dominate such policies, even if they could be carried out in the short run. Additionally, 'beggar-thy-neighbour' policies offer little hope for a small country like Ireland, which is relatively less industrialized than most other EU countries. An export-led growth path could entail the 'Brazilianization' of Irish society, lowering average living standards to Third World levels in order to make the Irish labour force competitive with low-wage economies.

The other side of this dilemma is that the policy options that are available to government, most notably enhancing wage flexibility and reducing labour costs (without increasing capital investment), can be enacted, but fail to address the central problem. Jobs that are created do not compete with the existing private economy, that is, they are in the so-called social economy and voluntary sector. In relation to their macro-economic impact, such policies are bound to be more ceremonial than instrumental. They have the appearance of effective action but essentially leave the economy unchanged. Given such a pessimistic prognosis, the only option left is to rethink the problem, to address anew the causes and consequences of mass unemployment in Ireland and the capitalist world in general.

The consequence of mass unemployment which should concern us is not the lost output created by this forced idleness, but the inability of the unemployed to participate fully in civil society. This social participation gap stems both from both the lack of adequate income caused by unemployment and from the fact that a job is one of the most important ways in which individuals connect with the community at large, tying them into the community as a whole, giving them a sense of self-worth and value that comes from being appreciated and acknowledging that they have made a valid contribution. Both of these costs, which have severe social and economic multiplier effects (drugs, alcohol abuse, abuse in the home, suicide, crime, and various other social ills), are at the heart of the sense of social decline in the developed countries. The solution to the real cost of unemployment lies in distribution and not in production, with increasing participation and not necessarily employment (meaning paid employment).

Progress in our rapidly changing society is there for everyone to see but not for everyone to share. The benefits of progress go to those with a socially recognized claim to a share in this progress, and under existing arrangements a validated claim to the benefits of progress is tied to market participation. It is not tied to how much one contributes to society, but to the holding of claims to a share in output, to the holding of

The world of work

assets (in the form of jobs, natural resources, financial wealth) which give one the power to claim a share. What is required is for society to recognize that there are many equally valid ways to contribute to society, including the social economy, and that all should be supported. This would necessitate the provision of a basic income and a change in social attitudes towards work and social participation (Clark and Kavanagh, 1996a, 1996b).

NOTES

1. These were the *Programme for National Recovery 1987–1990* (PNR), the *Programme for Economic and Social Progress 1991–1994* (PESP) and the *Programme for Competitiveness and Work 1994–1997* (PCW).
2. It is only in current negotiations that the unemployed are represented.

REFERENCES

Appelbaum, E. (1979), 'The labour market', in A. Eichner (ed.), *A Guide to Post Keynesian Economics*, Armonk, N.Y.: M.E Sharp.

Barry, F. (1993), 'Issues in the analysis of Irish unemployment', in J. Bradley, J. FitzGerald and D. McCoy (eds), *Medium Term Review, 1991–1996*, Dublin: ESRI.

Barry, F. and Bradley J. (1991), 'On the causes of Ireland's unemployment', *Economic and Social Review*, **22** (4): 253–86.

Barry, F. and Hannon, A. (1998), 'Education, industrial change and unemployment', in C.M.A. Clark and C. Kavanagh (eds), *'Unemployment in Ireland: Alternative Perspectives'*, Aldershot: Ashgate.

Calmfors, L. and Lang, H. (1995), 'Macroeconomic effects of active labour market programmes in a union wage-setting model', *Economic Journal*, **105**: 601–19.

Calmfors, L. and Driffill, J. (1988), 'Bargaining structure, corporatism and macroeconomic performance', *Economic Policy*, **6** (1): 13–61.

Clark, C.M.A. (1998). 'Unemployment in Ireland: a post Keynesian perspective', in C.M.A. Clark and C. Kavanagh (eds), *'Unemployment in Ireland: Alternative Perspectives'*, Aldershot: Ashgate.

Clark, C.M.A. and Kavanagh, C. (1995), 'Basic income and the Irish worker', in S. Healy and B. Reynolds (eds), *An Adequate Income Guarantee for All*, Dublin: CORI.

Clark, C.M.A. and Kavanagh, C. (1996a), 'Basic income, inequality, and unemployment: rethinking the linkage between work and welfare', *Journal of Economic Issues*, **30**, (2).

Clark, C.M.A. and Kavanagh, C. (1996b), 'Progress, values and economic indicators', in S. Healy and B. Reynolds (eds), *Progress, Values and Public Policy*, Dublin: CORI.

Cobb, C., Halstead, T. and Rowe, J. (1995), 'If the GDP is up, why is America down', *Atlantic Monthly*, **276** October: 59–78.

Davidson, P. (1994), *Post Keynesian Macroeconomic Theory*, Aldershot, Hants: Edward Elgar.

Dineen, D.A. (1984), 'Anti-unemployment policies in Ireland since 1970', in R. Henning and J. Richardson (eds), *Unemployment: Policy Responses of Western Democracies*, London: Sage Publications.

Duggan, C. (1993), 'Employment programmes: prospects and issues', paper presented at the conference on Employment Programmes in a Changing Labour Market, 15–16 November, Dublin Castle, Dublin.

Eatwell, J. (1995), 'Disguised unemployment: the G7 experience', UNCTAD Discussion Paper.

Eatwell, J. (ed.), (1994), *Global Unemployment: Loss of Jobs in the 90s*, Armonk, N.Y.: M.E. Sharpe.

European Commission (1993). *Employment in Europe 1993*, Luxembourg: Office for Publications of the European Communities.

Forfás (1996), *Shaping Our Future*, Dublin.

Glyn, A. and Rowthorn, B. (1994), 'European employment policies', in J. Michie and J. Grieve Smith (eds), *Unemployment in Europe*, London: Academic Press.

Kavanagh, C. (1998), 'A review of the role of active labour market policies in Ireland', in C.M.A. Clark and C. Kavanagh (eds), *Unemployment in Ireland: Alternative Perspectives*, Aldershot: Ashgate.

Kennedy, K. (1989), *Unemployment in Ireland*, Cork: Cork University Press.

Kennedy, K. (1998), 'Irish unemployment in a European context', in C.M.A. Clark and C. Kavanagh (eds), *Unemployment in Ireland: Alternative Perspectives*, Aldershot: Ashgate.

Keynes, J.M. (1936), *The General Theory of Employment, Interest and Money*, London: Macmillan.

Keynes, J.M. (1963), *Essays in Persuasion*, New York: W.W. Norton.

Layard, R., Nickell, S. and Jackman, R. (1994), *The Unemployment Crisis*, Oxford: Oxford University Press.

Leddin, A. (1991), 'An analysis of the Irish unemployment problem in the context of EMS membership', University of Limerick, mimeo.

Leddin, A. and Walsh, B. (1995), *The Macroeconomy of Ireland*, Dublin: Gill & Macmillan.

Lee, G. (1988–89), 'Hysteresis and the natural rate of unemployment in Ireland', *Journal of Statistical and Social Inquiry of Ireland*, **26** (2): 31–61.

McGettigan, D. (1994), 'The causes of Irish unemployment: a review', in *Economic Perspectives for the Medium Term*, Dublin: ESRI.

Michie, J. and Grieve Smith, J. (eds) (1994), *Unemployment in Europe*, London: Academic Press.

Michie, J. and Wilkinson, F. (1995), 'Wages, government policy and unemployment', *Review of Political Economy*, **7** (2): 133–49.

Munck, R. (1993), *The Irish Economy: Results and Prospects*, London: Pluto Press.

National Economic and Social Forum (1994), *Ending Long-term Unemployment*, Report no.4, Dublin: NESF.

Newell, A. and Symons, J. (1990), 'The causes of Ireland's unemployment', *Economic and Social Review*, **21** (24): 409–29.

O'Connell, P.J and Sexton, J.J (1993), *Evaluation of Operational Programme to Combat Long-term Unemployment Among Adults in Ireland: Objective 3 of the Community Support Framework*, Dublin: ESRI.

O'Connell, P.J. and Sexton, J.J. (1994), 'Labour market developments in Ireland, 1971–1993', in *Economic Perspectives for the Medium Term*, Dublin: ESRI.

OECD (1993), *Employment Outlook 1993*, Paris: OECD.

OECD (1994a), *Employment Outlook 1994*, Paris: OECD.

OECD (1994b), *OECD Jobs Study*, Paris: OECD.

OECD (1995a), *Economic Outlook 1995*, Paris: OECD.

OECD (1995b), *OECD Economic Surveys: Ireland*, Paris: OECD.

O'Hagan, J.W. (1995), 'Employment and unemployment', in J. O'Hagan (ed.), *The Economy of Ireland: Policy and Performance of a Small European Country*, Dublin: Gill & Macmillan.

Pressman, S. (1995), 'Deficits, full employment and the use of fiscal policy', *Review of Political Economy*, **7** (2): 212–26.

Pressman, S., Seccareccia, M. and Lavoie, M. (1995), 'High unemployment in developed Economies', *Review of Political Economy*, **7** (2): 125–32.

Rowthorn, R. (1995), 'Capital formation and unemployment', *Oxford Review of Economic Policy*, **11** (1): 26–39.

Standing, G. (1986), 'Meshing labour flexibility with security: an answer to British unemployment', *International Labour Review*, **125** (2): 87–106.

Standing, G. (1992a), 'The need for a new social consensus', in P. Van Perijs (ed.), *Arguing for Basic Income*, London: Verso.

Standing, G. (1992b), 'Structural adjustment and labour market policies: towards social adjustment', in G. Standing and V. Tokman (eds), *Towards Social Adjustment?*, Geneva: ILO.

Tansey, P. (1991), *Making the Irish Labour Market Work*, Dublin: Gill & Macmillan.

Walsh, B. (1987), 'Why is unemployment so high in Ireland today?', *Perspectives on Economic Policy*, **1**: 3–44.

Walsh, B. (1993), 'Unemployment and economic performance in Ireland: the background', *FAS Labour Market Review*, **4**: (2): Dublin.

Weeks, J. (1992), 'The myth of labour market clearing', in G. Standing and V. Tokman (eds), *Towards Social Adjustment?*, Geneva: ILO.

PART IV

A Policy Agenda

13. Employment as a human right

Marc R. Tool

A policy that knowingly excludes millions from the world of work inhabits the same moral universe as apartheid.
Will Hutton, 'A Nobel vision of fair shares for all'

Have we given up trying to gain full employment? If not, what should we be trying to do about it?
James Meade, *Full Employment Regained*

INTRODUCTION

The International Labour Organization reported in 1994 that 'nearly one out of three workers in the world's labour force either has no job or is earning too little to live decently'. The world confronts 'the worst global employment crisis since the Great Depression of the 1930s'. Worldwide, '120 million are registered as unemployed. ... 700 million more are under-employed, earning less than needed to support a minimum standard of living'. In western Europe, unemployment levels generally remain at or near double-digit levels; nearly 'half of the 35 million unemployed workers ... have been off the employment rolls for a year or more' (ILO, 1994, p. A9). An observer of French efforts to reduce unemployment contends that the 'crisis of unemployment in the West is, without doubt, the most serious of our many problems, and the one that feeds and compounds all the rest – from crime to family breakdown and ethnic tension' (Woollacott, 1995, p. 21). Conditions for the unemployed have not dramatically improved in 1997.

It is the purpose of this chapter to address this crisis by arguing for the principle of guaranteed paid employment for all persons in the labour force.

Although the official unemployment rate in the United States in 1995 was under 6 per cent (US Dept of Commerce, 1996, p. 413), there is good reason to believe that the actual jobless rate may well be nearly double the official estimate if absent job holders, partially employed civilians wanting full-time jobs, and discouraged workers are included in the aggregate estimate (Dembo and Morehouse, 1944, pp. 9–17; US Dept of Commerce, 1996, p. 402). Moreover, it is not the case in the US that income forgone through unemployment is adequately replaced by unemployment insurance (UI) and other welfare transfers. Only about half of income is offset by compensatory transfers and, because of eligibility requirements, only about a third of the jobless actually receive UI compensation (Layard *et al.*, 1991; cited in Michl, 1995, p. 71).

But persistent unemployment in the United States, although modestly reduced in the last couple of years, is nevertheless only the most obvious indicator of a deteriorating economic situation for many American workers. This unseemly condition is dramatically demonstrated by other indicators that show an increasing maldistribution of income, a significant erosion of comparative levels of income and loss of job access for many in the workforce.

Maldistribution

The distribution of aggregate money income of families has, in the last two decades, become significantly and increasingly more unequal. In 1994, the top 5 per cent with 20.1 per cent receive more income than the bottom 40 per cent with 14.2 per cent (US Dept of Commerce, 1996, p. 467; Dembo and Morehouse, 1994, p. 30). In 1991, the comparable figures were 17.1 per cent and 15.2 per cent, respectively (US Dept of Commerce, 1996, p. 467). The degree of inequality in the USA substantially exceeds that of any other developed economy, east or west (World Bank, 1990, p. 237; Luxembourg Income Study, 1995, p. A4).

Erosion of Comparative Income

As Professor Wallace Peterson (1994, pp. 35–48) shows, the USA, in the two decades after 1973, endured a 'Silent Depression'. Increases in annual constant dollar earnings of non-agricultural workers dropped from about 2 per cent to less than 1 per cent. Weekly earnings were lower in the 1990s than in the 1980s (US Dept of Commerce, 1996, p. 424). Annual constant dollar median family incomes dropped each year from 1989 to 1993, and were only modestly reversed in 1994 (ibid., p. 461). The annual constant dollar rate of increase in disposable income per person fell to half its previous level from 2.6 per cent in 1973 to 1.3 per cent in 1993. In the last three years, the rate has averaged only about 0.5 per cent (Economic Report of the President, 1996, p. 311).

In 1996, the minimum wage in the USA was increased by the Congress from $4.25 to $4.75 per hour for workers. It will increase to $5.25 after one year for such workers (US House, 1996). While this increase is helpful, note that over recent decades the minimum wage has not been increased commensurate with increases in average hourly earnings. For example, in 1950 the minimum wage was 54 per cent of the average hourly earnings of workers. By 1996, it had dropped to 34 per cent (US Dept of Commerce, 1996, p. 429). In 1995, nearly 2 million workers were working at the minimum wage of $4.25; over a million and a half were, in addition, employed at rates below the official minimum (ibid.).

Displacement

In addition, if account is taken of substantial worker displacements resulting from downsizing, robotizing, computer-driven production controls, off-shore assembly and the like, concerns over job access and job security become ever more significant for the workforce generally. In 1994, nearly four and a half million workers were displaced: 42 per cent from plant closures, 30 per cent from slack work and 28 per cent from abolished shifts or positions (US Dept of Commerce, 1996, p. 404). In sum, in the USA and the developed world, relative earnings levels and work options have been significantly reduced over the last quarter-century for middle- and lower-income working families. Aggressive job creation supported by the Clinton Administration in the USA has slowed the erosion in some sectors, but basic insecurity continues for many workers.

Confronted with this sampling of data and indications of the attendant consequences, it is my task here to address the unemployment aspects of this earnings deterioration by lending advocacy support for policy initiatives to make access to paid employment at adequate levels of remuneration an assured human right. Indeed, employment as a human right has been affirmed in various US legislative proposals, in United Nations declarations and by the International Labour Organization (details below, pp. 282–4). Every adult who wants to work would, under this proposal, be assured of paid employment at a livable wage in the private or public sector. This chapter is intended to contribute to the continuing dialogue on the urgency, significance and feasibility of an assured employment policy.

In the following sections, declarations in support of assured employment are briefly reviewed; 'employment as a human right' is supported theoretically using neo-institutionalist constructs; contributions of legally assured employment are explored; the fiscal feasibility of policy options to introduce assured employment is briefly considered; and obstacles to the achievement of assured employment are examined and assessed.

This chapter reflects a neo-institutionalist (and post-Keynesian) approach to inquiry in which belief systems, institutional structures and discretionary conduct (public and private) that promote or retard the realization of assured employment are analytically explored. For present purposes, the neoclassicists' normative advocacy of a 'free market' economy is not relevant. The presumption that a 'market-clearing equilibrium, involving a balance between demand and supply in each market, will ensure the full employment of labor' (Sawyer, 1995, p. 17) is viewed as not credible. In lieu of deference to 'market forces', the locus and use of economic power to frame and implement policy as institutional adjustments is seen as the relevant universe of discourse. As Sawyer (ibid., p. 16) observes, unemployment arises 'as a control mechanism, albeit a socially and economically inefficient one'. The quest, then, is to shift from residual ideological and undemocratic policies that generate or tolerate unemployment to public measures that move towards assured employment.

THE PAST AS PROLOGUE

The role of the worker has, over the years, been variously characterized as a curse, a punishment, a moral obligation, a natural right, a source of profit, an access to status, a post-capitalist joy, even a time-filler (Special Task Force, 1972, p. 1). But the instrumental function of work is to engage individuals in constructive activity that contributes significantly to their own development and well-being (and that of their families) and concurrently helps to provide for the continuity and efficiency of the social process – economically, socially, politically. The absence of paid employment for significant segments of the community threatens that qualitative and communal participatory continuity.

But the concept of assured employment is not unfamiliar. President Roosevelt's experience with a decade of economic insecurity in the Great Depression of the 1930s led him to advocate assured employment in his State of the Union message in 1944. He called for an Economic Bill of Rights that would guarantee '[T]he right to a useful and remunerative job. ... [T]he right to earn enough to provide adequate food and clothing and recreation. ... [T]he right of every family to a decent home' (Roosevelt, 1944; reprinted in Commager, 1948, p. 694).

The United Nations Charter of 1945 affirms in Article 55 that 'the United Nations shall promote: . . . higher standards of living, full employment, and conditions of economic and social progress and development' (US Dept of State, 1945; reprinted in Staff, Social Sciences 1, 1949, p. 776). The Charter was ratified by the United States Senate in 1945.

The initial US Full Employment Bill of 1945 affirms that: 'All Americans able to work and seeking work have the right to useful, remunerative, regular and full-time employment, and it is the policy of the United States to assure the existence at all times of sufficient employment opportunities to enable all Americans ... to freely exercise this right' (quoted in Ginsburg, 1983, pp. 14–15). This Bill was not passed by Congress. A substitute Employment Act of 1946 was adopted but all references to full, guaranteed or assured employment were, under political pressure, dropped.

The United Nations in 1948, in Article 23 of its Universal Declaration of Human Rights, affirms that: '1. Everyone has the right to work, to free choice of employment, to just and favourable conditions of work and to protection against unemployment. 2. Everyone, without any discrimination, has the right to equal pay for equal work. 3. Everyone who works has the right to just and favourable remuneration insuring for himself and his family an existence worthy of human dignity' (UN Doc. A/811 1948; republished in Staff, Social Sciences 1, 1949, p. 794).

In the United States, the effort to provide for guaranteed employment resurfaced in the mid-1970s coincident with a substantial economic downturn. The Equal Opportunity and Full Employment Act introduced in 1975 by Congressman Hawkins, was 'to establish and guarantee the rights of all adult Americans able and willing to work to equal opportunities for useful paid employment at fair rates of compensation' (US House, 1975, p.1). Under the Hawkins Bill, the federal government would take primary responsibility for promoting employment and growth. Macro-economic policy would be used to increase the overall demand for labour; most jobs, in consequence, were expected to be created in the private sector. The federal government, working with smaller jurisdictions, would create jobs for everyone still out of work. In intent and design, it remains as the benchmark policy option in the USA for assured and noninvidious employment.

In 1977, the Hawkins Bill was merged with the Balanced Growth and Economic Planning Bill, introduced by Senators Humphrey and Javits (US Senate, 1975) and was subsequently referred to as the Humphrey–Hawkins Bill. In pursuit of political support, successive versions of Humphrey–Hawkins were developed, each scaling down or abandoning most of the original equal opportunity, full employment and national-planning goals and provisions (Ginsburg, 1983, pp. 63–74). The heavily amended Full Employment and Balanced Growth Act of 1977 was signed into law, but even its affirmation of percentage goal and targets for low rates of unemployment and inflation were largely ignored (ibid., pp. 63–84). After 20 additional and frustrating years of default in achieving virtually full employment in the USA and elsewhere, it is time, in my view, to move the quest for assured employment back on to national and international political agendas.

Global support is available. The International Labour Organization continues to provide imaginative leadership in the quest for full employment policies in developed, transitional and underdeveloped countries. As Werner Sengenberger notes elsewhere in this volume (Chapter 14), the ILO supports the objective of full employment in its Employment Convention no. 122 adopted in 1964. In addition, the Declaration of the World Summit for Social Development, signed by some 117 heads of state in Copenhagen in 1995, followed 'principles of ILO standards of employment policy' and secured pledges 'to promote the goal of full employment as a basic priority' (Sengenberger, 1996, p. 2).

EMPLOYMENT AS A HUMAN RIGHT

The concept of affirmed access to employment need not be characterized as a natural right rooted in natural law philosophy or other extra-evidential referential sources. It can be characterized instead as a human right that is based on the continuum of evidential social inquiry and the causal sequences and connectivities disclosed therewith. The following characterization of a human right to employment is grounded in the pragmatic instrumentalist approach to discourse and analysis.

The concept of a human right to employment requires the making of a value judgement and the use of a criterion of appraisal. It affirms that people ought to have access to continuing and remunerative employment. The undergirding value premise incorporated is and must be both a product of and an operative criterion in any scientifically credible analysis of the determinants of employment. This premise is an integral part of the continuum of factual inquiry and rational appraisals of consequence and conduct. The value premise incorporated identifies the 'ought' as the fostering of the continuity and instrumental efficiency of the social process. I have elsewhere identified the instrumental value premise as pursuit of 'the continuity of human life and the noninvidious recreation of community through the instrumental use of knowledge' (Tool, 1985, p. 293). It is the criterion endemic to warranted inquiry; it precludes invidious (or ceremonial) assessments of structure and conduct; it is operationally pertinent. It discloses the character of the 'problem' of unemployment as the denial of effectual and continuing instrumentally productive participation in the economic process. It is the critical normative vehicle for problem solving through the creation and assessment of hypothetical modifications of existing institutional structures.

In contrast, the value premise of the natural right to employment is rooted in the tradition of natural law. Its rationale represents a metaphysical approach to discourse and analysis and has purported to distinguish between what is and what ought to be over the last three centuries and more in the west. God created Nature, ergo what is Natural is good. The value premise is conformity with what is perceived to be natural. But '[t]he doctrine of natural rights is ... not a theory, not an attempted description or ordering of facts, but a faith, the essential dogmatic basis of what Carl Becker has called the "heavenly city" of the eighteenth century' (Brinton, 1947, p. 300). Belief in the doctrine of natural rights was extensively and 'successfully' reflected, for example, in the French Declaration of the Rights of Man and in the American Declaration of Independence, as a vehicle with which to undercut unilateral governance by the mediaeval church and by later monarchies. But its 'oughtness' principle of 'inalienable rights' is distilled not from experiential analysis but as an *a priori* construct sanctioned by an outside-inquiry force, presence or determinant. Its 'validity' is a function not of causal demonstration but of antecedent reverential belief. It embodies and recommends a value premise that must be accepted prior to inquiry and is validated not through causal demonstration of connectedness but through *a priori* deference to God, Nature or other metaphysical determinant.

In sum, the natural right to employment is a non-empirical, non-experiential, extra-causal conception of what ought to be. Its credibility derives from the acceptance of an antecedent metaphysical belief which cannot be integratively incorporated into the inquiry process. The human right to employment is grounded in the continuum of factual experience and rational appraisals of actual consequences experienced and is validated by inquiry-embedded instrumental social value theory.

Neo-institutionalist concepts of rightness, participation and community reflect the normative, empirical and analytical value premise of the continuity and instrumental efficiency of the social process.

Rightness

The instrumentalists' democratic ethos historically affirms the fundamental human right to be and to belong. Legally assured employment affirms the human right to be a part of, to belong to and contribute to the economic community. It is obvious that specialization of labour, in all but the most underdeveloped countries, has proceeded to the point where receipt of a continuous money income provides the primary access to the material means of life and experience. All adult individuals, as a condition of their own psychological, physical and cultural continuity, need regular access to an adequate flow of money income that provides the 'tickets to participation' in most aspects of economic and social life. As Will Hutton (1996, p. 19) observes: 'Exclusion from work implies exclusion from mainstream society, which in turn means exclusion from the political preoccupations of the majority. A democratic government that deliberately runs the economy with high unemployment sets out to debar some of its citizens from their economic and social rights.'

The source, size and utilization of income are, in the main, specified and constrained by prevailing institutional structures. Such income may come as earnings from work performed or services rendered, from ownership of financial and real property, from grants from others or from coercive seizure. The first three are contractually, legislatively and/or culturally prescribed; the fourth is formally proscribed. Typically, most people, rich and poor, receive income from a combination of sources.

In any case, for all but the very rich, earned income, mainly as wages or salaries, is demonstrably a universal and continuous need; physical and social membership in a human community establishes the right to a continuous flow of income in that community. Obviously, the question of how membership is to be legally defined and delimited is a critical dimension. Beyond the reminder that such membership, in a democratic order, must needs be non-invidious, the matter cannot be pursued here. Communities would, with assured access to employment, become legally obligated to sustain minimum income flows to their individual members as a condition of providing for their own continuity.

Universal assurance of employment – access to adequate earned income as a human right – connotes, then, non-discriminatory status within the community. For an instrumentalist, universality means non-invidious access to political, social and economic processes. An individual's obligation, given access to employment and community membership, is significantly to contribute to the economic well-being of the community. Employment as an enforceable human right. then, is an affirmation of the right to be in, to belong to and to help reconstruct a human community.

Participatory Involvement

Employment generates significant democratically warranted pecuniary and psychological consequences for individuals. First, access to and discretion over pecuniary income, given adequate levels, is a major source of individual empowerment. Income receipt confers discretion. Choices, not just over a 'market basket' of commodities, but more generally over the actual character and extent of quality-of-life options, become available. Empowerment from pecuniary discretion defines access to relevant education, health care, artistic expression, political involvement and acceptance of communal responsibilities, as well as economic goods and services. This legally established empowerment tends to reduce workers' vulnerability to intimidation and coercion from employers, private and public. Worker empowerment, predictably, is and will remain a major reason for conservative opposition to assured employment.

Secondly, participatory involvement through employment contributes to psychological stability and maturation (Jahoda, 1982). Assured employment helps to provide continuing opportunities to define and redefine who the self is and might become. As individuals come to know themselves in a working context, they discover and create new understandings, skills, capacities and interests. The work undertaken becomes a major conditioner of thought and behaviour that contributes significantly to the shaping and character of an individual's psyche. Involuntary unemployment aborts such maturation of growth and capacity.

Thirdly, participatory involvement through assured employment provides continuing and extensive opportunities to fashion and to affirm one's own conception of self-worth in a context of social interaction and engagement (Goodwin, 1972, pp. 112–18). Use of these options compels repeated formulations and applications of distinctions between invidious and non-invidious characterizations both of the self and of associates with whom one works. For a female computer specialist, gender may be a constraint on upward mobility. For a status-hungry junior executive, rank held may be a sufficient indicator of 'merit'. For a personnel director, hiring options may be delimited by ethnicity. The invidious use of human differences may well be reflected in employment connections. If 'relative worth' is invidiously defined as denigrative attributes at and by work, and is perceived and accepted as such by others, the capacity to function and grow socially and psychologically is heavily and adversely affected.

In an important sense, we become what we do. This recognition of one's job as a major conditioner of mind and conduct dates back, of course, in different forms at least to Marx and Veblen. Recall that, for Marx, economic class membership (bourgeoisie and proletariat) determines behaviour and sentiments. Class membership is stipulated by the presence or absence of property ownership. For Veblen, differing employments are historically characterized as worthy or unworthy, as non-invidious ('industrial labor') or invidious ('warfare, politics, public worship and public merrymaking'). The former 'has to do with elaborating the material means of life'; the latter has to do with 'the coercive utilization of man by man' (Veblen, [1899] 1934, pp. 7–10). Indeed, employment provides opportunities for the development of what are for Veblen the constructive 'instincts', predispositions to workmanship, idle curiosity and parental bent, even as it also provides, for some, the pecuniary means for the destructive 'contaminants' of emulation and predation (ibid., pp. 1–50).

To claims that assured employment would necessarily imply the provision of merely menial jobs and offer little by way of intellectual or manipulative involvement or challenge, a neo-institutionalist response is persuasive. Having no job is more likely to be psychologically destructive than having a menial job. Moreover, 'menialness', as Veblen observed, has more to do with the status and/or esteem conventionally associated with the work than it has with its physical demands, dirtiness or complexity. A surgeon's work is hardly tidy. A car mechanic must now master and repair computer-driven mechanisms. Invidious characterizations of jobs tend to be reflected in differential wage and salary levels.

Participation through employment involves discretionary interaction with others in consequence of which identities are refashioned; habitual reflections are modified; expenditure patterns are revised; personal responsibilities are identified and perhaps fulfilled. Participative involvement through employment enhances discretion and provides in some measure for growth in causal understanding and technological capabilities.

Community

People live only in the presence of, and in interdependence with, other people, feral children and hermits notwithstanding. The construct of community refers to the extensive and always complex array of prescriptive and proscriptive institutional constraints that correlate patterns of belief and behaviour. Such constraints provide the networks that define, organize and regulate social and economic life. For neo-institutionalists, these institutional constraints, though residually habitual, are perceived as fundamentally developmental and evolutionary. The community's efforts to respond to structural problems will necessarily take the form of adjustments in existing interdependent institutional forms that have become habitual. Human behaviour, in consequence, must then be adaptable and changeable; habitual modes must be revamped.

A community is a necessary mesh of individual and institutional interdependencies affirming the inescapable fact that we are reliant one upon another. Legally assured employment provides one of the most critical demonstrations of such recognized interdependencies. Involuntary and continuing unemployment is a demonstration of a massive failure to acknowledge major economic interdependencies. The admonition holds: If any significant segment of the community is impaired in form and substance (for example, denied meaningful employment), the whole community is impaired to that extent: '[A]ny community in which any sort of mutilation is practiced is a mutilated community. Modern industry demands the full powers of all its participants' (Ayres, [1944] 1978, p. 233). Impairments preclude or erode such powers. The reconstruction of any community is a necessarily continuing task of reducing or ending impeding and misdirective precepts and behaviour. Impaired segments – here the dispirited, unorganized, unemployed workers – cannot (do not) effectively participate in this undertaking. Their voices are not heard. Those who receive the incidence, for example, of flawed stabilization and employment policies have little influence on the reconstructions allegedly addressed to the removal of impairing behaviour and judgements. Illustratively, on what indicators does the Federal Reserve Bank rely in administering interest rate changes? 'Natural rates' of unemployment? Poverty indices? The interests of the unemployed are not vested; they are economically marginalized. For conservatives, assured employment is a perceived inflationary and political threat, not an instrumental promise. The institutional adjustment to establish legally assured employment as a human right empowers workers, reduces impairment and helps restore a sense of economic community.

CONTRIBUTIONS OF LEGALLY ASSURED EMPLOYMENT

The achievement and maintenance of virtually full employment generates instrumentally warranted consequences across a broad spectrum of socially needed and constructive outcomes. In the following, some categorical sorting of contributions is suggested by identifying, in sequence, those affecting individuals, the social order, the economic order and the political order. Differentiations are unavoidably somewhat arbitrary and certainly not discrete.

When employment is legally assured individuals gain, as noted, from the enhanced sense of self-worth generated by the continuing opportunity to make a productive contribution to the economic process. The ensuing continuity in family income received materially and demonstrably assists in the reduction of tensions and disjunctions that impair or destroy family cohesion. Given an opportunity, individuals with jobs will generally enhance their own levels of knowledge and understanding, improve capacities and develop new skills.

However, separated workers returning to employment may not have that opportunity. As Michl (1995, p. 72) observes: 'Displaced workers are more likely to be re-employed part-time or at reduced hours, and even if they are fortunate enough to find a full-time replacement job, they tend to earn substantially less than in their previous job.' Opportunities and incentives to enhance skills, then, may not exist. But the argument for assured employment is not eroded. Regular full-time employment should afford increased discretion over one's own life and work. With assured employment, choices among jobs can more frequently be made in search of qualitatively demanding and growth-inducing work connections.

The character, then, as well as the fact of employment, obviously does matter: 'The more democratic and self-affirmative an individual is, the less he will stand for boring, dehumanized and authoritarian work. Under such conditions, the workers either protest or give in, at some cost to their psychological well-being' (Special Task Force, 1972, p. 22). Employees' interest and desire for meaningful work – work that matters and contributes and is recognized as such – surfaces time after time, for example, in Studs Terkel's (1974) interviews with ordinary people about their jobs across a broad spectrum of occupations.

When employment is legally assured the social order gains. Assured employment does not eliminate, but would materially reduce, the extent of invidious discrimination in employment. If the original Hawkins Bill (1975) had been passed and implemented, the need and demands for 'affirmative action' directives would surely have been significantly eroded. Competition for jobs, in the rivalry sense, would, of course, continue but with augmented and assured access to jobs, its ugly degeneration into racial, gender and ethnic conflict would be moderated.

Those who have long argued that substantially full employment is the most important and extensive welfare measure have both reason and experience on their side. Since the introduction of assured employment would probably be accompanied by an offsetting reduction in transfer income dispersed as welfare expenditures (on which more below, pp. 293–94), 'welfare-dependency', so abhorred by conservatives, would be diminished. Boulding's 'grants economy' can, in important respects, be reduced (for example, most unemployment insurance).

When employment is legally assured the economic order gains from the larger real product and service output that would be generated by a larger workforce. The social costs of lost output resulting in deprivation of livelihood and denial of participation are reduced. In the aggregate, forgone income, forgone output, forgone productivity growth, forgone expansion of productive knowledge, forgone human resource development, forgone reasoned management of the environment, combine to deprive a community of a significant fraction of its potential capacity for development. Instrumental judgements and creative and productive powers of the unemployed are wasted. Senator Humphrey, in arguing in support of the Humphrey–Hawkins Bill nearly two decades ago, observed that 'our failure to keep unemployment even at a 4 percent rate ... cost America over $600 billion in lost production and lost income in the [first 7 years of the] 1970s' (US Congress Record, 1977, p. 1). Similarly, Keyserling (1981, p. 227) observed that there have been 'gigantic forfeitures in production and employment [that] from the start of 1953 to the end of 1980 aggregated [a] loss of more than 8 trillion 1979 dollars worth of GNP ... loss of more than 83 million years of civilian employment opportunity' and 'a loss of above 2 trillion dollars in Federal, State and local tax revenues at existing tax rates'. Unemployment is a massive and needless social cost to the community.

Moreover, the human and material resources brought into productive use by assured employment could and should be directed to a comprehensive effort to rebuild the community's environment and infrastructure. Several areas of productive performance that in recent decades have been insufficiently addressed could be undertaken. A partial listing would include: (a) ecological enhancement: cleaning up hundreds of toxic waste sites, replanting clear-cut forests, developing an environmental restoration technology and industry, shifting to a largely organic agriculture; (b) improved health: providing universal access to quality health care that extends coverage to the 39.7 million (1994) in the USA without health insurance and therefore without adequate medical care (US Dept of Commerce, 1996, p. 120); (c) educational rehabilitation: universal access to quality learning, small classes, restored physical plant, expansion of technological resources; (d) macro stability: increased aggregate demand from rising aggregate incomes to stimulate the appearance of increased numbers of professional and commercial providers of goods and services and generate countercyclical pressures; (e) salvage of youth: assured employment to dramatically undercut the subculture among the young of gangs, drug dealing and public mischief. We sometimes forget that drug dealing is a major self-generated and self-controlled employment option. In the USA, unemployment rates in 1995 for young men (16–19 years) at 18.4 per cent and for young women at 16.1 per cent remain very high. Rates for young blacks at 35.7 per cent and for Hispanics at 24.1 per cent, respectively, are significantly higher (ibid., p. 413).

The finger pointed by Galbraith four decades ago at the deteriorating 'social balance' in the USA between private affluence and public squalor

(Galbraith, 1958, pp. 251–69 and passim) unfortunately still has descriptive merit. Federal budgets seem disproportionately to have supported programmes in defence, income security and healthcare services over the last two decades, but federal responsibilities in the areas of human, environmental and infrastructure investments remain, in my view, comparatively underfunded relative to need (ibid., pp. 330–36).

Human investments in young children, family preservation, education, workforce and national service, together with infrastructure investments in environmental restoration, transportation (highways, mass transit, railroads and air) and community development seem comparatively to be exceedingly modest. One example is the fact that in the USA nearly 15 million children live in poverty. In 1994, 16.32 per cent of the children in white families lived below the poverty line. Comparable figures for children in black families was 43.3 per cent and for children in Hispanic families 41.1 per cent (US Dept of Commerce, 1996, p. 472). The failure to develop more adequate public transport (fast urban and non-urban trains) is another. The failure to provide access to higher education for all young adults who could benefit from the experience (comparable to the GI Bill of Rights of post-Second World War that enrolled some 7–9 million veterans) is a third indicator. Access still depends, evidently, more on the 'ability to pay' than on the 'ability to learn'. The latter is a more instrumentally warranted standard (Bush, 1986, pp. 37–9).

In sum, assured employment would generate significant manpower resources and income to reduce poverty and augment investments in people, to ensure a co-evolutionary environment and to rebuild the public infrastructure. It would contribute substantial tax revenues to smaller jurisdictions as well as to the federal government.

When employment is guaranteed, the political order gains. Legally assured employment would help bring some significant part of the non-participating bottom 40 per cent of families (ranked by income) into the political process. Political participation (voting, campaigning, standing for office) is very low for those who have given up on the notion that public sector policies and programmes adequately address their concerns and conditions. Demeaned by poverty, viewed as a burden by the better-off, cynical about their views being heard or making a difference, and having been shut out of participative action, they do not perceive political involvement as having a significant bearing on their status and condition.

For example, delusiveness was generated by the following events: in the 1960s, the Johnson Administration introduced the Community Action Program (CAP) as part of the War on Poverty and did actually bring many living in poor neighbourhoods into the deliberative process of helping to draft community action programmes. Established urban politicians (mayors *et al.*) were confronted and challenged to make basic changes in, for example, job access, welfare delivery and urban amenities. The threat to the continuity and standing of local and conventional political power centres was substantial. In consequence, anxious political recipients of the CAP demands for change successfully pressured Congress to abandon the Program (Kravitz, 1969, pp. 52–69; Selover, 1969, pp. 159–87).

Establishing the human right to employment would demonstrate continuing and substantive public concern with conditions confronted by the unemployed and could help stimulate their interest in democratic participation and processes.

FISCAL FEASIBILITY OF ASSURED EMPLOYMENT

The question of fiscal feasibility must be considered. At issue is whether or not the national community can generate and provide the outlays that would be required fully to provide assured employment for virtually all members of the labour force.

Philip Harvey (1989, pp. 21–50) has recently addressed, and made informed statistical observations concerning, the fiscal feasibility of an assured employment policy in the USA. What follows is a brief characterization of his persuasive analysis. His basic argument is that the introduction of an assured employment programme funded in large part by a significant reduction in the existing welfare system is both possible and desirable. Although the numerical specifics and estimates in the following may now appear somewhat dated, the basic construct and proposal of redirecting public funding from transfers to assured employment retains its credibility and promise. In Harvey's words: 'The funding of a public employment program capable of providing jobs for all able-bodied persons unable to find work in the regular labor market would be enormously expensive, but the wages earned by the program's employees would substitute for a broad range of cash and in-kind transfer payments for which such persons are currently eligible' (ibid., p. 21).

Two basic changes in distributional structure then are contemplated: First, the federal government would, with two exceptions, terminate its existing 'gratuitous income maintenance assistance to able-bodied persons of working age and their dependents' (ibid., p. 22). No more welfare grants, food stamps or unemployment assistance except (a) where a parent of small children chooses to provide their home care and forgoes outside employment, and (b) where, for short-term unemployed persons, financial assistance as unemployment insurance is provided pending probable and timely re-employment in the private sector. Secondly, the federal government would 'henceforth guarantee employment at living wages to every man, woman, and youth in the country who is unable to find adequately remunerative work in the regular labor market' (ibid.).

It is assumed in Harvey's analysis of fiscal feasibility of assured employment (a) that there would be no eligibility constraints involving means-testing or waiting periods, (b) that governmentally funded jobs 'would pay wages sufficient to provide a family income at least equal to the official poverty line', and (c) that remaining gratuitous transfer payments 'would be limited to the elderly, the disabled, and to children lacking the support of both of their parents' (ibid.).

Utilizing data for the decade from 1977 to 1986, Harvey calculated the number of jobs needed to reduce unemployment in this expanded labour force to 2 per cent: 'Some frictional unemployment is unavoidable even in a fully employed economy' (ibid., p. 27). Brought back into this labour force would be separated workers, discouraged workers, part-time workers wanting full-time jobs, technologically displaced workers, and the like. The number of jobs needed, with generous estimates, ranged from a low of 7.4 million in 1979 to a high of 13.6 million in 1983 with an annual average over the decade of just over 10 million (ibid., p. 31). The wage rates incorporated take account variously of existing governmental wage schedules, going 'market' rates, and statutory minimum wage rates, but all such rates permit earners to live at or above the poverty line. He concludes that, in comparing year with year, the net cost of the assured jobs programme, less the cutbacks in other programmes, would generate a spending deficit of just over $200 billion for the decade ranging from $1.4 billion to $49.7 billion per year (ibid., p. 49). This $50 billion or less per year is the order of magnitude, on Harvey's assumptions, of the additional governmental revenues required to assure virtually full employment. A $200 billion plus decade deficit 'would have amounted to less than 2 percent of all government tax receipts for the period' (ibid., p. 50). The foregoing estimates will obviously require updating to contemporary figures when more exact and timely data are needed. However, as a portion of a $6 trillion GDP or a $1.5 trillion federal budget, this fiscal expenditure appears to be a singularly modest price tag for realizing the extensive and important gains generated by assured employment.

In the USA, as this is written in early 1997, the dismantling of the 60-year-old federal welfare system has been legislated. Remaining support mechanisms will become a responsibility mainly of the individual states. Each state will have some discretion over the character and extent of programmes made available to needy recipients. The federal government will provide 'block grants' to states to cover part of the costs of continuing some such support. Especially targeted is aid to dependent children and their 'welfare mothers'. Overall it is expected that aggregate support will be reduced and that support access and levels may vary to some extent among states. Present recipients are expected to find paid employment within a year or two. Some states will offer educational access and/or job training; the extent and character of these policies is presently unknown. What seems to be missing, however, is a binding governmental commitment to provide assured employment at the state or federal level. That a significant fraction of children now living in poverty will experience increased deprivation seems on present information to be highly probable.

OBSTACLES TO AN ASSURED EMPLOYMENT PROGRAMME

Even if fiscal feasibility is not, in substance, a decisive deterrent to the introduction of an assured employment policy, there are even so an array of other arguments which tend to derail dialogue and social action on institutional adjustments to achieve and sustain virtually full employment. Space constraints permit only a minimal consideration of such obstacles here but even a truncated review may help to set an agenda both for further inquiry and for policy exploration.

For convenience, obstacles are non-rigorously categorized as ideological and political. Ideological constraints here are derivative from the prevailing orthodox neoclassical mind-set. Political constraints reflect considerations of the locus and shifting of discretionary power over policy and income shares.

Ideological Constraints

1. An orthodox neoclassical contention is that high and rising wages, above what a free market would provide, cause unemployment: '[N]eoclassical theory has long predicted that in the short run, with perfect competition, a fixed capital stock and diminishing returns, an increase in the real wage in excess of the equilibrium level will induce a reduction in employment' (Riach, 1995, p. 163). 'If real wages increase more than productivity ... the real cost of marginal production increases, and employment must decline so that this increased cost does not exceed the real value of the marginal product' (de Laragentaye, 1979, p. 10; quoted in Riach, 1995, p. 163). 'Employers will substitute away from labour because of cost considerations' (ibid., p. 164). On orthodox assumptions, rising wages and fuller employment are mutually exclusive. Union pressure to raise wages, then, is counterproductive, especially for labour.

One counterargument is that the presumed free market determination of wages is fatally flawed. Its undergirding marginal productivity theory of factor pricing rests on behavioural and institutional assumptions of unfettered markets that cannot be empirically sustained. For neo-institutionalists, 'the term market refers only to a structured process of interaction between actual or potential buyers and sellers, not to a domain within which a single equilibrium price is presumed to emerge or exist' (Ramstad, 1993, p. 196). Wage rates, as with major prices generally, are for the most part administered by those possessing discretionary power in the pertinent institutional complexes of corporate management, regulatory bodies, trade unions and professional associations. Actual markets in the area of wage-setting require explicit examination of the differing structures and functions, segments and levels of the labour market and the loci of actual discretion over differing wage and salary rates. An implication, then, is that there is no necessarily unique connection between high wages and unemployment.

Another counterargument is provided by Michael Perelman (1995, pp. 145–62). The gains from high wages include stimulation of demand, leading to augmented economies of scale that enable firms to pay higher wages. Higher wages 'encourage employers to develop improved technologies to save labour'. In addition, 'high wages stimulate workers to be more productive ... workers respond to higher wages by contributing more effort' to their jobs and by developing their productive skills and capacities. In sum, 'low wages ensure low, not high productivity' (ibid., p.145). An increased wage income to workers is a stimulus to enhanced productivity and boost to worker morale through empowerment.

2. An orthodox neoclassical contention is that virtually full employment, generated by assured employment, would necessarily produce inflation. The trade-off between employment levels and inflationary price increases is reduced to a monocausal account 'at the core of which stands the concept of the natural rate of unemployment' (Palley, 1995, p. 137). 'The argument behind this theory is that if unemployment falls below the natural rate, inflation will increase; moreover, inflation will accelerate as long as unemployment remains below the natural rate' (ibid., p. 140). 'Proper' policy is to endure the 'natural rate' presumed to lie in the unemployment range of 6–7 per cent. Its influence on analysis and policy is extensive (for example, UNCTAD, 1995, pp. 163–70). This neoclassically warranted, problem-evading, theory of a natural rate of unemployment – NAIRU, the infamous 'non-accelerating-inflation rate of unemployment' (Klein, 1994, pp. 273–80; Brockway, 1995, pp. 897–910) – implies that macro-management, and especially an activist monetary policy, can

only corrupt the operation of a competitive market-price economy. The late William Vickrey (1993, p. 2) characterized NAIRU as 'one of the most vicious euphemisms ever coined'.

A counterargument is that there is nothing 'natural', meaning non-discretionary, about any rate of unemployment or, for that matter, of inflation. There is no necessary trade-off. The determinants of inflationary increases are multiple, complex and often transitory. Administered pricing is the norm, not the exception. The determinants of employment levels are similarly multiple, complex and often transitory, but different. The bearing of aggregate demand on employment is substantial. Following Keynesian and Kaleckian arguments, 'in a decentralized monetary economy there is no automatic market mechanism which ensures that aggregate demand is sufficient to purchase full employment aggregate supply' (Sawyer, 1995, p. 19). Insufficient aggregate demand could forestall virtually full and assured employment. Only inquiry into a particular context of employment and pricing will permit identification of which causal factors are operative and significant and how they bear on the larger economic outcome. It is clear, however, that no economy can successfully depress its way out of an inflation by augmenting unemployment (Klein, 1994, p. 277): 'inflation and unemployment are not "natural" and both point to failures of the economy to perform in an acceptable way'.

3. An orthodox neoclassical contention is that assured employment would erode the work ethic (Sawyer, 1995, pp. 22–3). A personal reflection illustrates the argument: as an undergraduate, I was admonished by an orthodox professor (A.D.H. Kaplan) to accept the view that it was necessary to have significant unemployment (5–7 per cent) – to have people without jobs clamouring at the plant gates – so that those working inside the plants, in fear of job loss, would retain their work effort and ethic.

A counterargument would grant that work incentives are of course significant, but their character is not explained by the orthodox notion that the threat of unemployment is the source of the work ethic. Orthodoxy notwithstanding, we can no longer argue that coercive human relations are more productive than non-coercive relations. Committed, imaginative and creative productive efforts are not generated by fear and intimidation.

The so-called revolution in management theory and behaviour of the last quarter-century has led to a variety of semi-participatory models of productive organizations: worker ownership schemes, worker profit-sharing plans, worker teams, mid-management co-operative panels, job enrichment seminars, worker amenities, consultative exploration of innovations and technological enhancements, and the like (see, for example,

Rock and Kliendinst, 1992; Ellerman, 1990). While these reflect a significant erosion of the old hierarchical worker–boss arrangements, where
rank and status were a function of 'the number of men under me', the
basic question of where discretion actually rests and remains is pivotal:
'The new spirit of teamwork may be taking place', but is it not 'a game in
which the rules are still dictated by management' (Champlin and Olson,
1994, p. 455)? Should not recognition derive from workers' contributions
to co-operative co-ordination in which a variety of skills and specialized
knowledges are collectively employed and assessed? 'High levels of productivity' are enhanced by mechanisms of 'worker involvement and
participation in effective decision making' (Sawyer, 1995, p. 23), but that
employee participation must be substantive and continuing: 'Workers
have power, after all, only as long as they can keep their jobs' (Champlin
and Olson, 1994, p. 456).

A genuine shift from coercion and intimidation in employment relations to democratic and participatory relations does not erode the work
effort; it enhances it. But such relations must not be *pro forma*, symbolic
'window dressing'; they must reflect *de facto* shared discretion for which
the employment connection is a precondition. Assured employment,
because it empowers workers, is not the 'enemy' of high productivity; it is
a means for its realization.

Political Constraints

At issue is the question of whose interests are to be served by the character and magnitude of macro-stabilization policies that include assured
employment. Those in the top 5 or 10 per cent, ranked by family income?
Those in the bottom 40 per cent? Those in the middle 50 per cent? Or
some combination? Would assured employment help democratize controls over the level of employment?

The underclass (bottom 40 per cent) is hurt by inflationary increases in
prices (in the absence of cost-of-living adjustments on earned and transfer income), by job losses and by an inability through policy to alter their
circumstances. The fact of their economic deprivation renders them
largely politically impotent: the fact or threat of unemployment is politically intimidating. Sawyer agrees that 'unemployment is the most
powerful of all economic controls'. He argues that 'the ideal is to replace
the arbitrary undemocratic "control" of unemployment by conscious
controls, operated democratically in the public interest' (Sawyer, 1995,
p. 16). But 'conscious controls' are directed not to reductions in unemployment but to deflationary, especially, constrictive monetary policies of
rising interest rates, shrinking of access to credit, and the like. In Michl's
(1995, p. 63) words: 'Inflation ... creates a natural lobby for disinflation-

ary policy ... To the extent that the wealthiest citizens, who depend on interest and capital income substantially more than the average citizen, are also disproportionately represented in the political process (and who would seriously dispute that?) this creates a very strong bias toward disinflationary economic policies'.

An attentive observer recognizes that the Federal Reserve Bank, and the financial community generally, are centrally and continuously transfixed on suppressing inflation, whatever the costs in unemployment. Macro-policy is reduced mainly to demand constraints, rising interest rates and a tolerance of higher unemployment. 'The natural rate' provides a continuing apologia for inaction in reducing unemployment.

Unemployment falls most heavily on middle- and lower-income groups of workers with the minimal resources to respond. 'The incidence of unemployment is highly regressive' (Michl, 1995, p. 71). Such groups are at the mercy both of national monetary authorities and of corporate hierarchies which decide on the extent, character and locale of employment connections: 'Employers are in a much stronger relative position when unemployment is high' (Sawyer, 1995, p. 19). Large corporations shift to contingency hiring and the use of temporary workers; they reduce or abandon fringe benefits for new hires. With the steady erosion of union organizations, only recently slowed, and a continuing indifference to legislative restoration of negotiational institutions, empowerment of workers has a low priority. In some instances, workers, individually and organized, can still have some participatory impact on particular employment and wage decisions, but only inquiry will disclose its extent and significance.

Political resistance to assured employment is to be expected from those who now benefit from the fact of continuing and significant unemployment (ibid.). Assured employment would erode, but not eliminate, the capacity of employers to intimidate workers, for example, with threats of separation or off-shore displacement. Assured employment would encourage, if not require, more formal structures through which to negotiate terms and conditions of employment. This passing of significant political power from corporate employers back to workers through institutional adjustments will be resisted politically. Only through federal legislation can assured employment be instituted to generate economic benefits and democratization of wage-setting.

In sum, assured employment would significantly enlarge the economy's capacity to produce, modestly reduce the degree of income inequality, enhance the productive capabilities of workers, reduce some economic conflict, relieve outright human misery and broaden political participation in policy formation. Any inflationary consequences that might emerge can be successfully addressed through national policies of macro-management and regulatory action as needed.

REFERENCES

Arestis, P. and Marshall, M. (eds) (1995), *The Political Economy of Full Employment: Conservatism, Corporatism and Institutional Change*, Aldershot, Hants: Edward Elgar.

Ayres, C.E. ([1944] 1978), *The Theory of Economic Progress*, Kalamazoo, Mich.: New Issues Press, Western Michigan University.

Brinton, C. (1947), 'Natural rights', in E.R.A. Seligman (ed.), *The Encyclopaedia of the Social Sciences*, New York: Macmillan.

Brockway, G.P. (1995), 'The NAIRU delusion', *Journal of Economic Issues*, **29**: 897–910.

Bush, P.D. (1986), 'On the concept of ceremonial encapsulation', *Review of Institutional Thought*, 3 December: 25–45.

Champlin, D. and Olson, P. (1994), 'Post-industrial metaphors: understanding corporate restructuring and the economic environment of the 1990s', *Journal of Economic Issues*, **28**: 449–59.

Colander, D.C. (ed.) (1981), *Solutions to Unemployment*, New York: Harcourt Brace Jovanovich.

Collins, S.D., Ginsburg, H.L. and Goldberg, G.S. (1994), *Jobs for All: A Plan for the Revitalization of America*, New York: New Initiatives for Full Employment (Council on International and Public Affairs).

Commanger, H.S. (ed.) (1948), *Documents of American History*, New York: Appleton-Century-Croft.

de Crespigny, A. and Wertheimer, A. (eds) (1970), *Contemporary Political Theory*, New York: Atherton Press.

Dembo, D. and Morehouse, W. (1994), *The Underbelly of the U.S. Economy*, New York: Apex Press.

Eatwell, J. (ed.) (1995), *Global Unemployment: Loss of Jobs in the 90s*, Armonk, N.Y.: M.E. Sharpe.

Ellerman, D. (1990), *The Democratic Worker-owned Firm*, Boston, Mass.: Unwin Hyman.

Economic Report of the President (1996), Washington, D.C.: US Government Printing Office.

Galbraith, J.K. (1958), *The Affluent Society*, Boston, Mass.: Houghton Mifflin.

Ginsburg, H. (1983), *Full Employment and Public Policy: The United States and Sweden*, Lexington, Mass.: D.C. Heath.

Goodwin, L. (1972), *Do the Poor Want to Work? A Social-psychological Study of Work Orientations*, Washington, D.C.: Brookings Institution.

Green, P. and Levinson, S. (eds) (1970), *Power and Community: Dissenting Essays in Political Science*, New York: Vintage Press.

Harvey, P. (1989), *Securing the Right to Employment*, Princeton, N.J. : Princeton University Press.

Hutton, W. (1996), 'A Nobel vision of fair shares for all', *Manchester Guardian Weekly*, 7 January: 19.

International Labour Organization (1994), 'Job crisis grips globe ...', *Sacramento Bee*, 7 March: A9.

Jahoda, M. (1982), *Employment and Unemployment: A Social-psychological Analysis*, Cambridge: Cambridge University Press.

Keyserling, L.H. (1981), 'The Humphrey–Hawkins Act since its 1978 enactment', in D.C. Collander (ed.), *Solutions to Unemployment*, New York: Harcourt Brace, pp. 225–9.

Klein, P.A. (1994), *Beyond Dissent*, Armonk, N.Y.: M.E.Sharpe.

Kravitz, S. (1969), 'The Community Action Program – past, present, and its future?', in J.L. Sundquist (ed.), *On Fighting Poverty*, New York: Basic Books, pp. 52–69.

Luxembourg Income Study (1995), 'US has biggest income gap in study of rich, poor families', *San Francisco Chronicle*, 15 August.

Meade, J.E. (1995), *Full Employment Regained*, Cambridge: Cambridge University Press.

Michl, T.R. (1995), 'Assessing the costs of inflation and unemployment', in P. Arestis and M. Marshall (eds), *The Political Economy of Full Employment*, Aldershot, Hants.: Edward Elgar, pp. 54–78.

Palley, T.I. (1995), 'Full employment and the inflation constraint', in J. Eatwell (ed.), *Global Unemployment: Loss of Jobs in the 90s,* Armonk, N.Y.: M.E. Sharpe, pp. 137–46.

Perelman, M. (1995), 'High wages, enlightened management and economic productivity', in P. Arestis and M. Marshall (eds), *The Political Economy of Full Employment*, Aldershot, Hants: Edward Elgar, pp. 145–62.

Peterson, W.C. (1994), *Silent Depression*, New York: W. W. Norton.

Ramstad, Y. (1993), 'Institutional economics and the dual labor market theory', in M.R. Tool (ed.), *Institutional Economics: Theory, Method, Policy*, Boston, Mass.: Kluwer Academic Publishers, pp. 173–233.

Riach, P.A. (1995), 'Wage-employment determination in a post-Keynesian world', in P. Arestis and M. Marshall (eds), *The Political Economy of Full Employment*, Aldershot, Hants: Edward Elgar, pp. 163–75.

Rock, C.P. and Kliendinst, M.A. (1992), 'Worker-managed firms, democratic principles and the evolution of financial relations', *Journal of Economic Issues*, 26 June: 605–13.

Roosevelt, [President] F.D. (1944), 'An economic bill of rights', *New York Times*, 12 January, reprinted in H.S. Commager (ed.), *Documents of American History* vol. II, New York: Appleton-Century-Croft, 1948, pp. 693–5.

Sawyer, M. (1995), 'Obstacles to full employment in capitalist economies', in P. Arestis and M. Marshall (eds), *The Political Economy of Full Employment*, Aldershot, Hants.: Edward Elgar, pp. 15–35.

Selover, W.C. (1969), 'The view from Capitol Hill: harassment and survival', in J.L. Sundquist (ed.), *On Fighting Poverty*, New York: Basic Books, pp. 158–87.

Sengenberger, W. (1996), 'Full employment: past, present and future – an ILO perspective', paper presented at meetings of the European Association for Evolutionary Political Economy, Antwerp, Belgium, November (Chapter 14 in this volume).

Special Task Force (1972), *Report to Secretary of Health, Education and Welfare: Work in America*, Cambridge, Mass.: MIT Press.

Staff, Social Sciences 1, College of the University of Chicago (eds) (1949), *The People Shall Judge: Readings in the Formation of American Policy*, vol. II, Chicago: University of Chicago Press.

Sundquist, J.L. (ed.) (1969), *On Fighting Poverty*, New York: Basic Books.

Terkel, S. (1974), *Working*, New York: Pantheon Books.

Tool, M.R. ([1979] 1985), *The Discretionary Economy: A Normative Theory of Political Economy*, Boulder, Col.: Westview Press.

Tool, M.R. (ed.) (1993), *Institutional Economics: Theory, Method, Policy*, Boston, Mass.: Kluwer Academic Publishers.

United Nations Conference on Trade and Development (UNCTAD) (1995), *Trade and Development Report*, Geneva: United Nations.

United Nations, General Assembly (1948), *Universal Declaration of Human Rights*, UN Doc. A/811, Art. 23, reprinted in Staff, *The People Shall Judge*, vol. II, pp. 792–95.

US Congress (1977), *Congressional Record*, vol. 123, no 193, 6 December.

US Department of Commerce, Bureau of the Census (1996), *Statistical Abstract of the United States*, Washington, D.C.: US Government Printing Office.

US Department of State (1945), *Charter of the United Nations*, Publication no. 2353, Conference series, no. 74. Washington, D.C.: US Government Printing Office, reprinted in Staff, *The People Shall Judge*, vol. II, pp. 766–84.

US House (1975), Committee on Education and Labor. Equal Opportunity and Full Employment Act, HR 50. 94th Cong., 1st sess. Subcommittee print.

US House (1996), Personal Responsibility and Work Opportunity Reconcilation Act, HR 3734, 104th Cong., 2nd sess.

US Senate (1975), Balanced Growth and Economic Planning Act, S Doc. 1795, 94th Cong., 1st sess.

Veblen, T.B. ([1899] 1934), *The Theory of the Leisure Class*, New York: Modern Library.

Veblen, T.B. ([1914] 1946), *The Instinct of Workmanship*, New York: Viking Press.

Vickrey, W. (1993), 'Today's task for economists', *American Economic Review*, **83**, March: 1–10.

Woollacott, M. (1995), 'A sickness sans frontières', *Manchester Guardian Weekly*, 4 June: 21.

World Bank (1990), *World Development Report*, New York: Oxford University Press.

14. Full employment: past, present and future. An ILO perspective

Werner Sengenberger

THE ILO MAINTAINS THE OBJECTIVE OF FULL EMPLOYMENT

For the ILO the idea of full employment is not out of date. The widespread unemployment and underemployment in nearly all quarters of the world is neither inevitable nor irreversible. The ILO upholds, and has in fact just reconfirmed, the basic objectives laid down in its main Employment Policy Convention no. 122, adopted in 1964. This Convention, which has been ratified by 88 countries, calls upon member states of the ILO to 'declare and pursue, as a major goal, an active policy designed to promote full, productive and freely chosen employment'. It requires the members to 'stimulate growth and development, raising levels of living, meeting manpower requirements and overcoming unemployment and underemployment'.

The continued belief in full employment as a universal concept also finds expression in the Declaration of the World Summit for Social Development that took place in Copenhagen in March 1995. In the largest gathering yet of world leaders, 117 heads of state or government pledged to make the conquest of poverty, full employment and the goal of fostering stable, safe and just societies their overriding objectives. Following principles of ILO standards of employment policy, the world leaders committed themselves to promote the goal of full employment, as a basic priority of their governments' economic and social policies, and to enable all men and women to attain secure and sustainable livelihoods through freely chosen productive employment and work. Moreover, these objectives would have to be pursued with full respect for workers' rights and with the participation of employers, workers and their respective organizations, giving special attention to the problems of structural, long-term unemployment and underemployment of youth, women, people with disabilities and all other disadvantaged groups and individuals (Commitment 3 of the Copenhagen Declaration and Programme of Action).

The latest confirmation of the full employment objective in the ILO dates from the International Labour Conference in June 1996. The Conference adopted a policy statement by the Employment Policy Committee entitled 'The achievement of full employment in a global context: the responsibility of governments, employers and trade unions'. In these conclusions full employment is considered a valid and achievable goal for all countries regardless of their level of development. However, it was recognized that the concept may have to be interpreted differently for developing countries. Since in most of these countries only a minority of the employed are in formal wage employment in the modern sector, the rest being in peasant farming, casual and contract labour or low-productivity self-employment in the informal sector, progress towards full employment must be measured by using a combination of indicators. These include the rate of growth in modern sector employment and changes in real average earnings, and the degree of open and disguised unemployment and underemployment in the rural and informal sectors.

But even for the developed countries the definition of full employment, while remaining fundamentally valid, needs to take into account changes in the structure of employment, such as new forms of flexible employment and a growing trend towards shorter and flexible working hours in a significant number of countries. Measures of unemployment catch only one aspect of the employment problem in a given country: that of total lack of work. Less obvious situations, such as partial lack of work, low employment income, underutilization of skills or low productivity, are not accounted for in unemployment statistics at all. Furthermore, underemployment which has traditionally been regarded as a phenomenon largely affecting developing countries, has assumed greater relevance for industrialized countries in recent years. There, the economic crisis of the last decade has increasingly generated a multitude of small jobs and irregular activities similar to those of the informal sector of the developing countries.

THE ORIGINS OF THE FULL EMPLOYMENT OBJECTIVE

Historically, the call for full employment, both at the national and the international level of the economy, came as a reaction to the traumatic experience of mass unemployment during the Great Depression affecting the industrialized world in the 1920s and 1930s. John Maynard Keynes, who inspired the economic thinking at the time, came forward with a message saying that mass involuntary unemployment was a preventable evil and that it was possible for economic policies to ensure full employment which for him was reached at the point at which aggregate demand could not further increase employment and output. This basic idea was translated later on by William Beveridge into a practical policy concept. In his book *Full Employment in a Free Society*, published in 1944, he defined full employment as a state in which there were 'more vacant jobs than unemployed men', and where there were jobs 'at fair wages of such a kind, and so located, that the unemployed men can reasonably be expected to take them'.

At the international level, the ILO spearheaded the combat against mass unemployment when it adopted its Declaration of Philadelphia in 1944. This Declaration contained a strong commitment to the pursuit of full employment and redefined the ILO's mandate in the area of employment policy.

What should be noted in these early drives to a full employment policy is that the attainment of full employment should not be at any price but should recognize the need for adequate pay and working conditions. Full employment is more than the absence of unemployment. The objective must be 'more and better jobs', or jobs that respect labour standards. There must be the fullest possible opportunity for each worker to qualify for and to use his or her skills and endowments in a job for which he or she is well suited, irrespective of race, colour, gender, religion, political opinion, national extraction or social origin.

It is precisely this combination of attributes of full employment, low unemployment, low inequality, and adequate social protection which is at stake today when, for example, a trade-off is constructed between the level of wages and the level of employment, or when the only successful road to job creation is said to come through encroachments upon labour standards.

THE PRESENT EMPLOYMENT SITUATION

The present employment situation[1] falls drastically short of the objectives of fully productive, freely chosen and adequately remunerated employment.

Many developing countries have experienced a rise in poverty, unemployment and underemployment since the early 1980s, while mass unemployment has emerged in the transition economies since 1990. In the OECD countries we have seen the rise and persistence of unemployment in most countries since 1973. Presently, 34 million workers are out of work in the industrialized world. In the European Union unemployment rose from just over 5 per cent in 1979 to around 11 per cent in 1994.

While joblessness is still relatively low in Japan (around 3 per cent), it is also emerging as a problem there. In the United States, unemployment increased steeply between 1979 and 1982 to nearly 10 per cent, but has subsequently declined to the 5 per cent level of 1997. The figures on open unemployment do not tell us the full extent of joblessness. In addition to the 34 million unemployed in the industrialized countries there are 4 million discouraged workers and 15 million who involuntarily work part-time. In transition countries, especially in eastern Europe, registered unemployment reveals only a minor fraction of the total unemployment of labour. Unemployment has been concentrated among the young, unskilled workers and migrants, and the proportion of long-term unemployed has risen markedly.

Parallel to the secular rise in unemployment levels, we observe an increasing number of part-time and fixed-term contacts and other forms of atypical work which are widely seen as a sign of the increasing precariousness of employment. Furthermore, we notice a broad tendency towards rising wage and income inequality, both within and between countries. The evolution of greater wage dispersion has been most pronounced in the United States, Canada and the United Kingdom. While the first of these two developments constitutes an obvious deviation from the goal of full employment, it might be argued that the second one also undermines the idea of full employment because jobs at the bottom fall below widely held normative standards for an acceptable job. Many of these jobs fail to pay a living wage, giving rise to a growing number of 'working poor'.

The consequences of the lack of employment for countless men and women who are available for and actively seek work are serious and multifarious. Mass joblessness amounts to a waste of human resources; it gives rise to feelings of anxiety and insecurity; it contributes to mass poverty, not only in developing countries but today also in industrialized countries and transition economies; it aggravates the position of vulnerable and disadvantaged groups in the labour market; it breeds social exclusion which in turn fosters crime and threatens social cohesion; and it tends to affect negatively the quality of employment, including the safety of jobs and other working conditions, which traditionally are of as much concern to the ILO as the level of employment. Strains are heaped upon the security system at a time when the viability of that system is vital for adequate income protection. Trade unions and employers' organizations are weakened when sound industrial relations are required for consensus and concerted action to redress the employment problems. Recognizing all these threats, it is clear that more and better jobs are urgently needed for the prevention of social disintegration and the achievement of the

ILO's fundamental objectives of democracy, the protection of the working people, the alleviation of poverty and social justice.

ALTERNATIVE EXPLANATIONS OF THE HIGH AND PERSISTENT UNEMPLOYMENT

The persistence of mass unemployment in the developed and developing countries, the onslaught of large-scale joblessness in the transition countries after the political turnaround, and hence the steady drift away from full employment, have led analysts and policy-makers alike to reopen the debate on the nature and causes of the employment problem, and also to question the usefulness of the full employment concept.

Generally, four major strands of thinking and interpretation about the origins and causes of the employment problem can be identified:

1. full employment has fallen victim to the increasing globalization of the world economy;
2. unemployment is due to labour market rigidities and excessive levels of social protection;
3. the nature of technology and work is fundamentally changing, rendering the conventional notion of full employment, and the conventional means to achieve it, obsolete;
4. unemployment is due to insufficient economic growth;

In the course of preparing the ILO's report *World Employment 1996–97*, explanations of the rising unemployment were examined. In the following I summarize the results.

International Trade

As we said earlier, in all industrialized countries unemployment has hit the less-qualified workers particularly hard. In addition, in the Anglo-Saxon countries the wages of un- and semi-skilled workers have deteriorated. This has led analysts to believe that the expansion of trade with low-wage countries is a major cause of the secular rise in unemployment and the downward pressure on wages in high-income countries.

This explanation may be doubted, however, in view of the fact that most trade occurs between the industrialized countries, whereas north–south trade still remains relatively modest. The share of imports from the dynamic Asian economies plus China to the OECD countries represented only 1.5 per cent of the GDP of OECD countries in 1993, compared with 0.19 per cent in 1962. Furthermore, their trade with the developing countries, especially with the Asian countries, has been in balance or in surplus, which means that such trade tends to be job-creating rather than job-destroying. However, trade may have some job displacement effects in certain sectors, as imports tend to concentrate on products with low-skilled labour-intensive content, while exports tend to be more capital-intensive and embody a high-skilled labour content. Nevertheless, studies by the ILO and others have shown that the competition from the developing countries has had only a marginal impact on overall employment levels in the industrialized countries.

Labour Market Rigidities and Social Protection

The persistence of mass unemployment, especially in Europe, has been attributed to imperfections in the labour market. It has been argued that rigid labour markets inhibit employment creation. Moreover, labour market distortions due to legal or contractual protection of employment and incomes would cause economic recovery to quickly generate inflationary pressures unacceptable to the monetary authorities, which then take steps to curb economic activity. As a result, employment fails to grow.

Again, it is difficult to observe or measure the effects of these competitive imperfections in reality. In most European countries, minimum wages and the various forms of employment and income protection have not been increased since the 1960s. On the contrary, concerning the level of labour market regulation, governments have attempted to make labour markets numerically more flexible by reviewing and reforming their labour market legislation. Yet this has not had any major positive effect on employment.

With regard to social charges leading to high non-wage labour costs, it is true that they represent a high proportion of the total cost of employing labour in most OECD countries. It is feared that this affects both the demand for labour, by reducing incentives to hire, and the supply of labour, by decreasing the motivation to search for a job because of high social benefits. Moreover, such costs are said to contribute to unemployment by undermining international competitiveness.

There is no clear evidence from international comparisons that the level of social charges has a negative impact on competitiveness. While it is true that social expenditure has risen, this may be attributed to rising levels of unemployment. In order to diminish this cost the proper response would seem to be to combat unemployment rather than lower protection and income replacement for the unemployed. Downscaling social protection tends to reduce the acceptability of economic restructuring, increase poverty and undermine social cohesion and social stability.

The End of the Work and Labour Society

The most fundamental challenge of the (conventional) concept of full employment is posed by those who argue the case of massive technological unemployment and 'jobless growth' in a 'post-industrial' society. Fewer and fewer workers would be needed to produce the same output. These views of inevitable labour displacement, notably among blue-collar workers in the old industrialized world, are inspired by reports about massive layoffs in traditional industries and corporate downsizing in Europe and North America. This labour saving happens at a time when an increasing number of the developing countries are undergoing their own industrial revolution and are not available to absorb the surplus goods from the north. These observations have led analysts and policy-makers to call for a new concept of work and a basic re-engineering of society, including the delinking of income from employment. Some observers have hailed the advent of a 'post-materialist' age in which human labour is replaced by machines. It would finally permit society to be free and classless (see, for example, Gorz, 1985). Reference is made to the writings of Aristotle, Thomas Morus, Francis Bacon and Karl Marx.

According to ILO research, it is premature to speak of the end of the work society. There appears to be no clear evidence that rapid technological changes have brought about an environment of jobless growth, to the point where the growth of output no longer generates employment. For example, process innovations could be expected to lead to higher productivity growth, thus diminishing the increase of jobs. Yet the average yearly labour productivity growth in the business sector in the 1980s and 1990s was less than half of the productivity growth in the 1960s and 1970s. According to recent ILO estimates, there is also no evidence that the job content of growth has decreased. On the contrary, there are signs that the opposite has happened. Growth has become more employment intensive. Thus, in the United States before the first oil shock in 1973, an annual growth rate of 2 per cent was required for net job increases, whereas today new jobs are created as soon as growth reaches 0.6 per cent. In Europe, the corresponding required growth rate has decreased from 4.3 per cent to 2 per cent. The ILO has also not found any evidence of 'jobless growth' in developing countries, including the rapidly industrializing countries. The same basic findings were received when the responsiveness of employment to growth was examined through estimates of the employment-to-GDP elasticity in the period between 1975 and 1993.

Those who argue that our societies have run out of work must confront the fact that the rate of employment growth in industrialized countries has remained almost unchanged over the last three-and-a-half decades. The rise in European unemployment does not reflect a decline in the amount of work provided. Rather, the rise in European unemployment is largely related to the fact that employment growth lagged behind labour force growth. Furthermore, there is no unequivocal downward trend in the total amount of weekly working hours. In Canada, Japan and the United States there has been a clear tendency for total working hours to increase, while France, Italy, Sweden, Germany and the United Kingdom show either stable or decreasing trends. Seen in this light, the data suggest that after the Second World War, at least in part of the industrialized world, the compensation effects of technology have been more than fully effective. The story looks different, however, if one compares the hours worked to the hours available and to the GDP produced. In the United States, which shows the strongest evidence of 'continuing work', work hours have increased by 68 per cent since 1960, the labour force by 82 per cent, and GDP by 1 per cent. In Japan, the corresponding figures were 17 per cent, 46 per cent and 537 per cent.

Finally, contrary to popular belief, there do not appear to be any dramatic changes in personal attitudes towards employment. The unemployed continue to be clearly less happy or less satisfied with their lives than are those who have jobs. This suggests *inter alia* that most unemployment is still involuntary.

Slow and Inadequate Economic Growth

According to the ILO, slow and insufficient growth is a major factor behind increased unemployment. Consequently, a strategy of more rapid economic expansion to raise demand and promote job-intensive growth will have to be the driving force for a reduction in joblessness. In the industrialized countries the rate of growth has slowed down considerably for more than two decades. In the United States this took the form of a halt in the secular rise in individual incomes as a result of a slow-down in labour productivity gains. In Europe, productivity gains remained at a more constant level and labour earnings continued to increase, but the decline in growth was reflected in a strong upward trend in unemployment.

While there is no single cause for the decline in growth in the industrialized world, the adoption of restrictive monetary policies to combat inflation may be regarded as a major factor. The rise in real interest rates, pushed up by financial deregulation, did relieve pressures on prices but at the cost of a lasting reduction in economic activity. This, in turn, fuelled public debt, without this being attributable to lax budgetary policy.

Low actual growth tends to reduce potential growth. It reduces the accumulation of capital and production capacity, since enterprises reduce investment in anticipation of limited markets for their output. Weak growth also worsens the quality and availability of labour by keeping workers out of employment for long periods and making their skills successively obsolete. The quantitative impact of the activity growth rate on the available labour force is clearly evident over the recent period in the European Union: during the years 1986–90, annual growth was 3.3 per cent and the growth in the available active population (employed and unemployed) was 0.9 per cent a year. During the years 1991–95, when actual growth was only 1.5 per cent, the available active population showed no increase.

Finally, poor growth weakens public finance which, in turn, hampers the development of public infrastructure which is necessary for economic restructuring.

A POLICY AGENDA FOR RENEWED FULL EMPLOYMENT

In the perspective of the ILO, a policy framework for full employment must comprise the following essential components: creating an enabling global environment; pursuing macro-policies for sustained growth; enhancing the adaptability of the labour market through structural policies and the efficient use of human resources; targeting policies to improve the situation of the vulnerable groups; and strengthening social dialogue at the national and international level for solidaristic action.[2]

Creating an Enabling Global Environment

Globalization requires an appropriate enabling policy framework to contain its potential risks, such as mass job loss, job relocation, insecurity and heightened disparities, and to maximize the potential benefits of economic integration, such as achieving a higher growth of output and employment and a more equitable distribution of these benefits.

Full employment can only be achieved in a stable political, economic and social environment and through international co-operation. This requires:

- that all countries commit themselves to adherence to common rules in maintaining open economic and trade policies and refrain from policies that confer on them unfair comparative advantage. In a number of countries the loss of jobs, especially among the low skilled, risks igniting protectionist sentiments. Universal compliance with basic labour standards contributes to equity and respect for

human rights in the face of rising international competition (ILO
and OECD studies are under way to examine the social dimension of
the liberalization of trade). The ILO's Tripartite Declaration on
Multinational Enterprises and Social Policy provides a reference
point for foreign direct investment;

- effective arrangements to overcome problems associated with the
  increasing globalization of international markets, such as the rapid
  increase of volatile short-term financial flows which destabilize economic growth and employment; and means to discourage speculation
  and promote productive employment;

- in view of the difficulties which many developing countries have in
  meeting intensified international competition and in compensating
  for the negative social outcomes of structural adjustment programmes, increased international assistance is needed to reverse
  their marginalization, reduce their burden of external debt and
  bring about a desirable reduction in international inequalities and
  world poverty. In line with the commitment made at the World
  Summit for Social Development, effective development-orientated
  and durable solutions to external debt problems should be found (it
  may be recalled that the United Nations and also delegates to the
  Social Summit called for a '20:20 compact', in which developing
  countries devote 20 per cent of their government spending to basic
  social services and the industrial countries put 20 per cent of their
  foreign aid budget towards such people-centred efforts).

Macro-economic Policies for Sustained Economic Growth

Improved international economic co-operation and implementation of
macro-economic policy for higher growth among major industrial
economies will provide a major boost to world output and promote sustainable economic and social development, including in transition and
developing countries. In his address to the G7 Employment Conference
in Lille in April 1996, the Director-General of the ILO called upon the
governments of the largest industrialized countries to embark on a co-
ordinated programme of economic growth in order to increase the
demand for labour and the creation of jobs.

The mechanisms both of international policy co-ordination and of
that between monetary fiscal policy-makers must be strengthened.
Individual action by any single actor is at best ineffective and at worst
counterproductive. The increasing complexity of society does allow policies to be subordinated to a single objective, such as the regulation of
money supply. Budgetary, fiscal and monetary decision-makers must act
in concert to complement a *declared* and well-co-ordinated monetary

policy with a *declared* and co-ordinated fiscal policy to promote growth without excessive inflation.

In the industrialized countries there is room for the reduction of short-term and long-term interest rates. Action by the central banks should be co-ordinated to avoid excessive and counterproductive fluctuations of exchange rates. In the area of budgetary policy, an assessment should be made of whether stabilizing or decreasing public debt should be a short-term or medium-term objective and whether such stabilization should be introduced gradually while strengthening the capacity of the economy to generate jobs. Economic growth and lower unemployment are effective means of attaining a sustained reduction in public debt and deficits through increased tax revenues from higher growth and savings on social security spending.

Both the credibility of fiscal and monetary policies and the room to manoeuvre must be supported by non-inflationary wage strategy. This can only work in the context of a sound industrial relations system, requiring a strong commitment by all partners in the labour market to the objective of non-inflationary employment-intensive growth and to the use of an appropriate negotiating mechanism for that purpose.

Enhanced Functioning of the Labour Market

Countries at all levels of development should set clear priorities to create and expand employment and improve its quality, including conditions of work. Labour market and human resource policies are essential tools to that end. There is a need to provide universal access to basic education, opportunities for further education, vocational training skill development and opportunities for lifelong education.

The development of small and medium-sized enterprises should be assisted in order to encourage job creation by facilitating their access to capital markets and credit.

Special policies and programmes should be designed to enhance the employability of vulnerable groups, reintegrate the long-term unem-ployed as active members of the labour market and provide equal employment opportunities for women and men.

Measures should be established to allow workers to adjust to the changing pattern of international production and trade and to promote their security of employment. Employment security and flexibility in the utilization of labour can be combined through, among other means, labour management co-operation at the enterprise level and workplace, collective bargaining and investment in appropriate skills. Different means of reorganizing and restructuring working time with a view to increasing employment opportunities should be considered.

Strengthening Social Dialogue on Employment

In view of the increasing interdependence of national economies, complex labour markets and widespread disillusionment with policies on
unemployment, the success of any strategy to promote employment and
growth and combat social exclusion will depend on the ability of the government to secure broad support for the chosen policy package. The
achievement of a genuine consensus on the appropriate components of
an employment strategy is highly desirable and a precondition for its
acceptability and successful implementation. It can also have beneficial
effects on investor confidence and volatile capital markets.

Tripartite forms of social dialogue among governments and workers'
and employers' organizations in support of employment generation are
seen by the ILO as a priority item on the national policy agenda. Such
national consultation and negotiation should concentrate on raising production through enlarging capacity as well as improving productivity.
Moreover, national tripartite consultation can cover, as has been the case
in central and eastern Europe in recent years, diverse regulatory items
such as taxation, social security, employment services, vocational training, legal rules concerning working time and job security, the promotion
of private investment and the direction of public investment, and so on.

Social and economic dialogue and solidaristic action for employment
should also be promoted at the international level. At this level, the ILO's
role has been reinforced by the mandate given to it by the UN World
Summit for Social Development to lead the international inter-agency
effort to promote full, productive and freely chosen employment. It is
becoming more widely accepted that closer co-operation is needed
between international agencies with an economic and social vocation,
such as the Bretton Woods organizations, the WTO, OECD and the ILO,
with a view to promoting a better mutual understanding of the interrela-
tionship between economic, social and employment policies. In this
connection, the ILO's role is to stress the merits of programmes of economic reform which are based on consensus among the social partners,
which allow for raising both the quantity and the quality of employment
and adequate compensatory programmes in social safety nets. The introduction of employment targets into structural adjustment targets should
be taken into account.

Employment-centred Research and Policy Assessment

The International Labour Conference 1996 has also requested the ILO's
secretariat to continue to undertake comparative analysis of common

employment policy issues that are relevant to countries at all levels of development. These will serve as a basis for advice to constituents and for discussion with the Bretton Woods institutions. Issues for research should include the following:

1. the impact of trade and financial liberalization on the level and quality of employment, particularly with respect to women's employment;
2. appropriate forms of government support for infrastructural development and training, in order to achieve higher levels of productivity and international competitiveness;
3. forms of support for the development of small and medium-sized enterprises, including the provision of appropriate credit schemes, infrastructure, and so on, paying particular attention to the problems of women entrepreneurs;
4. the design of labour market institutions and regulations which can best satisfy the twin imperatives of higher employment growth and competitiveness, on the one hand, and employment security and an adequate level of social protection on the other.

It is in these areas of research and policy assessment that the ILO seeks the collaboration of the external research community and academic institutions. The ILO welcomes the interest of research associations in the problems of unemployment and employment creation. It appeals to these groups to support the ILO in combating the pressing social ills.

NOTES

1. A full account of the global employment situation is presented in ILO (1995b, 1996a).
2. This section is largely based on the Conclusions of the Employment Policy Committee of the ILO's International Labour Conference, 1996.

REFERENCES

Gorz, A. (1985), *Paths to Paradise: On the Liberation from Work*, trs. M. Imrie, Boston, Mass.: Sunt End Press.

International Labour Office (ILO) (1995a), 'Controversies in labour statistics', in ILO.

International Labour Office (ILO), (1995b), *World Employment 1995*, Geneva: ILO.

International Labour Office (ILO), (1996a), *World Employment 1996/97*, Geneva: ILO.

International Labour Office (ILO), (1996b), *Combating Unemployment and Exclusion: Issues and Policy Options*, contribution to the G7 Employment Conference submitted by the Director-General of the International Labour Office, Lille, 1–2 April, Geneva: ILO.

International Labour Office (ILO), (1996c) International Labour Conference: *Employment Policies in a Global Context*, Report of the Committee on Employment Policies, Provisional Record 13, Geneva: ILO.

United Nations Development Programme (UNDP) (1996), *Human Development Report 1996*, London: Oxford University Press.

United Nations. World Summit for Social Development (1995), *The Copenhagen Declaration and Programme of Action*, New York: UN.

15. Reforming the labour market through guaranteed incomes: a US perspective

Jeff Manza and Fred Block

INTRODUCTION

For most of the post-Second World War period, social and economic policy debates in Europe and the USA have centred around full employment as the preferred means to promote economic growth and to reduce poverty. Theorists of full employment have argued that minimizing unemployment will enhance the bargaining power of even the least skilled workers, resulting in an overall reduction in social and economic inequality. To be sure, even with full employment there must be a welfare safety net to support the basic needs of the relatively small number of non-elderly households without a wage earner, but the assumption has been that such transfer programmes to those outside the labour force will play a subordinate role in social policy.

In both the United States and western Europe, recent economic developments have stimulated a search for alternatives to the full employment strategy. In the USA in the 1990s, poverty rates have remained stubbornly high despite vigorous employment growth. The official measure of unemployment has fallen as low as 5.5 per cent in the last several years,[1] but there has been no reversal in the dramatic trend towards greater inequality in the distribution of income and wealth. It remains unclear how low the unemployment rate would have to be pushed before there would be significant progress in the reduction of poverty and inequality. In western Europe, persistently high rates of unemployment for a decade and a half have made full employment seem like an increasingly distant and unattainable goal. And the persistence of high unemployment has created growing strains on government budgets and continuing pressure to cut back on unemployment benefits. While intense debate continues over the causes and possible cures for high European unemployment, some analysts have argued that new circumstances require a new policy paradigm.

One of the most promising alternative policy paradigms centres on the idea of providing a guaranteed income for all citizens through government transfers. Over the last decade, there has been a lively debate in western Europe over the idea that it is time to simply provide all citizens with a guaranteed minimum income, sufficient to cover basic needs. The debate over 'basic' or 'citizen's' income proposals has involved social scientists and politicians from different intellectual and political traditions and has received serious attention in several countries.[2]

In this chapter, we review proposals for universal income guarantees, considering some of the implications their adoption would have for the functioning of the labour market and for the reduction of poverty and income inequality. We begin our discussion with an overview of the problem of poverty in post-industrial societies, and the emerging dilemmas of anti-poverty policies. Next, we provide a brief introduction to proposals for a guaranteed income, concentrating mainly on 'negative income tax' and 'basic income' proposals. While our thinking has been shaped largely in response to conditions in the United States, we think the analysis is also relevant to the European situation.

THE DILEMMAS OF ANTI-POVERTY STRATEGIES

The current structure of poverty in the United States provides a useful window into the broader policy dilemmas that confront all the developed market societies. In 1991, there were 21.6 million people in the United States living in non-elderly households with income below the poverty line after government transfers. Almost 20 per cent of these people were in households with a full-time and full-year wage earner. Another 40 per cent lived in households where someone worked only part-time or part-year. The remaining 40 per cent lived in households without significant wage earnings either because of illness, disability, school attendance or inability to find work. In about a fifth of this last group – accounting for 8 per cent of the non-elderly poor – there was someone who was actively looking for work but had been unable to find it.

This diversity in the causes of poverty means that any concerted effort to reduce poverty must do three things simultaneously. First, income levels of the poorest workers must be raised. This means, most obviously, that poor families dependent on a part-time or a very poorly paid full-time wage earner must see its income level rise. The second necessary step is to expand the availability of employment. This means providing more working time for many of those working part-time or part-year, and job opportunities for at least some of those in the group who have no earned income. Thirdly, income transfers have to be increased for that still substantial group of poor households who cannot take advantage of expanded opportunities to earn income.

To be sure, there is room for considerable disagreement about the priority that should be given to these different tasks. For example, many analysts suggest that the first two objectives – increasing the compensation for work and expanding the availability of jobs – are far more urgent than taking care of those households which have no employment income at all. But any anti-poverty strategy that completely ignores this latter group has two obvious flaws. Even if it were entirely successful on the other two fronts, it would still leave a significant number of people, including children, living in poverty and accumulating further disadvantages. Secondly, even if jobs were abundantly available, there are a variety of contingencies – disabilities, mental problems, addiction, illness of other family members, and unanticipated family breakup – that can leave households without earned income. Just as a simple matter of fairness, people need to be protected from these contingencies. Once it is recognized that a morally defensible anti-poverty strategy needs to move forward on all three fronts, it becomes apparent that there is a serious policy trilemma.[3] Efforts to achieve one of these three goals tend to interfere with accomplishing one or both of the other goals.

The first horn of the trilemma results from efforts to raise the income of low-wage workers. When this is done by raising wages, either through higher minimum wages or some system of wage-bargaining, it is likely that the creation of new employment opportunities will be slowed. Conservatives, of course, take this argument even further and insist that any increase in the minimum wage will lead to a net contraction of available employment. While this extreme formulation is both theoretically and empirically dubious,[4] there can be little doubt that with sharp increases in the price of unskilled labour, employers will attempt to save on labour costs by hiring fewer employees. Some of the sharp divergence between the western European and the US labour market experience over the past 15 years can be traced to precisely this difference in the relative cost of unskilled labour. Labour market regulations in western Europe ensure that most employees at the bottom of the labour market make sufficiently high wages to escape poverty. As a consequence, the creation of new jobs has been relatively slow, leading to very high rates of unemployment. In the USA, with its far weaker labour market regulation, compensation for low-wage employees has fallen relative to average wages and to the poverty line. The result has been much more dynamic employment creation in the USA, but with the cost that significant numbers of workers at the low end of the labour market remain in poverty.[5]

Governments can circumvent this policy conflict, but their actions produce a second problem. It is possible to keep minimum wage levels and other labour market regulation low in order to maximize job creation, but then use transfer payments to bring low-wage workers out of poverty. This policy choice makes it easier to raise income levels of the working poor and expand employment opportunities simultaneously. But if such a programme is successful in expanding the total supply of low-wage jobs, the aggregate cost of the income transfer is likely to be quite high.[6] The second horn of the trilemma is that such expensive transfers to the working poor will generally come at the expense of transfers to the non-working poor. Since politics limits the total amount of funds available at any particular time for anti-poverty efforts, more-generous income subsidies for the working poor means less-generous transfers to those who are outside the labour force. The consequence is that those who are entirely dependent on transfers are likely to remain well below the poverty line.

This second horn of the trilemma is also evident when government seeks to address the need for more employment opportunities by deliberately creating more public sector jobs – whether of a temporary or a permanent kind. Such a strategy of government as the employer of last resort often appears to be a desirable response to the inadequate number of private sector jobs that are provided when the minimum wage is set at a particular level. The problem, however, is that public sector job creation tends to be even more expensive than the policy of tax credits for the working poor. There are two reasons for this. First, there are usually strong pressures on government to compensate such public service jobs at higher than the minimum wage in order to protect existing public sector workers from being replaced by cheaper labour. Secondly, in order to protect such programmes from the charges of patronage and corruption, the people employed need to be carefully monitored. But the hiring of many supervisory employees substantially escalates the cost of the programme. The consequence is that deliberate public sector job creation also tends to come at the expense of generosity to those who are entirely dependent on transfers.

The third horn is the one that has dominated recent debates on welfare and unemployment benefits. If transfer payments are generous enough to allow those without earned income – including the unemployed – to escape poverty, some people who would otherwise look for work have incentives to rely completely on transfer payments. This drives up the budgetary costs of the transfer payments and reduces the resources that might otherwise be available for public sector job creation or for subsidies to low-wage employees. Moreover, when the reliance on transfers becomes widespread, subcultures can develop in which neither employment nor preparation for employment are important factors in people's lives.

While the trilemma is common to any developed market society, its severity depends critically on two factors. The first is the strength of certain 'post-industrial trends' such as the expansion of women's participation in the paid labour force, the growth of part-time work, the rise in female-headed households, and the more rapid turnover of skills in the labour market.[7] These trends tend to increase the number of households at any point in time that do not include a full-time earner. Many of these households will be in danger of slipping into poverty without transfer payments. The second factor is the level of redistributive spending. In countries where comparatively high social spending is possible, enough funds can be distributed across all three programme categories to manage the trilemma. But as nations face mounting pressures to cut government budgets, the trilemma looms ever larger.

THE GUARANTEED INCOME ALTERNATIVE

While proposals for a universal guaranteed income (GI) represent a dramatic departure from existing welfare state regimes, they could provide a means for better managing the policy trilemma. Existing transfer programmes provide benefits to selected categories of citizens through means-testing or other eligibility criteria,[8] but guaranteed income programmes replace most categorical programmes with a universal benefit available to all citizens, without means-testing or work requirements.[9] The two best-known GI proposals are the negative income tax (NIT) and the basic income grant (BI). The NIT was initially popularized by the libertarian economist Milton Friedman, who in his 1962 book *Capitalism and Freedom* proposed scrapping most welfare state programmes in favour of a single cash transfer to all households below a certain income level. The grant came in the form of a 'negative income tax' in the sense that as the income of a household went up, the grant would be taxed back, usually at a rate of 50 per cent, until it disappeared altogether.[10] Friedman's NIT proposal, or the substantially more generous version endorsed by several hundred US economists in the late 1960s, is not a true universal programme in that it is paid to households and is income-dependent. Some more recent proposals for a NIT – such as a proposal we have recently developed in the US context – come closer to providing a universal income guarantee by providing the grant to individuals rather than households and making it available to those who need it through monthly cheques.[11]

Proposals for a basic income grant go one step further than NIT schemes by abandoning any income test whatsoever. Whereas NIT schemes build in an *ex post* mechanism to tax back some or all of the universal grant upon the receipt of market incomes by an individual or household, BI schemes make no such adjustments. All citizens would simply receive the grant, irrespective of their ability or opportunity to perform paid labour. BI schemes eliminate all categories of eligibility, producing what the political theorist Robert Goodin has called a 'minimally presumptuous welfare state'.[12] Considerable debate has taken place over the size of the grant that post-industrial economies could afford; some have called for a 'partial' BI which might be expanded over time while others have called for 'full' basic income that would provide a sufficient minimum income to fund basic needs universally. Proponents of full BI have even suggested that it might over time produce 'a capitalist road to communism'.[13]

While there are important differences between basic income and negative income tax proposals,[14] they share much in common. First, BIs and NIT's can be structured to provide very similar post-tax, post-transfer income distributions. Secondly, both eliminate the 'traps' common to many types of income-maintenance programmes, in which recipients face sharp disincentives to taking employment. For example, where eligibility for unemployment benefits is means tested, an individual who takes a part-time job might face the loss of 100 per cent of the benefits – resulting in an actual reduction in income. Thirdly, both end bureaucratic programme administration and the stigmas which claimants experience in proving eligibility under many current (categorical, means-tested) welfare state programmes.[15] Finally, both provide workers at the bottom end of the wage structure an alternative to accepting poor quality jobs.

However, the two types of income guarantees have very different budgetary consequences. Since the NIT targets its payments very specifically at low-income households and individuals, its budgetary costs will be more modest than unconditional BI proposals that require much larger initial budgetary outlays to finance transfers to middle- and even upper-income households.[16] If one had the luxury of constructing a system of transfers and taxation from scratch, this difference would be of little importance, but in the current environment of budgetary constraint, this gives NIT proposals an obvious advantage.

Given this advantage, the NIT has better potential to manage the policy trilemma by simultaneously increasing the incomes of households that are largely dependent on wage income and those that lack wage income. By loosening the linkage between *work* and *income*, the NIT avoids the trap of over-reliance on employment to secure citizens' well-being. At the same time, it promises to achieve the objectives historically favoured by advocates of full employment – a tighter labour market in which even low-skilled workers have substantially more bargaining power than at present – by adjusting micro-level labour market decisions in the direction of reduced work effort (as we discuss in more detail below, pp. 324–5).

THE NIT AND THE LABOUR MARKET

Since it is difficult to think through the consequences of a NIT in the abstract, it is useful to provide some details of our proposal for the USA as a starting point. In our conception, all adult, resident[17] citizens[18] under 65 are entitled to an income supplement that would guarantee them an income of $6,000 in 1990 dollars.[19] (We concentrate on the under-65 population because we believe that existing programmes, such as Social Security, already provide sufficient income support for the elderly.) Children who are between 18 and 20 are eligible for a benefit of $2,500, and for children under 18 the custodial parent is entitled to $2,500 for the first child, $2,000 for the second child, and $1,500 for each additional child.[20] These benefit levels are designed to bring all households within about 90 per cent of the Federal poverty line. For example, the poverty threshold for single adults in 1990 was $6,802, so the grant for a single adult with no income would provide 88.2 per cent of that amount. A family of two adults and two young children with no income would be entitled to transfers of $16,500 – well above the poverty line of $13,359.

Households with income below the threshold for eligibility would be taxed 50 per cent on that income. For example, if the four-person family mentioned above were to earn $5,000 in income, the grant they would receive would be reduced by $2,500, making their after-tax income $19,000. If they earned $10,000, their after tax income would be $21,500. Even with $30,000 of earned income, they would still be entitled to a transfer of $1,500, bringing their total income to $31,500. It is only at income above $33,000 – double their benefit level – that they would no longer be eligible for any income supplement.

This design ensures that the NIT will provide very substantial benefits to those households which are currently just above the Federal poverty line. The family of four earning $20,000 a year will receive an annual transfer of $6,500. This means that even as many of the poor are raised up to the Federal poverty line, these non-poor but hard-pressed families will also experience a dramatic improvement in their living standards.

Based on an analysis of the 1990 census data, we estimate that this programme would cost somewhere around $208 billion – an estimate that includes an adjustment for work disincentive effects. However, we also estimate that much of this cost – $153 billion – would be offset by eliminating a variety of existing transfer programmes that would no longer be needed. Hence, the actual increase in budgetary outlays to eliminate poverty in the USA might be as little as $55 billion in 1990 dollars.

In our view, this NIT design could achieve many of the objectives of full employment advocates: a tighter labour market in which even low-skilled workers have substantially more bargaining power. It can do this by taking advantage of some of the same post-industrial labour market trends that have rendered the full employment model problematic. The key to the argument is a distinction between two techniques for tightening the labour markets: a 'macro' strategy and a 'micro' strategy. The macro strategy assumes that people's preferences about work and leisure are relatively stable and that the labour market can be tightened by adding new jobs at decent wages until virtually everyone who wants a job is employed. This is the approach that advocates of full employment have taken. If we use the United States as an example and assume an employed labour force of 100 million people, it might take 6–8 million new full-time jobs to bring about the desired level of labour market tightness given the numbers of the unemployed, the underemployed and people who have been discouraged from seeking employment.[21] (In many European countries, of course, the proportion of full-time jobs that would be required would be quite a bit higher.) In contrast, the micro strategy begins from the observation that at any given moment, there are tens of millions of people – both employed and thinking about employment – who are engaged in a complex calculation as to how many hours of paid labour they need to perform. Among the factors that such individuals are weighing are family responsibilities, the option to pursue education or training, the demands of various avocational interests, their budgetary needs, and the rate of compensation of available work. If a GI programme placed a floor under income, it could influence many of these calculations in the same direction by giving people the economic security to reduce their hours of work.[22] With such reductions, it would be possible to tighten the labour market by reducing the aggregate hours of work supplied by those who are already in the labour force. With the same example of an employed labour force of 100 million people, an average reduction in annual hours of work of just 6 per cent could open year-round, half-time jobs for as many as 9 million people who are currently not working.[23]

What makes the micro strategy viable is employers' interest in expanding the quantity of part-time jobs. The availability of part-time jobs, along with the growing flexibility in time schedules associated with the new technologies now being deployed in many industries, means that many people no longer face a binary choice between a full-time job or full-time leisure.[24] Rather, they face a graduated choice of working anywhere from zero hours per week to as many as 60 hours a week. To be sure, this 'flexibility' is being produced by post-industrial labour market volatility. Old jobs are being eliminated, new jobs have limited durations, skill requirements are constantly shifting, and the role of self-employment has been expanding dramatically. The old expectation that millions of people would be employed at full-time jobs for the duration of their work lives in a single enterprise is now completely anachronistic. But the GI would help people to cope more effectively with this volatility.

Universal income grants are vulnerable to 'free lunch' criticisms since they encourage some people to reduce their work effort. Critics suggest that millions of poor households would choose to live entirely on their grant, producing absolute shortages of workers in low-end jobs. The resulting tightening of the labour market would result in severe inflationary pressures. But there are several powerful reasons for doubting this scenario. First, a poverty-level income – whatever criterion is used to define the poverty line – is hardly a comfortable level of existence; it involves doing without many of the consumer goods that most people now see as necessities. The temptation for most people to earn money to live at a higher standard of living than that provided by the grant will be very strong. Secondly, analyses of the work-disincentive effects of the negative income tax experiments in the United States in the 1970s generally found a reduction of somewhere between 5 per cent and 15 per cent.[25] This means that someone who had been working 2,000 hours per year might be expected to reduce his or her annual hours by 100–300 hours. Even at the larger figure, this would represent a smaller shock to the economy than the legislated or bargained reductions in working hours that occurred in most countries between the late nineteenth century and the 1940s. Thirdly, the work disincentive effects for those currently in the labour force have to be weighed against the positive incentives for those who are currently provided with transfer payments under categorical programmes and face 'welfare traps'. When categorical programmes are replaced by a GI grant, these individuals will experience a sharp reduction in these effective tax rates, and they will have more incentives (and opportunities) to take paid employment.

In fact, from a macro-economic point of view, it is hardly desirable for everyone to choose to work as many hours as possible. Even with the successes of the US economy in job creation, that society has come nowhere near providing full-time employment for even the two-thirds of adults below 65 who are currently in the labour force. Given the realities of post-industrial labour markets, there are neither good moral nor good economic arguments against using transfers to encourage people to reduce their hours of paid work.

Indeed, the opposite objection – that the reduction in work effort will be too small to have an appreciable effect – may have as much or more force than the free lunch criticism. The force of this objection depends very much on the level of the negative income grants. If the maximum grant level for a household were, for example, only 50 per cent of the poverty line, these households would face extremely strong pressure for earned income and the risks of the Speenhamland scenario would be considerable.[26] However, if the grant level were closer to 100 per cent of the poverty line (or above), individuals and families would be able to manage without earned income for months at a time by reducing current consumption. This, in itself, would make the Speenhamland scenario unlikely because employees would have the option of walking away if employers were reducing wage levels or degrading working conditions. In short, even if a higher grant did not appreciably tighten the labour market by reducing hours of work, it would still improve the bargaining power of low-wage workers by eliminating the danger that unemployment would necessarily result in hunger or homelessness.

But what about the less extreme objection that even if the effects are not disastrous, the resulting tightening of the labour market and improved bargaining power of low-wage employees will significantly increase inflationary pressures in the economy? Our view is that the mainstream of the economics profession has overstated the degree to which reductions in unemployment below some 'natural' level will automatically produce inflation. Our view is that as long as employers are operating in competitive product markets where their ability to pass higher wages through to consumers is limited, they will have strong incentives to raise productivity along with wages. And we see a universal guaranteed income as helping to support the kind of flexibility in labour markets that employers need to assure continuous productivity improvements.

In sum, when the NIT is evaluated in relation to the trilemma, the results are generally positive. A NIT would provide a substantial improvement in the living standard of those households with a full-time wage earner, and ensures that households with either no or limited earned incomes will be brought close to (or above) the poverty line. And if the work disincentive effects are relatively strong, then the NIT will also provide more opportunities for employment for many of those who are currently unable to find additional hours of paid work.

FUNDING A GUARANTEED INCOME REFORM

While GI programmes are obviously expensive, they can be financed in part by replacing existing programmes that provide either universal or targeted benefits. The magnitude of savings will vary from one country to another. Depending on the particular plan, some or all of the following types of typical transfers might be replaced by the GI:

- public pension benefits that flow to those under age 65;
- disability benefits;
- income maintenance programmes, including unemployment benefits, benefits to poor individuals and households without market incomes, and subsidies for low-wage workers;
- food, energy and other consumption subsidies;
- veterans' benefits;
- housing subsidies for individuals or families;
- agricultural subsidies;
- children's or family benefits;
- educational subsidies.

Some centrist and conservative supporters of GI schemes would limit the grant to the amount saved from these already existing programmes divided equally among the entire population. However, it is also possible to structure the introduction of a GI so that almost no current recipients are made worse off than they were under the previous transfer regime. That would mean programme cuts will have to be selectively adjusted at the individual level so that the total transfers received remains unchanged. Adjustments may also be necessary for individuals who currently receive benefits from more than one programme exceeding the total amount provided by the GI grant, or for particular categories of citizens (for example, those with extreme disabilities or mental problems) who might require more than a GI grant.

If the level of the GI grant is low enough, the entire programme might be revenue neutral, although there will be wide variation from country to country. In already generous social democratic welfare states such as Sweden, the cost savings achieved from existing welfare state programmes could fund a significantly larger GI grant than in liberal welfare state regimes such as those in North America.[27] But it is likely that a GI grant sufficient to bring all households at least up to the poverty line would require some additional revenues in all countries. In the US case (which is the most extreme of the OECD countries), we have estimated that additional transfers amounting to approximately 1.3 per cent of GDP would be required to guarantee all households an income approximating the official poverty line.

Given the fiscal pressures on virtually all governments, raising *any* additional revenue to fund a GI programme is, of course, problematic.

With strong anti-tax sentiment everywhere, we suspect that advocacy of increased personal income or VAT taxes to fund a GI programme are probably politically unfeasible. Additional taxes on most types of corporate revenues may similarly be politically problematic in an age of intense global competition. However, there are a variety of other approaches to raising the necessary revenues that might be considered. Although the era of the Cold War and superpower conflict has ended, many countries have achieved only modest savings in their defence budgets. Since a GI programme would provide a safety net for those likely to face unemployment as a result of military cutbacks, it would make sense to combine the implementation of GI with reductions in defence spending.

Recently, several other ideas have been suggested that would also generate a large portion of the needed revenue. In a study of the growing inequality of wealth distribution in the United States, Edward Wolff has suggested that a wealth tax would be a means both to increase equity and ensure more productive uses of existing wealth. This would be a tax of around 0.5 per cent on the value of assets (both financial holdings and real property) that excludes pension holdings and the first $129,000 of other assets for a family of four. Wolff's simulation suggests that a wealth tax following this model would have raised $67.5 billion in 1989 in the USA.[28]

Robert Pollin and Dean Baker have recently argued that a transaction tax on financial exchanges would both raise very substantial revenues and dampen some of the excess volatility that currently exists in stock, bond and derivative markets. The idea is that if traders had to pay a small transaction tax on each trade, it would discourage certain speculative strategies that tend to destabilize the markets. Their estimates are that a 0.5 per cent transaction tax would generate between $30 billion and $60 billion per year in revenue.[29] Recently, there has also been renewed discussion of international agreement to establish a 'Tobin tax' on foreign exchange transactions which is also designed to reduce excess volatility in those markets. One recent study finds that such a tax at the rate of 0.25 per cent would have generated revenues of $46.8 billion for the United States and $300 billion globally based on the 1995 level of foreign exchange trading.[30]

Some combination of these different expedients could raise the necessary revenue to finance a GI programme without the need for further increases of personal income tax or VAT. Over the medium term, a well-developed GI scheme could contribute to a faster rate of increase in tax revenues. As that happens, it would be possible gradually to increase the generosity of the income supplement to ensure that it was completely effective in eliminating poverty. Finally, as with any major shift in social policy, it would be desirable to phase in the GI over a period of several years. Such a phase-in strategy would mean that all the additional revenue would not have to be raised in one year, but could be generated more slowly and with less shock to the economy.

IMPLEMENTING A GUARANTEED INCOME SCHEME

In discussing the savings from the elimination of existing programmes, we have not included any 'administrative savings'. While it is notoriously difficult to estimate accurately such savings, we expect that they could be considerable. Eliminating the need for government officials to evaluate eligibility for a host of current categorical programmes would free considerable resources. But rather than see thousands of eligibility workers lose their jobs, we think that in many countries those resources could be redeployed to improve the functioning of the labour market. In particular, there is room in a number of countries for increased effort to improve both the enforcement of labour market regulations and to develop better arrangements for matching people to employment.

The main forms of cheating in many labour markets occur when employers ignoring existing laws on minimum wages, overtime, documentation and working conditions and when employees work 'off the books' to avoid taxation. The growth of the 'second' or 'underground' economy is a well-documented phenomenon.[31] While a GI should provide most low-wage employees with a greater ability to refuse substandard pay and working conditions, there is a distinct risk that even more people would attempt to receive part or all of their wages 'off the books', so that employees would be able to maximize income by combining their NIT grant with a larger amount of unreported income. Unscrupulous employers may be tempted to offer non-reporting of income as a *quid pro quo* for the acceptance of substandard working conditions.

Current government employees could be redeployed to ensure both that employers follow existing labour laws and that employees are more scrupulous in reporting earned income. While both individuals and employers will continue to have incentives to cheat, the enforcement effort could reinforce incentives to co-operate. Greater enforcement for labour market regulations can create a 'level playing field' where employers do not have to worry about competition from firms paying subminimum wages, reinforcing the stabilizing features that union–management co-operation have traditionally fostered in the union sector. On the employee side, we think that it is reasonable to expect a higher level of voluntary compliance when an individual knows that the tax system will provide him or her with a subsistence level of income in bad times. In such a context, it is harder to justify tax avoidance in good times. In fact, it is possible that the combination of greater voluntary compliance and improved enforcement could bring a substantial amount of legal but unreported – 'underground' – income into the tax system.

The GI should also make it far easier for people to devote more time to additional training and education during adulthood. By providing an income floor, people will be better able to devote periods of time to more-intensive study. Similarly, the security of the safety net would encourage more individuals to pursue entrepreneurial initiatives, since they would recognize that even if their small business were to fail, their families would be protected from economic disaster.

But the largest economic benefit of implementing a GI scheme would come from having a more balanced labour market in which the bargaining position of low-wage employees was enhanced. Employers would be under pressure to create training and advancement opportunities for low-wage employees, and this should generate continuous improvements in the society's 'human capital'. Employers would also have stronger incentives to invest in new equipment that would eliminate the most dangerous and degraded types of work. In a word, the tighter labour market provided by the GI would encourage employers to shift from low value-added to high value-added production, and adopt more co-operative relationships with their workforce.

Since a guaranteed income redistributes income downwards, it would also strengthen the economy by giving a boost to consumer demand. This effect would be strongest in poor communities where a GI would increase purchasing power, and this could help to establish an economic base for entrepreneurial initiatives that could provide more jobs for impoverished inner-city neighbourhoods.

In short, it is easy to imagine a scenario in which a GI scheme combined with institutional restructuring in government and firms would quickly cover the costs of the grant through higher levels of economic growth. The resulting reduction in poverty rates can also be expected to produce a decline in the crime rate while also slowing the growth in the costs of incarceration of offenders that many countries are currently experiencing. Similarly, less poverty should mean more years of schooling for poor children, which should translate into future productivity gains. Hence, there are multiple reasons for believing that the ultimate benefits of implementing a guaranteed income programme will exceed the costs.

THE CULTURAL CONTEXT

Conservative critics of guaranteed income proposals have argued that the consequences of income guarantees cannot simply be reduced to questions of labour market behaviour. In the present US context, where conservative cultural objections to virtually all types of social provision have broad political influence, the claim that giving people money for doing nothing only serves to reinforce and encourage familiar pathologies such as teen childbearing, drug addiction and criminality is widely voiced. Our view is that such behaviours are the consequence of poverty rather than of the measures intended to alleviate poverty. But whatever one's views of causality, the important question is: How does a society go about persuading people to abandon these less-desirable behaviours?

In the United States, the answer over the past 20 years has been policies designed to impose stricter behavioural standards: more prisons, an ongoing war on drugs, and repeated efforts to tighten welfare rules to force recipients into the labour force. Some conservative governments in Europe have sought to develop similar policies, although the USA remains by far the leader in turning to punitive measures for dealing with its poor population. These policies are often justified as 'tough love' measures that are ultimately in the interests of the poor, who need to be held to strict standards of conduct if they are ever to change their behaviours. But while such 'tough love' measures have led to an explosion of the prison population,[32] they have had little visible effect in transforming the culture of poor neighbourhoods. In our view, this 'strict parenting'[33] model has failed for two reasons. First, genuine 'tough love' requires showing the individual that there is another path – if they abandon the undesirable behaviours, they will be helped to pursue that other path. Such help has been noticeably absent in recent social policy. Secondly, when 'tough love' is effective, it is because the new behavioural requirements are being imposed not by some impersonal authority but by close family members or friends.

In short, if the cultural arguments are taken seriously, changed behaviour will only come when new behavioural standards are strongly reinforced within poor communities themselves. As long as those communities continue to feel victimized by the larger society, significant change is unlikely. This is the hope of a guaranteed income approach. Both the income grant itself and its expected consequence of greater employment opportunities would be perceived by poor communities as opening up genuine possibilities for escaping poverty. In this new context, those insisting on new behavioural standards would be far more persuasive.

A GI programme could also play a significant role in facilitating community development initiatives. It would make it more practical for

millions of people to devote additional hours to voluntary activities in
support of community activities. Organizations could offer idealistic
young people quite minimal salaries for full-time work because the grant
would ensure a subsistence level of income for them. By the same logic,
the resources of community organizations could be stretched further. For
example, a programme in a poor community to teach construction skills
to young people through the rehabilitation of substandard housing would
be able to hire more young people because it could reduce the amount of
compensation for each of the apprentices.

But the political fate of GI proposals is also linked to a second important cultural issue: the question of family stability. One important,
although contested, finding of the income maintenance experiments conducted in the USA in the 1970s was that the NIT schemes used in the
experiments tended to increase the level of marital break-up.[34] It was generally assumed that this was because women who wanted to leave a bad
marriage had better economic options with the NIT than they had without
it. It has been suggested that this finding was the major factor in explaining
the disappearance of the NIT from US politics since politicians did not
want to be associated with policies that accelerated family break-up.

With the passage of 20 years, this finding no longer seems like a significant defect with a GI programme. At the time of the NIT experiments,
feminist critiques of the traditional family had not penetrated very deeply
into American culture. The old value that women and men were obligated
to remain in unsatisfactory marriages 'until death do us part' was still
widespread, and awareness of problems of spousal abuse was still quite
limited. But over the past 20 years, cultural norms have changed fundamentally; women and men are now far less willing to remain in a bad
marriage. The increasing number of female-headed households suggests
that economic coercion is no longer a very effective glue in keeping
households together. In short, by now most of the marriages that were
simply hanging by a thread have already been dissolved, so that the availability of income support for women should not lead to heightened levels
of marital break-up.

THE POLITICS OF A GUARANTEED INCOME

It is difficult to anticipate the precise political circumstances under which
one or another country might decide to implement a guaranteed income,
particularly since politicians of the centre and the right have occasionally
flirted with GI proposals. It must be remembered that the United States
came quite close to adopting a Guaranteed Income plan in the early 1970s

under the Nixon Administration. In the aftermath of the urban turmoil of the late 1960s, that Administration proposed quite minimal income guarantees. The proposal passed one house of Congress and was only defeated in the US Senate.[35] To be sure, the terms of policy debate in the USA shifted radically in the aftermath of that near miss, with both policy intellectuals and politicians becoming far less supportive of any income transfers to non-elderly adults. This shift culminated in the passage in 1996 of 'welfare reform' legislation designed to withdraw transfers from many non-working parents to ensure that they moved into the workforce.

While the immediate prospects of reviving interest in the GI in the USA appear bleak, the possibilities in Europe appear somewhat better. In the short term, of course, the pressures for budget balancing in preparation for monetary union make it difficult to gain serious consideration for such a dramatic policy shift within a single country. However, if the decision is made to delay the project of monetary union, pressures could build for unique national solutions to the strains of high unemployment. Alternatively, if the movement to monetary union remains on track, the GI idea might re-emerge as a European-wide strategy to create a simpler and more flexible safety net.

But in either case, the ultimate prospects for the implementation of a GI are likely to depend on the orientation of the trade unions. While a GI proposal might be placed on the political agenda by politicians of the centre, left or right, the stance of labour is likely to be crucial in determining its ultimate political fate. Historically, most trade unions have been unenthusiastic about GI proposals because of their preference for full employment policies as the best way to improve workers' bargaining power.

Our view is that unions and their allies increasingly face a choice between a defensive and an offensive political strategy. The defensive strategy rests on the premise that the current period of high unemployment, pressures for greater labour market flexibility and demands for budgetary austerity will ultimately give way to a period that will be more favourable to traditional full employment policies. Hence, the goal in the short term is to defend as much as possible of existing labour market rules and existing social benefit programmes with the idea that when the political situation improves, it will be possible to restore high employment and expansive, universal social programmes.

The danger in this strategy is that the structural situation will not improve and that defensive battles will fail to halt a series of incremental 'reforms' that gradually erode existing wage levels and social protections. In this scenario, Europe will gradually retrace the path of the United States over the last quarter century towards increasing economic inequality and a much weakened political position for unions and their allies.

The offensive strategy starts from the premise that pressures for labour market flexibility and for budget restraint will be continuous and that fighting purely defensive battles is a losing approach. Without offering a positive vision of how societies should adapt to these new circumstances, labour will be perceived as increasingly irrelevant. The positive vision would embrace the GI as a mechanism that could tighten the labour market and put a secure floor under the standard of living for all citizens. Certainly, this approach makes important concessions to labour's opponents in accepting greater labour market flexibility, including removing obstacles to the spread of part-time work, and in substituting income-tested benefits for universal programmes. But the key idea is that if a sufficiently generous GI could be implemented, it would immediately establish a more productive terrain on which to continue the fight for improved wages and working conditions and for greater economic equality.

In sum, as long as the current employment crisis continues, GI proposals deserve serious consideration and debate. They could represent the only politically feasible path towards a society that provides a decent standard of living for all citizens.

NOTES

1. The US employment outlook is not as rosy as the official data indicate since the data exclude employees involuntarily working part-time and those who are too discouraged to look for work. Even so, the official data shapes the perceptions of economic actors, and there is considerable fear in the business community that unemployment rates below 5.5 per cent will produce powerful inflationary pressures.
2. The European Basic Income Network (BIEN) has been the most active organization involved in this debate. They have produced a lively newsletter since 1988, back issues of which are accessible on the world-wide web (along with much other information about the basic income movement) at *http://www.econ.ucl.ac.be/etes/bien/bien.html*. In Britain, the Citizens' Income Research Group has also produced a regular journal (*Citizens' Income*) devoted to issues surrounding basic income ideas. For an introduction to some of the major debates that have engaged social scientists and philosophers over universal income proposals, see Philippe Van Parijs (ed.), *Arguing for Basic Income*, London: Verso, 1992.
3. We have borrowed the idea of a policy trilemma from Peter Swenson, who elaborates it in *Fair Shares: Unions, Pay, and Politics in Sweden and West Germany*, Ithaca, N.Y.: Cornell University Press, 1989.
4. The important study by David Card and Alan B. Krueger, *Myth and Measurement: The New Economics of the Minimum Wage*, Princeton: Princeton University Press, 1995, has forcefully debunked many of the most exaggerated claims about the labour market consequences of raising the minimum wage.
5. To be sure, the USA has also been far more successful than many European countries in expanding the number of well-paying employment opportunities. Estimates are that half of the remarkable 10 million jobs created between 1992 and 1996 paid above the median.
6. There is also an economic cost if such transfers encourage employers to shift the employment mix towards labour-intensive, low-productivity jobs. See, for example, John Myles, 'Decline or impasse? The current state of the welfare state', *Studies in Political Economy* **26** (1987): 73–107.

7. These are identified as post-industrial trends in Fred Block, *Postindustrial Possibilities*, Berkeley, Cal.: University of California Press, 1990. See also Judith Stacey, *In the Name of the Family*, Boston, Mass.: Beacon University Press, 1996, and Frances Fox Piven (ed.), *Labor Parties in Postindustrial Societies*, Cambridge: Polity Press, 1991.

8. We distinguish between income testing that is done through routine tax procedures and the more intrusive and demeaning means testing that has determined eligibility for certain categorical programmes.

9. Proposals for universal income grants have gone under a wide range of names: 'state bonus', 'social credit', 'negative income tax', 'demogrant', 'universal grant', 'basic income', 'citizen's income' and most commonly today, 'basic income'. The term 'guaranteed income' is used in this chapter as an umbrella term to describe all proposals which would provide an income floor for citizens through a grant paid to individuals without work requirements. For a recent survey of the variety of policy proposals which can loosely be grouped under the 'guaranteed income' heading, see Robert Haveman, 'Reducing poverty while increasing employment: a primer on alternative strategies, and a blueprint', *OEDC Economic Studies* **26** (1996): 7–42.

10. Milton Friedman, *Capitalism and Freedom*, Chicago: University of Chicago Press, 1962.

11. See Fred Block and Jeff Manza, 'Could we end poverty in a postindustrial society? The case for a progressive negative income tax', *Politics & Society* **25** (1997): 473–511. See also Claus Offe, Ulrich Muckenburger and Ilona Ostner, 'A basic income guaranteed by the state: a need of the moment in social policy', in Claus Offe, *Modernity and the State*, Cambridge, Mass.: MIT Press, 1996, pp. 201–21 (which defends a basic income approach which includes features of the negative income tax).

12. Robert Goodin, 'Towards a minimally presumptuous social welfare policy', in Van Parijs (ed.), *Arguing for Basic Income*, pp. 195–214.

13. For advocates of a partial BI, see, for example, Hermione Parker, *Instead of the Dole: An Enquiry into the Integration of the Tax and Benefit Systems*, London: Routledge, 1989; the most forceful advocate of an unconditional full basic income grant is the Belgian political enonomist Philippe Van Parijs; see especially his recent *Real Freedom for All: What, if Anything, Can Justify Capitism?*, Oxford: Oxford University Press, 1995. The 'capitalist road to communism' argument was originally developed in Robert van der Veen and Philippe Van Parijs, 'A capitalist road to communism', *Theory and Society* **15** (1986): 635–55.

14. In particular, Van Parijs has insisted on these differences (and the advantages of basic income). See his 'Competing justifications of basic income', in Van Parijs (ed.), *Arguing for Basic Income*, pp. 4–6; and *Real Freedom for All*, pp. 35–7. For an earlier, systematic comparison of the two types of programmes, see Jonathan R. Kesselman and Irwin Garfinkel, 'Professor Friedman, meet Lady Rhys-Williams: NIT v, CIT', *Journal of Public Economics* **10** (1978): 179–216.

15. It is important to note briefly that the stigmas associated with means-tested programmes can – at least in a polity where receipt of 'welfare' is actively discouraged by the larger political culture – result in significant numbers of poor individuals who forgo public programmes for which they are otherwise eligible. The economists Rebecca Blank and Patricia Ruggles have estimated that in the United States the overall 'take-up' rate for the major programme of income support for low-income households (Aid to Families with Dependent Children) has been 60–72 per cent of eligible households, while the take-up rate for the major food subsidy programme (the Food Stamp programme) is 41–54 per cent. Further, they find that fewer than 35 per cent of households who become eligible for these programmes for short periods take benefits. Rebecca Blank and Patricia Ruggles, 'Multiple program use in a dynamic context: data from the SIPP', Report to the United States Census Bureau 91–24, December 1992, pp. 70–71.

16. John Myles and Paul Pierson, 'Friedman's revenge: the reform of "liberal" welfare states in Canada and the United States', *Politics & Society* **25** (1997): 443–72, argue that NIT designs will be of increasing interest to budget-cutting politicians because they target benefits so effectively.

17. Residency is a requirement to prevent US citizens from collecting their cheques abroad where a lower standard of living might allow someone to live in luxury with an amount of money that was not intended to support luxury.

18. The relationships between transfer programme and immigration are difficult and complex, and require much further elaboration. Briefly, our view is that the entitlement of legal immigrants to the NIT transfer could be handled through a vesting process. Adult legal immigrants might become eligible for a certain number of months of a NIT transfer for every two or three years of gainful employment. Those in the USA without proper documentation would not be eligible for the NIT, but we also think that improving the bargaining leverage of citizens who are low-wage workers requires stricter enforcement of existing laws against employing undocumented individuals. However, the special character of the US–Mexico border calls for some kind of more imaginative solution because there are tens of thousands of people who have constructed some kind of 'binational' existence. These people could be granted some form of quasi-citizenship rights that included legal protections in the US labour market.

19. We use 1990 dollars because our estimates of the cost of such a programme are drawn from 1990 census data, but we would increase grant levels to keep pace with inflation. Since the cost of living as measured by the Consumer Price Index (CPI) has risen approximately 15 per cent from 1990 to 1996, the actual grant level that we are proposing for adults would be $6,900. In order to adjust for differences in the cost of living across states, grant levels could vary from 90 per cent to 110 per cent of this central amount depending upon where a state ranked in its relative cost of living.

20. Young people between 18 and 20 who are emancipated – living on their own and not claimed as dependants on someone else's income tax return – would receive the adult grant level. Hence, a 19-year-old single mother of one child living on her own would be entitled to $8,500. The parents or custodians of a teen mother under 18 would receive the child's benefit for both the daughter and the grandchild. Single mothers under 18 could receive the adult grant if they were living in a supervised group home. The latter option would help teen mothers to escape from abusive home situations.

21. These examples are meant only to be illustrative, since actual labour markets are far more complex than this kind of static analysis can indicate. Moreover, in these scenarios, we would expect that some who are currently working part-time would move into full-time positions and some who are currently unemployed would move into part-time positions.

22. A similar version of this argument is made by Georg Voruba, 'Redistribution of work and income in the crisis: actors' problems of working time reduction and a guaranteed basic income', *Contemporary Crisis* **14** (1990): 57–67.

23. If the GI grant comes in the form of negative income tax, the reduction in working time would be concentrated among the bottom half of earners, both because they would be the primary beneficiaries and because salaried employees often have little control over their working hours. Hence, the 6 per cent reduction in hours of work given in the example should be thought as a 10 per cent average reduction extending over the bottom 60 per cent of wage earners.

24. To be sure, in some employment situations employees still have very little control over their hours – with employers inposing mandatory overtime or being unwilling to afford employees any flexibility. But there has already been considerable movement towards greater flexibility in negotiating working time and we would expect further progress as a result of both legislation and greater employee bargaining power.

25. This is the standard range of work reduction estimates from the negative income tax experiments carried out in the 1970s in the United States. See Philip K. Robins and Richard W. West, 'Labor supply response', in *Final Report of the Seattle/Denver Income Maintenance Experiment*, vol. 1, Stanford, Cal.: SRI International, 1983, pp. 91–108; and Gary Burtless, 'The work responses to a guaranteed income: a survey of experimental evidence', in Alicia Munnell (ed.), *Lessons from the Income Maintenance Experiments*, Boston, Mass.: Ferderal Reserve Bank, 1989, pp. 22–52.

26. Speenhamland refers to the classic discussion in Karl Polanyi, *The Great Transformation*, Boston, Mass.: Beacon Press, 1957, of the impact on the rural poor in

England of an income guarantee system at the end of the eighteenth century that led to a sharp reduction in wages and standards of living. Our view is that these negative consequences were linked to the low level of the income guarantee and the prohibition on trade union activity. A more generous income guarantee combined with trade union rights should lead to an improvement in the wage levels of the poorest workers.

27. If the grant takes the form of an unconditional basic income grant, and all subsidies to middle- and upper-income households are included in the programme to be collapsed into the BI grant, it is possible on paper to make the cost of implementation revenue-neutral. However, in practice most middle- and upper-income households would face additional tax burdens to cover the cost of a more equitable sharing of welfare state benefits across all households.
28. Edward Wolff, *Top Heavy: A Study of the Increasing Inequality of Wealth in the United States*, New York: Twentieth Century Fund, 1995, p. 43.
29. Robert Pollin and Dean Baker, 'Taxing the big casino', *Nation*, 9 May 1994.
30. David Felix and Ranjit Sau, 'On the revenue potential and phasing in of the Tobin tax', in Mahbub up Haq, Inge Kaul and Isabelle Grunberg (eds), *The Tobin Tax: Coping with Financial Volatility*, New York: Oxford University Press, 1996, pp. 223–45. Their estimates include an adjustment for lower levels of trading as a consequence of the tax.
31. See, for example, Alejandro Portes, Manuel Castells and Lauren Benton (eds), *The Informal Economy: Studies in Advanced and Less Developed Countries*, Baltimore, Md: Johns Hopkins University Press, 1989.
32. In June 1996, the USA had an extraordinary 1.63 million people in prison. See Fox Butterfield, 'Slower growth in the number of inmates', *New York Times*, 20 January 1997, p. a-10.
33. The role of 'parenting' in social policy debates in the United States is a central theme of George Lakoff, *Moral Politics: What Conservatives Know that Liberals Don't*, Chicage: University of Chicago Press, 1996.
34. See, for example, Glen G. Cain, 'The income maintenance experiments and the issues of marital stability and family composition', in Munnell (ed.), *Lessons from the Income Maintenance Experiments*, pp. 60–93.
35. Daniel Patrick Moynihan, *The Politics of a Guaranteed Income: The Nixon Administration and the Politics of the Family Assistance Plan*, New York: Random House: 1973; Jill Quadagno, *The Color of Welfare*, New York: Oxford University Press, 1994, ch. 5.

16. The reduction of working time as a means of solving the unemployment problem

Angelo Reati*

THE PROBLEM

In Chapter 5 of this volume I argued that the most likely medium- to long-term trend for employment stemming from the diffusion of the technological revolution in computer and information technologies will be stagnation (or perhaps even a slight decline). This is because the present technical change in processes has an historically unique characteristic which differentiates it from the technological revolutions of the past: pervasiveness. The new technology covers not only the whole industry but also a substantial and growing part of services. Thus, we cannot expect that, as in the past, the service sector will absorb the labour shaken out by industry.

Of course, product innovations could redress such a situation, but unfortunately the scene is dominated by process innovations and, in spite of the many potentialities which exist, there are no signs that the situation will be reversed in the next few years (let us say five to ten years).[1] The problem then is how to restore full employment in a situation where labour demand will be stationary and where, at the beginning, there is a very high number of unemployed people. I think that the solution can only be found in measures to reduce total labour supply and, subsidiarily, by developing labour-intensive activities in the service sector.

Ways to reduce labour supply are well known: lengthening the compulsory education period, early retirement, part-time jobs, sabbatical periods and reduction of working time. In most European countries the first two have already been widely followed and therefore we should not expect too

* I thank Ernesto Screpanti for comments and discussions on the first version of this chapter. Usual disclaimers apply.

much from them. Part-time employment and sabbatical periods can provide some results, but they are necessarily limited in scope. Of course, part-time jobs must be chosen and not imposed. There remains the reduction of working time.

THE SIMPLE ARITHMETIC OF EMPLOYMENT AND THE REDUCTION OF WORKING TIME

In this section I shall show that the reduction of working time could suit the purposes of solving the problem of unemployment without cutting wages and, at the same time, avoiding inflation.

The relationship between the reduction of working time and employment growth is easily seen by writing the identity which describes the factors determining the level of physical output at any period of time:

$$Y \equiv LH\pi_h \qquad (16.1)$$

where: Y is the physical output of any commodity for a given period of time (one week, one year, and so on)

L is the number of workers

H is the individual working time for the same period of time (for example, weekly hours per worker)[2]

π_h is the hourly productivity level: $\pi_h = Y/(LH)$.

We see that for any given level of output and productivity, employment (L) can increase by reducing the working time (H) of present workers. Identity (16.1) holds at both the micro and the macro level, because I am considering here the phenomenon from its additive aspect (total employment is the sum of employment in individual enterprises, and it is the same for output). However, we shall see later that, when we go beyond this simple characteristic of additivity and take into account the mechanisms which determine sectoral demand, one cannot simply extrapolate the micro-economic results to the whole economy.

Box 16.1 provides an illustration of the micro-economic aspects. Let us consider at the start (point A) a small enterprise employing ten workers under normal conditions: eight hours a day for five days per week for a total of 400 hours per week and a (hypothetical) output of 1,200 units of commodity. Hourly productivity is thus three units.

Box 16.1 The effects of the reduction of working time*

(I) Employment

(A) The situation at the start
Working hours for the enterprise:
  10L × 8H/d × 5d = 400h/week
  (L = number of workers; H = hours; d = days)
π_h (hourly productivity):   3 units
Weekly output (Y):   1,200 units

(B) Reduction of working time by 10 per cent and lengthening of the working time for the enterprise
Working hours for the enterprise:
  present workers: 10L × 9H/d × 4d =   360 h/week
  new workers: 10L × 9H/d × 2d =   180 h/week
  total: 540 h/week
π_h (hourly productivity):   3 units
Weekly output (Y):   1,620 units

(C) Reduction of working time by 10 per cent, lengthening of the working time for the enterprise and increase in productivity by 11.1 per cent
Working hours for the enterprise:
  present workers: 10L × 9H/d × 4d =   360 h/week
  new workers: 7L × 9H/d × 2d =   126 h/week
  total: 486 h/week
π_h (hourly productivity):   3.33 units
Weekly output (Y):   1,620 units

(II) Costs and profits

Selling price of the commodity (p)   5 ecu
Other costs per unit of output
  (raw materials, energy, etc.)(p_m)   2 ecu

(A) Situation at the start
Labour costs per week (400h × 6 ecu/h) 2,400 ecu
  (wage rate: 6 ecu per hour)
Other costs (2 ecu × 1,200 units)   2,400 ecu
Total: 4,800 ecu

Revenues (5 ecu × 1,200 units)	6,000 ecu
Profit (S)	1,200 ecu
Weekly wage per worker: 40 h × 6 ecu/h = 240 ecu/week	
Labour cost per unit of output	2 ecu
Profit share	33.33%

(B) Reduction of working time keeping the weekly wage unchanged

Labour cost per week:

present workers:	10L × 240 ecu	2,400 ecu	
new workers:	10L × 120 ecu (2 days)	1,200 ecu	3,600 ecu
Other costs: 2 ecu × 1,620 units			3,240 ecu
Total costs			6,840 ecu
Revenue: 5 ecu × 1,620 units			8,100 ecu
Profit (S)			1,260 ecu
Wage rate (w)			6.67 ecu
Labour cost per unit of output			2.22 ecu
Profit share			25.9%

(C) Reduction of working time, 11.1 per cent increase in productivity and weekly wage unchanged

Labour costs per week:

present workers:	10L × 240 ecu	2,400 ecu	
new workers:	7L × 120 ecu (2 days)	840 ecu	3,240 ecu
Other costs: 2 ecu × 1,620 units			3,240 ecu
Total costs			6,480 ecu
Revenue: 5 ecu × 1,620 units			8,100 ecu
Profit (S)			1,620 ecu
Wage rate (w)			6.67 ecu
Labour cost per unit of output			2.00 ecu
Profit share			33.33%

*I thank A. Dramais for suggesting this example.

In the first example (point B) I make a double assumption: (a) a relatively important reduction in working time, let us say 10 per cent; and (b) an increase in capacity utilization by reducing weekly idle time for plant and equipment. Employees will thus work 36 hours per week (instead of 40) – spread over a four-day week of nine hours a day – while the enterprise will produce for six days per week (nine hours per day). Consequently, with no change in productivity (three units per hour), output will increase by 35 per cent and employment by 50 per cent. In fact, the enterprise must now engage ten new workers for two days, which corresponds to half of the hours worked by its old employees. If another firm reduces the working time under the same conditions, the new employees would obtain a full-time job by taking a second part-time job in this enterprise. We see that, if all enterprises in the European Union behaved like the enterprise in question, something like 40 million new jobs would be created in the market sector (EUR-15), an amount which is bigger than present unemployment levels (even taking into account hidden unemployment).

Note that what we are considering here is just the direct employment effect. If we take into account the overall effect (that is, the direct plus the indirect effect) the employment increase would be much larger, probably 20 to 40 per cent higher than the direct effect.

Box 16.1 also shows another example (point C), where employment growth is lower (35 per cent instead of 50 per cent) because I assume a productivity increase of 11.1 per cent (each worker produces 3.33 units per hour instead of 3 units). This example is particularly useful for considering the question of wages.

Wages are, in fact, the *punctum dolens*: whenever trade unions propose a reduction in working time, employers and governments – if they say yes – add a condition: the weekly pay must be reduced proportionally to the reduction in working time. Of course, it could be objected that, at present, the rate of profit is very high – at the level it reached in the 1960s[3] – but this argument may have little success in collective bargaining since unemployment puts workers in a weak position. We live in a capitalist society – a society which is conceived for profits, not people – and so we cannot ignore the constraints imposed by profit.

However, if the reduction of working time goes together with an increase in productivity, it becomes simultaneously possible to satisfy a double constraint: (a) to leave unchanged the level of the individual wage (for example, the weekly pay per worker); and (b) to keep constant the share of profits in value added. Let us start from the second constraint and reason, as before, at the micro-economic level. To understand the trade-off between working time, productivity, wages, growth in output and employment let us write the expression for the profit share:

$$\frac{S}{pY - p_m Y} = \frac{pY - wHL - p_m Y}{pY - p_m Y} \qquad (16.2)$$

where: S is the mass of profits

w is the wage rate (hourly wage)

p is the unit price of output

p_m is the unit price of intermediate output (raw materials, energy, and so on).

Equation (16.2) can be written as follows:

$$\frac{S}{pY - p_m Y} = 1 - \frac{w}{\pi_h} \frac{1}{p - p_m} \tag{16.3}$$

Calculating the derivative with respect to time of (16.3) and equating it to zero (since the profit share must be constant), after some manipulations we obtain:

$$\dot{\pi} = \dot{w} \tag{16.4}$$

where: $\dot{w}$ is the (instantaneous) percentage rate of change of the wage rate

$\dot{\pi}$ is the (instantaneous) percentage rate of change of productivity.

This well-known condition for the constancy of the profit share is indeed the result of three separate movements: a decrease in working time and an increase in employment and output. To see it precisely let us rewrite equation (16.3) as follows:

$$\frac{S}{pY - p_m Y} = 1 - w \frac{HL}{Y} \frac{1}{p - p_m} \tag{16.5}$$

Calculating, as before, the derivative with respect to time and equating it to zero, after several passages we have:

$$\dot{w} + (-\dot{H}) + \dot{L} = \dot{Y} \tag{16.6}[4]$$

where: $\dot{H}$ is the (instantaneous) percentage change of working time

$\dot{L}$ is the (instantaneous) percentage increase of employment

$\dot{Y}$ is the (instantaneous) percentage increase of output.

Taking into consideration equation (16.4) we have the following, which shows clearly the trade-off in question:

$$\dot{\pi} - \dot{H} + \dot{L} = \dot{Y}. \tag{16.7}$$

This is illustrated by the last numerical example in Box 16.1 (part II, point C). The stability of the individual wage (W) implies that the percentage growth of the wage rate (w) is identical to the percentage change in working time (H). In fact:

$$W = wH. \tag{16.8}$$

Taking the derivative with respect to time (W = constant) and proceeding as before to obtain the (instantaneous) percentage rates of change, we have:

$$\dot{w} = \dot{H}. \tag{16.9}[5]$$

Finally, let us note that in this case the percentage increase of output is exactly matched by the increase of the purchasing power of employees. In fact, the wage bill paid by the enterprise (W_{tot}) is:

$$W_{tot} = wHL \tag{16.10}$$

which means that:

$$\dot{W}_{tot} = \dot{w} + \dot{H} + \dot{L}. \tag{16.11}$$

Taking into consideration equation (16.6) we have:

$$\dot{W}_{tot} = \dot{Y}. \tag{16.12}$$

At the macro-economic level we could perform the same reasoning and derive equations (16.2)–(16.12). Within this logical framework we could say that, if the double constraint of the stability of individual wage and profit share is satisfied, the economic system could enter into a virtuous circle of self-fulfilling expectations. Capitalists know that if they increase their output, the mass of wages will increase correspondingly (equation (16.12)) and the same holds for the mass of profits; consequently, they will expect an increase in demand. However, as we shall see in the next section things are not so simple. But before proceeding further let us draw some first conclusions.

The previous analysis shows that the reduction of working time can solve the unemployment problem without creating difficulties on the income distribution side, provided that five conditions are fulfilled. Such a reduction must:

1. be important;
2. be sudden;
3. involve a large part of the economy;
4. be coupled with an increase in the degree of capital utilization;
5. be concomitant with an increase in productivity.

The first and second conditions guarantee the effectiveness of the measure from the point of view of job creation. In fact, if the reduction of working time were not important and, moreover, if it were implemented gradually, enterprises could adapt to the new situation either by trying to increase their productivity or by accepting a lower level of output, without hiring new workers. The fourth and fifth conditions are of particular importance since we have seen that they allow a solution to the problem of the conflict between profits and wages. Within this framework, it is essential that firms not producing around the clock reduce the working time for their present employees from five to four days per week, since this reorganization favours the hiring of new personnel.

DISCUSSION

Several difficulties arise. Before addressing them, let us clarify one point concerning productivity.

The numerical example above indicates that productivity growth must be large (11.1 per cent in this case), and it may be questioned whether this is realistic in present circumstances.[6] The reply is positive, because enterprises adopting radical process innovations experience a substantial leap in their productivity level. For instance, according to a recent microeconomic study of a representative sample of large American corporations, the introduction of computer capital increased the productivity level by more than 50 per cent (Brynjolfsson and Hitt, 1993).

However, at the sectoral level the increase in productivity is more gradual, since it depends on the pattern and length of the diffusion of technical change: enterprises in the same industry do not adopt new technology simultaneously, so that it normally takes 10–15 years for the new technique to completely replace the old one. This means that an important and sudden reduction of the working time can be feasible only for the innovators; therefore, we would wait several years before the reduction spreads to the whole sector.[7]

Problems arise on the *demand* side. Equation (16.12) shows that if all the enterprises of an economic system reduce working time, at a global level the growth of output is exactly matched by an identical percentage increase of the purchasing power of wage earners. For instance, in the numerical example in Box 16.1, both output and wages grow by 35 per cent. Apparently there are no problems; however, this is a case where my previous arithmetic is simplistic.

Indeed, if *global* demand grows at the same rate as output, this does not mean that for all *sectors* (and all enterprises) the growth of demand for their commodities will be exactly equal to the potential increase of their output. In fact, when per capita income grows, the demand for different

categories of goods increases at a rate which is different from the rate of
increase of income. This is an old result in economic theory, known as
Engel's Law. For subsistence goods (food and other necessities) the growth
of demand is less than the percentage growth of per capita income; for
other commodities demand growth exceeds or is below the growth of
income according to the different categories of goods. In other words, in
an economy where there is technical change, the growth of the various sectors is non-proportional (for a complete model of structural change see
Pasinetti, 1981). For our problem this means that the reduction of working time should be varied according to the sectoral perspectives of
demand, and this could drastically reduce the possibility of increasing
employment in some sectors on the basis of the above mechanism.

Of course, this does not mean that the reduction of working time to
absorb unemployment is not feasible, but rather that it requires public
intervention in the form of some fiscal incentive. It is worth mentioning
the French de Robien law, which was approved in June 1996 under the
then Conservative government. The law grants a considerable reduction in
employers' social security contributions for seven consecutive years to
enterprises which substantially reduce working time (by 10 or 15 per cent)
and which increase employment by the same percentage amount.[8] When
the reduction in working time is 10 per cent, the cut in social security contributions is 40 per cent for the first year and 30 per cent for the following
years; it becomes respectively 50 per cent and 40 per cent when working
time is reduced by 15 per cent (and employment increased by 15 per cent).
A recent econometric estimate by the semi-official body OFCE
(Observatoire Français des Conjonctures Economiques), (Timbeau, 1997)
shows that this measure is very promising. A generalized cut in working
time of 10 per cent could generate two million permanent new jobs – and
a decrease of 1.5 million in the number of unemployed – with a relatively
modest increase in net borrowing by the government (a supplementary 2.2
per cent of GDP in 1996).

Other obstacles arise from the profound *reorganization of enterprises* as
well as from the *flexibility of labour* that is required by the reduction of
working time. For instance, managers do not always have the skills to
implement the changes in the organization of their company and moreover
they could not necessarily find enough financial incentives for doing this.
Some resistance to change could also arise from workers, because a large
proportion of employees would be obliged to accept two part-time jobs
and to work on Saturdays. However, it should not be too hard to overcome
such resistance since the flexibility which is required is a 'positive' one,
which is directly linked to an increase in employment. This is completely
different from flexibility in the current (neoclassical) sense, whose primary

goal is to submit workers to the requirements of profit by making jobs precarious, by wage cuts, by reduced social protection and by easy dismissal.

A *cultural* change is also required, which concerns both the working environment and leisure. Within the enterprise a reduction of working time imposes a change of mentality on managers as well as employees, since everybody has to work with an increased number of colleagues. This would be particularly hard for managers to accept: they will have to share part of their supervisory functions with somebody else.

On the other hand, increased spare time presents the problem of its good use: passing from the 'empty' time of unemployment to 'empty' leisure needs to be avoided. Thus, there is a personal effort involved in reorganizing activity and also a societal effort to offer sufficient opportunities at the cultural and social participation level.

The reduction of working time poses a formidable challenge in the field of *education* and *vocational training*. The overwhelming majority of new jobs will be linked, directly or indirectly, with the information and communication technologies: the new demand for labour will thus concern qualified labour. Also, for many presently unemployed people (particularly the elderly and long-term unemployed), there is a large gap between their skills and what is required by the new jobs. There is a serious bottleneck here, which could be overcome only at the price of huge investment by public authorities and serious efforts from the individuals involved.

CONCLUSION

In this chapter I have presented a numerical example to show that the reduction of working time is potentially able to solve the unemployment problem. This possibility – which already appears when considering the *direct* employment effect – is strongly reinforced when we take into account the overall (direct plus indirect) effect of the suggested measure.

To be effective, the reduction of working time should fulfil a number of conditions: it should be significant (for instance, the weekly working time should be cut by 10 per cent); it should be enforced suddenly; it should concern a substantial part of the economy; and, above all, it should accompany an increase in the rate of capacity utilization by a lengthening of the weekly running time of plants (for example, from five to six days per week). If this is coupled with productivity growth (a modernization of the present production structure by the adoption of new technologies), it would even be possible to avoid conflict on income distribution because the increase of employment could be obtained without cutting wages.

What this implies is that for some sectors (those adopting radical technical change by means of computer and information technologies and which benefit from strong demand) it is technically possible to attain the above objectives for employment and income. No public incentives are needed but enterprises have to overcome the cultural and organizational obstacles which arise every time a substantial reduction of working time is envisaged. Considering that one of the main characteristics of information technologies is pervasiveness, the share of the economy that is susceptible to benefit from that possibility is large and rapidly growing.

For enterprises and sectors which miss out on radical technical change and which face weak demand, it will be necessary to provide some fiscal incentives. Some interesting proposals are available (Rocard, 1996; Larrouturou, 1995) and also a promising experiment has been initiated in France with the de Robien law.

In conclusion, contrary to the well-known thesis which links the solution of the unemployment problem to the growth of output, in this chapter I have tried to show that it is rather the inverse which is true. In fact, it is the reduction of working time which will induce the growth of output and employment and, moreover, with growth public authorities will dispose of the resources to finance social activities (the 'third sector') which could provide jobs for those who remain excluded from the development of the market sector.

NOTES

1. The conditions for an upsurge of product innovation are more extensive and difficult to satisfy than those required by process innovation; see Tylecote (Chapter 6 in this volume).
2. Note that in the numerical example in Box 16.1, H refers to the length of the working day.
3. See, for instance, European Commission (1997, fig. 9 p. 28).
4. The minus sign on H is because, by assumption, there is a reduction of working time $(dH/dt < 0)$.
5. In the second part of Box 16.1 (point C) the percentage increase in the wage rate (11.1 per cent) is higher than the percentage reduction of working time (10 per cent) because equation (16.9) holds only for small changes (the *instantaneous* percentage changes).
6. Note that the 11.1 per cent increase is one shot and not per annum.
7. It is in this sense that the proposal of those who suggest a gradual reduction in working time, at the same pace as the growth of total economy productivity, needs to be modified (compare Jossa, 1996).
8. The new personnel must be kept on for at least two years.

REFERENCES

Brynjolfsson, E. and Hitt, L. (1993), 'Is information system spending productive? New evidence and new results', *Communications of the ACM*, **36** (12): 47–64.

European Commission (1995), *Local Development and Employment Initiatives*, Luxembourg: Office des Publications Officielles des Communautés Européennes.

European Commission (1997), Annual Economic Report 1997, *European Economy*, **63**.

Jossa, B. (1996), 'Working time reduction as a remedy against unemployment', *Economic Notes by Banca Monte dei Paschi di Siena SpA*, **25** (1): 1–20.

Larrouturou, P. (1995), *Du temps pour vivre. La semaine de quatre jours à la carte*, Paris: Flammarion.

Pasinetti, L.L. (1981), *Structural Change and Economic Growth: A Theoretical Essay on the Dynamics of the Wealth of Nations*, Cambridge: Cambridge University Press.

Rocard, M. (1996), *Les Moyens d'en sortir*, Paris: Seuil.

Timbeau, X. (1997), 'Réduction du temps de travail: quelles modalités?' *Observations et diagnostiques économiques, Lettre de l'OFCE*, n. 158, 31 January.

Index